Obesity and Reproductive Health

Edited by

Philip Baker, Adam Balen, Lucilla Poston and Naveed Sattar

RCOG PRESS

Philip Baker DM FRCOG
Professor of Maternal and Fetal Health, Maternal and Fetal Health Research Centre, The University of Manchester, St Mary's Hospital, Hathersage Road, Manchester M13 0JH

Adam H Balen MD FRCOG
Professor of Reproductive Medicine and Surgery, Clarendon Wing, Leeds General Infirmary, Belmont Grove, Leeds LS2 9NS

Lucilla Poston PhD FRCOG
Professor of Maternal and Fetal Health, Head of Division of Reproduction and Endocrinology (King's College London), Maternal and Fetal Research Unit, 10th Floor, North Wing, St Thomas' Hospital, London SE1 7EH

Naveed Sattar MBChB PhD FRCP (Glas) FRCPath
Professor Metabolic Medicine, BHF Glasgow Cardiovascular Research Centre, University of Glasgow, 4th Floor QEB, Glasgow Royal Infirmary, Glasgow G31 2ER

Published by the **RCOG Press** at the Royal College of Obstetricians and Gynaecologists, 27 Sussex Place, Regent's Park, London NW1 4RG

www.rcog.org.uk

Registered charity no. 213280

First published 2007

. ISBN 978-1-904752-39-4

Cover image: © 2007 Paul Whitehill/Science Photo Library

RCOG Editor: Andrew Welsh
Original design by Karl Harrington, FiSH Books, London
Typesetting by Andrew Welsh
Index by Liza Furnival, Medical Indexing Ltd
Printed by Henry Ling Ltd, The Dorset Press, Dorchester DT1 1HD

Obesity and
Reproductive Health

Since 1973 the Royal College of Obstetricians and Gynaecologists has regularly convened Study Groups to address important growth areas within obstetrics and gynaecology. An international group of eminent clinicians and scientists from various disciplines is invited to present the results of recent research and to take part in in-depth discussions. The resulting volume, containing enhanced versions of the papers presented, is published within a few months of the meeting and provides a summary of the subject that is both authoritative and up to date.

SOME PREVIOUS STUDY GROUP PUBLICATIONS AVAILABLE

Contents

SECTION 4 LONG-TERM HEALTH

SECTION 5 CONSENSUS VIEWS

Participants

Philip Baker
Convenor of RCOG Study Groups and Professor of Maternal and Fetal Health, Maternal and Fetal Health Research Centre, The University of Manchester, St Mary's Hospital, Hathersage Road, Manchester M13 0JH, UK.

Adam H Balen
Professor of Reproductive Medicine and Surgery, Clarendon Wing, Leeds General Infirmary, Belmont Grove, Leeds LS2 9NS, UK.

Lisa Bodnar
Assistant Professor of Epidemiology, Psychiatry and Obstetrics/Gynecology, Graduate School of Public Health and School of Medicine, University of Pittsburgh, A742 Crabtree Hall, 130 DeSoto Street, Pittsburgh, PA 15261, USA.

Patrick Catalano
Professor and Chair, Reproductive Biology, MetroHealth Medical Center, 2500 MetroHealth Drive, Cleveland, OH 44109, USA.

Martin Dresner
Head of Obstetric Anaesthesia, Department of Anaesthesia, The General Infirmary at Leeds, Great George Street, Leeds LS1 3EX, UK.

David B Dunger
Professor of Paediatrics, Department of Paediatrics, University of Cambridge, Level 8, Box 116, Addenbrooke's Hospital, Hills Road, Cambridge CB2 2QQ, UK.

Cynthia Farquhar
Postgraduate Professor, Department of Obstetrics and Gynaecology, University of Auckland, Private Bag 92019, Auckland 1142, New Zealand.

Georgina Jones
Non-clinical Senior Lecturer, Health Services Research Section, ScHARR, University of Sheffield, 30 Regent Court, 30 Regent Street, Sheffield S1 4DA, UK.

Siân Jones
Consultant Obstetrician and Gynaecologist, c/o M1 Maternity, Bradford Teaching Hospitals Foundation Trust, Duckworth Lane, Bradford BD9 6RJ, UK.

Sean Kehoe
Professor of Gynaecological Cancer, Oxford University, Level 3, The Women's Centre, John Radcliffe Hospital, Headington, Oxford OX3 9DU, UK.

John G Kral
Professor of Surgery and Medicine, Department of Surgery, SUNY Downstate Medical Center, 450 Clarkson Avenue, Box 40, Brooklyn, New York 11203-2098, USA.

Mike Lean
Professor of Human Nutrition, Department of Human Nutrition, University of Glasgow, Queen Elizabeth Building, Royal Infirmary, Glasgow G31 2ER, UK and Professor of Human Nutrition, University of Otago, Dunedin, New Zealand.

Diana Mansour
Head of Contraception and Sexual Health Services, Deputy Medical Director, Community Services, Newcastle Primary Care Trust, Graingerville Clinic, Newcastle General Hospital, Westgate Road, Newcastle upon Tyne NE4 6BE, UK.

Nadia Micali
Clinical Lecturer, Department of Child and Adolescent Psychiatry, Box 85, Institute of Psychiatry, King's College London, De Crespigny Park, London SE5 8AF, UK.

Lucilla Poston
Professor of Maternal and Fetal Health, Head of Division of Reproduction and Endocrinology (King's College London), Maternal and Fetal Research Unit, 10th Floor, North Wing, St Thomas' Hospital, London SE1 7EH, UK.

Jane E Ramsay
Consultant Obstetrician and Gynaecologist, Ayshire Maternity Unit, Crosshouse Hospital, Kilmarnock KA2 0BE, UK.

Margaret CP Rees
Reader in Reproductive Medicine, University of Oxford and Honorary Consultant in Medical Gynaecology, Level 4, Women's Centre, John Radcliffe Hospital, Oxford OX3 9DU, UK.

James M Roberts
Professor of Obstetrics, Gynecology and Reproductive Sciences and Epidemiology, University of Pittsburgh and Senior Scientist, Magee-Womens Research Institute, 204 Craft Avenue, Pittsburgh PA 15213, USA.

Stephen Robinson
Consultant Physician, Unit of Metabolic Medicine, Mint Wing, St Mary's Hospital, Paddington, London W2 1PG, UK.

Naveed Sattar
Professor Metabolic Medicine, BHF Glasgow Cardiovascular Research Centre, University of Glasgow, 4th Floor QEB, Glasgow Royal Infirmary, Glasgow G31 2ER, UK.

Anthony Smith
Consultant Urogynaecologist, The Warrell Unit, St Mary's Hospital, Hathersage Road, Manchester M13 0JH, UK.

John Wilding
Professor of Medicine and Honorary Consultant Physician, Clinical Sciences Centre, University Hospital Aintree, Longmoor Lane, Liverpool L9 7AL, UK.

Additional contributors

M Lynn Ahmed
Research Assistant, Department of Paediatrics, Women's Centre, Room 2103, John Radcliffe Hospital, Oxford OX3 9DU and Department of Paediatrics, Addenbrooke's Hospital, Box 116, Level 8, Cambridge CB2 2QQ, UK.

Simon Biron
Professor of Surgery, General Surgery Service, Laval Hospital, Laval University, 2725, Chemin Ste-Foy, Quebec, Canada GIV 4G5.

Margaret Eckert-Norton
Nurse Practitioner, Diabetes Treatment Center, SUNY Downstate Medical Center, 450 Clarkson Avenue, Box 123, Brooklyn, New York 11203, USA.

Ingrid Flight
Research Officer, CSIRO Human Nutrition, PO Box 10041, Adelaide SA 5000, Australia.

Eleanor Gate
Clinical Teaching Fellow, Ayshire Maternity Unit, Crosshouse Hospital, Kilmarnock KA2 0BE, UK.

Bramara Guruwadayarhalli
Specialist Registrar, M1 Maternity, Bradford Teaching Hospitals Foundation Trust, Duckworth Lane, Bradford BD9 6RJ, UK.

Frederic-Simon Hould
Associate Professor of Surgery, General Surgery Service, Laval Hospital, Laval University, 2725, Chemin Ste-Foy, Quebec, Canada GIV 4G5.

Sharif Ismail
Consultant Obstetrician and Gynaecologist, Department of Obstetrics and Gynaecology, Yeovil District Hospital, Yeovil BA21 4AT, UK.

Eugene J Kongnyuy
Lecturer in Sexual and Reproductive Health, Department of Child and Reproductive Health, Liverpool School of Tropical Medicine, Liverpool L3 5QA, UK.

Picard Marceau
Professor of Surgery, General Surgery Service, Laval Hospital, Laval University, 2725, Chemin Ste-Foy, Quebec, Canada GIV 4G5.

Simon Marceau
Associate Professor of Surgery, General Surgery Service, Laval Hospital, Laval University, 2725, Chemin Ste-Foy, Quebec, Canada GIV 4G5.

Robert Norman
Professor, Department of Obstetrics and Gynaecology, University of Adelaide, Queen Elizabeth Hospital, Woodville Road, Adelaide SA 5011, Australia.

Ken K Ong
Group Leader in Epidemiology, MRC Epidemiology Unit, Strangeways Research Laboratory (Room 328), Wort's Causeway, Cambridge CB1 8RN, UK.

Thelma Patrick
Assistant Professor of Health Promotion and Development, Obstetrics and
Gynecology and Reproductive Sciences, University of Pittsburgh and Assistant
Investigator, Magee-Womens Research Institute, 445 Victoria Building, 3500
Victoria Street, Pittsburgh PA 15261, USA.

Vyjayanthi Srinivasan
Specialist Registrar, M1 Maternity, Bradford Teaching Hospitals Foundation Trust,
Duckworth Lane, Bradford BD9 6RJ, UK.

Paul Taylor
Lecturer, Maternal and Fetal Research Unit, Division of Reproduction and
Endocrinology, King's College London, 10th Floor, North Wing, St Thomas'
Hospital, London SE1 7EH, UK.

Christina KH Yu
Subspecialty Trainee in Maternal and Fetal Medicine, St Mary's Hospital, Praed
Street, London W2 1NY, UK.

DECLARATION OF INTEREST

All contributors to the Study Group were invited to make a specific Declaration of Interest in relation
to the subject of the Study Group. This was undertaken and all contributors complied with this
request. Martin Dresner is a member of the Obstetric Anaesthetists Association. Georgina Jones is a
consultant to PCOS UK. Sean Kehoe is a consultant to an Advisory Group of Sanofi Pasteur. Diana
Mansour receives honoraria and sponsorship to attend conferences, sits on the Advisory Boards of
Schering, Organon, Wyeth, Novo Nordisk and Janssen Cilag, and her department conducts research
trials sponsored by industry, including Organon, Schering and Janssen Cilag. John Wilding has
received research funding and lecture fees and undertaken consulting for a number of companies
involved in development of drugs for obesity, including Roche, Abbott, Sanofi Aventis, GSK,
Johnson & Johnson and SlimFast Foods Ltd, he is the chair of the Association for the Study of Obesity,
he has written commissioned articles for a number of journals, and he is on the editorial boards of
IFO (unpaid), Diabetes, Obesity and Metabolism (unpaid) and Cardiometabolic Risk and Weight
Management (paid). Stephen Robinson has lectured doctors regarding obesity at meetings funded
by Roche Pharmaceuticals. John Kral has Swedish stocks in Astra-Zeneca Pharmaceuticals. Adam
Balen has received honoraria for lectures, research income from Serono, Ferring, Organon, Schering
Pharmaceuticals and fees for editorial work from BICOG. Siân Jones is a member of the Northern
European Medical Advisory Board of Cytyc. Lucilla Poston holds shares in CORRA Life Sciences and
holds patents in diagnosis of pre-eclampsia (EP01980756PCTB1044892) and detecting and predicting
pre-eclampsia (P517376GB3, pending).

Preface

Obesity, defined as a body mass index above 30 kg/m^2, is the major public health issue of our time. Rates of obesity have gone up nearly four-fold since the 1980s and currently 1 in 4 adult women are obese. The effect of adiposity is manifest in nearly every aspect of female reproductive life, whether as a metabolic or reproductive complication or as a technical problem affecting clinical issues such as ultrasonography and surgery. Indeed, obesity is present in 35% of maternal deaths in the UK.

While obesity has been widely discussed in the context of chronic diseases such as diabetes and heart disease, far less attention has been focused on the reproductive issues. This book, a product of the 53rd RCOG Study Group, provides a comprehensive review of the effects of obesity on reproductive health and gives some indication as to how such risks can best be managed.

Each chapter has been written by an expert in the field and the book also discusses the optimal care for pregnant women who are obese, including advice on managing surgical and anaesthetic risks. Other reproductive issues influenced by obesity, such as polycystic ovary syndrome and quality of life, are also covered. There are also sections on surgery in women who are obese and drugs that are relevant to management of obesity in nonpregnant women. Finally, the measurement of adiposity in pregnancy and the effects of maternal obesity on the future risks for offspring, both short and long term, are discussed. The book is thus relevant for all healthcare workers in obstetric and gynaecology disciplines, as well as others with a general interest in the management of obesity in women.

Philip Baker
Adam Balen
Lucilla Poston
Naveed Sattar

Section 1

Epidemiology of obesity

Chapter 1

Overview and prevalence of obesity in the UK

John Wilding

Introduction

The rising prevalence of obesity in the UK, that now affects nearly 25% of the adult population, is well documented. The reasons for this are complex and are thought to relate to changes in energy intake and energy expenditure (specifically physical activity) that have occurred over the last three decades. The consequences of this for the health of the nation are significant and include a rapidly rising incidence of type 2 diabetes, and impending reversal in the current trend for reduction in rates of vascular disease in the population.[1] Other consequences of obesity have, however, been less discussed and include important effects on the reproductive health of women, with greater rates of infertility that may be resistant to conventional treatment, and a greater chance of complications of pregnancy, macrosomia and requirement for operative delivery.

This review will predominantly deal with the epidemiological changes in adiposity that have occurred in the population of the UK over the past 25 years, particularly focusing on the consequences for women of childbearing age.

Obesity and epidemiology: prevalence in the general population

Obesity is usually defined epidemiologically using the body mass index (BMI), calculated as weight (in kg) divided by the square of height (in metres squared). A BMI of 18–25 kg/m^2 is considered as a healthy weight, a BMI > 30 kg/m^2 as obese, and > 40 kg/m^2 as morbidly obese.[2]

For the past 25 years the Health Survey for England has documented a progressive rise in the proportion of the population who are obese, from about 8% in 1980 to 24% in 2004.[3] Nearly two-thirds of the adult population are sufficiently overweight or obese to be putting their health at risk. The prevalence of severe or morbid obesity has also risen dramatically, from under 0.2% in 1980 to 0.9% of men and 1.9% of women in 2004. It is important to recognise, however, that BMI is an imperfect estimate of body fatness, which does not take into account differences in lean body mass between individuals of the same height and weight, or differences in body fat distribution that may be important determinants of the risk of disease. For this reason, researchers are increasingly considering other measures, such as waist circumference and waist:hip ratio as better measures of total body fatness for use in epidemiological research.[4,5] Studies have shown that such measurements better predict total body fatness than BMI, as measured by more sophisticated techniques such as dual-energy X-ray absorptiometry (DEXA) scanning and underwater weighing, and most importantly that they independently predict important disease consequences of obesity, such as diabetes and heart disease more accurately than BMI.[6]

Basic biology of energy balance

When considering the biology of energy balance, it is important to remember that weight gain develops on a background of day-to-day fluctuations in energy intake and expenditure, but that a relatively small cumulative imbalance can lead to a very significant weight gain over time. For example, a 100 kcal energy imbalance (equivalent to a small bar of chocolate, or 30 minutes of walking) will lead to an accumulation of 36 500 kcal of energy over a year. This energy is mostly stored as fat, and will result in a 5.1 kg gain in weight. If continued for 5 years, a person with a starting weight of 70 kg and a healthy BMI of 23 kg/m^2 would gain 26 kg and increase their BMI to 31 kg/m^2, which is in the obese category. As most of the population are weight stable, or only gaining weight slowly, it is evident that the regulation of body weight is under powerful biological control. A detailed description of this is beyond the scope of this review, but current understanding recognises that there are both short-term circulating and neural factors, largely derived from the gut, that regulate individual meal size and duration, and long-term factors that are largely regulated by hormonal and neural signals from body fat stores. The central nervous system, particularly the brainstem and hypothalamus, plays a key role in integrating these signals to determine energy intake and expenditure (Figure 1.1).[7,8]

Causes of obesity

Genetic predisposition

Obesity develops as a result of chronic energy imbalance, i.e. from intake exceeding output over a period of time. There is good evidence that the mechanisms regulating body weight are under powerful biological control, but this homeostatic system is (probably for good reasons) biased towards promotion of weight gain rather than weight loss. Twin studies have demonstrated that heritable factors account for about 80% of the variation in BMI[9] and, in identical twins, discordance for BMI is unusual; hence genetic factors are certainly important in the regulation of adiposity. Single-gene disorders that result in extreme obesity phenotypes are, however, rare. They have mostly been found in the context of severe early onset childhood obesity, and include mutations in the fat-derived hormone leptin and its receptor, the melano-cortin-4 receptor, and pro-opiomelanocortin (POMC) mutations.[10–12] Together, such mutations may account for up to 5% of severe early onset childhood obesity, but are rare in adult populations. Syndromic conditions, such as Prader–Willi syndrome and Bardet–Beidel syndrome are also associated with obesity, but the precise mechanisms how these lead to energy imbalance are poorly understood.[13]

Changes in energy expenditure

Despite the important contribution of genetic background, it is clear from the rapidly changing prevalence of obesity that the current epidemic is due to changes in the environment rather than genes, although it is also clear that, in an obesogenic environment, those genetically predisposed are most likely to gain weight. The environmental factors that are most likely to have contributed include a progressive decrease in physical activity of the population, which has declined to the point that the average person in the UK is now walking a marathon distance per week less than they would have done in 1950.[1] Physical activity has also declined in other ways, with changing leisure activity patterns, particularly increased time spent watching television and playing computer games, and increasing use of labour-saving devices. Studies have repeatedly shown that women are less likely to be physically active than men at all ages, but of particular concern is the observation from the Health Survey for England that only 30% of women of reproductive age are achieving the minimum physical activity guideline of five bouts of 30 minutes of brisk walking or the equivalent each week.[3]

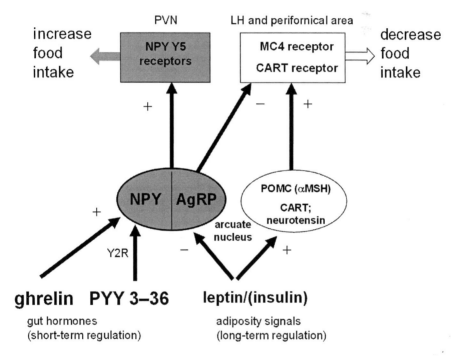

Figure 1.1. Hypothalamic pathways integrate peripheral signals to control food intake; peripheral signals indicating fat stores, such as leptin and probably insulin, provide long-term regulation by increasing expression in the hypothalamus of signals that decrease appetite through their respective receptors such as αMSH, CART and neurotensin, and decreasing expression of orexigenic (food intake increasing) signals such as NPY and AgRP; some short-term (within meal) signals such as PYY 3-36 (which decreases food intake) and ghrelin (which increases food intake) also converge on these same hypothalamic neurons; AgRP = agouti-related protein; CART = cocaine- and amphetamine-regulated transcript; LH = lateral hypothalamus; MC4 = melanocortin-4; NPY = neuropeptide Y; POMC = pro-opiomelanocortin; PVN = hypothalamic paraventricular nucleus; PYY 3-36 = peptide YY 3-36; Y2R = neuropeptide Y Y2 receptor; αMSH = α-melanocyte-stimulating hormone

Changes in energy intake

Patterns of food intake have also changed and, although fat consumption overall has declined slightly on household food surveys, these do not include snacks or other food consumed outside the home. Carbonated soft drinks and fast food have been a particular concern, as there is epidemiological evidence linking high consumption of these products with weight gain and development of type 2 diabetes.[14,15] The key factor linking these products appears to be energy density, as energy-dense foods are less satiating and more likely to lead to the phenomenon of 'passive overconsumption'.

Other causes

Given the central role of the hypothalamus in appetite regulation, it is not surprising that people with hypothalamic–pituitary disease have a high prevalence of obesity and related problems[16] and this should always be considered in women with obesity and reproductive problems, but will usually be identified during the course of investigation. Many drug treatments also predispose to weight gain and the following treatments have been implicated: corticosteroids; some atypical antipsychotic agents such as olanzapine; pizotifen; antidiabetic drugs such as sulphonylureas, thiazolidenediones and insulin; some antidepressants; and β-blockers. Long-acting depot contraceptives, notably medroxyprogesterone acetate, are also an important cause of increased appetite and weight gain and are of particular relevance to women of reproductive age.

Who is affected most?

When studying the way the population has gained weight over the past 25 years, it is clear that the epidemic has not affected all sections of the population equally. Firstly the 'bell-shaped' distribution curve of BMI has not only shifted to the right, but it has also flattened, resulting in a disproportionate increase in the number of people with severe obesity (Figure 1.2); such severe obesity may have very serious consequences for health. Studies of the distribution curves of body weight in relation to age show that the prevalence of obesity rises with age but is rising particularly rapidly in young people. Older people seem to be less affected, perhaps because of a cohort effect but also because of the decreased life expectancy associated with obesity.

International studies have also found that ethnicity may be another important factor to consider when assessing the affect of adiposity on health. Some groups, for example people of south Asian origin, may be susceptible to diabetes and other metabolic consequences of obesity at lower BMI and waist circumference measurements than white populations.[17]

Social class, health inequalities and obesity

It is also important to recognise that the socially disadvantaged are much more likely to develop obesity and to suffer from its consequences. From Health Survey for England data, this can be seen to affect women more than men, and is of particular importance because other risk factors for future ill health, such as smoking, are also more commonly found in those women from less-advantaged social groups.

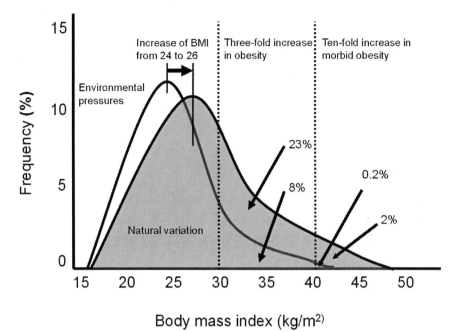

Figure 1.2. How the population distribution of body mass index (BMI) has changed; a small shift in mean BMI can lead to a large change in the proportion of individuals with obesity and severe obesity

Rising obesity in women of childbearing age

Despite the perceived pressure from the media and fashion industry for girls and young women to be slim, obesity has now become a significant problem for girls and young women. This mostly seems to affect women of childbearing age (Table 1.1), and this is of particular relevance given the current trend for women to wait until their 30s before having children. In the age group 35–44, 24 % of women are now obese, and 3% have morbid obesity; in this latter group, the difficulties conceiving and potential problems in pregnancy and childbirth are very real threats to women's health. These population trends are clearly reflected in the progressive increase in BMI at booking for antenatal care reported in Glasgow in the past 25 years. Over this time the proportion of women with a BMI greater than 30 kg/m^2 at booking has increased from 10% to nearly 20%, while the proportion of healthy weight has progressively fallen.[18]

Table 1.1. Prevalence of obesity and severe obesity in women of childbearing age in England; data from Health Survey for England (2004)[3]

Age group (years)	Prevalence		Mean BMI (kg/m²)
	BMI > 30 kg/m²	BMI > 40 kg/m²	
16–24	12.1%	1.8%	24.4
25–34	16.9%	2.2%	25.7
35–44	24%	3.0%	26.8

Consequences of obesity: focusing on women's health

In addition to the adverse effects of obesity on general health, certain obesity-related complications may specifically affect women. This is thought to be mainly a result of hormonal changes that occur in obesity, but other factors including increased systemic inflammation and mechanical effects may also be relevant. Women who are obese are two to three times more likely to develop hormone-dependent malignancies, including breast, ovarian and endometrial cancer, and have menstrual irregularities, often in association with polycystic ovary syndrome (PCOS).

Effects of obesity on reproductive health

The effects of obesity on reproductive health are significant. They include difficulty in conceiving, which may be related to insulin resistance and PCOS. For those women who are obese and able to conceive, there is a greater risk of pregnancy-related complications, notably diabetes, pre-eclampsia and thromboembolic disease, and of subsequent operative delivery.[19] Congenital abnormalities are also more common in babies born to women who are obese.

Summary

In summary, obesity rates are continuing to rise year-on-year in the UK. Younger, more deprived individuals are the most likely to be affected, a fact that has significant consequences for women of reproductive age. These changes are related to low levels of physical activity in the population, coupled with easy availability of energy-dense, often high-fat food. These rising levels of obesity are associated with significant risks to general, and particularly reproductive, health of women, and urgent action is required to reverse these worrying trends.

References

1. *Tackling Obesity in England*. Report by the Comptroller and Auditor General. HC 220. London: The Stationery Office; 2001.
2. World Health Organization. *Obesity – Preventing and Managing the Global Epidemic*. 24. Geneva: WHO; 1998.
3. Department of Health. *Health Survey for England 2004*. London: Department of Health; 2006.
4. Lemieux S, Prud'homme D, Bouchard C, Tremblay A, Despres JP. A single threshold value of waist girth identifies normal-weight and overweight subjects with excess visceral adipose tissue. *Am J Clin Nutr* 1996;64:685–93.
5. Yusuf S, Hawken S, Ounpuu S, Bautista L, Franzosi MG, Commerford P, et al. Obesity and the risk of myocardial infarction in 27,000 participants from 52 countries: a case–control study. *Lancet* 2005;366:1640–9.
6. Despres JP, Lemieux I, Prud'homme D. Treatment of obesity: need to focus on high risk abdominally obese patients. *BMJ* 2001;322:716–20.
7. Wilding J. Neuropeptides and appetite control. *Diabet Med* 2002;19:619–27.
8. Huda MSB, Wilding JPH, Pinkney JH. Gut peptides and the regulation of appetite. *Obes Rev* 2006;7:163–82.
9. Pietilainen KH, Kaprio J, Rissanen A, Winter T, Rimpela A, Viken RJ, et al. Distribution and heritability of BMI in Finnish adolescents aged 16 y and 17 y: A study of 4884 twins and 2509 singletons. *Int J Obes Relat Metab Disord* 1999;23:107–15.
10. Farooqi IS, Jebb SA, Langmack G, Lawrence E, Cheetham CH, Prentice AM, et al. Effects of recombinant leptin therapy in a child with congenital leptin deficiency. *N Engl J Med* 1999;341:879–84.

11. Farooqi IS, Yeo GS, Keogh JM, Aminian S, Jebb SA, Butler G, et al. Dominant and recessive inheritance of morbid obesity associated with melanocortin 4 receptor deficiency. *J Clin Invest* 2000;106:271–9.

12. Yeo GSH, Farooqi IS, Aminian S, Halsall DJ, Stanhope RC, O'Rahilly S. A frameshift mutation in MC4R associated with dominantly inherited human obesity. *Nat Genet* 1998;20:111–2.

13. Chung WK, Leibel RL. Molecular physiology of syndromic obesities in humans. *Trends Endocrinol Metab* 2005;16:267–72.

14. Pereira MA, Kartashov AI, Ebbeling CB, Van Horn L, Slattery M, Jacobs DR, et al. Fast-food habits, weight gain, and insulin resistance (the CARDIA study): 15-year prospective analysis. *Lancet* 2005;365:36–42.

15. Ludwig DS, Peterson KE, Gortmaker SL. Relation between consumption of sugar-sweetened drinks and childhood obesity: a prospective, observational analysis. *Lancet* 2001;357:505–8.

16. Daousi C, Dunn AJ, Foy PM, Macfarlane IA, Pinkney JH. Endocrine and neuroanatomic features associated with weight gain and obesity in adult patients with hypothalamic damage. *Am J Med* 2005;118:45–50.

17. World Health Organization. *The Asia-Pacific Perspective: Redefining Obesity and Its Treatment.* Australia: Health Communications Australia; 2000.

18. Kanagalingam MG, Forouhi NG, Greer IA, Sattar N. Changes in booking body mass index over a decade: retrospective analysis from a Glasgow Maternity Hospital. *BJOG* 2005;112:1431–3.

19. Ramsay JE, Greer I, Sattar N. ABC of obesity – Obesity and reproduction. *BMJ* 2006;333:1159–62.

Chapter 2

Prevalence and causes of obesity in adolescence

David B Dunger, M Lynn Ahmed and Ken K Ong

Introduction

Adolescence is characterised by rapid changes in growth and psychological development. During puberty, around 16% of mature adult height is gained, and young men and women gain 42% and 47%, respectively, of adult weight. As well as the development of secondary sexual characteristics, the hormonal changes of puberty lead to dramatic metabolic effects that help to drive pubertal growth and the acquisition of lean body and fat mass. There is clear sexual dimorphism, with young women having an earlier growth spurt, usually early during pubertal development and young men having a later growth spurt. The longer period of prepubertal growth and the increased magnitude of the pubertal growth spurt in young men contribute to the mean adult difference in male and female heights of around 13 cm. There are also profound sex differences in the acquisition of body composition as, during the later stages of puberty, after their pubertal growth spurt, young women have a steady gain in fat mass, whereas in men, after the pubertal growth spurt, the gains are largely in lean body mass. Given the rapid changes in growth and weight gain during puberty, it is not surprising that, together with prenatal and early postnatal development, adolescence has been identified as a critical risk period for the development of obesity.[1]

Prevalence of obesity during adolescence

The prevalence of overweight and obesity in children and adolescents is increasing around the world and this is a major public health concern. In the USA, the prevalence of obesity and overweight, based on body mass index (BMI), has doubled in the past 25 years.[2] This is graphically demonstrated from the US Preventative Services Task Force study,[2] which shows the increase in obesity risk particularly in older children and adolescents (Figure 2.1). Data from the National Health and Nutrition Examination Survey (NHANES), a nationally representative sample from the USA, suggest that the percentage of 'overweight' children (i.e. BMI ≥ 95th centile) increased from 13.8% in 1999/2000 to 16% in 2003/04 in girls; and the rise was even greater in boys, from 14% to 18.2%.[3] In a survey of data from ten countries between 1970 and 2000, Cole[4] noted that the highest prevalences and the fastest rates of increase in overweight have occurred in the USA and Canada, while in China the prevalence remains low but is slowly increasing, and in Russia it is falling. In other countries (Germany, Finland, Brazil, England, Scotland and Australia), rates of overweight are increasing by around 4% every 10 years (Figure 2.2).

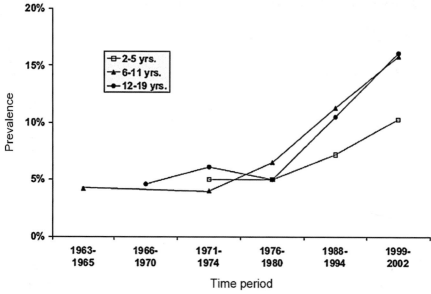

Figure 2.1. Overweight (BMI ≥ 95th centile) in US children and adolescents. Reproduced with permission from Whitlock *et al.*,[2] data from Ogden *et al.*[72]

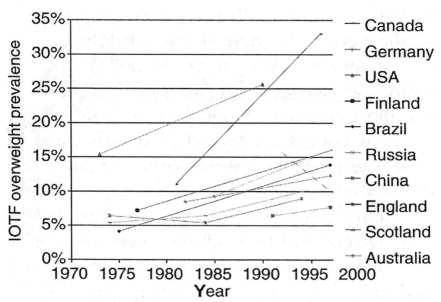

Figure 2.2. Trends over time in the prevalence of overweight in boys from ten countries based on the International Obesity Task Force (IOTF) cut-offs; reproduced with permission from Cole[4]

The escalation of childhood obesity in the UK took off in the late 1980s. Figure 2.3 shows the dramatic rise in the prevalence of obese children between 1990 and 1996.[5] It is clear that the greatest increase has been during the adolescent years, similar to that seen in the USA. In the 2002–04 Health Survey for England (HSE), 14% of 2- to 11-year-olds and 25% of 11- to 15-year-olds were obese (BMI ≥ 95th centile).[5] The first report of the UK National Childhood Obesity Database (NCOD), for 2005–06, included data on 538 400 children measured in schools at ages 4–5 years and 10–11 years.[6] In the older age group, the prevalences of overweight (BMI > 85–95th centile) and obesity (BMI ≥ 95th centile) was 18.9% and 13.6%, respectively, in boys, and 15.4% and 13.5% in girls. Rates of uptake for this noncompulsory survey were poor at only around 48%; higher response rates were associated with higher apparent prevalences of obesity, and it is therefore likely that this exercise significantly underestimated the true prevalence of overweight and obesity.

Causes of obesity during adolescence

Numerous factors have been suggested to play a role in the trend towards increasing overweight and obesity, including changes in diet, with increases in intake of total calories, consumption of fast foods high in saturated fat, sugar and low in fibre and the intake of soft drinks.[7] Attention has also been focused on declining levels of physical activity in children and adolescents. Several studies have reported that children with higher BMI have lower levels of physical activity[8,9] or longer duration of TV watching,[10,11] and this may have particular relevance for adolescent obesity because pronounced declines in levels of physical activity are typically observed during the later school years.[12]

The debate as to whether increasing rates of adolescent overweight and obesity are mainly due to 'gluttony' or 'sloth' will no doubt continue,[13] and these factors are likely to be closely interrelated. In a European multicentre study of around 2000 children, TV viewing was associated with increasing rates of obesity, while objectively measured physical activity was separately associated with the metabolic risk markers of obesity.[14] The authors suggested that snacking while watching TV increased obesity, regardless of physical activity levels. Certainly, there is good evidence to promote pub-

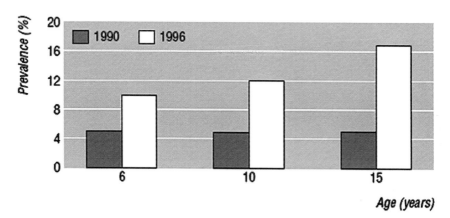

Figure 2.3. Increase in prevalence of UK childhood obesity (BMI ≥ 95th centile); reproduced with permission from Reilly et al.[5]

lic health strategies in both nutrition and physical activity,[15] but further research is also needed to identify the optimal targets. For example, recent data suggest that physical activity levels should be much higher than the current international guidelines of a minimum of 1 hour of physical activity each day, of at least moderate intensity, to prevent clustering of cardiovascular disease risk factors.[16]

Others have argued that the evidence for the role of physical activity and nutrition in the obesity epidemic is only circumstantial, and that there are several other plausible factors that have shown secular changes in parallel to those in obesity.[17] The authors provided evidence for a further ten putative additional explanations for the trend in obesity over the last few decades:

1. sleep debt
2. environmental endocrine disrupters
3. central heating and the reduction in the variability of ambient temperatures
4. decreased smoking
5. use of pharmaceutical agents, such as antipsychotics and antidepressants
6. changes in the distribution of ethnicity and age
7. increasing mother's age at pregnancy
8. intrauterine and intergenerational effects, such as birthweight and maternal obesity
9. increasing reproductive fitness of obesity related genotypes
10. assorted mating for adiposity.

The causes of the increasing prevalence of obesity during adolescence are likely to be complex and may vary with age of obesity onset and the aetiology may determine its persistence into adult life.

Obesity in adolescence tends to persist into adult life. In a population of adolescents aged 13–18 years with a BMI greater than the 95th centile, 50% of boys and 66% of girls were obese as adults.[18] The risk may be even higher if at least one parent is obese.[5] 'Tracking' of obesity from childhood to adult life is more likely to be seen if the children are still obese after sexual maturation is achieved.[19] Recent UK studies indicate tracking of obesity risk during adolescence. In a 5 year longitudinal study of 5863 London school children aged 11–12 years at baseline, Wardle et al.[20] concluded that obesity, which is evident after the age of 11 years, is much more likely to be persistent. The authors found that BMI correlations between subsequent years were around 0.9, and were only slightly lower for 2, 3 and 4 year intervals, and concluded that the data highlighted the need to target efforts to prevent obesity even before adolescence.

Childhood overweight and the timing of puberty

Frisch and Revelle[21,22] suggested that there might be a lower limit of fat mass required for pubertal development and, in particular, for a normal menstrual cycle. Although this 'critical weight' hypothesis provoked controversy, the idea that there was a 'sensor' of body fat levels that fed back to the brain to activate central gonadotrophin secretion was borne out with the discovery of leptin.[23] Leptin is secreted by adipocytes and is believed to have a permissive effect on the onset of puberty through the regulation of gonadotrophin secretion.[24,25] Women with delayed puberty due to excessive exercise who have been given recombinant leptin move rapidly into puberty with restored gonadotrophin secretion.[26] However, in the converse situation where rapid early weight gain stimulates pubertal development, the mechanisms are less clear. It could be that the early rise in leptin levels is the stimulus to signal early pubertal development but there are many other circulating hormones such as insulin-like growth factor-I (IGF-I) and insulin, through its effects on sex hormone-binding globulin, which also could be a signal for early pubertal development. Data from our group highlight the importance of insulin resistance in the possible onset and transition through puberty.[27]

Studies stretching back over 50 years have noted that children who enter puberty earlier are more likely to be overweight or to have some measure of increased adiposity.[28–37] Wang[38] observed a sex difference in the association between weight and the timing of puberty through analysis of data from the third NHANES survey (1988–94) of 1501 girls and 1520 boys aged 8–14 years. That study observed that early maturity was associated with being overweight or obese in girls whereas early maturing boys were thinner. Biro et al.[39] and Vizmanos et al.[40] observed similar findings. However a UK study by Sandhu et al.[41] suggested that boys who entered puberty early also had a higher childhood BMI. Negative relationships between body fat and menarche were observed in the Amsterdam Growth and Health Study[36] and in both white and black girls in the Bogalusa Heart Study.[42] Data from an Australian study reported by Tam et al.[43] showed increased adiposity in girls who entered puberty early.

These various studies suggest that early puberty is related to increased adiposity and weight gain but they do not necessarily imply causality.[43,44] It has been suggested that the link between increased weight gain and adiposity and age at pubertal onset are independent events or perhaps the consequence of an additional factor determining both weight gain and rate of maturation.

Early infancy weight gain and the timing of puberty

Secular trends towards earlier age at menarche have been observed in many populations over the past 50 years with a surprisingly consistent rate of around 3.6 months per decade.[45] This has generally been attributed to improvements in nutrition and reductions in infection.[46,47] These changing nutritional and socio-economic factors had their greatest impact during the first 2 years of life and are most evident in more rapid height gain.[46] The UK 1946 Birth Cohort Data also indicated that weight gain during the first 2 years of life was an important predictor of timing of pubertal development and early puberty was particularly marked in children showing rapid weight gain during the first 2 years of life.[48] Similar observations have been seen in the contemporary Avon Longitudinal Study of Pregnancy and Childhood (ALSPAC) where early weight gain during the first 2 years of life appears to be an important determinant of the tempo of puberty and risk for obesity and that these associations are highly heritable and reflect patterns of weight gain and early menarche in the mothers.[49]

It appears that rapid gains in weight and height during early infancy contribute not only to the risk of obesity during childhood and of early maturation but also, as will be discussed later, to the variation in metabolic risk associated with obesity in adults. The underlying biological mechanisms that drive weight gain and early pubertal development are unknown.

Thus, links between the timing of puberty, excess weight gain and obesity may be largely determined at a very early stage of postnatal development. The subsequent effects on rates of weight gain during puberty and, in particular, body composition may be very relevant to the metabolic and diabetes risk associated with the prevalence of obesity and overweight during adolescence.

Obesity, body composition and disease risk

The startling increases in adolescent obesity have been received with alarm in the USA and UK and have led to headlines which suggest that the next generation may have a shorter life expectancy than their parents. However, these interpretations of the population obesity risk assume that all adolescents who are obese are at equal risk of developing long-term complications and, in particular, cardiovascular disease (CVD) and type 2 diabetes. Recent reports indicate that only 21% of adolescents who are extremely obese (BMI z-score ≥ 3) will have evidence of impaired glucose tolerance[50] and 4% will have evidence of type 2 diabetes. Similarly, only around 33% of adolescents who are extremely obese in the UK will have other evidence of risk for the metabolic syndrome.[51,52] Thus, not all adolescents who are obese seem to be at equal risk of developing type 2 diabetes and CVD. The risk of developing type 2 diabetes is increased if there is a family history[53] and if there are clear ethnic differences in the risks of developing early markers of diabetes risk such as insulin resistance.[54,55] It is clear that not all adolescents who are obese carry the same risk for the development of type 2 diabetes or the metabolic syndrome. Genetic factors, reflected in the family history, ethnicity, early developmental influences and the distribution of body fat are also important determinants of disease risk associated with obesity.

Similar to the early timing of childhood weight gain that appears to promote earlier puberty, rapid weight gain from birth during the first years of postnatal life may have a greater impact on subsequent obesity-related metabolic risk than weight gain in later childhood.[56,57] Caprio et al.[58] in a study of severely obese youth showed that those with impaired glucose tolerance or other features of the metabolic syndrome had increased central adiposity and ectopic deposition of lipid in the liver. The relationship between central fat deposition and insulin resistance is well established.[59] Studies have identified the importance of prenatal and early postnatal nutritional exposure to the subsequent risk for the development of obesity and, in particular, the development of increased visceral adiposity.[60] Children whose weight gain was restrained in utero and who showed rapid postnatal weight gain appear to be at increased risk for the development of obesity, increased visceral adiposity and insulin resistance.[61,62] In a longitudinal study of young Swedish adults, rapid weight gain very early in the first 6 months of life predicted greater overall adiposity and also increased metabolic syndrome risk at age 17 years.[56,57] In addition to insulin resistance, there is also evidence that low birthweight may independently be associated with reduced insulin secretion,[62] a risk factor for the development of impaired glucose tolerance and, through glucotoxicity, with increased risk for type 2 diabetes and other features of the metabolic syndrome.[53]

Gender-specific effects of obesity on metabolism

The association between adolescent obesity and risk for the metabolic syndrome and type 2 diabetes shows clear sexual dimorphism with an apparent increase in risk in women compared with men.[63] In the UK ALSPAC birth cohort study, increasing BMI had a significantly greater impact on blood lipid profiles and other metabolic markers of disease risk in girls than in boys.[64] The sexual dimorphism in the association between adiponectin levels and type 2 diabetes risk during adolescence is particularly marked (Figure 2.4). A series of detailed longitudinal studies of girls who were born small and then showed postnatal catch-up weight gain indicates that this pattern of growth may be associated with early pubertal development, rapid transition through puberty and reduced final height,[65] and also an increased risk for the development of central adiposity and other features of the metabolic syndrome.[60] The mechanism for this pattern of growth and metabolic risk are unclear but is related to increased central adiposity and increased insulin resistance. This may be of central importance as insulin sensitisation with metformin can slow the tempo of pubertal development and reverse many of the metabolic risk factors.[27,66]

Studies of Catalan girls presenting with precocious pubarche also highlighted the importance of hyperandrogenism in the development of metabolic disease risk in women. Early weight gain is associated with increased adrenal androgen production[67] and subsequent risk for ovarian hyperandrogenism.[62] Low birthweight followed by postnatal catch-up growth can be associated with premature pubarche and the early development of polycystic ovary syndrome in some populations where preliminary data suggest that women may be more susceptible through genetic variation in the androgen receptor and the aromatase gene.[68,69] Hyperandrogenism has itself been associated with the development of abnormal body composition in women with a more android distribution of fat and the development of insulin resistance.[70] The extent to which high androgen levels contribute over and above the insulin resistance subsequent upon low birthweight and postnatal catch-up, or childhood development of adiposity, has yet to be determined but preliminary studies, using combinations of metformin and flutamide, an androgen receptor blocker, have shown greater efficacy than metformin used alone.[71]

Prenatal and postnatal weight gain, genetic and gender differences, as well as postnatal environmental exposures, combine to determine diabetes and metabolic risk associated with increasing adiposity during adolescence. They need to be considered when determining intervention strategies.

Conclusion

The prevalence of obesity and overweight is increasing during adolescence and this is a major public health concern. The avoidance of excessive weight gain is a major focus of public health policy and should include measures to promote exercise and reduce calorie intake in adolescent populations. However, identification of adult

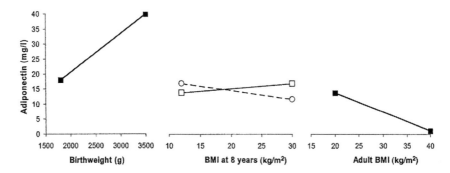

Figure 2.4. Schematic diagram showing the changing relationships between adiponectin levels and body size; left panel: at birth in both sexes; middle panel: at age 8 years in boys (□) and girls (○); and right panel: in adults of both sexes; derived from data reported by Ong *et al.*[64]

health risk associated with obesity during adolescence should be more focused, as it is important to identify high-risk individuals who, through early perinatal exposures, or genetic or ethnic background, have an increased risk for the development of type 2 diabetes and the metabolic syndrome. There is a need to identify people with markers of future disease risk, such as hyperandrogenism in women, increased visceral adiposity, ectopic deposition of fat in liver and muscle, markers of inflammation and cardiovascular disease risk, abnormal lipids and lipoprotein, and elevated blood pressure, for more detailed study and exploration of interventional strategies.

References

1. Dietz WH. Critical periods in childhood for the development of obesity. *Am J Clin Nutr* 1994;59:955–9.
2. Whitlock EP, Williams SB, Gold R, Smith PR, Shipman SA. Screening and interventions for childhood overweight: a summary of evidence for the US Preventive Services Task Force. *Pediatrics* 2005;116:e125–44.
3. Ogden CL, Carroll MD, Curtin LR, McDowell MA, Tabak CJ, Flegal KM. Prevalence of overweight and obesity in the United States, 1999–2004. *JAMA* 2006;295:1549–55.
4. Cole T. Childhood obesity: assessment and prevalence. In: Cameron N, Norgan N, Ellison G, editors. *Childhood Obesity, Contemporary Issues*. Boca Raton: CRC Press, Taylor & Francis Group; 2006. p. 3–12.
5. Reilly JJ, Wilson D. ABC of obesity. Childhood obesity. *BMJ* 2006;333:1207–10.
6. Crowther R, Dinsdale H, Rutter H, Kyffin R. *Analysis of the National Childhood Obesity Database 2005–06: A report for the Department of Health*. 2006.
7. Malik VS, Schulze MB, Hu FB. Intake of sugar-sweetened beverages and weight gain: a systematic review. *Am J Clin Nutr* 2006;84:274–88.
8. Rennie KL, Livingstone MB, Wells JC, McGloin A, Coward WA, Prentice AM, et al. Association of physical activity with body-composition indexes in children aged 6–8 y at varied risk of obesity. *Am J Clin Nutr* 2005;82:13–20.
9. Wareham NJ, van Sluijs EM, Ekelund U. Physical activity and obesity prevention: a review of the current evidence. *Proc Nutr Soc* 2005;64:229–47.
10. Andersen RE, Crespo CJ, Bartlett SJ, Cheskin LJ, Pratt M. Relationship of physical activity and television watching with body weight and level of fatness among children: results from the Third National Health and Nutrition Examination Survey. *JAMA* 1998;279:938–42.
11. Dietz WH Jr, Gortmaker SL. Do we fatten our children at the television set? Obesity and television viewing in children and adolescents. *Pediatrics* 1985;75:807–12.
12. Caspersen CJ, Pereira MA, Curran KM. Changes in physical activity patterns in the United States, by sex and cross-sectional age. *Med Sci Sports Exerc* 2000;32:1601–9.
13. Prentice AM, Jebb SA. Obesity in Britain: gluttony or sloth? *BMJ* 1995;311:437–9.
14. Ekelund U, Brage S, Froberg K, Harro M, Anderssen SA, Sardinha LB, et al. TV viewing and physical activity are independently associated with metabolic risk in children: the European Youth Heart Study. *PLoS Med* 2006;3:e488.
15. Sjostrom M, Yngve A, Poortvliet E, Warm D, Ekelund U. Diet and physical activity – interactions for health; public health nutrition in the European perspective. *Public Health Nutr* 1999;2:453–9.
16. Andersen LB, Harro M, Sardinha LB, Froberg K, Ekelund U, Brage S, et al. Physical activity and clustered cardiovascular risk in children: a cross-sectional study (The European Youth Heart Study). *Lancet* 2006;368:299–304.
17. Keith SW, Redden DT, Katzmarzyk PT, Boggiano MM, Hanlon EC, Benca RM, et al. Putative contributors to the secular increase in obesity: exploring the roads less traveled. *Int J Obes (Lond)* 2006;30:1585–94.
18. Guo SS, Wu W, Chumlea WC, Roche AF. Predicting overweight and obesity in adulthood from body mass index values in childhood and adolescence. *Am J Clin Nutr* 2002;76:653–8.

19. Guo SS, Chumlea WC, Roche AF, Siervogel RM. Age- and maturity-related changes in body composition during adolescence into adulthood: the Fels Longitudinal Study. *Int J Obes Relat Metab Disord* 1997;21:1167–75.

20. Wardle J, Brodersen NH, Cole TJ, Jarvis MJ, Boniface DR. Development of adiposity in adolescence: five year longitudinal study of an ethnically and socioeconomically diverse sample of young people in Britain. *BMJ* 2006;332:1130–5.

21. Frisch RE, Revelle R. Height and weight at menarche and a hypothesis of critical body weights and adolescent events. *Science* 1970;169:397–9.

22. Frisch RE, Revelle R. Height and weight at menarche and a hypothesis of menarche. *Arch Dis Child* 1971;46:695–701.

23. Zhang Y, Proenca R, Maffei M, Barone M, Leopold L, Friedman JM. Positional cloning of the mouse obese gene and its human homologue. *Nature* 1994;372:425–32.

24. Cheung CC, Thornton JE, Kuijper JL, Weigle DS, Clifton DK, Steiner RA. Leptin is a metabolic gate for the onset of puberty in the female rat. *Endocrinology* 1997;138:855–8.

25. Clayton PE, Gill MS, Hall CM, Tillmann V, Whatmore AJ, Price DA. Serum leptin through childhood and adolescence. *Clin Endocrinol (Oxf)* 1997;46:727–33.

26. Welt CK, Chan JL, Bullen J, Murphy R, Smith P, DePaoli AM, *et al.* Recombinant human leptin in women with hypothalamic amenorrhea. *N Engl J Med* 2004;351:987–97.

27. Ibanez L, Ong K, Valls C, Marcos MV, Dunger DB, de Zegher F. Metformin treatment to prevent early puberty in girls with precocious pubarche. *J Clin Endocrinol Metab* 2006;91:2888–91.

28. Adair LS, Gordon-Larsen P. Maturational timing and overweight prevalence in US adolescent girls. *Am J Public Health* 2001;91:642–4.

29. Anderson SE, Dallal GE, Must A. Relative weight and race influence average age at menarche: results from two nationally representative surveys of US girls studied 25 years apart. *Pediatrics* 2003;111:844–50.

30. Beunen G, Malina RM, Lefevre J, Claessens AL, Renson R, Simons J, *et al.* Size, fatness and relative fat distribution of males of contrasting maturity status during adolescence and as adults. *Int J Obes Relat Metab Disord* 1994;18:670–8.

31. Buckler J. *A Longitudinal Study of Adolescent Growth.* London, UK: Springer-Verlag. p. 1990.

32. Cameron N, Demerath EW. Critical periods in human growth and their relationship to diseases of aging. *Am J Phys Anthropol* 2002;Suppl 35:159–84.

33. Kaplowitz PB, Slora EJ, Wasserman RC, Pedlow SE, Herman-Giddens ME. Earlier onset of puberty in girls: relation to increased body mass index and race. *Pediatrics* 2001;108:347–53.

34. Morrison JA, Barton B, Biro FM, Sprecher DL, Falkner F, Obarzanek E. Sexual maturation and obesity in 9- and 10-year-old black and white girls: the National Heart, Lung, and Blood Institute Growth and Health Study. *J Pediatr* 1994;124:889–95.

35. Stark O, Peckham CS, Moynihan C. Weight and age at menarche. *Arch Dis Child* 1989;64:383–7.

36. van Lenthe FJ, Kemper CG, van Mechelen W. Rapid maturation in adolescence results in greater obesity in adulthood: the Amsterdam Growth and Health Study. *Am J Clin Nutr* 1996;64:18–24.

37. Wattigney WA, Srinivasan SR, Chen W, Greenlund KJ, Berenson GS. Secular trend of earlier onset of menarche with increasing obesity in black and white girls: the Bogalusa Heart Study. *Ethn Dis* 1999;9:181–9.

38. Wang Y. Is obesity associated with early sexual maturation? A comparison of the association in American boys versus girls. *Pediatrics* 2002;110:903–10.

39. Biro FM, Lucky AW, Huster GA, Morrison JA. Pubertal staging in boys. *J Pediatr* 1995;127:100–2.

40. Vizmanos B, Marti-Henneberg C. Puberty begins with a characteristic subcutaneous body fat mass in each sex. *Eur J Clin Nutr* 2000;54:203–8.

41. Sandhu J, Ben-Shlomo Y, Cole TJ, Holly J, Davey Smith G. The impact of childhood body mass index on timing of puberty, adult stature and obesity: a follow-up study based on adolescent anthropometry recorded at Christ's Hospital (1936–1964). *Int J Obes (Lond)* 2006;30:14–22.

42. Freedman DS, Khan LK, Serdula MK, Dietz WH, Srinivasan SR, Berenson GS. The relation of menarcheal age to obesity in childhood and adulthood: the Bogalusa heart study. *BMC Pediatr* 2003;3:3.

43. Tam CS, de Zegher F, Garnett SP, Baur LA, Cowell CT. Opposing influences of prenatal and postnatal growth on the timing of menarche. *J Clin Endocrinol Metab* 2006;91:4369–73.

44. Demerath EW, Li J, Sun SS, Chumlea WC, Remsberg KE, Czerwinski SA, et al. Fifty-year trends in serial body mass index during adolescence in girls: the Fels Longitudinal Study. *Am J Clin Nutr* 2004;80:441–6.

45. Ong KK, Ahmed ML, Dunger DB. Lessons from large population studies on timing and tempo of puberty (secular trends and relation to body size): the European trend. *Mol Cell Endocrinol* 2006;254–255:8–12.

46. Cole TJ. Secular trends in growth. *Proc Nutr Soc* 2000;59:317–24.

47. Tanner JM. Growth as a measure of the nutritional and hygienic status of a population. *Horm Res* 1992;38 Suppl 1:106–15.

48. dos Santos Silva I, De Stavola BL, Mann V, Kuh D, Hardy R, Wadsworth ME. Prenatal factors, childhood growth trajectories and age at menarche. *Int J Epidemiol* 2002;31:405–12.

49. Ong KK, Northstone K, Wells JC, Rubin C, Ness AR, Golding J, Dunger DB. Earlier mother's age at menarche predicts rapid infancy growth and childhood obesity. *PLoS Med* 2007;4:e132.

50. Sinha R, Fisch G, Teague B, Tamborlane WV, Banyas B, Allen K, et al. Prevalence of impaired glucose tolerance among children and adolescents with marked obesity. *N Engl J Med* 2002;346:802–10.

51. Viner RM, Segal TY, Lichtarowicz-Krynska E, Hindmarsh P. Prevalence of the insulin resistance syndrome in obesity. *Arch Dis Child* 2005;90:10–4.

52. Weiss R, Caprio S. The metabolic consequences of childhood obesity. *Best Pract Res Clin Endocrinol Metab* 2005;19:405–19.

53. Arslanian SA. Type 2 diabetes mellitus in children: pathophysiology and risk factors. *J Pediatr Endocrinol Metab* 2000;13 Suppl 6:1385–94.

54. Arslanian S, Suprasongsin C. Differences in the *in vivo* insulin secretion and sensitivity of healthy black versus white adolescents. *J Pediatr* 1996;129:440–3.

55. Ehtisham S, Crabtree N, Clark P, Shaw N, Barrett T. Ethnic differences in insulin resistance and body composition in United Kingdom adolescents. *J Clin Endocrinol Metab* 2005;90:3963–9.

56. Ekelund U, Ong K, Linne Y, Neovius M, Brage S, Dunger DB, et al. Upward weight percentile crossing in infancy and early childhood independently predicts fat mass in young adults: the Stockholm Weight Development Study (SWEDES). *Am J Clin Nutr* 2006;83:324–30.

57. Ekelund U, Ong KK, Linne Y, Neovius M, Brage S, Dunger DB, et al. Association of weight gain in infancy and early childhood with metabolic risk in young adults. *J Clin Endocrinol Metab* 2007;92:98–103.

58. Weiss R, Dufour S, Taksali SE, Tamborlane WV, Petersen KF, Bonadonna RC, et al. Prediabetes in obese youth: a syndrome of impaired glucose tolerance, severe insulin resistance, and altered myo cellular and abdominal fat partitioning. *Lancet* 2003;362:951–7.

59. Freedman DS, Srinivasan SR, Burke GL, Shear CL, Smoak CG, Harsha DW, et al. Relation of body fat distribution to hyperinsulinemia in children and adolescents: the Bogalusa Heart Study. *Am J Clin Nutr* 1987;46:403–10.

60. Ibanez L, Ong K, Dunger DB, de Zegher F. Early development of adiposity and insulin resistance after catch-up weight gain in small-for-gestational-age children. *J Clin Endocrinol Metab* 2006;91:2153–8.

61. Ong KK, Ahmed ML, Emmett PM, Preece MA, Dunger DB. Association between postnatal catch-up growth and obesity in childhood: prospective cohort study. *BMJ* 2000;320:967–71.

62. Ong KK, Petry CJ, Emmett PM, Sandhu MS, Kiess W, Hales CN, et al. Insulin sensitivity and secretion in normal children related to size at birth, postnatal growth, and plasma insulin-like growth factor-I levels. *Diabetologia* 2004;47:1064–70.

63. Arslanian S. Type 2 diabetes in children: clinical aspects and risk factors. *Horm Res* 2002;57 Suppl 1:19–28.

64. Ong KK, Frystyk J, Flyvbjerg A, Petry CJ, Ness A, Dunger DB. Sex-discordant associations with adiponectin levels and lipid profiles in children. *Diabetes* 2006;55:1337–41.

65. Ibanez L, Ferrer A, Marcos MV, Hierro FR, de Zegher F. Early puberty: rapid progression and reduced final height in girls with low birth weight. *Pediatrics* 2000;106:E72.

66. Ibanez L, Valls C, Ong K, Dunger DB, de Zegher F. Metformin therapy during puberty delays menarche, prolongs pubertal growth, and augments adult height: a randomized study in low-birth-weight girls with early-normal onset of puberty. *J Clin Endocrinol Metab* 2006;91:2068–73.

67. Ong KK, Potau N, Petry CJ, Jones R, Ness AR, Honour JW, *et al.* Opposing influences of prenatal and postnatal weight gain on adrenarche in normal boys and girls. *J Clin Endocrinol Metab* 2004;89:2647–51.

68. Ibanez L, Ong KK, Mongan N, Jaaskelainen J, Marcos MV, Hughes IA, *et al.* Androgen receptor gene CAG repeat polymorphism in the development of ovarian hyperandrogenism. *J Clin Endocrinol Metab* 2003;88:3333–8.

69. Petry CJ, Ong KK, Michelmore KF, Artigas S, Wingate DL, Balen AH, *et al.* Association of aromatase (CYP 19) gene variation with features of hyperandrogenism in two populations of young women. *Hum Reprod* 2005;20:1837–43.

70. Ibanez L, Ong K, de Zegher F, Marcos MV, del Rio L, Dunger DB. Fat distribution in non-obese girls with and without precocious pubarche: central adiposity related to insulinaemia and androgenaemia from prepuberty to postmenarche. *Clin Endocrinol (Oxf)* 2003;58:372–9.

71. Ibanez L, Valls C, Ferrer A, Ong K, Dunger DB, De Zegher F. Additive effects of insulin-sensitizing and anti-androgen treatment in young, nonobese women with hyperinsulinism, hyperandrogenism, dyslipidemia, and anovulation. *J Clin Endocrinol Metab* 2002;87:2870–4.

72. Ogden CL, Flegal KM, Carroll MD, Johnson CL. Prevalence and trends in overweight among US children and adolescents, 1999–2000. *JAMA* 2002;288:1728–32.

Chapter 3
Eating disorders and their effect on pregnancy

Nadia Micali

Introduction

The eating disorders – anorexia nervosa, bulimia nervosa, binge-eating disorder (BED) and eating disorders not otherwise specified (EDNOS) – are common in young women in developed countries. The average prevalence rates for anorexia and bulimia are 0.3% and 1%, respectively,[1] in young Western women, but are higher, up to 5–7% of young women, if partial syndromes are included. The onset of these disorders is typically in adolescence or young adulthood, i.e. in a critical phase of a woman's reproductive life. These disorders are not self-limiting and many have a chronic course with notable psychiatric and medical co-morbidities and sequelae.

Definitions

The defining criteria for eating disorders are provided by both of the main psychiatric classificatory systems, ICD-10[2] and DSM-IV.[3]

Anorexia is defined as follows:

1. weight loss leading to a body weight at least 15% below the expected for age and height. The body mass index (BMI) is also used, with the normal range being 20–25 kg/m^2. Anorexia is defined by this ratio being less than 17.5 kg/m^2 and severe anorexia by less than 13.5 kg/m^2. In children and adolescents, this is most evident by failure to grow at a normal rate

2. self-induced weight loss by avoidance of 'fatty foods'

3. an intrusive dread of fatness, leading to a self-imposed weight threshold

4. a widespread endocrine disorder involving the hypothalamic–pituitary–gonadal axis is manifest in women as amenorrhoea and in men as a loss of sexual interest and potency. In prepuberty, the endocrine disorder is observed as a delayed onset of puberty.

The DSM-IV classification subtypes the illness into restricting and bingeing/purging.

Bulimia is characterised by:

1. recurrent episodes of overeating (at least twice a week over 3 months) where large amounts of food are consumed in short periods of time

2. persistent preoccupation with eating and a strong craving to eat.

3. partial attempts to counteract the 'fattening' effects of food by at least one of the following:
   (a) self-induced vomiting
   (b) self-induced purging (i.e. laxative, diuretic use)
   (c) alternating periods of starvation
   (d) use of drugs, e.g. appetite suppressants, thyroid preparations, diuretics, or insulin therapy neglect in people with diabetes
4. self-perception of being too fat, with an intrusive dread of fatness (usually leading to underweight).

The DSM-IV classification subtypes the disorder into purging and non-purging.

Although these conditions are regarded as distinct disorders, the possibility exists of an overlap: if both occur, anorexia is considered the primary diagnosis.

If not all the criteria above are met, the particular illness is defined as atypical or as 'eating disorder not otherwise specified' – EDNOS. DSM-IV includes a definition of 'binge-eating disorder' – BED – among EDNOS, as a provisional eating disorder diagnosis in need of further study. Research criteria for BED are available. BED is characterised by:

1. recurrent episodes of binge eating. An episode of binge eating is characterised by both of the following:
   (a) eating, in a discrete period of time (e.g. within any 2 hour period), an amount of food that is definitely larger than most people would eat in a similar period of time under similar circumstances
   (b) a sense of lack of control over eating during the episode (e.g. a feeling that one cannot stop eating or control what or how much one is eating)
2. binge-eating episodes associated with three or more of the following:
   (a) eating much more rapidly than normal
   (b) eating until feeling uncomfortably full
   (c) eating large amounts of food when not feeling physically hungry
   (d) eating alone because of being embarrassed by how much one is eating
   (e) feeling disgusted with oneself, depressed, or very guilty after overeating
3. marked distress regarding binge eating
4. binge eating, on average, at least 2 days a week for 6 months
5. binge eating *not* associated with regular use of inappropriate compensatory behaviours (e.g. purging, fasting, excessive exercise) and not occurring exclusively during the course of anorexia or bulimia.

Epidemiology

The incidence of full-syndrome anorexia is around 8/100 000,[1] with a prevalence in women of 0.1–1.5%. Bulimia has approximately twice these rates: an incidence of 12/100 000 and a prevalence of about 1%.[4] Both illnesses are ten times more common in women than in men; both present mostly in late adolescence, with a median onset of 17–18 years, but both early and late onset cases certainly do occur, in childhood and in later life, although both disorders are very rare below the age of 8 years. Research suggests that, contrary to media reports, there is no clear evidence of increasing rates in anorexia,[5,6] although the incidence of anorexia among 15- to 19-year-old young women increased significantly in a study carried out in the Netherlands.[6] These epidemiological studies have also suggested that, although there was an increase in the incidence of bulimia in the early 1990s, incidence rates declined or remained the same in the late 1990s.[5,6] Atypical eating disorders/ EDNOS are deemed to be the most frequent eating disorder, but difficulties in common definitions of this category have hampered the establishing of prevalence rates. In a review of the literature, Fairburn and Bohn[7] suggested EDNOS is the most common diagnosis of eating disorder in an outpatient setting, accounting for about 60% of cases.

Three studies have investigated prevalence rates for BED in Europe and in the USA. All have suggested rates between 0.4% and 0.77%.[4] Striegel-Moore et al.[8] found a difference in prevalence rates according to race, with white women having higher risk than black women. In clinical samples, the onset of BED seems to be later than anorexia and bulimia.[4]

Anorexia is a universal disorder across the globe with equal prevalence in non-Western countries; bulimia, in contrast, does seem restricted to the West. Contrary to popular belief, there is only a slight over-representation in upper and middle social classes, but certain occupational groups, combining an emphasis on perfection, competition and looks, such as modelling and dancing, have higher rates.[1]

Reproductive function

Past research has shown that fertility is decreased among women with eating disorders. However, recent advances in fertility treatment make it possible for women with eating disorders to conceive even at a low weight and irrespective of recovery from the eating disorder. Two studies that have looked at women attending fertility clinics have found a high rate of eating disorders.[9,10] Stewart et al.[9] found that, among 66 women attending a fertility clinic, 7.6% had anorexia or bulimia.

Follow-up studies of women with eating disorders have shown discordant results in terms of the reduction in fertility. Three long-term follow-up studies have investigated this. One study, of 141 women with anorexia who had been hospitalised in the past, found the fertility rate for women with anorexia to be reduced to one-third of that expected over 4–22 years.[11] The second study investigated 748 women who had been hospitalised for anorexia in adolescence 9–14 years previously, finding pregnancy rates to be one-half of those in control women.[12] A similar follow-up of 70 women who had been assessed or treated for anorexia 10 years previously found similar rates of pregnancy for women who had recovered from anorexia or had active anorexia and for control women.[13] Differences in findings might be due to differences in length of follow-up, and also to different levels of disorder severity across studies: possibly the first two studies focused on women who received treatment in hospital, i.e. more severe cases.

Women with bulimia seem to have fewer problems with reproductive function,[14] given that they are often at a normal weight and more frequently in a sexual relationship. A case–control study of 43 women with bulimia followed up 5–10 years later found that 19% had been investigated for infertility at follow-up.[15] Another follow-up of 173 women with bulimia who were studied over 10–15 years found no impairment of fertility.[16]

No studies have investigated the effects of EDNOS or BED on reproductive function and no conclusions can therefore be drawn on this.

Pregnancy outcomes

Although reproductive function is most likely to be impaired in women with eating disorders while they are ill with the disorder, many women with a past or current eating disorder eventually do become mothers. Pregnancies are often unplanned in this population group, given that many women wrongly believe that they cannot conceive because of menstrual abnormalities or amenorrhoea. There is still limited literature on the effects of a maternal eating disorder on pregnancy and pregnancy outcomes and the effects of pregnancy on eating disorders. Most of the studies in this field have either been small or have only relied on clinical samples; the issue of generalisability of results is thus a problem. Often studies have investigated pregnancy outcomes in women with eating disorders without studying each disorder separately. Many rely on retrospective assessments of eating disorder and/or pregnancy outcomes of varying degrees of validity and reliability. Moreover, few studies have contemporaneously assessed eating disorder symptoms and pregnancy status.

In a follow-up study of 141 women with anorexia, the rate of prematurity in their offspring was increased two-fold and perinatal mortality was increased six-fold.[11] Lower birthweights, more preterm births and a higher number of miscarriages were found in 66 women with anorexia compared with control women in a self-report retrospective study, with no differences between women with active and remitted symptomatology.[12] Stewart et al.[17] and Waugh and Bulik[18] found lower birthweights in the offspring of women with lifetime anorexia and bulimia. A register-based study by Sollid et al.[19] investigated birthweight and preterm delivery in 302 women who had been hospitalised for an eating disorder, comparing them with control women. The authors found a significantly higher risk in women with a history of an eating disorder for delivering a preterm and small-for-gestational-age (SGA) baby. Two studies have reported similar findings for women with anorexia, i.e. a birthweight reduction in women with a history of anorexia. One, based on the Avon Longitudinal Study of Parents and their Children (ALSPAC), comprising 14 000 women enrolled for a prospective longitudinal study on pregnancy and childhood, focused on 171 women who had a lifetime history of anorexia.[20] The study found a significantly lower birthweight in babies of women with a history of anorexia, and the risk was mainly accounted for by a low BMI before pregnancy. The second study used a national register to link women who had had a diagnosis of anorexia with perinatal outcomes, finding that women who had been diagnosed with anorexia had babies who were slightly lighter (43 g) than controls.[21] The only significant difference across the two groups was for instrumental delivery, which was less common for women with anorexia.

Two longitudinal studies, on the same sample, reported results contrasting with previous studies. One focused on live births and miscarriages in a cohort of 54 women with anorexia and bulimia, finding a slightly lower rate of live births and a normal rate of miscarriages than expected in women with eating disorders.[22] Franko and colleagues,[23] comparing women with anorexia ($n = 18$) and bulimia ($n = 31$), 22 of whom had a current eating disorder in the 9 months before conception, found no differences in birthweight, duration of pregnancy, pregnancy or neonatal problems.

With respect to the effects of bulimia on pregnancy, most of the literature seems to suggest an effect on fetal loss and miscarriages. In two small studies on the outcome of pregnancy in women with bulimia, a higher than expected number of fetal complications[24] and a two-fold increase in miscarriage rate was reported.[14] Mitchell et al.[25] also found rates of fetal loss that were twice those of controls in 20 women with active bulimia, even though these results were not significant. These results have been confirmed in a retrospective case–control comparison of women previously treated for bulimia ($n = 122$), which found an increased risk for miscarriages (OR 2.6) and of premature birth (OR 3.3).[26] In the longitudinal study of women with eating disorders who had given birth, women with bulimia ($n = 195$) were significantly more likely (OR 2.0) than controls to have had two or more miscarriages in the past, even after controlling for relevant confounders.[20] The possible mechanism for the higher risk of miscarriages in women with bulimia is still debated. Possible explanations include polycystic ovary syndrome (PCOS) and leptin abnormalities.[26]

Conti et al.,[27] in a retrospective case–control study of 88 women delivering low-birthweight (LBW) babies found a significant association between LBW and retro-spectively generated diagnosis of eating disorders. SGA status was predicted by low maternal prepregnancy weight, low maternal weight gain during pregnancy and higher eating disorder psychopathology. Preterm birth was not related to disturbed eating behaviours.

As for studies on pregnancy outcomes, no study has investigated women with EDNOS or BED. It is likely, however, that the effect of low maternal weight before pregnancy observed in women with anorexia applies to women with EDNOS or atypical anorexia who are underweight.

Several reports are available in the obstetric literature on the effect of maternal weight on fetal outcomes. Women with a lower body weight at conception or who fail to gain weight in pregnancy have been shown to be at higher risk of adverse obstetric outcomes, including low birthweight, prematurity and intrauterine growth restriction.[28–30] High prepregnancy body weight, on the other hand, was related to higher risk of late fetal deaths.[29]

Most of the research in the literature suggests that eating disorders, either active or remitted, may have a negative effect on pregnancy outcomes, mainly on birthweight, prematurity and miscarriages. Low body weight before and during pregnancy is very likely to account for most of the risk for low birthweight in the offspring.

A separate mention is needed for hyperemesis gravidarum and gestational diabetes mellitus (GDM): both of these conditions have been found in some studies to occur at higher rates in women with eating disorders. Abraham et al.[14] found a 10% rate of hyperemesis gravidarum among 25 women with active bulimia. These results were consistent with previous findings.[31]

High rates of GDM have been reported in women with eating disorders. Morgan[32] found an increased risk of GDM in 94 women with active bulimia in pregnancy. In another study, a four-fold higher rate of GDM was found in women with a past history of anorexia and bulimia compared with controls.[20]

Symptoms of eating disorders in pregnancy

Few studies evaluate the course of eating disorder symptomatology during pregnancy and those that do have reported conflicting results. Moreover, most studies are likely to be biased because only clinical samples are investigated. Two different hypotheses have been postulated from previous literature. The first is that eating behaviours (and associated symptoms) will improve during the early part of the pregnancy because of concern for the wellbeing of the fetus. The second is that the weight gain during pregnancy may exacerbate or rekindle latent weight and shape concerns which may lead to a relapse of the eating disorder in the postpartum period.

In one of the first studies in this field, Lacey and Smith[24] reported an absence of symptoms in 15 of 20 women with bulimia by the third trimester of pregnancy. Most of these women returned to prepregnancy levels of bulimic behaviour in the postpartum period. Lemberg and Phillips[33] reported similar findings. In a longitudinal study of 54 women receiving treatment for anorexia and bulimia, Blais and colleagues[22] found that, in the majority of cases, bulimic symptoms will improve during pregnancy and for a period of time after the birth, as the woman is aware of needing to eat healthily for the good of the baby. However, in women with anorexia, symptoms seemed to improve less. This study included full pregnancies as well as terminations and miscarriages, which makes it difficult to determine whether eating disorder symptomatology changed according to pregnancy outcome. A further long-term follow-up study assessed women who had received treatment for bulimia and investigated the change in bulimic symptoms during pregnancy. In this study, while bingeing and purging improved, abstinence rates from these behaviours were not affected by pregnancy and body dissatisfaction worsened during pregnancy.[34] A follow-up of women with bulimia who had been included in a treatment randomised controlled trial reported a non-significant decrease in eating disorder symptomatology in the year of childbirth, with a trend towards lower levels of symptomatology.[35] Another study of 150 pregnant women, of whom 11 had an active eating disorder, found an improvement in body dissatisfaction and eating attitudes. A trend was shown also for a reduction in compensatory behaviours.[36]

The presence in pregnancy of eating disorder behaviours and shape and weight concerns has been investigated in women with a recent episode of eating disorder, in women with a past history of eating disorder, and in obese and non-obese controls, in the ALSPAC cohort.[37] Women with a recent or past eating disorder had a significantly higher risk of using laxatives during the first 4 months of pregnancy (OR 49.6 and OR 4.7, respectively) and of self-induced vomiting (OR 51.9 and OR 5.9, respectively) compared with normal-weight controls and with obese controls. High exercise in pregnancy was more common in women with a recent eating disorder (33%) and in women with past eating disorder (31%) compared with obese (20%) and non-obese controls (21%). Dieting for weight loss before pregnancy was highly prevalent > 80%) among women with eating disorders and women who were obese and more common than among non-obese controls (57%). The reported prevalence of dieting for weight loss during pregnancy decreased dramatically (about four times lower) in all groups. The prevalence of dieting in the eating disorder and obese groups remained higher than non-obese controls: women with recent eating disorders had the highest prevalence (11%), followed by women who were obese (8%) and women with past eating disorders (4%). During the third trimester of pregnancy, more women with past or recent eating disorder reported a strong desire to lose weight (63% and 31%, respectively), that they 'felt they had put on too much weight' (past eating disorder 77% and recent eating disorder 65%), a high concern about weight gain (past eating disorder 79% and recent eating disorder 66%) and loss of control over eating (past eating disorder 72% and recent eating disorder 43%) compared with non-obese controls. Women who were obese shared high prevalence rates of 'feeling they had put on too much weight' (62%) and a strong desire to lose weight (37%) but not a high concern about weight gain or loss of control over eating. Women with recent eating disorders and women who were obese had high pre-pregnancy weight and shape concerns (as measured by the Eating Disorders Examination Questionnaire (EDEq)) and their scores tended to change in a similar way (significant decrease) during pregnancy compared with prepregnancy. The findings suggest that, although pregnancy might improve eating disorder symptoms in women with a recent onset eating disorder, eating disorder symptoms and cognitions remain elevated in this group of women. Moreover, women with a past history of eating disorder do experience some eating disorder symptoms and cognitions during pregnancy. In addition, the study suggested that, although the appraisal of weight gain and desire to lose weight in women who are obese is higher compared with those who are not obese, women who are obese have fewer concerns compared with those with eating disorders. The study was not able to test effective weight gain in the women who were obese, which might in effect be higher and therefore explain the appraisal of weight gain in this group. Weight and shape concerns declined in pregnancy in women who were obese, although they still remained more similar in values to women with eating disorders than non-obese controls, which suggests that pregnancy might have a similar effect on weight and shape concern in women who are obese and women with eating disorders.

In summary, the evidence on the impact of pregnancy on eating disorder symptoms is scarce. Some studies are available that have focused on bulimia; however, fewer have investigated women with anorexia. Most of these studies rely on small clinical samples. The studies published so far seem to suggest that, on the whole, eating disorder symptomatology decreases in a significant proportion of cases during pregnancy. Importantly however, although most symptoms decrease, they do not disappear completely. There is some evidence that women with past eating disorders have some eating disorder behaviours and concerns. Women who are obese share some of these concerns in pregnancy.

Conclusion

Eating disorders are relatively common disorders in women of childbearing age. Owing to their effect on sexual hormones, eating disorders have important effects on fertility as well as on perinatal outcomes. Research in this field, however, has been hampered by a changing nosology and difficulties in conducting sufficiently large studies. In general, expert advice suggests informing women of the risks involved in conceiving when still ill with an eating disorder and that assisted conception should not be offered until there is remission from the illness.[38,39] When women with an active eating disorder do become pregnant, they and their partners need to be made aware of the risks that this entails for mother and baby. Obstetric staff or other healthcare providers should be alert as to when a careful assessment of eating disorder symptoms during pregnancy might be needed.

References

1. Van Hoeken D, Seidell J, Hoek H. Epidemiology. In: Treasure J, Schmidt U, van Furth E, editors. *Handbook of Eating Disorders*. 2nd ed. Chichester: Wiley; 2003. p. 1134.

2. World Health Organization. *International Classification of Diseases*. Geneva: World Health Organization; 1992.

3. American Psychiatric Association. *Diagnostic and Statistical Manual of Mental Disorders*. 4th ed. Washington DC: American Psychiatric Association; 1994.

4. Striegel-Moore R, Franko D, Ach E. Epidemiology of eating disorders: an update. In: Wonderlich S, Mitchell J, deZwaan M, Steiger H, editors. *Annual Review of Eating Disorders. Part 2*. Oxford: Radcliffe Publishing; 2006. p. 65–80.

5. Currin L, Schmidt U, Treasure J, Jick H. Time trends in eating disorders incidence. *Br J Psychiatr* 2005;186:132–5.

6. Van Son G, van Hoeken D, Bartelds A, van Furth E, Hoek H. Time trends in the incidence of eating disorders: a primary care study in the Netherlands. *Int J Eat Disord* 2006;39:565–9.

7. Fairburn CG, Bohn K. Eating disorder NOS (EDNOS): an example of the troublesome 'not otherwise specified' (NOS) category in DSM-IV. *Behav Res Ther* 2005;43:691–701.

8. Striegel-Moore RH, Dohm FA, Kraemer HC, Taylor CB, Daniels SR, Crawford PB, et al. Eating disorders in black and white young women. *Am J Psychiatry* 2003;160:1326–31.

9. Stewart DE, Robinson E, Goldbloom DS, Wright C. *Am J Obstet Gynecol* 1991;163:1196–9.

10. Thommen M, Vallach L, Kiencke S. Prevalence of eating disorders in a swiss family planning clinic. *Eat Disord* 1995;3:324–31.

11. Brinch M, Isager T, Tolstrup K. Anorexia nervosa and motherhood: reproduction pattern and mothering behavior of 50 women. *Acta Psychiatr Scand* 1988;77:611–17.

12. Hjern A, Lindberg L, Lindblad F. Outcome and prognostic factors for adolescent female in-patients with anorexia nervosa: 9 to14-year old follow-up. *Br J Psychiatry* 2006;189:428–32.

13. Bulik CM, Sullivan PF, Fear JL, Pickering A, Dawn A, McCullin M. Fertility and reproduction in women with anorexia nervosa: a controlled study. *J Clin Psychiatry* 1999;60:130–5.

14. Abraham SF, Benit L, Mason C, Mitchell H, O'Connor N, Ward J, et al. The psychosexual histories of young women with bulimia. *Aust N Z J Psychiatry* 1985;19:72–6.

15. Abraham S. Sexuality and reproduction in bulimia nervosa patients over 10 years. *J Psychosom Res* 1998;44(3–4):491–502.

16. Crow SJ, Thuras P, Keel PK, Mitchell JE. Long-term menstrual and reproductive function in patients with bulimia nervosa. *Am J Psychiatry* 2002;159:1048–50.

17. Stewart DE, Raskin J, Garfinkel PE, MacDonald OL, Robinson GE. Anorexia nervosa, bulimia, and pregnancy. *Am J Obstet Gynecol* 1987;157:1194–8.

18. Waugh E, Bulik CM. Offspring of women with eating disorders. *Int J Eat Disord* 1999;25:123–33.

19. Sollid CP, Wisborg K, Hjort J, Secher NJ. Eating disorder that was diagnosed before pregnancy and pregnancy outcome. *Am J Obstet Gynecol* 2004;190:206–10.

20. Micali N, Simonoff E, Treasure J. Risk of major adverse perinatal outcomes in women with eating disorders. *Br J Psychiatry* 2007;190:255–9.

21. Ekeus C, Lindberg L, Lindblad F, Hjern A. Birth outcomes and pregnancy complications in women with a history of anorexia nervosa. *BJOG Int J Obstet Gynaecol* 2006;113:925–9.

22. Blais MA, Becker AE, Burwell RA, Flores AT, Nussbaum KM, Greenwood DN, et al. Pregnancy: outcome and impact on symptomatology in a cohort of eating-disordered women. *Int J Eat Disord* 2000;27:140–9.

23. Franko DL, Blais MA, Becker AE, Delinsky SS, Greenwood DN, Flores AT, et al. Pregnancy complications and neonatal outcomes in women with eating disorders. *Am J Psychiatry* 2001;158:1461–6.

24. Lacey JH, Smith G. Bulimia nervosa. The impact of pregnancy on mother and baby. *Br J Psychiatry* 1987;150:777–81.

25. Mitchell JE, Seim HC, Glotter D, Soll EA, Pyle RL. A retrospective study of pregnancy in bulimia nervosa. *Int J Eat Disord* 1991;10:209–14.

26. Morgan JF, Lacey JH, Chung E. Risk of postnatal depression, miscarriage, and preterm birth in bulimia nervosa: retrospective controlled study. *Psychosom Med* 2006;68:487–92.

27. Conti J, Abraham S, Taylor A. Eating behavior and pregnancy outcome. *J Psychosom Res* 1998;44(3–4):465–77.

28. Carmichael SL, Abrams B. A critical review of the relationship between gestational weight gain and preterm delivery. *Obstet Gynecol* 1997;89(5 Pt 2):865–73.

29. Cnattingius S, Bergstrom R, Lipworth L, Kramer MS. Prepregnancy weight and the risk of adverse pregnancy outcomes. *N Engl J Med* 1998;338:147–52.

30. Schieve LA, Cogswell ME, Scanlon KS, Perry G, Ferre C, Blackmore-Prince C, et al. Prepregnancy body mass index and pregnancy weight gain: associations with preterm delivery. The NMIHS Collaborative Study Group. *Obstet Gynecol* 2000;96:194–200.

31. Stewart DE. Reproductive functions in eating disorders. *Ann Med* 1992;24:287–91.

32. Morgan JF. Eating disorders and reproduction. *Aust N Z J Obstet Gynaecol* 1999;39:167–73.

33. Lemberg R, Phillips J. The impact of pregnancy on anorexia nervosa and bulimia. *Int J Eat Disord* 1989;8:285–95.

34. Crow SJ, Keel PK, Thuras P, Mitchell JE. Bulimia symptoms and other risk behaviors during pregnancy in women with bulimia nervosa. *Int J Eat Disord* 2004;36:220–3.

35. Carter FA, McIntosh VVW, Joyce PR, Frampton CM, Bulik CM. Bulimia nervosa, childbirth, and psychopathology. *J Psychosom Res* 2003;55:357–61.

36. Rocco PL, Orbitello B, Perini L, Pera V, Ciano RP, Balestrieri M. Effects of pregnancy on eating attitudes and disorders: A prospective study. *J Psychosom Res* 2005;59:175–9.

37. Micali N, Treasure J, Simonoff E. Eating disorders symptoms during pregnancy in women with current and past eating disorders. *Br J Psych* 2007;190:255–59.

38. van der Spuy ZM, Steer PJ, McCusker M, Steele SJ, Jacobs HS. Outcome of pregnancy in underweight women after spontaneous and induced ovulation. *Br Med J* 1988;296:962–5.

39. Abraham S, Mira M, Llewellyn-Jones D. Should ovulation be induced in women recovering from an eating disorder or who are compulsive exercisers? *Fertil Steril* 1990;53:566–8.

Chapter 4
Obesity: age, ethnic and social variations

Naveed Sattar

Background

As in many parts of the world, the UK has seen substantial increases in the prevalence of obesity since the 1980s. In 1980, 6–8% of men and women were obese but by 2002 these figures had tripled to 22–23%. Further projections suggest that prevalence figures will continue to rise so that, by 2010, a remarkable one-third of UK adults could be obese. Obesity levels appear to be rising in men and women to similar extents, although obesity levels vary by age, ethnicity and social variations and such variations are discussed below in greater detail.

Older adults

People continue to gain weight until they reach their 50s and 60s. Currently, near 30% of people aged between 65 and 74 years in the UK are obese, with chronic disease, mobility problems and depression aggravated by obesity.[1,2] Beyond the age of 74 years, the prevalence of obesity declines, in part due to survival bias of leaner individuals.

Children

The epidemic of paediatric obesity in the UK began in the late 1980s. The prevalence has continued to increase rapidly and obesity is the most common disorder of childhood and adolescence. Obesity in children often leads to low self-esteem and 'unwanted' comments from other children. Obesity is more common in older children and adolescents than in younger children. The Health Survey for England 2004 showed that 14% of 2- to 11-year-olds and 25% of 11- to 15-year-olds were obese, with a body mass index (BMI) greater than the 95th centile.[3]

Ethnic variations

Prevalence of obesity by ethnicity

Table 4.1, derived by Rennie and Jebb[4] from Health Survey for England, shows that while the prevalence of obesity in men from black Caribbean and south Asian origin is either similar or lower than in the general population, the prevalence of obesity in women from these ethnic groups is higher, especially for black Caribbean and Pakistani women. These findings are of relevance to metabolic complications.

Table 4.1. Prevalence of obesity (percentage with BMI > 30 kg/m²) in adults (16 to 55+ years) by ethnic group; data from Health Survey for England (1999)[18]

	Men (n = 3204)	Women (n = 3699)
Black Caribbean	18.3%	31.9%
Indian	11.9%	19.6%
Pakistani	12.6%	25.6%
Bangladeshi	5.4%	9.5%
Chinese	6.2%	4.5%
Irish	20.4%	21.2%
General population	18.9%	20.9%

Enhanced sensitivity to adverse metabolic effects of obesity in south Asians

There is now greater awareness of the different physical characteristics of south Asians and Europeans. South Asians have a different distribution of body fat compared with Europeans. They tend to have thinner limbs, suggestive of smaller muscle mass. Despite their relative 'peripheral' thinness, they are centrally obese, with a higher waist:hip ratio and higher subscapular:triceps skinfold ratio (indicating central obesity) than European counterparts.[5] South Asians have been shown to have more body fat per body mass compared with white Europeans.[6,7] In other words, south Asians carry more fat tissue (and less muscle tissue) and that fat is more centrally located, a finding that may have both genetic and developmental origins. It is of importance that south Asians generally exercise less than white Europeans, but data on dietary factors are not conclusive in either direction.

The recent International Diabetes Federation (IDF) definition of the metabolic syndrome acknowledges ethnic differences in fat distribution.[8] In defining central obesity, this document specifies different waist circumference cut-off values for various ethnic groups. For south Asian women, the cut-off point is the same as for European women (≥ 80 cm), but for south Asian men, the cut-off point is lower than for their European counterparts (≥ 90 cm versus ≥ 94 cm). The increased visceral adiposity in south Asians compared with Europeans may be pivotal to the greater burden of risk factors associated with the development of cardiovascular disease and diabetes in south Asians.[9]

South Asians have two- to four-fold higher rates of diabetes than Europeans and also develop both type 2 diabetes mellitus and cardiovascular disease, on average, a decade earlier.[10] They also develop diabetes at lower average BMI, consistent with lower waist cut-offs to define obesity.[10] In BMI terms, south Asians are considered to be overweight once BMI exceeds 23 kg/m² and obese at BMI beyond 27.5 kg/m².[11] South Asians also account for most childhood cases of diabetes in the UK. This latter finding is consistent with early differences in metabolism, which may also be apparent at birth.

In keeping with greater insulin resistance at any given BMI, south Asians have higher triglyceride and glucose levels, lower levels of high density lipoprotein (HDL) cholesterol and also higher markers of inflammation and vascular dysfunction.[9]

Afro-Caribbeans

Like south Asians, Afro-Caribbean individuals tend to have higher rates of type 2 diabetes than white Europeans, even with similar BMI. They also tend to have a higher prevalence of hypertension and stroke but, paradoxically, a lower prevalence (or mortality) of coronary heart disease (CHD) than white European groups in the UK.[12] In the Southall study, Afro-Caribbeans had a higher prevalence of diabetes (15% compared with 5% in Europeans) and higher systolic blood pressure (128 versus 121 mmHg). However, paradoxically, lipid profiles in this group of people are healthier (i.e. less atherogenic) than in Europeans, and HDL cholesterol (1.37 versus 1.25 mmol/l) and triglyceride (1.09 versus 1.48 mmol/l) levels are lower.[13] The more favourable lipid profile in British Afro-Caribbeans has also been shown by others[14] and may relate to their ability to store more fat in subcutaneous tissues than in visceral areas.

African-Americans, in contrast, exhibit a different pattern compared with people of African ancestry in the UK, with cardiovascular disease as the leading cause of death. It has been suggested that the higher CHD risk in African-Americans compared with UK-based people of African/Caribbean origin might relate to factors such as greater levels of obesity, lower socio-economic status and poorer access to health care. It is also suggested that sudden cardiac death is more common among African-Americans compared with white Americans.

Obesity rates around the world

The prevalence of adult obesity has exceeded 30% in the USA, is over 20% in most of Europe (5–23% in men, 7–36% in women), and is 40–70% in the Gulf states and Polynesian islands. Obesity is also present in low-income countries, and the lower socio-economic groups are affected most. In most countries, the prevalence of obesity now exceeds 15%, the figure used by the World Health Organization (WHO) to define the critical threshold for intervention in nutritional epidemics.[15] Obesity is therefore a global problem (Figure 4.1).

Obesity variation by socio-economic status

Obesity is slightly more common in children from socio-economically deprived families, for reasons that are unclear. In the UK, obesity is also more common among women from socio-economically deprived areas. In 2003, the prevalence of obesity among women was lower in managerial and professional households (18.7%) and in intermediate households (19.6%) than in routine and manual households (29.0%).

Figure 4.2 demonstrates the association of income (in quintiles) with obesity rates measured by all of BMI, waist circumference and waist:hip ratio in women in Scotland.[16] It is clear that all three measures of obesity are inversely associated with income status. The same association is not seen in men and the reason why women from low socio-economic areas experience more obesity is not clear but requires greater attention.

In a study of women booking for antenatal care in Glasgow,[17] women from the intermediate or deprived deprivation category were 3.7 time more likely to be obese than women from the most affluent areas. This analysis took account of maternal age, parity, booking gestational age and smoking and thus is in keeping with data in the general non-pregnant population.

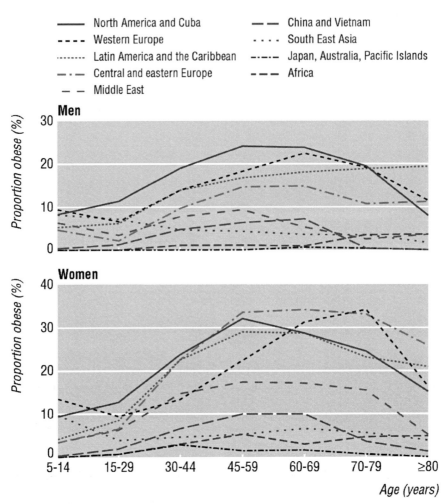

Figure 4.1. Prevalence of obesity worldwide; reproduced with permission from Haslam *et al.*[1] and adapted with permission from Haslam and James[15]

Finally, it must be remembered that obesity is increasing in all social classes and thus it would be wrong to focus attention on any particular group. Rather, strategies for obesity prevention and management should target all socio-economic status groups from a societal perspective.

Key messages

- By 2010, 33% of UK adults could be obese.
- Obesity levels tend to reach a maximum at around 50 years of age and decline after 60 years.
- Obesity levels are higher in south Asian and Afro-Caribbean women (but not men) compared with European counterparts.

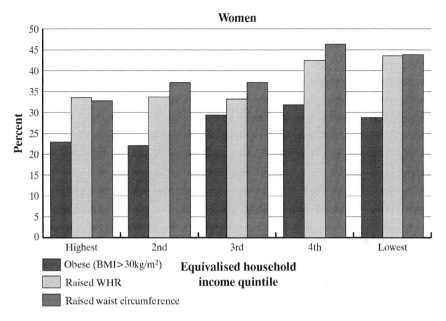

Figure 4.2. Prevalence of general and central obesity (age-standardised), by equivalised household income and sex; reproduced with permission from the Scottish Health Survey (2003)[16]

- South Asians are more sensitive than white Europeans to the effects of obesity and develop diabetes and CHD at lower average age and BMI.
- Afro-Caribbean people in the UK tend to have higher blood pressure and experience more stroke and diabetes but, paradoxically, have less CHD than white Europeans.
- Obesity is slightly more common in children from socio-economically deprived families in the developed world.
- Obesity is more common especially among women (but not men) from socio-economically deprived areas.

References

1. Haslam D, Sattar N, Lean M. ABC of obesity. Obesity – time to wake up. *BMJ* 2006;333:640–2.
2. Lean M, Gruer L, Alberti G, Sattar N. ABC of obesity. Obesity – can we turn the tide? *BMJ* 2006;333:1261–4.
3. Reilly JJ, Wilson D. ABC of obesity. Childhood obesity. *BMJ* 2006;333:1207–10.
4. Rennie KL, Jebb SA. Prevalence of obesity in Great Britain. *Obes Rev* 2005;6:11–12.
5. Yajnik CS. The insulin resistance epidemic in India: fetal origins, later lifestyle, or both? *Nutr Rev* 2001;59:1–9.
6. Banerji MA, Faridi N, Atluri R, Chaiken RL, Lebovitz HE. Body composition, visceral fat, leptin, and insulin resistance in Asian Indian men. *J Clin Endocrinol Metab* 1999;84:137–44.
7. Deurenberg P, Deurenberg-Yap M, Guricci S. Asians are different from Caucasians and from each other in their body mass index/body fat per cent relationship. *Obes Rev* 2002;3:141–6.
8. The IDF consensus worldwide definition of the metabolic syndrome. International Diabetes Federation; 2005 [www.idf.org/webdata/docs/IDF_Metasyndrome_definition.pdf].

9. Forouhi NG, Sattar N. CVD risk factors and ethnicity – a homogeneous relationship? *Atheroscler Suppl* 2006;7:11–19.

10. Mukhopadhyay B, Forouhi NG, Fisher BM, Kesson CM, Sattar N. A comparison of glycaemic and metabolic control over time among South Asian and European patients with Type 2 diabetes: results from follow-up in a routine diabetes clinic. *Diabet Med* 2006;23:94–8.

11. WHO Expert Consultation. Appropriate body-mass index for Asian populations and its implications for policy and intervention strategies. *Lancet* 2004;363:157–63.

12. Wild S, McKeigue P. Mortality by country of birth in England and Wales, 1970–1992. *Br Med J* 1997;314:689–762.

13. McKeigue PM, Shah B, Marmot MG. Relation of central obesity and insulin resistance with high diabetes prevalence and cardiovascular risk in South Asians. *Lancet* 1991;337:382–6.

14. Chaturvedi N, McKeigue PM, Marmot MG. Resting and ambulatory blood pressure differences in Afro-Caribbeans and Europeans. *Hypertension* 1993;22:90–6.

15. Haslam D, James WP. Obesity. *Lancet* 2005;366:1197–209.

16. Scottish Executive. *The Scottish Health Survey 2003. Volume 2: Adults.* Edinburgh: Scottish Executive; 2005 [www.scotland.gov.uk/Resource/Doc/76169/0019729.pdf].

17. Kanagalingam MG, Forouhi NG, Greer IA, Sattar N. Changes in booking body mass index over a decade: retrospective analysis from a Glasgow Maternity Hospital. *BJOG* 2005;112:1431–3.

18. Department of Health. *Health Survey for England 1999.* London: Department of Health; 2000.

Section 2

Obesity and female health

Chapter 5
Treating menstrual disturbance including pelvic pain (excluding PCOS)

Siân Jones, Vyjayanthi Srinivasan and
Bramara Guruwadayarhalli

Introduction

Obesity is a growing health problem worldwide. The overall reported prevalence of obesity (defined as a body mass index (BMI) greater than 30 kg/m^2) in women in the UK is 23%, with a further 33% being overweight (BMI > 25 kg/m^2).[1] The incidence of obesity is rising, particularly in adolescents and children. Koliopoulos et al.[2] studied the prevalence of obesity in an adolescent gynaecology clinic in Kettering and showed that 24% were obese and a further 17% overweight. There are few anti-obesity strategies that work. The only evidence-based approaches that are of proven benefit are bariatric surgery, drug treatments and multi-component weight-loss programmes that include diet, exercise and behavioural therapy.[3]

Studies have shown that there is an increased incidence of menstrual disorders in women who are obese.[4,5] Although a significant proportion of women who are obese have polycystic ovary syndrome (PCOS), studies have shown that women who are obese but without PCOS also experience menstrual cycle problems such as oligomenorrhoea, amenorrhoea and irregular menstrual cycles. A study by Castillo-Martinez et al.[6] in 2003 showed that, among a group of women without PCOS who were obese, 18.3% had oligomenorrhoea, 11.7% had amenorrhoea and 30% had menstrual cycle irregularities. They also showed that obesity grade is independently associated with menstrual cycle disturbances and the risk of amenorrhoea and oligomenorrhoea were increased two-fold for each unit increase of obesity grade. Rowland et al.[7] also showed a similar dose–response relation between BMI and long and irregular menstrual cycles.

Apart from the degree of obesity, evidence indicates that abnormal fat distribution rather than the degree of obesity plays an important role. Douchi et al.[8] studied the relative contribution of upper and lower body obesity to obesity-related menstrual disorders and concluded that upper body obesity (intra-abdominal visceral adiposity), and not lower body obesity, is associated with menstrual disorders.

Epidemiology

Some gynaecological conditions are more common in women who are obese than in those who are lean. Apart from the increased incidence of hormonal disturbances leading to anovulatory cycles, women who are obese are also found to be at increased risk of developing fibroids, endometrial polyps and endometrial hyperplasia, which cause abnormal uterine bleeding. Although other conditions are less common, on balance it can be expected that women who are obese will be over-represented among women presenting with gynaecological problems in both primary and secondary care.

Endometrial polyps

There are conflicting reports in the literature regarding the relationship between obesity and the incidence of endometrial polyps. Obesity associated with hypertension may act as an important factor in the pathogenesis of endometrial polyps. Reslova et al.[9] examined the characteristics of 245 women with endometrial polyps: 39% were overweight and 26% were obese. Savelli et al.[10] looked at the histological diagnosis of 509 endometrial polyps and showed that 70.3% were benign, 25.7% had simple or complex endometrial hyperplasia, 3.1% had hyperplasia with atypia and 0.8% were malignant. Age, menopausal status, obesity and hypertension were significantly associated with malignant or atypical polyps. Giordano et al.[11] studied six cases of endometrial cancer arising in polyps. They concluded that postmenopausal status, hypertension and obesity could all be considered risk factors for carcinomatous transformation within endometrial polyps in women with no history of breast cancer or tamoxifen treatment. In general, there is a paucity of data in the literature and more research studies are needed.

Fibroids

Several authors have studied the relationship between body fat and the risk of developing fibroids. The risk of having fibroids increases with increasing BMI and heavier women are at a two- to three-fold greater risk than the leanest women.[12–14] However, there are other studies that do not show such correlation.[15,16] Wise et al.[17] performed a prospective investigation regarding the risk of self-reported uterine fibroids (ultrasound/hysterectomy) in relation to BMI in a large cohort of black American women. BMI and weight gain exhibited a complex relation with risk of uterine leiomyomas. The BMI association was inverse J-shaped and findings were stronger in parous women. Weight gain was positively associated with risk among parous women only.

Apart from the BMI, occult obesity (BMI < 24 kg/m^2 and percentage body fat > 30%) and upper body fat distribution may lead to the development of uterine fibroids.[18] In one study, analyses were performed separately for uterine leiomyomas confirmed by ultrasound only as opposed to those confirmed by hysterectomy: the association with BMI was consistently stronger for women with hysterectomy-managed disease.[19] This study showed that excess weight in early adulthood was not associated with risk. Shikora et al.[20] in their retrospective study investigated the relationship between symptomatic uterine fibroids and obesity by reviewing hospital records of women undergoing myomectomy/hysterectomy for fibroids. They found 51% of the study population were obese and 15% severely obese and concluded that symptomatic fibroids were another co-morbid disease state associated with obesity. Schwartz,[21] in a review article on the epidemiology of fibroids, concluded that there is a lack of a consistent association with BMI. Obesity may contribute to risk, primarily by enhancing the growth of uterine fibroids, but does not influence the initial development of these tumours. Obesity either promotes the development or increases the severity of symptoms in women and may also reduce the effectiveness of non-surgical approaches to managing uterine fibroids.

From the above studies it can be concluded that symptomatic fibroids needing intervention are more common in women who are obese. From a practical point of view, conservative management should be considered as women who are obese are at high surgical risk.

Endometrial hyperplasia

Endometrial hyperplasia is a precursor to endometrial cancer. Women at any age with unopposed estrogen from any source are at an increased risk. Endometrial hyperplasia is more common, both pre- and postmenopausally, in women who are obese, as androgens produced by the adrenal glands and adipose tissues are converted into estrogens (estrone) by aromatase.

In premenopausal women, unopposed estrogen from anovulatory cycles (more common in women who are obese) has been shown to increase the likelihood of endometrial hyperplasia and cancer. A classification system for endometrial hyperplasia has been developed based on the complexity of endometrial glands and cytological atypia. Untreated, fewer than 2% of hyperplasias without atypia progress to carcinoma and the mean duration of progression is 10 years. If untreated, atypical hyperplasia progresses to carcinoma in 23% of cases over a mean duration of 4 years.[22] The risk of concomitant carcinoma in the uterus with atypical hyperplasia has been reported to be as high as 17–25%.[23]

Endometriosis

The prevalence of endometriosis is estimated to be 10–15% in women of reproductive age. Studies have shown that women with endometriosis have lower BMI and are less frequently obese than control subjects.[24] In a cohort study of women undergoing laparoscopy, women with endometriosis were taller and thinner and had significantly lower BMI. Higher BMI was statistically protective for a diagnosis of endometriosis: for every unit increase in BMI there was approximately a 12–14% decrease in the likelihood of being diagnosed with endometriosis.[25] Data from the Nurses' Health Study II showed an inverse relationship with BMI at age 18 years but no association with waist:hip ratio (WHR). An inverse relationship with current BMI was observed only when there was concurrent infertility.[26]

Obesity may cause hyper-estrogenism and, because endometriosis is ectopic endometrium, hyper-estrogenism could theoretically cause hyperplasia or transformation into cancer. Zanetta et al.[27] studied cancers arising from endometriosis over a 10 year period and found that there was a trend towards higher risk of development of cancer in women with high BMI or with prolonged use of unopposed estrogens. They also found that, when obesity and unopposed estrogen were combined, the difference was statistically significant and hence concluded that hyper-estrogenism is a significant risk factor for the development of cancer from endometriosis.

Adenomyosis

There are no data available relating to obesity, but extrapolating from endometriosis one might conclude there would be a lower incidence of adenomyosis in women who are obese. There are few data regarding treatment options but hysterectomy or the levonorgestrel-releasing intrauterine system (LNG-IUS) are the mainstays of treatment.[28]

Dysmenorrhoea

Hirata et al.[29] studied nearly 3000 Japanese adolescents and found that dysmenorrhoea was less common in obese teenagers than in thin teenagers.

Initial assessment

History

A weight history should be taken and the common pathologies should be kept in mind.

Examination

General practitioners referring women who are obese should clearly indicate the BMI in the referral letter. This enables appropriate equipment and staff to be planned in advance. Women who are obese will need bigger chairs, beds, operating tables and examination couches. They may need hoists and assistants. Gynaecological examination poses difficulties for women who are obese: they may develop dyspnoea in the supine position and may have to be examined in a propped-up position. Abdominal masses can be difficult to detect in women who are obese unless the mass is large. Assessing uterine size correctly can make the difference between an abdominal or vaginal approach to surgery. If size is difficult to determine, imaging is appropriate.[30]

Pelvic assessment may require retraction of the pannus to gain access to the perineum. Long and wide speculums may be needed. Viewing the cervix may be easier in the left lateral position with a Sims speculum. Bimanual examination in women who are obese is often unhelpful. Padilla et al.[31] studied the limitations of pelvic examinations in evaluating the pelvic organs. The study was double blinded and compared the assessments of examiners and surgical findings. It considered obesity as an effect-modifying variable and significantly reduced the detection of adnexal masses, although uterine assessment was found to be more accurate.

Cervical cytology and swabs

There may be difficulty in accessing the cervix – see above.

Endometrial biopsy

The H Pipelle®, a device used for 'no touch' biopsy during 'no touch' hysteroscopy, may be the most suitable sampling device for women who are obese.[32] It is 60 cm long, whereas the standard Pipelle® is 23 cm long. It also develops a higher suction pressure and obtains a greater volume of material, ensuring a good sample of endometrium at the first attempt.[33]

Imaging

Imaging is often suboptimal. Currently, imaging technology has limited ability to accommodate women who are obese and to provide the desired quality of images. Radiologists are more interested in actual weight and body diameter than BMI as these measurements determine whether the woman will fit on or in the imaging equipment. Table weights and aperture diameters differ between machines being used. This information should be easily available to clinicians who request imaging. For ordinary radiology, the woman's surface area may be too large to fit the standard 14 × 17 inch cassette. Multiple cassettes may be used.[34]

In sonography, obesity may limit appropriate positioning for good images and is also limited because:

▨ increased thickness of the body results in poor penetration of the ultrasound beam beyond the focal depth of the probe

▨ the increased attenuation of the ultrasound beam at it passes through adipose tissue further compounds the issue of beam penetration.

Solutions to improve image quality include using the lowest frequency transducers available, imaging the organ of interest within the focal length of the transducer and determining the amount of adipose tissue from other imaging, e.g. computed tomography (CT) or magnetic resonance imaging (MRI).

Computed tomography

If a woman can fit on the CT scanner, image quality is generally adequate. Details of small structures are visible in most people who are obese.

Magnetic resonance imaging

An MRI scan table has a weight limit of 159 kg and a body diameter limit of 60 cm.[34]

Transvaginal ultrasound scanning

A transvaginal ultrasound scan (TVS) is used to assess the uterine size, myometrial and endometrial structural abnormalities and adnexal masses. In the NICE clinical guideline for heavy menstrual bleeding published in January 2007,[35] pelvic scanning is recommended to detect structural and histological abnormalities. The NICE Guideline Development Group evaluated all the evidence on TVS, diagnostic hysteroscopy and saline infusion sonography, including two recent systematic reviews, and found a wide variation in published results on accuracy of each modality.[36,37] Following the consultation process, NICE recommended that imaging should be undertaken in the following circumstances:

▨ the uterus is palpable abdominally

▨ vaginal examination reveals a pelvic mass of uncertain origin

▨ pharmaceutical treatment fails.

The NICE guideline also recommended the following in terms of diagnosis:

▨ ultrasound is the first-line diagnostic tool for identifying structural abnormalities

▨ if imaging shows the presence of uterine fibroids, appropriate treatment should be planned based on size, number and location of the fibroids

▨ saline infusion sonography should not be used as a first-line diagnostic tool

▨ MRI should not be used as a first-line diagnostic tool.[35]

Hysteroscopy

Hysteroscopy is the gold standard for investigating and treating intracavitary anomalies such as polyps and fibroids, and for assessing the cavity for suitability for ablative techniques. Ambulatory hysteroscopy will be more appropriate for women who are obese to avoid the risks of general anaesthesia.[38] Longer hysteroscopes will need to be developed to allow better access to the uterine cavity in women who are obese. The Greenberg speculum can reduce the intra-speculum distance from the handle on the hysteroscope to the external cervical os by an average of 28 mm compared with the Graves speculum.[39] A vaginoscopic approach may be more comfortable as speculum and tenaculum are avoided and thus this approach is associated with considerably less discomfort.[40]

Laparoscopy

Diagnostic laparoscopy in women who are obese may be technically challenging but there are some techniques that can be adopted to reduce risk.[41] Although it is generally recommended to perform an open (Hasson) technique for primary entry for women who are morbidly obese, it is clear that even this technique is fraught with difficulties. If a Veress needle approach is used, it is important to make the vertical incision deep in the base of the umbilicus since this is the area where skin, deep fascia and parietal peritoneum of the anterior abdominal wall meet. In this area there is little opportunity for the parietal peritoneum to tent away from the Veress needle and allow retroperitoneal insufflation and surgical emphysema. In this situation, as long as the needle is inserted vertically, the average distance from the lower margin of the umbilicus to the peritoneum is 6 ± 3 cm, which will allow the placement of a standard-length needle even in those who are extremely obese.[42] Any attempt to introduce a needle at 45° means that the needle has to traverse distances of 11–16 cm, which is too long for a standard Veress needle.[43] Complete assessment of the pelvis for pathology may be difficult, owing to the excessive fat pad in the abdomen, omentum and around the bowel.

Transvaginal hydrolaparoscopy

Gordts et al.[44] showed that transvaginal hydrolaparoscopy (THL) in the office setting allowed early and complete endoscopic screening for women who are infertile. In a study of 157 women, access to the pouch of Douglas was achieved in 95% of cases. Failure was more common in women who were obese. Rectal perforation occurred in one woman, and this was treated conservatively. A multinational retrospective survey of nearly 4000 procedures showed that the risk of bowel injury during THL was 0.25%. Most tended to be minor and 92% were treated expectantly. Data on the use of THL in women who are obese are not available.[45]

Treatment options

Menorrhagia

If the history and investigations indicate that pharmaceutical treatment is appropriate and either hormonal or non-hormonal treatments are acceptable, treatments should be considered in the following order:

1. LNG-IUS, provided that long-term (at least 12 months) use is anticipated
2. tranexamic acid or nonsteroidal anti-inflammatory drugs (NSAIDs) or combined oral contraceptives (COCs)
3. norethisterone (15 mg) daily from days 5 to 26 of the menstrual cycle, or injected long-acting progestogens.

In women wishing to conceive, tranexamic acid or NSAIDs are recommended as first-line agents.[35]

With regard to menstrual disorders in women who are obese, the need for management of BMI as part of the treatment process has not been well recognised. Anti-obesity drugs have, however, been used to treat both obesity and menstrual disorders successfully.[46]

LNG-IUS

Controlled trials supported by observational studies show that the use of LNG-IUS can reduce the menstrual loss by 79–97% at 3–6 months with a continuation rate of 65–88%.[47,48] LNG-IUS has the advantage of avoiding the systemic effects of hormones, but provides similar beneficial effect on the endometrium and hence would provide the best first-line option in women who are obese with menstrual disorders. In view of the high risk of endometrial hyperplasia in women who are obese with amenorrhoea/oligomenorrhoea, these women need to have regular endometrial shedding either with hormones or LNG-IUS as this has a protective effect on the endometrium. Hence LNG-IUS could be recommended as a first-line treatment in women who are obese. LNG-IUS is more effective than cyclical norethisterone for 21 days as a treatment for heavy menstrual bleeding.[49]

Tranexamic acid

Tranexamic acid has also been found to be effective in controlling ovulatory bleeding. There are no data available within randomised controlled trials (RCTs) that record the frequency of thromboembolic events.[50] However large-scale studies in Scandinavia have shown that the incidence of thrombosis in women treated by tranexamic acid is no different from the spontaneous incidence of thrombosis in women.[51] Therefore, it can be presumed that tranexamic acid does not add to the background risk of thrombosis and so could be used safely in women who are obese. Tranexamic acid causes a greater reduction in objective measurements of heavy menstrual bleeding when compared with placebo or other medical therapies (NSAIDs or luteal phase progestogens).[50]

Nonsteroidal anti-inflammatory drugs

NSAIDs have been shown to be effective in reducing menstrual blood loss (30–50%) in women with menorrhagia, particularly those who are ovulatory.[52] They could also be used as an adjunct to progestogens in women with anovulatory bleeding. The evidence with regard to NSAIDs on the Cochrane database shows that NSAIDs reduce heavy menstrual bleeding but are less effective than tranexamic acid or danazol. There were no statistical differences between NSAIDs and the oral contraceptive pill, luteal progestogen or an intrauterine system. There was no evidence of a difference between individual NSAIDs in reducing heavy menstrual bleeding.[53]

Progestogens

The major role of progestogens is in the management of anovulatory bleeding. Prolonged use of cyclical systemic progestogens is associated with adverse effects such as weight gain, mood changes and deleterious effects on lipid profile. These adverse effects have the potential to worsen the metabolic profile in women who are obese. Hence systemic progestogens have only a short-term role in the management of heavy menstrual bleeding in women who are obese. The Cochrane review on treatment options available for heavy menstrual bleeding was published in 2006. With regard to cyclical progestogens for 21 days, a reduction in menstrual loss was noted but women found the treatment less acceptable than LNG-IUS.[54]

Summary

A review of the evidence with regard to heavy menstrual bleeding and obesity shows that systemic progestogens should only be used in the short term. The agent of first choice for heavy menstrual bleeding would be LNG-IUS owing to its high efficacy, minimal adverse effects and strong suppression effect on the endometrium, thereby protecting against endometrial hyperplasia. Tranexamic acid could be safely used as an adjunct and in the treatment of acute bleeding episodes.

Endometrial polyps

The optimal therapy for endometrial polyps is hysteroscopic resection to ensure removal of the endometrial basalis, to prevent persistence or recurrence of the polyp.[55]

It is possible to remove polyps in the outpatient setting, which would be of particular advantage to women who are obese. Bettocchi et al.,[56] in a study of nearly 5000 cases of operative office hysteroscopy, showed that with scissors, graspers and forceps he was able to remove polyps up to 3.7 mm in diameter with good patient satisfaction. In a small RCT of 40 women diagnosed with endometrial polyps at outpatient hysteroscopy, Marsh et al.[57] studied the use of different methods of removal: immediate removal using graspers or a bipolar electrode or elective removal under general anaesthetic with a resectoscope. The study showed that outpatient polypectomy was better tolerated, led to a significantly shorter time away from home or work, allowed for faster recovery and was preferred by the women. Other authors have suggested that the bipolar electrode or formal resectoscopy is a better modality to prevent recurrence.[58] This study also suggested that the bipolar electrode is better for small, non-fundal polyps and resectoscopy is better for polyps larger than 2 cm, or if they are fundal.[58]

Endometrial hyperplasia

Endometrial hyperplasia without atypia responds well to progestogens but women with atypical hyperplasia should be treated with hysterectomy unless there are other factors precluding surgery. A retrospective analysis of 351 women diagnosed with endometrial hyperplasia showed that 80% of women with atypical hyperplasia were managed by hysterectomy compared with 30% without atypia. Of those women managed conservatively, 36% had persistent or progressive disease (mean follow-up 36 months).[59]

In a retrospective study of 602 women with complex and atypical hyperplasia, 86% were obese. In untreated women, 2% of the complex hyperplasias progressed into endometrial cancer and 10.5% into atypical hyperplasia. Of the atypical hyperplasias, 52% progressed to endometrial cancer but 20.3% regressed spontaneously. In the treated women, 61% of the atypical hyperplasias regressed with progestin therapy.[60]

Cyclic or continuous progestogens, intrauterine progestogens, gonadotrophin-releasing hormone agonists (GnRHa), aromatase inhibitors, danazol and hysterectomy are all options for treatment. Choice of treatment depends on the woman's age, need to retain fertility, surgical risk and presence of cytological atypia. As people who are obese pose high surgical risk, these women are more likely to be offered conservative management.

The anti-proliferative effect of progestogens on the human endometrium is well known and they have been widely used in the treatment of hyperplasias for over 40 years. Treatment is commonly accompanied by the finding of an inactive or suppressed endometrium after therapy. However, 30% of endometrial hyperplasia cases do not respond to progestogens and hyperplastic glands persist.

Systemic progestogens

Cyclical or continuous progesterones have been used in the treatment of endometrial hyperplasia. Cyclic medroxyprogesterone acetate has been used effectively to treat premenopausal women with hyperplasia without atypia. Regression was noted in 80% of women, 92% had normal endometrium at 12 months and after a mean of 7 years follow-up showed no cases of endometrial carcinoma.[61] In the same study, atypical hyperplasia was treated with continuous medroxyprogesterone acetate but only 25% reverted to normal endometrium and 25% were diagnosed with endometrial cancer within a mean of 5.5 years. This study also emphasised the higher incidence of resistance to regression of atypical hyperplasia to benign endometrium.[61]

If women with atypical hyperplasia choose to avoid surgery, or are unsuitable for surgery, and take progestogens, they need close follow-up with biopsy every 3–6 months and the progesterone dose should be altered according to the histology.

LNG-IUS

Local hormone delivery with the LNG-IUS device causes high levonorgestrel levels in endometrial tissue but low levels in the systemic circulation. In turn, this leads to strong endometrial suppression. In a retrospective cohort study, Vereide et al.[62] showed that LNG-IUS is superior to oral treatment with medroxyprogesterone acetate for endometrial hyperplasia. They showed that women with hyperplasia of the highest malignant potential might benefit most from LNG-IUS. They also showed that LNG-IUS causes complete downregulation of progesterone receptor (PR) expression and considerable downregulation of estrogen receptor (ER) expression in both glands and stroma. Although downregulation of PR and ER receptors were noted with systemic treatment, it was more pronounced with LNG-IUS.[63]

Gonadotrophin-releasing hormone agonists

Several studies have demonstrated the efficacy of conservative management with progestogens and GnRHa in women with endometrial hyperplasia with and without atypia. Using GnRHa alone resulted in regression in 87% of a group of women including those with hyperplasia and hyperplasia with atypia at 6 months. Adding progestogens gives favourable results even in women with atypical hyperplasia. Perez-Medina et al.[64] reported regression in 16 out of 19 women treated with norethisterone (NET) and triptorelin after 6 months.

GnRHa and tibolone as add-back therapy for endometrial hyperplasia achieved complete remission in all women but found 19% recurrence at 2 years of follow-up.[65] Subsequently, however, it has been shown by the Million Women Study that tibolone increases the risk of endometrial cancer.[66]

Aromatase inhibitors

Aromatase inhibitors interrupt endogenous peripheral estrogen production (from C19 steroids), avoid the adverse effects of high-dose progestogens and may be an effective hormone therapy for women who are obese. They have shown their potential either as single agents or in combination with progestogens. Anastrozole (1 mg/day) for 12 months has been used to treat 11 postmenopausal women who were obese with endometrial hyperplasia, who were not fit for surgery. At a mean of 10 months follow-up, all of them had atrophic endometrium.[67]

Endometrial hyperplasia has often been associated with diabetes. Session et al.[68] describe the case of a 37-year-old woman whose atypical endometrial hyperplasia was resistant to progestogen therapy. The endometrium had regressed to normal 1 month after initiating metformin therapy. A comprehensive review of current thinking was published in 2006.[69]

Transcervical resection of the endometrium

Vilos *et al.*[70] showed resectoscopic surgery may be effective therapy for endometrial hyperplasia without atypia, especially in women at high risk for medical therapy or hysterectomy. An earlier study of hysteroscopic resection of endometrial hyperplasia without atypia in 73 women by Cianferoni *et al.*[71] showed resection was effective in achieving regression of endometrial hyperplasia and prevents its recurrence. Follow-up was for 3 years.

Summary

A review of the evidence shows that, in women who are obese, hyperplasia is more common. Although conservative modes of treatment would be ideal in these women, they need very close follow-up given the high rate of concomitant endometrial carcinoma in women with cytological atypia. Further studies to look into the response rate of treatment with LNG-IUS in this subgroup of women are required. Anastrozole holds promise for the future but more RCTs are needed.

Medical treatments for fibroids

Gonadotrophin-releasing hormone agonists

Many studies of GnRHa in women with fibroids have reported between 35% and 61% reduction in fibroid and uterine volume after 3–6 months of treatment.[72] There is no evidence that one is superior to the other. By the 3rd or 4th month, maximal effect of tumour reduction is achieved. In addition, the estradiol level at week 12 and the weight of women affect the degree of shrinkage. Heavier women show less shrinkage probably owing to extragonadal estradiol.[72] Peripheral adipose tissue can contribute significantly to the circulating estrogen pool, which is formed independently of pituitary function. Obesity can therefore interfere with GnRHa treatment as there can be normal circulating estrogen levels despite gonadotrophin suppression.[73] Once treatment stops, the uterus rapidly returns to pretreatment volumes, often within weeks. This makes long-term treatment ineffective but there is still a role for using short-term GnRHa for preoperative therapy.

Progesterone antagonists/antiprogesterones

These drugs have been in use for more than 25 years and their safety and efficacy is proven.

Mifepristone

Steinauer *et al.*[74] conducted a systematic review of mifepristone for the treatment of uterine leiomyomas. There were no RCTs. The authors concluded that mifepristone showed reduction in leiomyoma size (ranging from 26% to 74%), pain and bleeding. A notable adverse effect was development of endometrial hyperplasia. Transient elevation in transaminases occurred in 4%.

A subsequent RCT of low-dose mifepristone (5 mg versus 10 mg) for a period of 1 year showed good response rates with reduction in myoma volume by 52% at 12 months.[75] Endometrial hyperplasia was noted in the 10 mg group and uterine volumes increased in 9 out of 10 women at 6 months post-treatment, although remaining on average 42% less than baseline, i.e. re-growth occurs slowly in contrast to treatment with GnRHa.

A further RCT has studied the effect of mifepristone for symptomatic leiomyomas on uterine size and quality of life.[76] Mifepristone 5 mg daily was given to the women in the treatment arm for 26 weeks and the results showed that there was reduction in the uterine volume by 47% as opposed to an increase by 10% in the placebo arm. Improvement was also noted with regard to bleeding and other fibroid-related symptoms. There were no cases of endometrial hyperplasia or abnormal liver function.

More studies are needed into this treatment option, particularly as this would benefit women who are obese and at high surgical risk.

Selective estrogen or progesterone receptor modulators

There are several reports on the use of raloxifene, a selective estrogen receptor modulator (SERM), to prevent growth of fibroids. Jirecek et al.[77] gave 180 mg (high dose) raloxifene to 25 premenopausal women for 3 months, with reduction in fibroid volume. A lower dose has been used in conjunction with GnRHa with similar results.[78] This area remains controversial.

Selective progesterone receptor modulators (SPRMs) are a more recent treatment strategy for fibroids. The most promising one seems to be asoprisnil (J867), which exhibits endometrial anti-proliferative effects in primates. It has also been used in women with fibroids where it was noted to suppress bleeding and reduced fibroid volume in the absence of hypo-estrogenism. Asoprisnil has also been used in endometriosis, reducing nonmenstrual pain and dysmennorhoea.[79]

LNG-IUS

The available clinical data on LNG-IUS in reducing the size of fibroids are controversial. Several case reports and trials have shown a reduction in leiomyoma size in women using LNG-IUS. However, in the VUOKKO trial, no marked change was noticed in the size of fibroids.[80] Further evaluation revealed that some had grown and some had reduced in size. Mauro et al.[81] suggested that progesterone may have dual actions on uterine leiomyoma growth. However, when LNG-IUS is used in women with fibroids, it does not cause a progression of symptoms.

Uterine artery embolisation

First described in 1995 for the treatment of uterine fibroids,[82] uterine artery embolisation (UAE) was the subject of NICE interventional procedure guidance in 2004.[83] The systematic review that informed the guidance concluded that there was a reduction in mean fibroid volume of between 40% and 75%. However, symptom improvement occurred in 62–95% of women. There was a large variation in reported complication rates: the need for hysterectomy varied from 0.5% to 11.8% and late expulsion of a fibroid from 2.2% to 7.7%. Ovarian dysfunction ranged from 2.5% to 14%.

A Cochrane review on UAE for symptomatic uterine fibroids was published in January 2006.[84] Three trials were included in the review: two RCTs comparing UAE with abdominal hysterectomy and the third comparing UAE with myomectomy. With regard to improvement of fibroid-related symptoms, 85% showed an improvement in bleeding and a 30–46% reduction in fibroid volume was achieved. The authors concluded that UAE offers an advantage over hysterectomy with regard to hospital stay and return to normal activities. The higher minor complication rate and readmission rates require more long-term trials to comment on effectiveness and safety.

The Fibroid Registry for Outcomes Data (FIBROID) was established and funded by the Society of Interventional Radiology in 1999 to serve as a prospective multicentre database of women undergoing UAE (www.fibroidregistry.org). Enrolment of 3319 women occurred over a 2 year entry period between December 2000 and December 2002.

In the first report on short-term outcomes on 3005 women, at 2 days, 90 women experienced 94 adverse events, 20 of which were major. Of the 74 minor complications, groin haematomas were the most common. The average hospital stay was 1.68 days, and women resumed normal activities after 2 weeks. At 1 month, 710 women reported adverse events, 111 were major (4%) but only 32 women needed surgical intervention. Obesity was not linked to complications in the short term.[85,86] The symptom and quality of life status was assessed in 1797 women, 1 year after UAE, and this showed that most women (82%) were satisfied with the outcome. Predictors of greater improvement of symptoms were noted in women with smaller leiomyoma size, submucosal location and presenting symptom of heavy menstrual bleeding. Only 2.9% of women needed a hysterectomy in the first year of follow-up.[87] Baseline demographics showed that 12.1% of the original cohort of women were morbidly obese (BMI > 35 kg/m^2). The mean BMI was 27.9 kg/m^2. Every unit increase in BMI gave a better symptom score at 6 months and 1 year review although this was not statistically significant.

These studies show that UAE is of benefit to women as a conservative option that avoids surgery. The response rates and complication rates observed in women who are obese are no different when compared with the general population (MA Lumsden, personal communication).

However, Chapman et al.[88] undertook a UK survey of surgical and radiological management of uterine fibroids in 2006. The option of UAE was only used by 50% of respondents: hysterectomy and myomectomy remained the mainstay of treatment. Almost 50 % of UK gynaecologists carry out hysteroscopic myomectomy and just over 10% perform laparoscopic myomectomy.

Summary

A review of the evidence with regard to fibroids and obesity shows that symptomatic fibroids are more common in women who are obese. UAE holds great promise as a conservative form of management thereby avoiding surgery. However further long-term follow-up studies are needed to look into the regrowth rates and long-term complications. Mifepristone also seems to hold great promise as an alternative option in these women, although further RCTs are needed to look into the long-term success rates and adverse effects.

Surgical treatment for fibroids

Hysteroscopic surgery

Submucous fibroids can be removed by hysteroscopic resection. Most authors would agree that type 0 and type 1 fibroids of up to 5 cm can be treated hysteroscopically. Small fibroids (less than 2 cm) can be removed using the Versapoint bipolar spring electrode through the operating channel of an outpatient hysteroscope, which is of obvious advantage to women who are obese. Larger fibroids will require formal resection under regional or general anaesthesia. Pretreatment with GnRHa is advised to make the fibroid smaller and less vascular and to decrease operating time and fluid intravasation.[89] In women who are obese, preparation with GnRHa is not as effective because of the peripheral production of estrogens in the adipose tissue.[73]

Laparoscopic and abdominal myomectomy

Mais *et al.*[90] compared laparoscopic with abdominal myomectomy in a small prospective randomised trial. They demonstrated that there was no difference in blood loss or operative time between the two groups, although the laparoscopic approach was associated with less pain and shorter recovery time. Landi *et al.*[91] undertook a prospective study of 368 women undergoing laparoscopic myomectomy. They concluded that laparoscopic myomectomy was safe and effective. However neither studies commented on the BMI of their patients.

Alessandri *et al.*[92] conducted a randomised study of laparoscopic versus minilaparotomic myomectomy for uterine myomas. Again laparoscopic myomectomy was associated with less pain and quicker recovery, but higher costs. He excluded women with BMI > 29 kg/m^2 and the findings of this study cannot be applied to women who are obese.

Theoretically, myomectomy should carry increased risks in women who are obese; however, there is no evidence to support this.

Temporary uterine artery occlusion

Dickner *et al.*[93] studied Doppler-guided transvaginal uterine artery identification. This study of 109 women showed the ease of undertaking this irrespective of parity, uterine size or position. They postulated that the use of a Doppler-guided device to occlude the uterine arteries is an alternative to invasive procedures (UAE or laparoscopic uterine artery occlusion) in the treatment of women with symptomatic fibroids. A subsequent case report showed that it was possible to occlude both uterine arteries with a Doppler-directed clamp for 6 hours. This was successful in reducing symptoms of menorrhagia, uterine volume decreased by 48.9% and volume of dominant fibroid by 77.2%.[94] A more recent case report confirms this.[95] Results from a larger group of women, (post-treatment fertility and outcome in relation to BMI) are yet to be analysed. Temporary uterine artery occlusion can be postulated as a safe and effective alternative for women who are obese wishing to conserve their fertility and avoid a hysterectomy.

Endometrial ablation

The MISTLETOE (Minimally Invasive Surgical Techniques – Laser, EndoThermal or Endoresection) survey audited complications related to the first-generation techniques of endometrial resection and ablation.[96] BMI was not one of the demographic issues studied and it can only be hypothesised that complication rates might be higher. Theoretically, procedures might take longer for women who are obese if the surgeon has problems with access to the uterus, if priming has been inadequate or if standard instruments are too short to reach the whole of the uterine cavity. Hysterectomy rates after first-generation techniques are 25% at 5 years.

Second-generation techniques require less skill than those of the first generation and are inherently safer owing to shorter operating times, avoidance of fluid overload and suitability for local anaesthesia. Second-generation techniques are limited to certain maximum cavity lengths and presence of only small fibroids. There is no evidence to indicate that women who are obese have larger uterine cavities than women who are lean but are more likely to have fibroids. Hysterectomy rates after microwave endometrial ablation (MEA) are as low as 16% at 5 years.[35] Loffer[97] reviewed whether the presence of fibroids limited the ability to undertake endometrial ablation. He also studied whether fibroids affected the postoperative course and long-term outcome.

He concluded that fibroids are not a contraindication to ablation or its immediate success, but do increase the subsequent hysterectomy rates.

Necrosis of a fibroid has been described after ThermaChoice and MEA, needing further surgical intervention to remove the fibroid.[98] It should be noted that there are case reports of endometrial carcinoma after endometrial resection for dysfunctional uterine bleeding (DUB).[97]

The NovaSure impedance-controlled system for endometrial ablation may be ideal for women who are obese. No pretreatment is required and it can be readily performed under local anaesthesia. Mean treatment time is 90 seconds. The device, which is dependent on impedance developing in the tissues being ablated, calculates the treatment time. The ablation of the endometrium is a low-impedance process owing to the high level of liquid in the endometrium. When the ablation process reaches the higher density myometrium, desiccation occurs and impedance rises. Once impedance has reached 50 Ω, the device switches off. Follow-up after 3 years suggests a very low subsequent hysterectomy rate of only 3%.[99]

Sabbah et al.[100] undertook a prospective study using the NovaSure System in 65 women with heavy menstrual bleeding who all had submucous type 1 and 2 fibroids up to 3 cm. At 12 months, 95% of the women were satisfied with the procedure, including 69% with complete amenorrhoea. Results are comparable to those obtained in women with normal cavities.

Major surgery in women who are obese

There will be women who are obese who cannot be managed conservatively or where conservative approaches have failed. In these cases, surgeons should pay particular attention to the three main areas of risk: bleeding, infection and venous thromboembolism (VTE). Preoperative preparations require a multidisciplinary approach: minimally, a surgeon and anaesthetist at consultant level with two experienced assistants. A standard operating table can support a patient weighing 130–160 kg. Surgeons may need to reserve a table capable of holding more weight and which has side extensions for overlap. Full blood count and crossmatch will be necessary.[101]

Many people who are obese have associated medical problems, such as diabetes, hypertension and hypercholesterolaemia, and require appropriate preoperative investigations. Electrocardiogram, chest X-ray and peak respiratory flow rate may all be required.

Counselling and consent for the procedure and for the risks in relation to obesity should also be carefully undertaken.[3,102] Incisions for abdominal hysterectomy should be planned in advance with some thought about access, infection risk and subsequent wound integrity on an individual patient basis.[103]

Surgeons need to ensure that they have long instruments and appropriate retractors and pay particular attention to good haemostasis. Wounds should be closed with a non-absorbable/delayed absorption suture for the rectus sheath. Antibiotic prophylaxis is imperative in view of the high risk of sepsis; the dose should be calculated using body weight. Thromboprophylaxis is also essential and would include thromboembolic deterrent stockings and low molecular weight heparin. The dose should be calculated using body weight.[103]

Blomfield et al.[104] undertook a retrospective study of safety and efficacy of panniculectomy in women who were obese undergoing gynaecological surgery. The procedure improved surgical access, facilitated radical surgery, was considered to have acceptable morbidity and was cosmetically acceptable to the women.

If hysterectomy is necessary, which is the optimum route? A number of studies have evaluated the outcomes of different methods of hysterectomy in women who are obese.

Abdominal hysterectomy

Pitkin[105] retrospectively reviewed 300 women who were obese and who underwent total abdominal hysterectomy (TAH) during the period between 1948 and 1973 and compared them with matched controls weighing less than 91 kg. Women who were obese had a longer operative time, greater blood loss with consecutive transfusions, higher rate of second postoperative day pyrexia, a seven-fold increase in wound complications, and a three-fold longer length of hospital stay. There were three post-operative deaths in the obese group.

Vaginal hysterectomy

Pitkin[106] also conducted a retrospective study of 108 women who weighed more than 91 kg and compared them with matched controls weighing less than 91 kg. He showed that operating time and blood loss were greater in the obese group. He found no significant difference in the postoperative febrile morbidity, length of hospitalisation or mortality. In 1990, Pratt et al.[107] undertook a retrospective study of 471 women who were obese who had vaginal hysterectomy. They showed that the women who were obese had slightly more febrile morbidity, stayed in hospital 1 day longer and had slightly lower haemoglobin at 48 hours. They did not undertake any statistical analysis.

Abdominal versus vaginal hysterectomy

Isik-Akbay et al.[108] retrospectively compared perioperative outcomes in abdominal (369) and vaginal (180) hysterectomies for women who were obese (BMI > 30 kg/m^2). They reviewed the rate of operative and postoperative complications, operative time, perioperative change in haemoglobin concentration and length of hospital stay. Uterine weight was higher in the abdominal group and parity was greater in the vaginal group. The authors found vaginal hysterectomies were associated with shorter operative time and hospital stay and a decrease in postoperative morbidity due to fever and ileus and urinary tract infection. In the abdominal group, the wound infection rate was 3.7%. No difference was found in the need for blood transfusions.

Rasmussen et al.[109] studied the influence of BMI on the prevalence of complications after vaginal and abdominal hysterectomy. A retrospective review of 444 vaginal and 503 abdominal hysterectomies for benign indications was undertaken. Women who were obese who had TAH had larger blood loss than those who had a vaginal hysterectomy. He also found obesity predisposed to a longer operating time for both routes and this was more pronounced in the TAH group.

Laparoscopic hysterectomy

If women who are obese are at a significantly greater risk of complications when undergoing laparotomy, does laparoscopic surgery offer any benefits? In general surgery, several authors have shown that laparoscopic cholecystectomy is safe and well suited to women who are obese. These techniques offer a shorter hospital stay and more rapid recovery, and the surgical complications in women who are obese are often related to poor healing and infections.

Reich et al.[110] introduced their technique for laparoscopic hysterectomy in 1989. Heinberg et al.[111] undertook a retrospective study of operative and postoperative complications in women undergoing total laparoscopic hysterectomy (TLH), comparing women who were obese with those who were not. Although there was twice the chance of conversion to laparoscopically assisted vaginal hysterectomy (LAVH), and four times the chance of conversion to TAH in women who were obese, neither reached statistical significance. TLH for women who were obese was 60% more likely to take more than 2 hours and was associated with three times the risk of blood loss more than 500 ml, but only 3.8% of women who were obese required blood transfusion. Olsson et al.[112] compared laparoscopic with abdominal hysterectomy in a randomised prospective study. He found less operative blood loss, less postoperative pain and shorter hospital stay and convalescence and thus reduced loss of working hours in the laparoscopic group.

Laparoscopically assisted vaginal hysterectomy

Shen et al. in 2002[113] published a retrospective cohort study from Taiwan on the effects of weight on complications of LAVH. The authors classified women who were obese as having BMI > 25 kg/m^2 (Asian cut-off). There were 670 women of whom 162 had BMI > 25 kg/m^2. Overweight women had a higher chance of resort to laparotomy, and greater blood loss.

Holub et al.[114] studied laparoscopic hysterectomy in women who were obese in a comparative clinical prospective study. He compared LAVH with vaginal colpotomy against LAVH with laparoscopic colpotomy in 271 women. There were 54 women who were obese in this cohort. He also included women undergoing pelvic and infra-aortic lymph node dissections. He concluded that duration of procedure was longer (99.54 minutes versus 90.95 minutes) and major operative complications were higher (5.55% versus 3.22%) in women who were obese. There was no difference in blood loss, presence of adhesions, weight of the specimen, length of stay or postoperative complications between high and low BMI groups.

EVALUATE study

The EVALUATE RCT study compared the outcomes of abdominal, vaginal and laparoscopic hysterectomy routes and found the laparoscopic route to be associated with shorter hospital stay and less postoperative pain but associated with higher rate of complications and longer operative time. However, there was no long-term difference in women's satisfaction. The mean BMI of women in both arms of the study was 26 kg/m^2. In the abdominal arm, the incidence of major haemorrhage, bladder injury, anaesthetic problems, intraoperative conversions and postoperative morbidity was higher in the laparoscopic hysterectomy group.[115]

VALUE study

The VALUE sttudy retrospectively reviewed all types of hysterectomy conducted for DUB in the UK between 1994 and 1995. BMI was not measured. Laparoscopic techniques were associated with higher complication rates than other methods.[116]

Conclusion

There are many methods of conservative management available that are ideal for women who are obese. There is, however, scope for research in newer treatments.

As new medical managements become available, operating on women who are obese will become less common. Interventional radiology has much to offer. Those women who do need surgery need careful counselling and preparation for surgery by the multidisciplinary team. As endoscopic skills develop, women who are obese may be the ideal candidates for laparoscopic surgery because of its association with shorter hospital stays and lower complications rates. Gynaecologists are ideally placed to help women who are obese with their menstrual problems by assisting them in their battle against their weight and giving the best available evidence-based advice.

References

1. Balen AH. Editor's choice. *BJOG* 2006;113(10):i–ii.
2. Koliopoulos G, Wood PL, Papanikou E, Creatsas GJ. *J Pediatr Adolesc Gynecol* 2005;18:163–6.
3. National Institute for Health and Clinical Excellence, National Collaborating Centre for Primary Care. *Obesity: the Prevention, Identification, Assessment and Management of Overweight and Obesity in Adults and Children.* London: NICE; 2006 [www.nice.org.uk/CG043fullguideline].
4. Hartz AJ, Barboriak PN, Wong A, Katayama KP, Rimm AA. The association of obesity with infertility and related menstrual abnormalities in women. *Int J Obes* 1979;3:57–73.
5. Harlow SD, Matanoski GM. The association between weight, physical activity and stress and variation in the length of the menstrual cycle. *Am J Epidemiol* 1991;133:38.
6. Castillo-Martinez L, Lopez-Alvarenga JC, Villa AR, Gonzalez-Barranco J. Menstrual cycle length disorders in 18 to 40-y-old obese women. *Nutrition* 2003;19:317–20.
7. Rowland AS, Baird DD, Long S, Wegienka G, Harlow SD, Alavanja M, *et al.* Influence of medical conditions and lifestyle factors on the menstrual cycle. *Epidemiology* 2002;13:668–74.
8. Douchi T, Kuwahata R, Yamamoto S, Oki T, Yamasaki H, Nagata Y. Relationship of upper body obesity to menstrual disorders. *Acta Obstet Gynecol Scand* 2002;81:147–50.
9. Reslova T, Tosner J, Resl M, Kugler R, Vavrova I. Endometrial polyps. A clinical study of 245 cases. *Arch Gynecol Obstet* 1999;262:133–9.
10. Savelli l, De Iaco P, Santini D, Rosati F, Ghi T, Pignotti E, *et al.* Histopathologic features and risk factors for benignity, hyperplasia and cancer in endometrial polyps. *Am J Obstet Gynecol* 2003;188:927–31.
11. Giordano G, Gnetti L, Merisio C, Melpignano M. Postmenopausal status, hypertension and obesity as risk factors for malignant transformation in endometrial polyps. *Maturitas* 2007;56:190–7.
12. Ross RK, Pike M, Vessey MP. Risk factors for uterine fibroids: reduced risk associated with oral contraceptives. *BMJ* 1986;293:359–62.
13. Faerstein E, Szklo M, Roshenshein NB. Risk factors for uterine leiomyoma: a practice based case–control study. I. African American heritage, reproductive history, body size and smoking. *Am J Epidemiol* 2001;153:1–10.
14. Marshall LM, Spiegelman D, Barbieri RL. Variation in the incidence of uterine leiomyoma among premenopausal women by age and race. *Obstet Gynecol* 1997;90:967–73.
15. Chen CJ, Buck GM, Courey NG. Risk factors for uterine fibroids among women undergoing tubal sterilisation. *Am J Epidemiol* 2001;153:20–6.
16. Romieu I, Walker AM, Jick S. Determinants of uterine fibroids. *Post Market Surveil* 1991;5:119–33.
17. Wise LA, Palmer JR, Spiegelman D, Harlow BL, Stewart EA, Adams-Campbell LL, *et al.* Influence of body size and body fat distribution on risk of uterine leiomyomata in U.S. black women. *Epidemiology* 2005;16:346–54.
18. Sato F, Nishi M, Kudo R, Miyake H. Body fat distribution and uterine leiomyomas. *J Epidemiol* 1998;8:176–80.
19. Marshall LM, Spiegelman D, Manson JE. Risk of uterine leiomyomata among premenopausal women in relation to body size and cigarette smoking. *Epidemiology* 1998;9:511–17.
20. Shikora SA, Niloff JM, Bistrian BR, Forse RA, Blackburn GL. Relationship between obesity and uterine leiomyomata. *Nutrition* 1991;7:251–5.
21. Schwartz SM. Epidemiology of uterine leiomyomata. *Clin Obstet Gynecol* 2001;44:316–26.

22. Kurman RJ, Kaminski PF, Norris HJ. The behaviour of endometrial hyperplasia: a long-term study of untreated hyperplasia in 170 patients. *Cancer* 1985;56:403–12.

23. Montgomery BE, Daum GS, Dunton CJ. Endometrial hyperplasia: A review. *Obstet Gynecol Survey* 2004;58:368–78.

24. Ferrero S, Anserini P, Remorgida V, Ragni N. Body mass index in endometriosis. *Eur J Obstet Gynecol Reprod Biol* 2005;121:94–8.

25. Hediger ML, Hartnett HJ, Louis GM. Association of endometriosis with body size and figure. *Fertil Steril* 2005;84:1366–74.

26. Missmer SA, Hankinson SE, Spielgelman D, Barbieri RL, Marshall LM, Hunter DJ. Incidence of laparoscopically confirmed endometriosis by demographic, anthropometric and lifestyle factors. *Am J Epidemiol* 2004;160:784–96.

27. Zanetta GM, Webb MJ, Li H, Keeney GL. Hyperestrogenism: a relevant risk factor for the development of cancer from endometriosis. *Gynecol Oncol* 2000;79:18–22.

28. Farquhar C, Brosens I. Medical and surgical management of adenomyosis. *Best Prac Res Clin Obstet Gynaecol* 2006;20:603–16.

29. Hirata M, Kumabe K, Inoue Y. [Relationship between the frequency of menstrual pain and body weight in female adolescents]. *Nippon Koshu Eisei Zasshi* 2002;49:516–24. Japanese.

30. Cantuaria GHC, Angioli R, Frost L, Duncan R, Penalver MA. Comparison of bimanual examination with ultrasound examination before hysterectomy for uterine leiomyoma. *Obstet Gynecol* 1998;92:109–12.

31. Padilla LA, Radosevich DM, Milad MP. Limitations of pelvic examination for evaluation of the female pelvic organs. *Int J Gynecol Obstet* 2005;88:84–8.

32. Sharma M, Taylor A, di Speizio Sardo A, Buck L, Mastrogamvrakis G, Kosmas I, *et al.* Outpatient hysteroscopy: traditional versus the 'no touch' technique. *BJOG* 2005;112:963–67.

33. Di Spiezio Sardo A, Sharma M, Taylor A, Buck L, Magos A. A new device for 'no touch' biopsy at 'no touch' hysteroscopy: The H Pipelle. *Am J Obstet Gynecol* 2004;191:157–8.

34. Uppot RN, Sahani DV, Hahn PF, Gervais D, Mueller PR. Impact of obesity on medical imaging and image-guided intervention. *Am J Roentgenol* 2007;188:433–40.

35. National Collaborating Centre for Women's and Children's Health, National Institute for Health and Clinical Excellence. *Heavy Menstrual Bleeding.* London: RCOG Press; 2007 [www.nice.org.uk/CG044fullguideline].

36. Farquhar C, Ekeroma A, Furness S, Arroll B. A systematic review of transvaginal ultrasonography, sonohysterography and hysteroscopy for the investigation of abnormal uterine bleeding in premenopausal women. *Acta Obstet Gynecol Scand* 2003;82:493–504.

37. Dueholm M, Lundorf E, Olesen F. Imaging techniques for evaluation of the uterine cavity and endometrium in premenopausal patients before minimally invasive surgery. *Obstet Gynecol Surv* 2002;57:388–403.

38. Bakour SH, Jones SE, O'Donovan P. Ambulatory hysteroscopy: evidence-based guide to diagnosis and therapy. *Best Pract Res Clin Obstet Gynaecol* 2006;20:953–75.

39. Greenberg JA. The Greenberg hysteroscopy speculum: a new instrument for hysteroscopy. *JSLS*; 2006;10:129–30.

40. Bettocchi S. Selvaggi L. A vaginoscopic approach to reduce the pain of office hysteroscopy. *J Am Assoc Gynecol Laparosc* 1997;4:255–58.

41. Philips K, Sutton C. *Preventing Gynaecological Laparoscopic Injury.* RCOG Green-top Guideline. London: RCOG; 2007 Draft.

42. Holtz G. Insufflation of the obese patient. In: Corfman RS, Diamond MP, DeCherney AH, editors. *Complications of Laparoscopy and Hysteroscopy.* 2nd ed. Oxford: Blackwell Science; 1997.

43. Hurd WH, Bude RO, DeLancey JO, Gauvin JM, Aisen AM. Abdominal wall characterization with magnetic resonance imaging and computed tomography. The effect of obesity on the laparoscopic approach. *J Reprod Med* 1991;36:473–6.

44. Gordts S, Campo R, Brosens I. Office transvaginal hydrolaparoscopy for early diagnosis of pelvic endometriosis and adhesions. *J Am Assoc Gynecol Laparosc* 2000;7:45–9.

45. Gordts S, Watrelot A, Campo R, Brosens I. Risk and outcome of bowel injury during transvaginal pelvic endoscopy. *Fertil Steril* 2001;76:1238–41.

46.   Totoyan E, Frolowa N, Manyasan A, Akopyan M, Matevosyan A, Arutunyan J. Use of orlistat (xenical) in the treatment of women with obesity and disorders of the menstrual cycle. *Georgian Med News* 2006;139:20–2.

47.   Stewart A, Cummins C, Gold L. The effectiveness of the levonorgestrel-releasing intrauterine system in menorrhagia: a systematic review. *BJOG* 2001;108:74–86.

48.   Varma R, Sinha D, Gupta JK. Non-contraceptive uses of levonorgestrel-releasing hormone system (LNG-IUS) – A systematic enquiry and review. *Eur J Obstet Gynecol Reprod Biol* 2006;125:9–28.

49.   Lethaby AE, Cooke I, Rees M. Progesterone or progestogen-releasing intrauterine systems for heavy menstrual bleeding. *Cochrane Database Syst Rev* 2005;(4):CD002126.

50.   Lethaby A, Farquhar C, Cooke I. Antifibrinolytics for heavy menstrual bleeding. *Cochrane Database Syst Rev* 2000;(4):CD000249.

51.   Rybo G. Tranexamic acid therapy is effective treatment in heavy menstrual bleeding. *Clin Update Safety Ther Adv* 1991;4:1–8.

52.   Vargyas JM, Campeau JD, Mishell DR. Treatment of menorrhagia with meclofenamate sodium. *Am J Obstet Gynecol* 1987;157:944–50.

53.   Lethaby A, Augood C, Duckitt K. Nonsteroidal anti-inflammatory drugs for heavy menstrual bleeding. *Cochrane Database Syst Rev* 2002;(1):CD000400.

54.   Lethaby A, Irvine G, Cameron I. Cyclical progestogens for heavy menstrual bleeding. *Cochrane Database Syst Rev* 2000;(2):CD001016.

55.   Preutthipan S, Herabutya Y. Hysteroscopic polypectomy in 240 premenopausal and postmenopausal women. *Fertil Steril* 2005;83:705–9.

56.   Bettocchi S, Ceci O, Nappi L, Di Venere R, Masciopinto V, Pansini V, *et al.* Operative office hysteroscopy without anaesthesia: analysis of 4863 cases performed with mechanical instruments. *J Am Assoc Gynecol Laparosc* 2004;11:59–61.

57.   Marsh FA, Rogerson LJ, Duffy SR. A randomised controlled trial comparing outpatient versus day case endometrial polypectomy. *BJOG* 2006;113:896–901.

58.   Muzii L, Bellati F, Pernice M, Manci N, Angioli R, Panici PB. Resectoscopic versus bipolar electrode excision of endometrial polyps: a randomized study. *Fertil Steril* 2007;87:909–17.

59.   Clark TJ, Neelakantan D, Gupta JK. The management of endometrial hyperplasia: an evaluation of current practice. *Eur J Obstet Gynecol Reprod Biol* 2006;125:259–64.

60.   Horn LC, Schnurrbusch U, Bilek K, Hentschel B, Einenkel J. Risk of progression in complex and atypical endometrial hyperplasia: clinicopathologic analysis in cases with and without progestogen treatment. *Int J Gynecol Cancer* 2004;14:348–53.

61.   Ferenczy A, Gelfand M. The biologic significance of cytologic atypia in progestogen treated endometrial hyperplasia. *Am J Obstet Gynecol* 1989;160:126–31.

62.   Vereide AB, Arnes M, Straume B. Nuclear morphometric changes and therapy monitoring in patients with endometrial hyperplasia: a study comparing effects of intrauterine levonorgestrel and systemic medroxyprogesterone. *Gynecol Oncol* 2003;91:526–33.

63.   Vereide AB, Kaino T, Sager G, Arnes M, Orbo A. Effect of Levonorgestrel IUD and oral medroxyprogesterone acetate on glandular and stromal progesterone receptors (PRA and PRB) and estrogen receptors (ER-alpha and ER-beta) in human endometrial hyperplasia. *Gynecol Oncol* 2006;101:214–23.

64.   Perez-Medina T, Bajo J, Folguiera G. Atypical endometrial hyperplasia treatment with progestogens and gonadotrophin releasing hormone analogues: long-term follow-up. *Gynecol Oncol* 1999;73:299–304.

65.   Agostoras T, Vaitsi V, Pachopoulos M. Prolonged use of gonadotrophin releasing hormone agonist and Tibolone as add-back therapy for the treatment of endometrial hyperplasia. *Maturitas* 2004;48, 125–32.

66.   Million Women Study Collaborators. Endometrial cancer and hormone replacement therapy in the Million Women Study. *Lancet* 2005;365:1543–51.

67.   Agorastos T, Vaitsi V, Pantazis K. Aromatase inhibitor anastrozole for treating endometrial hyperplasia in obese postmenopausal women. *Eur J Obstet Gynecol Reprod Biol* 2005;118:239–40.

68.   Session DR, Kalli KR, Tunnon IS, Damario MA, Dumesic DA. Treatment of atypical endometrial hyperplasia with an insulin-sensitizing agent. *Gynecol Endocrinol* 2003;17:405–7.

69. Lai CH, Huang HJ. The role of hormones for the treatment of endometrial hyperplasia and endometrial cancer. *Curr Opin Obstet Gynecol* 2006;18:29–34.

70. Vilos GA, Harding PG, Ettler HC. Resectoscopic surgery in women with abnormal uterine bleeding and nonatypical endometrial hyperplasia. *J Am Assoc Gynecol Laparosc* 2002;9:131–7.

71. Cianferoni L, Giannini A, Frachini M. Hysteroscopic resection of endometrial hyperplasia. *J Am Assoc Gynecol Laparosc* 1999;6:151–54.

72. Chavez NF, Stewart EA. Medical treatment of uterine fibroids. *Clin Obstet Gynecol* 2001;44:372–84.

73. Hansen LM. Batzer FR, Corson SL, Bello S. Obesity and GnRH action. Report of a case with contribution by peripherally derived estrogens. *J Reprod Med* 1997;42:247–50.

74. Steinauer J, Pritts EA, Jackson R, Jacoby AF. Systematic review of mifepristone for the treatment of uterine leiomyomata. *Obstet Gynecol* 2004;103:1331–6.

75. Eisinger SH, Bonfiglio T, Fiscella K, Meldrum S, Guzick DS. Twelve-month safety and efficacy of low-dose mifepristone for uterine myomas. *J Minim Invasive Gynecol* 2005;12:227–33.

76. Fiscella K, Eisinger SH, Meldrum S, Feng C, Fisher S, Guzick DS. Effect of mifepristone for symptomatic leiomyomata on quality of life and uterine size: a randomized controlled trial. *Obstet Gynecol* 2006;108:1381–7.

77. Jirecek S, Lee A, Pavo I, Crans G, Eppel W, Wenzl R. Raloxifene prevents the growth of uterine leiomyomas in premenopausal women. *Fertil Steril* 2004;81:132–6.

78. Palomba S, Orio F, Russo T, Falbo A, Cascella T, Doldo P, *et al*. Long-term effectiveness and safety of GnRH agonist plus raloxifene administration in women with uterine fibroids. *Hum Reprod* 2004;19:1308–14.

79. Chwalisz K, Perez MC, Demanno D, Winkel C, Schubert G, Eiger W. Selective progesterone receptor modulator development and use in the treatment of leiomyomata and endometriosis. *Endocr Rev* 2005;26:423–38.

80. Inki P, Hurskainen R, Palo P. Comparison of ovarian cyst formation in women using the Levonorgestrel-releasing intrauterine system vs hysterectomy. *Ultrasound Obstet Gynecol* 2002;20:381–85.

81. Mauro T, Matsuo H, Shimomura Y, Kurachi O, Gao Z, Nakago S, *et al*. Effect of progesterone on growth factor expression in human uterine leiomyoma. *Steroids* 2003;68:817–24.

82. Ravina JH, Herbreteau D, Ciraru-Vigneron N, Bouret JM, Houdart E, Aymard A, *et al*. Arterial embolisation to treat uterine myomas. *Lancet* 1995;346:671–2.

83. National Institute for Clinical Excellence. *Uterine Artery Embolisation for the Treatment of Fibroids*. NICE Interventional Procedure Guidance 94. London: NICE; 2004 [www.nice.org.uk/ip020overview] and [www.nice.org.uk/IPG094].

84. Gupta JK, Sinha AS, Lumsden MA, Hickey M. Uterine artery embolization for symptomatic uterine fibroids. *Cochrane Database Syst Rev* 2006;(1):CD005073.

85. Myers ER, Goodwin S, Landow W, Mauro M, Peterson E, Pron G, *et al*.; FIBROID Investigators. Prospective data collection of a new procedure by a speciality society: The FIBROID registry. *Obstet Gynecol* 2005;106:44–51.

86. Worthington-Kirsch R, Spies JB, Myers ER, Mulgund J, Mauro M, Pron G, *et al*.; FIBROID Investigators. The Fibroid Registry for outcomes data (FIBROID) for uterine embolization: short-term outcomes. *Obstet Gynecol* 2005;106:52–9.

87. Spies JB, Myers ER, Worthington-Kirsh R, Mulgund J, Goodwin S, Mauro M; FIBROID Registry Investigators. The Fibroid registry: symptom and quality of life status 1 year after therapy. *Obstet Gynecol* 2005;10:1309–18.

88. Chapman L, Magos M. Surgical and radiological management of uterine fibroids in the UK. *Curr Opin Obstet Gynecol* 2006;18:394–401.

89. Bakour SH, Jones SE, Khan K. *Ambulatory Hysteroscopy: an Evidence-Based Guide to Diagnosis and Therapy in the Outpatient Setting*. London: RSM Press; 2006.

90. Mais V, Ajossa S, Guerriero S, Mascia M, Solla E, Melis GB. Laparoscopic versus abdominal myomectomy: A prospective, randomized trial to evaluate benefits in early outcome. *Am J Obstet Gynecol* 1996;174:654–8.

91. Landi S, Zaccoletti R, Ferrari L, Minelli L. Laparoscopic myomectomy: technique, complications and ultrasound scan evaluations. *J Am Assoc Gynecol Laparosc* 2001;8:231–40.

92. Alessandri F, Lijoi D, Mistrangelo E, Ferrero S, Ragni N. Randomized study of laparoscopic versus minilaparotomic myomectomy for uterine myomas. *J Minim Invasive Gynecol* 2006;13:92–7.

93. Dickner SK, Cooper JM, Diaz D. A non-incisional, Doppler-guided transvaginal approach to uterine artery identification and control of uterine perfusion. *J Am Assoc Gynecol Laparosc* 2004;11:55–8.

94. Istre O, Hald KH, Qvigstad E. Multiple myomas treated with a temporary, noninvasive, Doppler-directed, transvaginal uterine artery clamp. *J Am Assoc Gynecol Laparosc* 2004;11:273–6.

95. Vilos GA, Vilos EC, Romano W, Abu-Rafea B. Temporary uterine artery occlusion for treatment of menorrhagia and uterine fibroids using an incisionless Doppler-guided transvaginal clamp: case report. *Hum Reprod* 2006;21:269–71.

96. Overton C, Hargreaves J, Maresh M. A national survey of the complications of endometrial destruction for menstrual disorders. *BJOG* 1997;104:1351–59.

97. Loffer FD. Endometrial ablation in patients with myomas. *Curr Opin Obstet Gynecol* 2006;18:392–93.

98. Sagiv R, Ben-Shem E, Condrea A, Glezerman M, Golan A. Endometrial carcinoma after endometrial resection for dysfunctional uterine bleeding. *Obstet Gynecol* 2005;106:1174–6.

99. Gallinat A. NovaSure impedance controlled system for endometrial ablation: 3-year follow-up on 107 patients. *Am J Obstet Gynecol* 2004;191:1585–9.

100. Sabbah R, Desaulniers G. Use of the NovaSure impedance controlled endometrial ablation system in patients with intracavitary disease: 12-month follow-up results of a prospective, single-arm clinical study. *J Minim Invasive Gynecol* 2006;13:467–71.

101. Adams JP, Murphy PG. Obesity in anaesthesia and intensive care; *Br J Anaesth* 2000;85:91–108.

102. Royal College of Obstetricians and Gynaecologists. *Abdominal Hysterectomy for Heavy Periods.* Consent Advice 4. London: RCOG; 2004 [www.rcog.org.uk/resources/Public/pdf/consent4_hysterectomy.pdf].

103. Alexander CI, Listonwa. Operating on the obese woman – a review. *BJOG* 2006;113:1167–72.

104. Blomfield PI, Le T, Allen DG, Planner RS. Panniculectomy: a useful technique for the obese patient undergoing gynecological surgery. *Gynecol Oncol* 1998;70:80–6.

105. Pitkin RM. Abdominal hysterectomy in obese women. *Surg Gynecol Obstet* 1976;142:532–36.

106. Pitkin RM. Vaginal hysterectomy in obese women. *Obstet Gynecol* 1977;49:567–69.

107. Pratt JH, Daikoku NH. Obesity and vaginal hysterectomy. *J Reprod Med* 1990;35:945–49.

108. Isik-Akbay EF, Harmanli OH, Panganamamula UR, Akbay M, Gaughan J, Chatwini AJ. Hysterectomy in obese women: a comparison of abdominal and vaginal routes. *Obstet Gynecol* 2004;104:710–14.

109. Rasmussen KL. Neumann G, Ljungstrom B, Hansen V, Luaszus FF. The influence of body mass index on the prevalence of complications after vaginal and abdominal hysterectomy. *Acta Obstet Gynecol Scand* 2004;83:85–8.

110. Reich H, Decaprio J, McGlynn F. Laparoscopic hysterectomy. *J Gynecol Surg* 1989;5:213–6.

111. Heinberg EM, Crawford BL, Weitzen SH, Bonilla DJ. Total laparoscopic hysterectomy in obese versus nonobese patients. *Obstet Gynecol* 2004;103:674–80.

112. Olsson JH, Ellstrom M, Hahlin M. A randomised prospective trial comparing laparoscopic and abdominal hysterectomy. *BJOG* 1996;103:345–50.

113. Shen CC, Hsu TY, Huang FJ, Huang EY, Huang HW, Chang HY, *et al.* Laparoscopic-assisted vaginal hysterectomy in women of all weights and the effects of weight in complications. *J Am Assoc Gynecol Laparosc* 2002;9:468–73.

114. Holub Z, Jabor A, Kliment L, Fischlova D, Wagnerova M. Laparoscopic hysterectomy in obese women. *Eur J Obstet Gynecol Reprod Biol* 2001;98:77–82.

115. Garry R, Fountain J, Brown J, Manca A, Mason S, Sculpher M, *et al.* EVALUATE hysterectomy trial: a multicentre randomised trial comparing abdominal, vaginal and laparoscopic methods of hysterectomy. *Health Technol Assess* 2004;8:1–154

116. Maresh MJ, Metcalf MA, Overton MK, C, Hall V, Hargreaves J. The VALUE national hysterectomy study: description of patients and their surgery. *BJOG* 2002;109:302–12.

Chapter 6
Obesity and contraception

Diana Mansour

Introduction

The obesity epidemic is hitting all developed countries and it has been estimated that there are now more overweight than undernourished people in the world. For the UK, this is having a huge impact on health, with the direct cost of obesity to the NHS recently quoted as £0.5 billion per year. The indirect costs are even higher, being estimated at about £2 billion annually. Prevalence rates in developed countries have now reached record levels, with more than 25% of people in the USA and 20% in Australia being obese. In the UK, 22% of men and 24% of women are obese.[1]

How does this problem impact on contraception, and vice versa? Do certain birth control methods cause weight gain? Does body mass index (BMI) affect a method's contraceptive efficacy and will an increase in BMI alter the safety profile of these methods?

Contraceptive use in women who are obese

There is ample evidence reporting the impact of maternal obesity on increasing the risk of major pregnancy complications such as gestational diabetes mellitus (GDM), pre-eclampsia, respiratory complaints, venous thromboembolism (VTE), delivery complications and infection morbidity.[2] Obesity may also be an independent risk factor for neonatal complications, perinatal death and certain birth defects.[3,4] Maternal obesity increases the risk of delivering a large-for-gestational-age neonate, which in turn increases the risk of subsequent childhood obesity.[2-5] In an ideal world, women who are overweight should be advised of these complications well in advance of conception and be given effective contraception with adequate time for successful weight loss. In practice, this rarely happens.

In the UK, approximately 30% of all pregnancies are unplanned.[6] There is some evidence to suggest that women who are obese are less likely to use contraception and, even when contraception is used, they are still at increased risk of unintended pregnancy.[7,8] A retrospective study conducted in the USA found that obesity was a significant predictor of contraceptive non-use even when co-variables such as age, ethnicity, marital status, education and socio-economic status were controlled.[7] Why should this be? Perhaps women who are overweight think they are less fertile or are concerned that effective hormonal methods may increase their weight further.

There may, however, be more important psychosocial aspects underlying this issue. Weight-related problems and 'high risk' sexual behaviours have been explored in US college students.[9] Although there was a fairly low response rate to completing and returning questionnaires, results suggested that female students who were overweight were almost three times as likely to have reported having sex with a casual partner and being drunk when they last had sex.[9] Unhealthy weight-modifying behaviour in these students was significantly associated with casual sex, non-use of condoms and intoxication. Weight-related issues were not associated with sexual behaviours among college men in this study. This finding might have occurred by chance but there are data suggesting that body dissatisfaction is a risk factor for depression and low self-esteem in young people.[10,11] Perhaps these young women engaged in high-risk sexual behaviours in order to boost their self-esteem and demonstrate that they could attract a partner.

Weight gain and hormonal contraception

It is a common myth that 'the pill' causes weight gain and this is one of the most common reasons cited by young women for avoiding its use.[12] However, a Cochrane review identified three placebo-controlled randomised trials and could find no evidence supporting a causal association between combined oral contraception (COC) and weight gain.[13] Data for combined hormonal patches and the vaginal ring also suggest no association with weight gain.[14,15] It is of interest that, in a 13-cycle study comparing a combined hormonal ring with a 30 μg COC containing drospirenone, there were relatively small changes from baseline in mean body weight and body composition parameters, with no notable between-group differences.[15]

No studies have reported a significant association with weight change in progestogen-only pill (POP) users. A randomised comparative trial comparing the levonorgestrel-releasing intrauterine system (LNG-IUS) with a copper-containing intrauterine device failed to show an increase in weight with the LNG-IUS.[16] Weight change in etonogestrel contraceptive implant users has also been studied, with about 60% of women gaining at least 1 kg by 24 months and 37% gaining at least 3 kg.[17] A gradual increase in body weight has been shown in normal women of reproductive age so these findings may be attributable to normal increases over time. A US 2 year acceptability study investigating 330 women requesting an etonogestrel implant for contraception found no significant effect of this method on BMI and therefore supports this assumption.[18]

For users of depot medroxyprogesterone acetate (DMPA), studies have shown that the mean weight gain after 1 year is usually about 2 kg, rising to 9 kg with 5.5 years use.[19] It is thought that this is as a result of increasing appetite in users, leading to fat deposition and not fluid retention. Recent studies have also suggested that overweight users of DMPA gain additional weight compared with similar young women taking a COC or those in the control arm.[20] At 18 months, mean weight gain was 9.4, 0.2, and 3.1 kg for girls who were obese and receiving DMPA, receiving a COC, and control, respectively.[20] This finding has important counselling implications for overweight women requesting a long-acting hormonal contraceptive.

Effect of weight on efficacy of hormonal contraception

Does body weight and BMI have an effect on the efficacy of COC? An American multi-state database[8] was examined to investigate information on pregnancy intention, BMI and contraceptive use at the time of conception. Although there were a number of flaws in this study, after adjustments for known confounders, there did seem to be an association between increasing BMI and unintended pregnancy in women using contraception. Women who were overweight or obese and using contraception (particularly combined hormonal methods) were almost twice as likely to suffer from an unplanned pregnancy when compared with women of normal weight.[8] Is this a reliable finding and, if so, what is the explanation?

Most contraceptive efficacy studies recruit women of normal body weight so any effect of weight is unlikely to be seen. A retrospective cohort study from Puget Sound in the USA has suggested that body weight may affect hormone metabolism sufficiently to compromise contraceptive efficacy in COC users.[21] Analysis of data on 755 randomly selected women was performed, with 618 women being ever-users of COC. The authors stated that, during 2822 women-years of COC use, the pregnancy rate was 3.8 per 100 women-years of exposure. After controlling for parity, women who were 70.5 kg or more had a significantly increased risk of COC failure (RR 1.6; 95% CI 1.1–2.4) compared with women of a lower body weight. Those in the highest weight quartile using low dose (< 50 µg ethinylestradiol) and very low dose (< 35 µg ethinylestradiol) pills had between a four- and five-fold increased risk of pregnancy. Demographic confounders may affect these results, particularly with obesity being linked with social deprivation and this, in turn, may result in compliance issues. However, another analysis specifically investigated this point and found that the risk of pregnancy was more than doubled in consistent pill takers with a BMI greater than 27.3 kg/m^2 compared with those of normal weight.[22] The risk of pregnancy was over 70% higher in women weighing more than 74.8 kg and nearly doubled in women over 86.2 kg.[22] The authors concluded that, if this association is real, an additional 2–4 pregnancies will occur in 100 women who are overweight and using this method each year. Further supportive evidence comes from a small study comparing follicular suppression produced by three different oral contraceptive regimens. It was found that estrogen levels were more variable in women who were overweight and follicular suppression was reduced in women with a BMI > 25 kg/m^2.[23] Therefore, consideration should be given to the use of more effective birth control methods in women who are overweight.

Other studies comparing the combined hormonal patch with COCs included women who had a body weight up to 35% greater than normal. Contraceptive efficacy of the combined hormonal patch is similar to a COC.[24] Results of pooled data from three studies comparing efficacy of the patch with different COCs showed that five of the 15 on-therapy pregnancies that occurred were in a subgroup of women with baseline body weight ≥ 90 kg, which constituted 3% of the total study population.[24] The Summary of Product Characteristics for the patch suggests that it may be less effective in women weighing over 90 kg.[25]

A continuing area of controversy relates to a possible increased failure of POPs in women who are overweight. This has been appraised by the Clinical Effectiveness Unit (CEU) of the Faculty of Family Planning and Reproductive Health Care[26] and the authors concluded that, although there is no data showing that POPs are less effective in women weighing > 70 kg, two POPs per day may be advised. A large cohort study failed to find an association between failure rates and body weight, height or BMI. However, it is possible the study was insufficiently powered to either prove or disprove this hypothesis.[27] The CEU recommendation is based on the fact that higher failure rates were seen in women who were obese using the levonorgestrel-releasing vaginal ring and in women over 70 kg using the older hard-tubing formulation of Norplant.[28] However, changing to a softer tubing made the newer version of Norplant more effective in all women.

There are no data to support the giving of two tablets a day of the POP desogestrel in women over 70 kg. The main mechanism of action of this POP is inhibition of ovulation but it also has similar progestogenic effects to other POPs, producing secondary contraceptive effects by altering cervical mucus and endometrium. There are also no data to suggest that weight decreases the efficacy of the etonogestrel contraceptive implant, DMPA[29] or LNG-IUS.

An initial study reported that serum etonogestrel levels were higher in women of lower body weight using Implanon® (Organon Laboratories Ltd, Cambridge).[30] Therefore, the Summary of Product Characteristics[31] for Implanon states that 'the contraceptive effect of Implanon is related to the plasma levels of etonogestrel, which are inversely related to body weight, and decrease with time after insertion. The clinical experience with Implanon in heavier women in the third year of use is limited. Therefore it cannot be excluded that the contraceptive effect in these women during the third year of use may be lower than for women of normal weight. Clinicians may therefore consider earlier replacement of the implant in heavier women.'

However, over 2.5 million women have now used this implant to good effect with very few true failures reported (fewer than 0.01%). When studying the details of these failures, no association has yet been found linking body weight or BMI to efficacy (data on file, Organon Laboratories Ltd) and in this author's opinion it is not necessary to replace Implanon earlier than the usual 3 years in women who are overweight.

Safety of hormonal contraceptives in women who are overweight

Are there additional risks to prescribing combined hormonal contraception to women who are overweight? Data suggest that obesity alone increases the risk of VTE and cardiovascular disease. Studies[32,33] have shown a two- to five-fold increased risk of VTE in women with a BMI > 30 kg/m² who take the pill, while others[34] suggest two- to six-fold increases in women with a BMI > 25 kg/m². In a case–control study from the Netherlands adjusted for age and sex, obesity alone (BMI ≥ 30 kg/m²) doubled the risk of VTE. Obese individuals had higher levels of factor VIII and IX but not fibrinogen. Evaluation of the combined effect of COCs and obesity among women aged 15–45 years revealed that COCs further increased the effect of obesity on the risk of thrombosis, leading to a ten-fold increased risk among women with a BMI greater than 25 kg/m².[35]

Until recently, the guidance for prescribing combined hormonal contraception was vague, with the CEU suggesting that after counselling women who are overweight may choose to use a COC but consideration should be given to the use of alternative contraceptive methods.[36] The *British National Formulary* gave an upper limit with a recommendation that women with a BMI > 39 kg/m² should not use the COC.[37]

Very recent evidence suggests a much higher risk of VTE (four- to five-fold) in COC users[38] when compared with data issued by the Committee on Safety of Medicines in 1995. These post-marketing data demonstrate the true prevalence of VTE in women taking COCs in the 21st century, with 80% of index cases having risk factors present. A consensus group met in 2005 to explore these issues and adapt the World Health Organization Medical Eligibility Criteria for use in the UK. This work has now been published[39] and gives clear prescribing guidance. Women who have a BMI less than 30 kg/m² can use combined hormonal methods without restrictions. In women with a BMI between 30 kg/m² and less than 35 kg/m², the advantages of using these methods would appear to outweigh the theoretical or proven risks of VTE. Having a BMI over 35 kg/m² but less than 40 kg/m² brings the potential user into the category of UK Medical Eligibility Criteria 3 (UKMEC 3) where the theoretical or proven risks normally outweigh the advantages. Specialists in the field should be the only health professionals who prescribe these methods in this situation and only after careful consideration. An alternative contraceptive method is required for women with a BMI of 40 kg/m² or more. With almost one in four women being obese, and in view of recent data, safer prescribing of combined hormonal contraceptive methods by all health professionals is vital.

What is known about the combined hormonal patch or vaginal ring? Is there any interaction between weight and risk of VTE using these methods? It was initially thought that non-oral combined hormonal contraceptives would provide highly effective contraception with the theoretical advantage of steady, low-dose release mechanisms reducing troublesome adverse effects, and perhaps more serious adverse events. Unfortunately, in the case of the combined contraceptive patch, nuisance adverse effects were similar to the pill – if not a little worse – within the first few months, and efficacy data were unimpressive.[40] In 2005 the US Food and Drug Administration (FDA) updated its labelling for the Ortho Evra contraceptive patch after an increase in post-marketing reports of VTEs occurring in women using this patch.[41] Data on file with the FDA suggested there was a two-fold increased risk of developing a VTE while using a patch compared with a 35 μg COC. However, another published study showed no increased risk.[42] Overall, it was felt that patch users were exposed to 60% more estrogen compared with takers of a 35 μg COC although peak blood levels were about 25% lower than with the pill.[41] Women's health experts are recommending that potential patch users should have a BMI less than 30 kg/m².

Studies from 2005 confirmed that the exposure to ethinylestradiol was 3.4 times lower in vaginal ring users (releasing 15 μg/day) compared with the patch group (releasing 20 μg/day) and 2.1 times lower than the pill group containing 30 μg.[43] This clearly demonstrates the increased estrogen exposure of those using the patch compared with other methods. Serum ethinylestradiol levels showed much lower variation with the vaginal ring than with the patch or the COC. To date, there are no data linking the vaginal ring, weight and VTE.

There are no data to suggest that women who are obese using progestogen-only contraceptive methods face an increased risk of adverse effects compared with other women who are overweight. Progestogen-only methods alone have not been shown to increase the risks of VTE or cardiovascular disease.[44,45]

Obesity is an independent risk factor for arterial disease. However, there is a paucity of data linking the use of specific contraceptives with obesity and coronary heart disease events or stroke – probably because these events are so rare in women in their reproductive years.

Non-hormonal contraception and obesity

There are no effects of weight on the efficacy or safety of barrier methods or fertility awareness methods. However, women who gain or lose more than 7 lbs (3.2 kg) in weight should be advised to be re-measured for the diaphragm. Sterilisation under general anaesthesia poses increased risks for women who are obese. People who are overweight are more likely to suffer complications of general anaesthesia and their habitus increases the chance of a failed laparoscopic procedure, necessitating a mini-laparotomy. New hysteroscopic techniques such as Essure, a minimally invasive, transcervically placed microinsert that occludes the fallopian tubes, may offer advantages for such women. These micro-inserts can be inserted under hysteroscopic visualisation with intravenous sedation or paracervical block in over 85% of women.[46] Further research is under way investigating long-term safety and efficacy.

Conclusion

Much has been written in recent years about the global effects of diet, obesity and ill health. Health professionals working in the field of contraception need to sit up and take note. One of their roles is to advise women about the importance of normalising their BMI before pregnancy. They also have a duty to prescribe effective contraception safely and offer alternatives when obesity contraindicates the use of combined hormonal contraceptives.

References

1. Vlad I. Obesity costs UK economy £2bn a year *BMJ* 2003;327:1308.
2. Sebire NJ, Jolly M, Harris JP, Wadsworth J, Joffe M, Beard RW, *et al.* Maternal obesity and pregnancy outcome: a study of 287,213 pregnancies in London. *Int J Obes Relat Metab Disord* 2001;25:1175–82.
3. Callaway LK, Prins JB, Chang AM, McIntyre HD. The prevalence and impact of overweight and obesity in an Australian obstetric population. *Med J Aust* 2006;184:56–9.
4. Raatikainen K, Heiskanen N, Heinonen S. Transition from overweight to obesity worsens pregnancy outcome in a BMI-dependent manner. *Obesity (Silver Spring).* 2006;14:165–71.
5. Salsberry PJ, Reagan PB. Dynamics of early childhood overweight. *Pediatrics* 2005;116:1329–38.
6. National Collaborating Centre for Women's and Children's Health, National Institute for Health and Clinical Excellence. *Long-Acting Reversible Contraception: the Effective and Appropriate Use of Long-Acting Reversible Contraception.* Clinical Guideline 30. London: RCOG Press; 2005.
7. Chuang CH, Chase GA, Bensyl DM, Weisman CS. Contraceptive use by diabetic and obese women. *Women's Health Issues* 2005;15:167–73.
8. Brunner Huber LR, Hogue CJ. The association between body weight, unintended pregnancy resulting in a livebirth, and contraception at the time of conception. *Matern Child Health J* 2005;9:413–20.
9. Eisenberg ME, Neumark-Sztainer D, Lust KD. Weight-related issues and high-risk sexual behaviors among college students. *J Am Coll Health* 2005;54:95–101.
10. Paxton SJ, Neumark-Sztainer D, Hannan PJ, Eisenberg ME. Body dissatisfaction prospectively predicts depressive mood and low self-esteem in adolescent girls and boys. *J Clin Child Adolesc Psychol* 2006;35:539–49.
11. McLaren L, Gauvin L. The cumulative impact of being overweight on women's body esteem: a preliminary study. *Eat Weight Disord* 2002;7:324–7.
12. Fuchs N, Prinz H, Koch U. Attitudes to current oral contraceptive use and future developments: the women's perspective. *Eur J Contracept Reprod Health Care* 1996;1:275–84.
13. Gallo MF, Lopez LM, Grimes DA, Schulz KF, Helmerhorst FM. Combination contraceptives: effects on weight. *Cochrane Database Syst Rev* 2006;(1):CD003987.
14. Audet MC, Moreau M, Koltun WD, Waldbaum AS, Shangold G, Fisher AC, et al; ORTHO EVRA/EVRA 004 Study Group. Evaluation of contraceptive efficacy and cycle control of a transdermal contraceptive patch vs an oral contraceptive: a randomized controlled trial. *JAMA* 2001;285:2347–54.
15. Milsom I, Lete I, Bjertnaes A, Rokstad K, Lindh I, Gruber CJ, *et al.* Effects on cycle control and bodyweight of the combined contraceptive ring, NuvaRing, versus an oral contraceptive containing 30 microg ethinyl estradiol and 3 mg drospirenone. *Hum Reprod* 2006;21:2304–11.
16. Andersson K, Odlind V, Rybo G. Levonorgestrel-releasing and copper-releasing (Nova T) IUDs during five years of use: a randomized comparative trial. *Contraception* 1994;49:56–72.
17. Edwards JE, Moore A. Implanon. A review of clinical studies. *Br J Fam Plann* 1999;24(4 Suppl):3–16.
18. Funk S, Miller MM, Mishell DR Jr, Archer DF, Poindexter A, Schmidt J, *et al;* The Implanon US Study Group. Safety and efficacy of Implanon, a single-rod implantable contraceptive containing etonogestrel. *Contraception* 2005;71:319–26.

19. Bigrigg A, Evans M, Gbolade B, Newton J, Pollard L, Szarewski A, *et al*. Depo Provera. Position paper on clinical use, effectiveness and side effects. *Br J Fam Plann* 1999;25:69–76.

20. Bonny AE, Ziegler J, Harvey R, Debanne SM, Secic M, Cromer BA. Weight gain in obese and nonobese adolescent girls initiating depot medroxyprogesterone, oral contraceptive pills, or no hormonal contraceptive method. *Arch Pediatr Adolesc Med* 2006;160:40–5.

21. Holt VL, Cushing-Haugen KL, Daling JR. Body weight and risk of oral contraceptive failure. *Obstet Gynecol* 2002;99:820–7.

22. Holt VL, Scholes D, Wicklund KG, Cushing-Haugen KL, Daling JR. Body mass index, weight, and oral contraceptive failure risk. *Obstet Gynecol* 2005;105:46–52.

23. Schlaff WD, Lynch AM, Hughes HD, Cedars MI, Smith DL. Manipulation of the pill-free interval in oral contraceptive pill users: the effect on follicular suppression. *Am J Obstet Gynecol* 2004;190:943–51.

24. Zieman M, Guillebaud J, Weisberg E, Shangold GA, Fisher AC, Creasy GW. Contraceptive efficacy and cycle control with the Ortho Evra/Evra transdermal system: the analysis of pooled data. Fertil Steril 2002;77(2 Suppl 2):S13–18.

25. Janssen-Cilag International NV. Evra transdermal patch. Summary of Product Characteristics [www.janssencilag.co.uk/product/pdf/spc/00121.pdf].

26. de Souza A, Brechin S, Penney G. The members' enquiry service: frequently asked questions. *J Fam Plann Reprod Health Care* 2003;29:160–1.

27. Vessey M, Painter R. Oral contraception failures and body weight: findings in a large cohort study. *J Fam Plann Reprod Health Care* 2001;27:90–1.

28. Sivin I, Mishell DR, Darney P, Wan L, Christ M. Levonorgestrel capsule implants in the United States: a 5-year study. *Obstet Gynecol* 1998;92:337–44.

29. Jain J, Dutton C, Nicosia A, Wajszczuk C, Bode FR, Michell DR. Pharmacokinetics, ovulation suppression and return to ovulation following a lower dose subcutaneous formulation of Depo-Provera. *Contraception* 2004;70:11–18.

30. Huber J, Wenzl R. Pharmacokinetics of Implanon. An integrated analysis. *Contraception* 1998;58:85s–90s.

31. Organon Laboratories Limited. Implanon 68mg implant for subdermal use. Summary of Product Characteristics, document last updated on the eMC: Tue 23 May 2006 [www.emc.medicines.org.uk/].

32. Farmer RDT, Lawrenson RA, Todd JC, Williams TJ, MacRae KD, Tyrer F, Leydon GM. A comparison of the risks of venous thromboembolic disease in association with different combined oral contraceptives. *Br J Clin Pharmacol* 2000;49:580–90.

33. Lidegaard O, Erdstrom B, Kreiner S. Oral contraceptives and venous thromboembolism: a five year national case–control study. *Contraception* 2002;65:187–96.

34. Jick H, Kaye JA, Vasilakis-Scaramozza C, Jick SS. Risk of venous thromboembolism among users of third generation oral contraceptives compared with users of oral contraceptives with levonorgestrel before and after 1995: cohort and case–control analysis. *BMJ* 2000;321:1190–5.

35. Abdollahi M, Cushman M, Rosendaal FR. Obesity: risk of venous thrombosis and the interaction with coagulation factor levels and oral contraceptive use. *Thromb Haemost* 2003;89:493–8.

36. Faculty of Family Planning and Reproductive Health Care. Clinical Effectiveness Unit first prescription of combined oral contraception: recommendations for clinical practice. *J Fam Plann Reprod Health Care* 2000;26:27–38.

37. Joint Formulary Committee. *British National Formulary*. 52 ed. London: British Medical Association and Royal Pharmaceutical Society of Great Britain; 2006.

38. Heinemann LA, Dinger J. Safety of a new oral contraceptive containing drospirenone. *Drug Saf* 2004;27:1001–18.

39. Faculty of Family Planning and Reproductive Health Care. UK *Medical Eligibility Criteria for Contraceptive Use(UKMEC 2005/2006)*. London: FFPRHC; 2006 [www.ffprhc.org.uk/admin/uploads/UKMEC200506.pdf].

40. Faculty of Family Planning and Reproductive Health Care Clinical Effectiveness Unit. New Product Review (September 2003). Norelgestromin/ethinyl oestradiol transdermal contraceptive system (Evra). *J Fam Plann Reprod Health Care* 2004;30:43–5.

41. U.S. Food and Drug Administration. Ortho Evra (norelgestromin/ethinyl estradiol) Information [www.fda.gov/cder/drug/infopage/orthoevra/default.htm].

42. Jick SS, Kaye JA, Russmann S, Jick H. Risk of nonfatal venous thromboembolism in women using a contraceptive transdermal patch and oral contraceptives containing norgestimate and 35 microg of ethinyl estradiol. *Contraception* 2006;73:223–8.

43. van den Heuvel MW, van Bragt AJ, Alnabawy AK, Kaptein MC. Comparison of ethinylestradiol pharmacokinetics in three hormonal contraceptive formulations: the vaginal ring, the transdermal patch and an oral contraceptive. *Contraception* 2005;72:168–74.

44. Heinemann LA, Assmann A, Do Minh T, Garbe E. Oral progestogen-only contraceptives and cardiovascular risk: results from the Transnational Study on Oral Contraceptives and the Health of Young Women. *Eur J Contracept Reprod Health Care* 1999;4:67–73.

45. World Health Organization Collaborative Study of Cardiovascular Disease and Steroid Hormone Contraception. Cardiovascular disease and use of oral and injectable progestogen-only contraceptives and combined injectable contraceptives. Results of an international, multicenter, case–control study. *Contraception* 1998;57:315–24.

46. Kerin JF, Carignan CS, Cher D. The safety and effectiveness of a new hysteroscopic method for permanent birth control: results of the first Essure pbc clinical study. *Aust N Z J Obstet Gynaecol* 2001;41:364–70.

Chapter 7
Polycystic ovary syndrome, obesity and reproductive function

Adam H Balen

Introduction

Obesity is a common problem among women of reproductive age, with 56% of women in the UK being either overweight or obese. Obesity has a negative impact on spontaneous conception, miscarriage, pregnancy and the long-term health of both mother and child owing to both an increased rate of congenital anomalies and the possibility of metabolic disease in later life.

Polycystic ovary syndrome (PCOS) affects 20–25% of women. The prevalence appears to be rising because of the current epidemic of obesity.[1] PCOS accounts for 90–95% of women who attend infertility clinics with anovulation. At least 40% of women with PCOS are obese[2] and they are more insulin resistant than weight-matched individuals with normal ovaries. Increasing abdominal obesity is correlated with reduced menstrual frequency and fertility together with greater insulin resistance.[3]

Women who are obese respond less well to drugs that are used for ovarian stimulation for the treatment of both anovulation and assisted conception, although this does not always equate with a reduction in continuing pregnancy rates. Furthermore, obesity may affect the safety of procedures, for example the ability to see ovaries on ultrasound scan or the provision of safe anaesthesia for laparoscopy or oocyte retrieval. Obesity also has a major impact during pregnancy and at delivery.

Epidemiology of PCOS

PCOS is a heterogeneous collection of signs and symptoms that, gathered together, form a spectrum of a disorder with a mild presentation in some, while in others there is a severe disturbance of reproductive, endocrine and metabolic function. The pathophysiology of PCOS appears to be multifactorial and polygenic. The definition of the syndrome has been much debated. Key features include menstrual cycle disturbance, hyperandrogenism and obesity. There are many extra-ovarian aspects to the pathophysiology of PCOS yet ovarian dysfunction is central. At the 2003 Rotterdam joint consensus meeting between the European Society for Human Reproduction and Embryology (ESHRE) and the American Society for Reproductive Medicine (ASRM), a refined definition of PCOS was agreed, namely the presence of two out of the following three criteria:[4]

- oligo- and/or anovulation
- hyperandrogenism (clinical and/or biochemical)
- polycystic ovaries, with the exclusion of other aetiologies.

The morphology of the polycystic ovary (PCO) has been redefined as an ovary with 12 or more follicles measuring 2–9 mm in diameter and/or increased ovarian volume (> 10 cm³).[5]

There is considerable heterogeneity of symptoms and signs among women with PCOS and for an individual these may change over time.[2] Polycystic ovaries can exist without clinical signs of the syndrome, expression of which may be precipitated by various factors, most predominantly an increase in body weight.

Genetic studies have identified a link between PCOS and disordered insulin metabolism, and indicate that the syndrome may be the presentation of a complex genetic trait disorder.[6] The features of obesity, hyperinsulinaemia and hyperandrogenaemia that are commonly seen in PCOS are also known to be factors which confer an increased risk of cardiovascular disease and type 2 diabetes mellitus.[7] There are studies that indicate that women with PCOS have an increased risk for these diseases that pose long-term risks for health, and this evidence has prompted debate as to the need for screening women for polycystic ovaries. Because the phenotype of women with polycystic ovaries and the PCOS may be very variable[2] it is then difficult to elucidate the genotype. It is also likely that different combinations of genetic variants may result in differential expression of the separate components of the syndrome.[1]

There is debate about the prevalence of PCOS and, of course, this also depends upon the definitions used. Several studies have been performed to attempt to determine the prevalence of polycystic ovaries as detected by ultrasound alone in the general population, and these have found rates of between 17% and 33%.[1] The question of whether polycystic ovaries alone are pathological or a normal variant of ovarian morphology is still debated. While the spectrum of 'normality' might include the presence of polycystic ovaries in the absence of signs or symptoms of PCOS, there is evidence that women with polycystic morphology alone show typical responses to stresses such as weight gain or gonadotrophin stimulation during *in vitro* fertilisation (IVF) treatment. To date, there are no large-scale longitudinal prospective studies of women with polycystic ovaries that have explored the evolution of the syndrome or predictors of pathology.

In a study of 224 female volunteers between the ages of 18 and 25 years who considered themselves to be normal and who were not attending a physician with any medical problems, polycystic ovaries were identified using ultrasound in 33% of participants.[8] Fifty percent of the participants were using some form of hormonal contraception but the prevalence of polycystic ovaries in users and non-users of hormonal contraception was identical. Polycystic ovaries in the non-users of hormonal contraception were associated with irregular menstrual cycles and significantly higher serum testosterone concentrations when compared with women with normal ovaries. However, only a small proportion of women with polycystic ovaries (15%) had 'elevated' serum testosterone concentrations outside the normal range. Interestingly, there were no significant differences in acne, hirsutism, body mass index (BMI) or body fat percentage between women with polycystic ovaries and those with normal ovaries, and hyperinsulinism and reduced insulin sensitivity were not associated with polycystic ovaries in this group.

In this study, the prevalence of PCOS was as low as 8% using the US definition for PCOS, or as high as 26% if the broader Rotterdam consensus criteria were applied. The highest reported prevalence of PCO has been 52% among south Asian immigrants in Britain, of whom 49.1% had menstrual irregularity.[9] Rodin *et al.*[9] demonstrated that south Asian women with PCO had a degree of insulin resistance comparable with a control group of women with established type 2 diabetes mellitus.

Generally, there has been a paucity of data on the prevalence of PCOS among women of south Asian origin, both among migrant and native groups. Type 2 diabetes and insulin resistance have a high prevalence among indigenous populations in south Asia, with a rising prevalence among women. Insulin resistance and hyperinsulinaemia are common antecedents of type 2 diabetes, with a high prevalence in south Asians. Type 2 diabetes also has a familial basis, inherited as a complex genetic trait that interacts with environmental factors, chiefly nutrition, commencing from fetal life. It has already been found that south Asian women with anovular PCOS have greater insulin resistance and more severe symptoms of the syndrome than anovular white women with PCOS.[10] Furthermore, it has been found that women from south Asia living in the UK appear to express symptoms at an earlier age than their white British counterparts.[10]

Insulin resistance and visceral fat

Insulin resistance is also an important correlate of BMI and is perceived as a more accurate marker of the metabolic effect of obesity. There are also important ethnic variations in the expression of insulin resistance. A BMI > 30 kg/m^2 is usually considered to confer increased risk in white women whereas in those of south Asian origin a lower BMI > 25 kg/m^2 is sufficient to increase risk of metabolic defects.[10]

Insulin resistance is defined as a reduced glucose response to a given amount of insulin and may occur secondary to resistance at the insulin receptor, decreased hepatic clearance of insulin and/or increased pancreatic sensitivity. The measurement of insulin resistance is an imprecise science without universally accepted guidelines. Technical difficulties have given rise to a number of invasive tests, including the euglycaemic clamp method. This is considered to be a 'gold standard' but is complex and expensive, as is the measurement of fasting insulin concentrations which, combined with glucose, can provide formulae for the Homa and QUICKI calculations of insulin resistance. So, in practice, these are confined to the research setting in the UK and have not become established in clinical practice in reproductive medicine. Most clinicians resort to the standard 75 g oral glucose tolerance test (OGTT). Fasting glucose levels alone are poorly predictive of 2 hour levels in impaired glucose tolerance, suggesting that a full OGTT should be conducted.[11] Between 20% and 40% of women with PCOS have impaired glucose tolerance, which is significantly higher than the prevalence among age- and weight-matched premenopausal women.[12]

In a UK study of premenopausal women with type 2 diabetes, almost 30% had PCOS and 82% had PCO morphology.[13] Women with PCOS are between three and seven times more likely to develop type 2 diabetes than women in control groups.[11,14] Furthermore, the conversion rate is potentially rapid. When 54 normoglycaemic women and 13 women with impaired glucose tolerance (IGT) at baseline with PCOS were followed for an average 6.2 years, 9% of the normoglycaemic group developed impaired tolerance and 8% developed frank type 2 diabetes. Of the IGT group, 54% had frank type2 diabetes at follow-up. BMI at baseline was an independent significant predictor of conversion. The speed of change suggests regular surveillance is required, especially when BMI is high,[15] yet this is far from becoming part of standard UK health care for these women.

BMI is easy to measure and is a reproducible measurement. However, in metabolic terms, the distribution of body fat is more important than actual body weight. Visceral fat is more metabolically active and an increased waist circumference (or waist:hip ratio) correlates better with both metabolic risk and long-term disease.

Unfortunately, waist circumference is difficult to measure (subject to increased error) in obese individuals, while BMI is more consistent.

Although the insulin resistance may occur irrespective of BMI, the common association of PCOS and obesity has a synergistic deleterious impact on glucose homeostasis and can aggravate both hyperandrogenism and anovulation. An assessment of BMI alone is not thought to provide a reliable prediction of cardiovascular risk. It has been reported that the association between BMI and coronary heart disease almost disappeared after correction for dyslipidaemia, hyperglycaemia and hypertension.[16] Some women have profound metabolic abnormalities in the presence of a normal BMI whereas others have few risk factors with an elevated BMI.[17,18] Thus, it is the distribution of fat that is important rather than BMI itself, with android obesity being more of a risk factor than gynaecoid obesity. Hence the value of measuring waist: hip ratio, or waist circumference, which detects abdominal visceral fat rather than subcutaneous fat. It is the visceral fat that is metabolically active and which, when increased, results in increased rates of insulin resistance, type 2 diabetes, dyslipidaemia, hypertension and left ventricular enlargement.[17] Exercise has a significant effect on reducing visceral fat and reducing cardiovascular risk. Lord and Wilkin[17] have found a closer link between waist circumference and visceral fat mass, as assessed by computed tomography scan, than with waist:hip ratio or BMI. Waist circumference should ideally be less than 79 cm, while a measurement that is greater than 87 cm carries a significant risk.

The association between insulin resistance, compensatory hyperinsulinaemia and hyperandrogenism has provided insight into the pathogenesis of PCOS.[19] The cellular and molecular mechanisms of insulin resistance in PCOS have been extensively investigated and it is evident that the major defect is a decrease in insulin sensitivity secondary to a post-binding abnormality in insulin receptor-mediated signal transduction, with a less substantial, but significant, decrease in insulin responsiveness.[20] It appears that decreased insulin sensitivity in PCOS is potentially an intrinsic defect in genetically susceptible women, since it is independent of obesity, metabolic abnormalities, body fat topography and sex hormone levels. There may be genetic abnormalities in the regulation of insulin receptor phosphorylation, resulting in increased insulin-independent serine phosphorylation and decreased insulin-dependent tyrosine phosphorylation.[20,21]

Insulin acts through multiple sites to increase endogenous androgen levels. Increased peripheral insulin resistance results in a higher serum insulin concentration. Excess insulin binds to the insulin-like growth factor-I (IGF-I) receptors, which enhances androgen production in the theca cells in response to luteinising hormone (LH) stimulation.[22] Hyperinsulinaemia also decreases the synthesis of sex hormone-binding globulin (SHBG) by the liver. Therefore, there is an increase in serum free-testosterone (T) concentration, and consequent peripheral androgen action. In addition, hyperinsulinaemia inhibits the hepatic secretion of insulin-like growth factor binding protein-1 (IGFBP-1) leading to increased bioavailability of IGF-I and IGF-II,[23,24] the important regulators of ovarian follicular maturation and steroidogenesis.[25] Together with more IGF-II secretion from the theca cells, IGF-I and IGF-II further augment ovarian androgen production by acting on IGF-I receptors.[26,27]

Insulin may also increase endogenous androgen concentrations by increased cytochrome P450c17α enzyme activity, which is important for ovarian and adrenal steroid hormone biosynthesis. Insulin-induced overactivity of P450c17α and exaggerated serum 17-hydroxyprogesterone (17-OHP) response to stimulation by gonadotrophin-releasing hormone agonist (GnRHa) have also been demonstrated.[28–30] Intraovarian androgen excess is responsible for anovulation by acting directly on the ovary promoting the process of follicular atresia.[31,32] This latter process is characterised by apoptosis of granulosa cells. As a consequence, there is an increasingly larger stromal compartment, which retains LH responsiveness and continues to secrete androgens.

Women with PCOS, whether they are obese or not, are more insulin resistant and hyperinsulinaemic than age- and weight-matched women with normal ovaries.[33,34] Thus, there appear to be factors in women with PCOS which promote insulin resistance and that are independent of obesity.[35] Pancreatic β-cell dysfunction has been described in women with PCOS, whereby there is increased basal secretion of insulin yet an inadequate postprandial response.[36] This defect remains even after weight loss,[37] despite an improvement in glucose tolerance.

Insulin acts through its receptor to initiate a cascade of post-receptor events within the target cell. Phosphorylation causes insulin receptor substrates (IRS1–4) to promote glucose uptake via the transmembrane glucose transporter (GLUT4) and also to promote intracellular protein synthesis. Tyrosine phosphorylation increases the tyrosine kinase activity of the insulin receptor, while serine phosphorylation inhibits it, and it appears that at least 50% of women with PCOS have excessive serine phosphorylation and inhibition of normal signalling.[38] This affects only glucose homeostasis and not the other pleiotropic actions of insulin, so that cell growth and protein synthesis may continue. Serine phosphorylation also increases activity of P450c17 in both the ovary and adrenal gland, thus promoting androgen synthesis[38] and so this may be a mechanism for both insulin resistance and hyperandrogenism in some women with PCOS.

PCOS, the effect of weight loss and metformin

Several studies have shown that weight loss in women with PCOS improves the endocrine profile, menstrual cyclicity, rate of ovulation and likelihood of a healthy pregnancy.[39] Even a modest loss of 5–10% of total body weight can achieve a 30% reduction of central fat, an improvement in insulin sensitivity and restore ovulation. Lifestyle modification is clearly a key component for the improvement of reproductive function for women with anovulatory PCOS who are overweight.[40]

Weight loss should therefore be encouraged prior to ovulation induction treatments, such as clomifene citrate or gonadotrophin therapy, both to improve the likelihood of ovulation and to enhance ovarian response. Monitoring treatment is also harder in obese women as visualisation of the ovaries is more difficult, which raises the risk of multiple ovulation and multiple pregnancy. The national guideline in the UK for the management of women who are overweight with PCOS advises weight loss, preferably to a BMI of < 30 kg/m², prior to commencing drugs for ovarian stimulation.[40]

A study by Clark et al.[41] looked at the effect of a weight loss and exercise programme on women with a BMI > 30 kg/m² and anovulatory infertility who were clomifene resistant. The emphasis of the study was a realistic exercise schedule combined with positive reinforcement of a suitable eating programme over 6 months. Only 13 out of the 18 women enrolled completed the study, reinforcing the difficulties some individuals have in sustaining even moderate changes in lifestyle. Weight loss had a significant effect on endocrine function, ovulation and the chance of pregnancy. Fasting insulin and serum testosterone concentrations fell and 12 of the 13 women resumed ovulation: 11 becoming pregnant – five spontaneously and the remainder became responsive to clomifene. Thus, with appropriate support, these women may ovulate spontaneously without medical therapy. An extension of this study, on women with a variety of diagnoses, demonstrated that, in 60 out of 67 women, weight loss resulted in spontaneous ovulation with lower than anticipated rates of miscarriage and a significant saving in the cost of treatment.[42] Even a modest loss of 5% of total body weight can achieve a reduction of central fat, an improvement in insulin sensitivity, and restoration of ovulation.[43] Weight loss among women who are obese with anovulatory PCOS is therefore associated with significant improvements in the menstrual pattern (from 40% to 89%), and spontaneous resumption of regular ovulatory cycles (from 33% to 55%).[3,44,45] Lifestyle modification is clearly a key component for the improvement of reproductive function in women who are overweight with anovulation and PCOS. It is likely that starting to lose weight, by being in negative calorific balance, will provide early benefit.

There are a number of different diets that have been recommended and essentially any diet that is sustainable for an individual combined with a regimen of regular exercise is likely to achieve improvement in general health and reproductive function. There is no clear evidence that one type of diet will specifically benefit women with PCOS. There has been much interest in the potential value of low glycaemic index (GI) diets, with a relative balance of approximately 55% carbohydrate, 15% protein and 30% fat. A recent meta-analysis did not show a conclusive benefit compared with high GI diets;[46] neither has this been studied in detail in women with PCOS who are obese. A relative increase in protein (40% carbohydrate, 30% protein, 30% fat) has also received significant attention and may improve the metabolic profile, as shown in the only two randomised controlled trials that have compared different diets in women with PCOS,[47,48] although both studies demonstrated weight loss and improvement in reproductive function with both types of diet. Once weight has been lost, it is extremely difficult to maintain the improvement and considerable psychological support and encouragement is required. Another study looked at weight maintenance after an initial trial of weight loss over 8 weeks.[49] The number of women with weight loss greater than 5% decreased from 74% to 44% during a 6 month follow-up period, with approximately half of the subjects regaining weight during the maintenance phase, emphasising the difficulties that these women have in achieving long-term weight loss.[49]

Metformin

The use of insulin-lowering or insulin-sensitising agents has excited much interest in the management of PCOS but even metformin is less effective for women with anovulation and extreme obesity, although perhaps a higher dose is required than currently prescribed.[50] Many women who are obese and who wish to conceive are now prescribed metformin, often at body weights greater than would be permissible for treatment to induce ovulation. Those who ovulate and conceive while remaining obese will have to face considerable additional risks during pregnancy. Is it appropriate to treat these women with metformin if they have not already started to lose weight or achieved their target weight? At the very least, the risks of the pregnancy to mother and child should be explained, understood and actively managed before embarking on treatment.

It is logical to assume that therapy that achieves a fall in serum insulin concentrations should improve the symptoms of PCOS. Many studies have been carried out to evaluate the reproductive effects of metformin in women with PCOS. Most of the initial studies, however, were observational and any randomised studies only involved a small number of participants. Indeed, two systematic reviews published in 2003 revealed that the majority of the published studies on the effects of metformin alone on the menstrual cycle in women with PCOS had a sample size of fewer than

30 women.[51–53] It has been shown that metformin ameliorates hyperandrogenism and abnormalities of gonadotrophin secretion in women with PCOS and can also restore menstrual cyclicity. Metformin appears to be less effective in those who are significantly obese (BMI > 35 kg/m^2)[50,54,55] and there are still no agreed algorithms for its use. Furthermore, there is no agreement on predictors for response or the appropriate dose, and whether dose should be adjusted for body weight or other factors.

The largest appropriately powered prospective randomised double-blind, placebo-controlled multicentre study was published in 2006 and set out to evaluate the combined effects of lifestyle modification and metformin on women who were obese (BMI > 30 kg/m^2) with anovulatory PCOS.[50] All the women had an individualised assessment by a research dietician in order to set a realistic goal that could be sustained for a long period with an average reduction of energy intake of 500 kcal per day. Both the metformin-treated and placebo groups lost weight but the amount of weight reduction did not differ between the two groups. An increase in menstrual cyclicity was observed in those who lost weight but again did not differ between the two arms of the study.

The very variable findings from the published studies on the use of metformin reflect the large differences in study populations, particularly with respect to body weight. Insulin sensitivity decreases (or insulin resistance increases) with BMI. It has been shown that women with PCOS who are not obese respond better to metformin than women who are obese.[50,54,55] One might expect metformin to have a greater effect in those with the greater insulin resistance, however there may be either under-dosing or resistance to the effects of metformin at the doses used.

The thiazolidinedione derivatives, while potentially more effective than metformin for improving insulin sensitivity, are inappropriate for use in those seeking fertility, and they also have the unwanted effect of actually increasing weight.

Effect of obesity on treatment of anovulatory infertility

A study of 1880 women who were infertile and 40 023 control women showed that anovulatory infertility was three times more common in those with a BMI of > 27 kg/m^2.[56] Women who were overweight also required higher doses of clomifene and gonadotrophins[39] and were also harder to monitor accurately by transvaginal ultrasound scan, and it has been shown that they are at greater risk of over-response.[57] In this study, there was no significant influence of BMI on the rate of ovulation ($P = 0.363$) or pregnancy (as assessed by positive human chorionic gonadotrophin (hCG), $P = 0.596$; clinical pregnancy rate, $P = 0.781$; and continuing pregnancy rate, $P = 0.828$). The group with a BMI > 30 kg/m^2 produced more small follicles ($P = 0.005$) and fewer intermediate follicles ($P = 0.036$) than the women who were less overweight or had normal weight, despite a higher antral follicle count. Those with a BMI < 25 kg/m^2 had a better chance of a unifollicular response. An increasing BMI is associated with more treatment days, a higher total dose and a higher threshold dose of gonadotrophins.[57]

Many studies have historically excluded women with a BMI > 35 kg/m^2 or, in some cases, 30 kg/m^2, which has been based on general algorithms for the provision of ovulation induction. Some studies have included women who were very obese, for example, in a cohort of 270 women with PCOS who received either clomifene citrate or gonadotrophins for ovulation induction: the ovulation rate at 6 months was 79% in those with a BMI 18–24 kg/m^2, 15.3% in those with a BMI 30–34 kg/m^2 ($P < 0.001$) and 12% for BMI $\geq$ 35 kg/m^2 ($P < 0.001$).[58]

A meta-analysis of 13 studies confirmed a positive association between degree of obesity and amount of gonadotrophin required, with a weighted mean difference of 771 iu more needed (95% CI 700–842) and also a higher rate of cycle cancellation in those who were obese (pooled odds ratio (OR) 1.86; 95% CI 1.13–3.06).[59] There was also a reduction in ovulation rate associated with obesity compared with women who were not obese (OR 0.44; 95% CI 0.31–0.61). While there was no difference in pregnancy rates associated with obesity, there was a negative association with insulin resistance (pooled OR 0.29; 95% CI 0.10–0.80). Thus, the combination of obesity and insulin resistance appears to be the most significant determinant for the outcome of ovulation induction therapy, with degree of insulin resistance being more important.

Laparoscopic ovarian diathermy is an alternative to gonadotrophin therapy for clomifene citrate-resistant anovulatory PCOS.[60] However, those who are most likely to respond are women who are slim with elevated serum LH concentrations[60] rather than those who are overweight. Furthermore, obesity presents additional hazards during general anaesthesia.

Conclusion

PCOS is a heterogeneous condition. Ovarian dysfunction leads to the main signs and symptoms and the ovary is influenced by external factors, in particular the gonadotrophins, insulin and other growth factors, which are dependent upon both genetic and environmental influences. The diagnosis relies upon the presence of at least two of the features of menstrual disturbance, hyperandrogenism and/or the presence of polycystic ovaries. In 2003, international consensus definitions were agreed both for the morphological characteristics of the PCO and the diagnostic criteria for the syndrome. There are likely to be several potential routes by which an individual may develop PCOS, owing to a combination of genetic and environmental factors. At the heart of the pathophysiology for many women is insulin resistance and hyperinsulinaemia and, even if this is not the initiating cause in some, it is certainly an amplifier of hyperandrogenism in those that gain weight.

BMI is a reliable, reproducible and easy measurement but does not tell the whole story as it is an increase in visceral fat that correlates better with insulin resistance, metabolic disease, infertility and, in particular, anovulatory infertility, reduced response to ovarian stimulation, reduced outcome of infertility treatments and an increased risk of miscarriage and pregnancy complications. Therefore, an assessment of waist circumference is good practice and a more detailed measure of metabolic risk (OGTT, lipid profile, liver function tests) is advisable in those at high risk (BMI > 25 kg/m² if south Asian, BMI > 30 kg/m² if white, a family history of diabetes, or a past history of gestational diabetes).

It is therefore desirable that women should aim to reduce their BMI to 35 kg/m² or less before embarking upon any form of fertility treatment, irrespective of how it is funded. In those with a BMI > 35 kg/m² a loss of 5–10% body weight may be sufficient to enhance fertility but consideration needs to be given to the availability of facilities to provide safe treatment.

Women who are overweight and obese should be provided with detailed information about the association between weight and all aspects of reproductive outcome and success of fertility treatment. They should be provided with assistance to lose weight, including psychological support, dietary advice, exercise classes and, where appropriate, weight-reducing agents such as orlistat (sibutramine and rimonabant are not recommended in those trying to conceive) or bariatric surgery.

Metformin is not a substitute for weight loss. Evidence as to its efficacy is limited, it has little benefit in the most overweight and its role in the management of infertility is unclear.

PCOS affects 15–25% of the white UK population and approximately 50% of the south Asian population. It is the most common cause of menstrual irregularity and anovulatory infertility, accounting for 90% of cases. Between 40% and 50% of women with PCOS are overweight and increased body weight is associated with increased insulin resistance, reduced fertility and reduced reproductive outcomes.

Weight loss has been shown to improve endocrine and metabolic profiles and improve ovarian function and the outcomes of spontaneous and assisted conception. There is no particular diet or therapy that has been shown to be preferable in achieving weight loss in women with PCOS.

References

1. Balen AH, Michelmore K. What is polycystic ovary syndrome? Are national views important? *Hum Reprod* 2002;17:2219–27.

2. Balen AH, Conway GS, Kaltsas G, Techatraisak K, Manning PJ, West C, Jacobs HS. Polycystic ovary syndrome: The spectrum of the disorder in 1741 patients. *Hum Reprod* 1995;10:2705–12.

3. Pasquali R, Antenucci D, Caimirri F, Venturoli S, Paradis R, Fabbri R. Clinical and hormonal characteristics of obese amenorrheic hyperandrogenic women before and after weight loss. *J Clin Endocrinol Metab* 1989;68:173–9.

4. The Rotterdam ESHRE/ASRM-Sponsored PCOS consensus workshop group. Revised 2003 consensus on diagnostic criteria and long-term health risks related to polycystic ovary syndrome (PCOS). *Hum Reprod* 2004;19:41–7.

5. Balen AH, Laven JSE, Tan SL, Dewailly D. Ultrasound assessment of the polycystic ovary: international consensus definitions. *Hum Reprod Update* 2003;9:505–14.

6. Franks S, Gharani N, McCarthy M. Candidate genes in polycystic ovary syndrome. *Hum Reprod Update* 2001;7:405–10.

7. Rajkowha M, Glass MR, Rutherford AJ, Michelmore K, Balen AH. Polycystic ovary syndrome: a risk factor for cardiovascular disease? *BJOG* 2000;107:11–8.

8. Michelmore KF, Balen AH, Dunger DB, Vessey MP. Polycystic ovaries and associated clinical and biochemical features in young women. *Clin Endocrinol (Oxf)* 1999;51:779–86.

9. Rodin DA, Bano G, Bland JM, Taylor K, Nussey SS. Polycystic ovaries and associated metabolic abnormalities in Indian subcontinent Asian women. *Clin Endocrinol* 1998;49:91–9.

10. Wijeyaratne CN, Balen AH, Barth J, Belchetz PE. Clinical manifestations and insulin resistance (IR) in PCOS among South Asians and Caucasians: is there a difference? *Clin Endocrinol* 2002;57:343–50.

11. Ehrmann DA, Barnes RB, Rosenfield RL, Cavaghan MK, Imperial J. Prevalence of impaired glucose tolerance and diabetes in women with polycystic ovary syndrome. *Diabetes Care* 1999;22:141–6.

12. Legro RS, Kunselman AR, Dodson WC, Dunaif A. Prevalence and predictors of risk for type 2 diabetes mellitus and impaired glucose tolerance in polycystic ovary syndrome: a prospective, controlled study in 254 affected women. *J Clin Endocrinol Metab* 1999;84:165–9.

13. Conn JJ, Jacobs HS, Conway GS. The prevalence of polycystic ovaries in women with type 2 diabetes mellitus. *Clin Endocrinol (Oxf)* 2000;52:81–6.

14. Wild S, Pierpoint T, Jacobs H, McKeigue P. Long-term consequences of PCOS: results of a 31 year follow-up study. *Hum Fertil* 2000;3:101–5.

15. Norman RJ, Masters L, Milner CR, Wang JX, Davies MJ. Relative risk of conversion from normoglycaemia to impaired glucose tolerance or non-insulin dependent diabetes mellitus in polycystic ovarian syndrome. *Hum Reprod* 2001;16:1995–8.

16. Ashton WD, Nanchahal K, Wood DA. Body mass index and metabolic risk factors for coronary heart disease in women. *Eur Heart J* 2001;22:46–55.

17. Lord J, Wilkin T. Polycystic ovary syndrome and fat distribution: the central issue? *Hum Fertil* 2002;5:67–71.

18. Despres JP, Lemieux I, Prud'homme D. Treatment of obesity: need to focus on high risk, abdominally obese patients. *BMJ* 2001;322:716–20.

19. Balen AH. The pathogenesis of polycystic ovary syndrome: the enigma unravels. *Lancet* 1999;354:966–7.

20. Dunaif A. Insulin resistance and the polycystic ovary syndrome: mechanisms and implication for pathogenesis. *Endocr Rev* 1997;18:774–800.

21. Franks S. Polycystic ovary syndrome. *N Engl J Med* 1995;333:853–61.

22. Bergh C, Carlsson B, Olsson JH, Selleskog U, Hillensjo T. Regulation of androgen production in cultured human thecal cells by insulin-like growth factor I and insulin. *Fertil Steril* 1993;59:323–31.

23. Leroith D, Werner H, Beitner-Johnson D, Roberts CT Jr. Molecular and cellular aspects of the insulin-like growth factor I receptor. *Endocr Rev* 1995;16:143–63.

24. De Leo V, la Marca A, Orvieto R, Morgante G. Effect of metformin on insulin-like growth factor (IGF) I and IGF-binding protein I in polycystic ovary syndrome. *J Clin Endocrinol Metab* 2000;85:1598–600.

25. Adashi E. Intraovarian regulation: the proposed role of insulin-like growth factors. *Ann N Y Acad Sci* 1993;687:10–2.

26. Erickson GF, Magoffin DA, Cragun JR, Chang RJ. The effects of insulin and insulin-like growth factors-I and -II on estradiol production by granulosa cells of polycystic ovaries. *J Clin Endocrinol Metab* 1990;70:894–902.

27. Voutilainen R, Franks S, Mason HD, Martikainen H. Expression of insulin-like growth factor (IGF), IGF-binding protein, and IGF receptor messenger ribonucleic acids in normal and polycystic ovaries. *J Clin Endocrinol Metab* 1996;81:1003–8.

28. Rosenfield RL, Barnes RB, Cara JF, Lucky AW. Dysregulation of cytochrome P450c 17 alpha as the cause of polycystic ovarian syndrome. *Fertil Steril* 1990;53:785–91.

29. Nestler JE, Jakubowicz DJ. Lean women with polycystic ovary syndrome respond to insulin reduction with decreases in ovarian P450c17 alpha activity and serum androgens. *J Clin Endocrinol Metab* 1997;82:4075–9.

30. la Marca A, Egbe TO, Morgante G, Paglia T, Ciani A, De Leo V. Metformin treatment reduces ovarian cytochrome P-450c17alpha response to human chorionic gonadotrophin in women with insulin resistance-related polycystic ovary syndrome. *Hum Reprod* 2000;15:21–3.

31. Uilenbroek JTJ, Wonlersen PJA, Van der Schoot P. Atresia in preovulatory follicles: Gonadotropin binding in steroidogenic activity. *Biol Reprod* 1980;23:219–29.

32. Hsueh ADW, Billig H, Tsafiri A. Ovarian follicle atresia: A hormonally controlled apoptotic process. *Endocr Rev* 1994;15:707–24.

33. Dunaif A, Segal KR, Futterweit W, Dobrjansky A. Profound peripheral insulin resistance, independent of obesity in polycystic ovary syndrome. *Diabetes* 1989;38:1165–74.

34. Dunaif A, Segal KR, Shelley DR, Green G, Dobrjansky A, Licholai T. Evidence for distinctive and intrinsic defects in insulin action in polycystic ovary syndrome. *Diabetes* 1992;41:1257–66.

35. Tsilchorozidou T, Overton C, Conway GS. The pathophysiology of polycystic ovary syndrome. *Clin Endocrinol* 2004;60:1–17.

36. Ehrmann DA, Sturis J, Byrne MM, Karrison T, Rosenfield RL, Polonsky KS. Insulin secretory defects in polycystic ovary syndrome. Relationship to insulin sensitivity and family history of non-insulin dependent diabetes mellitus. *J Clin Invest* 1995;96:520–7.

37. Holte J, Bergh T, Berne C, Wide L, Lithell H. Restored insulin sensitivity but persistently increased early insulin secretion after weight loss in obese women with polycystic ovary syndrome. *J Clin Endocrinol Metab* 1995;80:2586–93.

38. Zhang LH, Rodriguez H, Ohno S, Miller WL. Serine phosphorylation of human P450c17 increases 17,20-lyase activity: implications for adrenarche and the polycystic ovary syndrome. *Proc Natl Acad Sci U S A* 1995;92:10619–23.

39. Norman RJ, Noakes M, Wu R, Davies MJ, Moran L, Wang JX. Improving reproductive performance in overweight/obese women with effective weight management. *Hum Reprod Update* 2004;10:267–80.

40. National Collaborating Centre for Women's and Children's Health, National Institute for Clinical Excellence. *Fertility: Assessment and Treatment for People with Fertility Problems*. London: RCOG Press; 2004.

41. Clark AM, Ledger W, Galletly C, Tomlinson L, Blaney F, Wang X, Norman RJ. Weight loss results in significant improvement in pregnancy and ovulation rates in anovulatory obese women. *Hum Reprod* 1995;10:2705–12.

42. Clark AM, Thornley B, Tomlinson L, Galletley C, Norman RJ. Weight loss in obese infertile women results in improvement in reproductive outcome for all forms of fertility treatment. *Hum Reprod* 1998;13:1502–5.

43. Falsetti L, Pasinetti E, Mazzani MD, Gastaldi A. Weight loss and menstrual cycle: clinical and endocrinological evaluation. *Gynecol Endocrinol* 1992;6:49–56.

44. Crosignani PG, Colombo M, Vegetti W, Somigliana E, Gessati A, Ragni G. Overweight and obese anovulatory patients with polycystic ovaries: parallel improvements in anthropometric indices, ovarian physiology and fertility rate induced by diet. *Hum Reprod* 2003;18:1928–32.

45. Guzick DS, Wing R, Smith D, Berga SL, Winters SJ. Endocrine consequences of weight loss in obese, hyperandrogenic, anovulatory women. *Fertil Steril* 1994;61:598–604.

46. Kelly S, Frost G, Whittaker V, Summerbell C. Low glycaemic index diets for coronary heart disease. *Cochrane Database Syst Rev* 2004;(4):CD004467.

47. Stamets K, Taylor DS, Kunselman A, *et al.* A randomized trial of the effects of two types of short-term hypocaloric diets on weight loss in women with polycystic ovary syndrome. *Fertil Steril* 2004;81:630–7.

48. Moran LJ, Noakes M, Clifton PM, *et al.* Dietary composition in restoring reproductive and metabolic physiology in overweight women with polycystic ovary syndrome. *J Clin Endocrinol Metab* 2003;88:812–19.

49. Moran LJ, Noakes M, Clifton PM, Wittert GA, Williams G, Norman RJ. Short-term meal replacements followed by dietary macronutrient restriction enhance weight loss in polycystic ovary syndrome. *Am J Clin Nutr* 2006;84:77–87.

50. Tang T, Glanville J, Hayden CJ, White D, Barth JH, Balen AH. Combined life-style modification and metformin in obese patients with PCOS. A randomised, placebo-controlled, double-blind multi-centre study. *Hum Reprod* 2006;21:80–9.

51. Costello M, Eden J. A systematic review of the reproductive system effects of metformin in patients with polycystic ovary syndrome. *Fertil Steril* 2003;79:1–9.

52. Lord JM, Flight IH, Norman RJ. Insulin-sensitising drugs (metformin, troglitazone, rosiglitazone, pioglitazone, D-chiro-inositol) for polycystic ovary syndrome. *Cochrane Database Syst Rev* 2003;(3): CD003053.

53. Lord JM, Flight IHK, Norman RJ. Metformin in polycystic ovary syndrome: systematic review and meta-analysis. *Br Med J* 2003;327:951–5.

54. Fleming R, Hopkinson Z, Wallace A, Greer I, Sattar N. Ovarian function and metabolic factors in women with oligomenorrhoea treated with metformin in a randomized double blind placebo-controlled trial. *J Clin Endocrinol Metab* 2002;87:569–74.

55. Maciel GA, Soares Júnior JM, Alves da Motta EL, Abi Haidar M, de Lima GR, Baracat EC. Nonobese women with polycystic ovary syndrome respond better than obese women to treatment with metformin. *Fertil Steril* 2004;81:355–60.

56. Grodstein F, Goldman MB, Cramer DW. Body mass index and ovulatory infertility. *Epidemiology* 1994;5:247–50.

57. Balen AH, Dresner M, Scott EM, Drife JO. Should obese women with polycystic ovary syndrome (PCOS) receive treatment for infertility? *Br Med J* 2006;332:434–5.

58. Al-Azemi M, Omu FE, Omu AE. The effect of obesity on the outcome of infertility management in women with polycystic ovary syndrome. *Arch Gynecol Obstet* 2004;270:205–10.

59. Mulders AG, Laven JS, Eijkemans MJ, Hughes EG, Fauser BC. Patient predictors for outcome with gonadotropin ovulation induction in women with normogonadotrophic anovulatory infertility: a meta-analysis. *Hum Reprod Update* 2003;9:429–49.

60. Balen A. Surgical treatment of polycystic ovary syndrome. *Best Pract Res Clin Endocrinol Metab* 2006;20:271–80.

Chapter 8
Obesity and fertility

Cynthia Farquhar

Introduction

Most developed nations are reporting increasing proportions of women in their re-productive years who are overweight. These proportions increase with increasing age. In addition to this, many women are now delaying their fertility until their 30s, when they may have gained extra weight. There are many unwanted health consequences of being overweight and reduced fertility is now recognised as one of them.

There is now a considerable body of evidence supporting the view that women who are overweight are more likely to be infertile compared with women of normal weight. This chapter will focus attention on the evidence for this association in women, including those with polycystic ovary syndrome (PCOS). It will also consider the impact of obesity on women undergoing assisted reproductive technology (ART) treatment. In the preparation of this chapter, MEDLINE and EMBASE were searched for appropriate studies up to October 2006. The following search terms were used: obesity, obese, overweight, increased body weight, body mass index, BMI, fertility, infertility, subfertility, IVF, anovulation, ovary and pregnancy outcomes. Studies with fewer than 50 women were not included. Only studies published in English were included.

Epidemiological studies of women with infertility and the impact of excessive weight

General population

There have been a number of large epidemiological studies that provide useful information on the impact of obesity on fertility.[1-11] These studies are summarised in Table 8.1. The studies are either large cohort studies or case–control studies. The largest study is the US-based Nurses' Health Study II, which recruited a cohort of 116 678 nurses in 1989. Within that cohort, there were 2527 infertile nulliparous women who were unable to conceive for more than 1 year. They were compared with 46 718 parous women with no history of infertility. The risk of anovulatory infertility was increased three-fold in women who had a body mass index (BMI) > 32 kg/m^2 at the age of 18 years (relative risk (RR) = 2.7; 95% CI 2.0–3.7).[1] In the BMI range 25–26.9 kg/m^2, there was no evidence of a difference.[1] A further report from the Nurses' Health Study II, published in 2002, reported a U-shaped curve with a two-fold increase in anovulatory infertility if the BMI was > 30 kg/m^2 (Figure 8.1). On the basis of the BMI findings in the Nurses' Health Study II, 25% of anovulatory

Table 8.1. Epidemiology studies of obesity and the association with fertility

Study	Population	Study design	Study group	Control group	Association	Notes
Hartz et al. (1979)[8]	US women, Wisconsin	Cohort study using postal survey	26 638 women who were members of a weight-reduction club	No comparator	Association found between weight and menstrual disorders and infertility	No data were provided on the BMI
Oxford Family Planning Study (1985)[10]	Women in a family planning clinic, UK	Prospective cohort study	4104 women stopping contraception in order to conceive		No association found between BMI and fertility	
Green et al. (1988)[7]	USA	Case–control study	204 women		BMI > 24 kg/m² was associated with increase in infertility (RR = 4.7 (95% CI 1.0–4.3))	
Rich-Edwards et al. (1994)[1] (The Nurses' Health Study II)	Nurses aged 25 to 42 years, USA	Nested case–control study	2527 infertile nulliparous with BMI ≥ 24 kg/m² at 18 years old	46 718 parous women	BMI ≥ 32 kg/m² was associated with increased anovulatory infertility (RR = 2.7 (95% CI 2.0–3.7)	Study was on the BMI at 18 years of age, not at the time of trying to conceive. Adjusted for age
Grodstein et al. (1994)[6]	7 US fertility clinics	Case control study, 1981–1983.	597 women with infertility	1695 women who had recently given birth	BMI > 27 kg/m² was associated with increased anovulatory infertility (RR = 3.1 (95% CI 2.2–4.4))	Adjustments were made for age and exercise. Only white women were included
Lake et al. (1997)[5] (British Birth Cohort study)	Women born in 1958	Cohort study	5799 women at 33 years	No comparator	Increased BMI ≥ 28 kg/m² at 23 years was associated with reduced likelihood of conceiving (RR = 0.70 (95% CI 0.56–0.87))	Adjusted for BMI at 7 years and social class at birth
Jensen et al. (1999)[9]	Antenatal women in Denmark	10 903 women in their first pregnancy			BMI ≥ 25 kg/m² was associated with reduced fertility rate (FR = 0.77 (95% CI 0.70–0.87))	FR = fecundability odds ratio was calculated as the odds of conceiving in a menstrual cycle. Adjustments were made for confounding
Bolumar et al. (2000)[4]	Pregnant women Denmark, Sweden, Germany, Sweden and Italy	Population-based survey of pregnant women from five European countries	2587 pregnant women who had planned their pregnancies	No comparator	Mean time to pregnancy was increased if BMI ≥ 30 kg/m²	Only 3% had BMI ≥ 30 kg/m². Adjusted for smoking (Figure 8.2)
Rich-Edwards et al. (2002)[2] (The Nurses' Health Study II)	Nurses aged 25–42 years at the cohort's inception in 1989	Nested case–control study	830 women with anovulatory infertility	26 125 parous women	U-shaped curve noted with two-fold increase in odds ratio for anovulatory infertility if BMI > 30 kg/m²	Adjusted for age. 25% of infertility in women with BMI ≥ 25 can be attributable to obesity (Figure 8.1)
Hassan and Killick (2004)[3]	Teaching hospitals in UK	Observational study	1976 pregnant women from antenatal clinics		Women who had BMI > 25 kg/m² took twice as long to conceive	Adjusted for other lifestyle variables, age and menstrual pattern
Wilcox et al. (1998)[11]	Volunteers	Observational study	104 women trying to conceive		No association found between weight and fertility	No information on actual BMI provided

infertility cases may be attributable to BMI ≥ 25 kg/m².[2] The length of time to conceive is also increased in women with increased BMI. A survey of 1976 consecutive pregnant women who were asked about the time to achieve a pregnancy reported that women who had a BMI > 25 kg/m² took twice as long to conceive as women with a normal BMI (19–24 kg/m²) and that, for women with a BMI > 39 kg/m², the RR for subfecundity (time to pregnancy > 12 months) was 3.8 (95% CI 2.3–6.2).[3] After adjusting for other factors such as age and coital frequency, the RR for subfecundity was 6.9 (95% CI 2.9–16.8).[3] Other studies also support the view that this delay is associated with increased BMI (Figure 8.2).[4] In the British Birth Cohort study of 5799 women born in 1958, it was found that women who were overweight at age 23 years were less likely to conceive within 12 months of unprotected intercourse after adjustment for confounders.[5] It was concluded that being overweight in early adulthood appears to increase the risk of menstrual problems and subfertility.

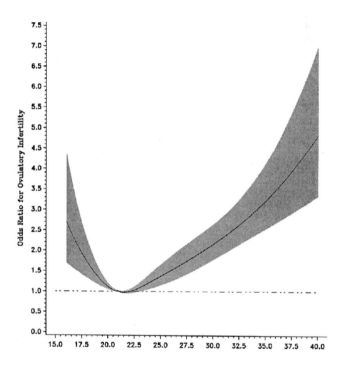

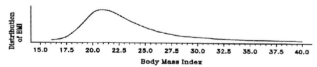

Figure 8.1. Multivariate odds ratios and 95% confidence intervals (shaded area) of ovulatory disorder infertility by body mass index (BMI, kg/m²) and distribution of BMI; Nurses' Health Study II, 1989–95; cubic spline model; knots were set, *a priori*, at the 5th, 35th, 65th and 95th percentiles of the BMI distribution; the reference BMI is 21 kg/m²; reproduced with permission from Rich-Edwards *et al.*[2]

The majority of the large epidemiological studies support the view that being overweight impacts negatively on fertility.[1–9] There are only two studies that do not provide evidence of this trend. One of these studies was the Oxford Family Planning Study of women stopping contraception in order to conceive. No association of increased body weight on fertility was found but more than half of the women were parous and no information was given on the proportion of women who were overweight.[10] A smaller study which followed 104 women while they were trying to conceive did not find an effect of weight or weight adjusted for height but once again the information on the weight of the subjects was not provided.[11]

Women who are obese with polycystic ovary syndrome

In general, the presentation of PCOS is more pronounced in women who are overweight. In women who are infertile, increased body weight is usually more prevalent and nearly 40% of women with PCOS also have a BMI > 25 kg/m^2.[12] It is likely that obesity acts both independently and in a synergistic way in women with PCOS.[13] Hyperinsulinaemia associated with obesity is the main mechanism by which being overweight impacts on ovarian function in women with PCOS. As in simple obesity, a hyperestrogenic state is also present in women with PCOS who are obese. Peripheral aromatisation (conversion) of androgens to estrogens occurs within adipose tissue, in parallel with decreased concentrations of sex hormone-binding globulin

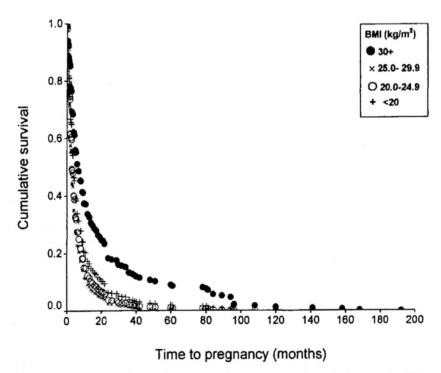

Figure 8.2.   Adjusted distribution of waiting time to pregnancy according to body mass index (BMI) at the beginning of the waiting time to pregnancy for European woman smokers whose pregnancies were planned, 1992; reproduced with permission from Bolumar et al.[4]

(SHBG). The excess estrogens exert positive feedback regulation on the pituitary release of gonadotrophins, which in turn leads to a rise in androgen production. When there is excess adipose tissue, the effect is exaggerated. The reduced levels of SHBG results in elevated free testosterone. In addition, elevated insulin levels stimulate ovarian stromal tissue to produce additional androgens. Furthermore, in women who are obese there is increased beta-endorphin secretion which in turn leads to increased insulin production.

As a result, women with PCOS are less likely to conceive if they are obese than if they are lean. There are many studies which support this finding. A systematic review by Mulders et al.[14] in 2003 summarised the findings of 13 studies and confirmed that women who were overweight (threshold varied from 25 to 30 kg/m^2) required greater amounts of gonadotrophin (weighted mean difference of 771 iu; 95% CI 700–842 iu) and that cycle cancellation was more likely (pooled OR 1.86; 95% CI 1.13–3.06).[14] The ovulation rate was reduced in those women with increased BMI compared with women with a normal BMI (OR 0.44; 95% CI 0.31–0.61). While there was no difference in pregnancy rates associated with increased BMI, for those women who conceived, miscarriage was three times more likely in women who were overweight (OR 3.05; 95% CI 1.45–6.44)

More recent studies have been published and confirm the findings of the systematic review. Loh et al. (2002)[15] reported that women with an abnormal BMI commonly required dosage adjustment and were more difficult to manage but that their potential for conception was normal. Al-Azemi et al.[16] reported on a cohort of 270 women with PCOS who received either clomifene citrate or gonadotrophins for ovulation induction and found that almost 80% of women with a BMI of 18–24 kg/m^2 ovulated at 6 months compared with only 12% of women with a BMI $\geq$ 35 kg/m^2. Balen et al.[17] reported on 335 women with World Health Organization (WHO) Group II anovulatory infertility with clomifene resistance who were given ovulation induction with gonadotrophins and found that body weight affected the gonadotrophin requirements only. There was no difference in the ovulation or clinical pregnancy rate in relation to body weight, although there was a limit on treatment provision to those with a BMI of < 35 kg/m^2.

Impact of excess body weight on women undergoing fertility treatment

In general, being overweight adversely affects the reproductive outcome of ovulation induction and ART cycles. Table 8.2 is a summary of the 35 studies that have considered the impact of obesity on fertility treatment.[16–50] Studies were only included if the data were presented for categories of BMI. There are a number of factors that influence fertility and these factors should be adjusted for in the studies. For example, increasing BMI is likely to be associated with increasing age, which is also an important factor in fertility. Other factors included the number of embryos transferred, number of cycles received, treatment type and cause of infertility. A major limitation with the published studies is the sparse reporting of live birth data. As miscarriage may be increased in women who are overweight, failing to report live birth data limits the interpretation of the results.

The published studies do not consistently report a negative association of increased BMI on the outcomes of fertility treatments. Of the 34 studies in Table 8.2, more studies have reported a negative impact of increased BMI on the pregnancy outcomes of ART cycles than not.[17–50] Ten of the 27 studies of *in vitro* fertilisation/intracytoplasmic

Table 8.2. Studies of the impact of body mass index on fertility treatments including assisted reproductive technology (ART) outcomes

Study	Population	Study design	Association	Notes
IVF/ICSI cycles				
Lewis *et al.* (1990)[18]	368 normally cycling women in an IVF programme, South Australia	Retrospective study	No relationship found between BMI and pregnancy rate but high BMI significantly reduced the number of oocytes recovered	Only 36 of participants had a BMI > 28 kg/m^2 and the heaviest woman was 106 kg. No adjustments were made for age
Crosignani *et al.* (1994)[19]	111 women with no evidence of PCOS undergoing IVF, Milan, Italy	Cohort study	Response to ovulation induction inversely related to BMI. Of the ten pregnancies, only one was in a woman with BMI ≥ 28 kg/m^2	Adjusted for age
Ramzy *et al.* (1996)[20]	118 women with IVF	Retrospective study	No relationship found between BMI and pregnancy rate but there was greater use of gonadotrophins	No adjustments for age
Wass *et al.* (1997)[21]	220 women undergoing IVF in Sweden	Prospective study of impact of android body fat distribution	Waist:hip ratio, but not BMI, was associated with reduced pregnancy rate by more than half (OR = 0.42; 95% CI 0.2–0.9)	Adjusted for age, BMI, smoking, indication for IVF, parity and number of embryos transferred
Tinkanen *et al.* (1999)[22]	74 women undergoing COH		No impact of BMI on outcomes or ampoule use	Mean BMI = 22 kg/m^2
Lashen *et al.* (1999)[23]	333 women undergoing IVF, England	Retrospective nested case–control study of prospectively collected database	No difference in the clinical pregnancy rate between the women with BMI > 27.9 kg/m^2 and those with BMI < 27.9 kg/m^2 (24% versus 20%) or in the requirements for gonadotrophins or the number of oocytes collected	Only 36 women (11%) had BMI > 30 kg/m^2. Only white women included. Age matching
Jones *et al.* (2000)[24]	247 women undergoing IVF cycles	Retrospective review	Pregnancy rate was significantly decreased when BMI > 30 kg/m^2 compared with normal BMI (17% compared with 45%)	No adjustments for age. Abstract only
Wittemer *et al.* (2000)[25]	398 women in an IVF programme, France	Retrospective study	Increase in the number of ampoules required and a decrease in the number of oocytes collected if BMI ≥ 25 kg/m^2. No difference in clinical pregnancy rate between groups	No adjustments were made for age
Wang *et al.* (2000)[26]	3586 women undergoing fertility treatment in South Australia. 25% of the women had PCOS	Retrospective analysis	Women with BMI ≥ 35 kg/m^2 had half the pregnancy rate than that of women with BMI 20–25 kg/m^2	Adjustments were made for effects of maternal age, number of embryos transferred, the number of cycles, treatment received and the cause of infertility
Loveland *et al.* (2001)[27]	139 women undergoing IVF, USA	Retrospective study	Women with a BMI > 25 kg/m^2 had reduced implantation and pregnancy rates, although 44% (8/18) of women with BMI > 35 kg/m^2 had a live birth	No adjustments made for age or number of cycles

Study	Population	Study design	Association	Notes
Salha et al. (2001)[28]	100 women undergoing IVF, England	Prospective cohort study.	Clinical pregnancy rate in the normal BMI group and in the BMI ≥ 25 kg/m² group was 37% and 26.6%, respectively (P = 0.042). There was also a reduced number of oocytes and lower fertilisation rate in the higher BMI group	Matched for age
Wang et al. (2002)[29]	2349 women undergoing ART in one tertiary fertility clinic, South Australia	Retrospective study	Women with increased BMI had increased risk of miscarriage compared with women with normal BMI	Adjusted for age and other risk factors
Engel et al. (2003)[30]	1881 women who were part of clinical trials of GnRH analogues for GnRH antagonists for IVF protocols	Pooled data from five RCTs of GnRH analogues for ovulation induction for IVF protocols	Increasing body weight was associated with increased requirements for gonadotrophins. No difference in the clinical pregnancy rate	No adjustment for increasing age with increasing weight
Merryman et al. (2003)[31]	192 embryo transfer cycles of women undergoing IVF, USA	Cohort study	BMI ≥ 27 kg/m² was associated with reduced ongoing and live birth rate compared with women with normal BMI (20% compared with 44.7%; P < 0.0061)	No data on age. Abstract only
Thum et al. (2003)[32]	6213 consecutive women undergoing IVF, London, UK	Cohort study	No difference in pregnancy detected between women with BMI 20–30 kg/m² and women with BMI > 30 kg/m². Small difference in live birth rate (28% with BMI 20–30 kg/m² and 23% with BMI > 30 kg/m², P = 0.04). Other outcomes such as number of oocytes collected and number of embryos transferred were also similar	No difference in age. Higher miscarriage rate. Abstract only
Nichols et al. (2003)[33]	372 women undergoing IVF, USA	Retrospective review	Women with a BMI ≥ 28 kg/m² had reduced live birth rate compared with BMI 20–27.9 kg/m² (OR = 0.53; 95% CI 0.32–0.86; P = 0.011)	Adjusted for age, number of embryos transferred, embryo quality and endometrial thickness.
Fedorcsak et al. (2004)[34]	5019 women undergoing IVF/ICSI Norway. 3.2% had PCOS	Retrospective review	Obesity is associated with lower chances for live birth after IVF and ICSI. Women with BMI ≥ 30 kg/m² had 17% live births compared with women with normal BMI who had 21% live births (P = 0.03). Obesity was also associated with an impaired response to ovarian stimulation	Adjusted for age and main infertility diagnoses
Ferlitsch et al. (2004)[35]	171 ovulatory women undergoing IVF in Vienna, Austria	Retrospective chart review	Raising BMI by one unit decreased the odds for pregnancy by 0.84 (95% CI 0.73–0.97). The RR of ovulatory infertility was 2.7 (95% CI 2.0–3.7) in women with BMI > 32 kg/m²	Multiple logistic regression analysis performed. The median BMI was 20.5 kg/m². Both BMI and follicle-stimulating hormone (FSH) levels were found to be independent predictors

Study	Population	Study design	Association	Notes
Ryley et al. (2004)[36]	6827 IVF cycles	Retrospective study	Clinical pregnancy rate reduced in women with BMI > 35 kg/m² (21.7%) compared with all other BMI groups. (31.3% in women with BMI 20–25 kg/m²)	Women with BMI > 40 kg/m² were not included. Women with BMI > 35 kg/m² were younger. No adjustments were made. Abstract only
Spandorfer et al. (2004)[37]	920 good-prognosis women undergoing IVF on New York, USA	Retrospective study	Women with a BMI > 27 kg/m² had increased cycle cancellation (15%) compared with women with BMI < 27 kg/m² (9%) but no difference in clinical pregnancy rates (56.3% and 56.4%)	Good prognosis was defined as age < 40 years, all with normal ovarian reserve. No difference in age for cancelled cycles
Lintsen et al. (2005)[38]	8457 women, The Netherlands	Large cohort study of prospectively collected data	Women with a BMI ≥ 27 kg/m² compared with women with BMI 20–27 kg/m² had a significantly lower delivery rate (OR = 0.67 (95% CI 0.48–0.94)	Logistic regression analysis
van Swieten et al. (2005)[39]	162 women undergoing IVF/ICSI	Prospective data	No evidence of a difference in cancellation rate or clinical pregnancy rate for women with BMI > 30 kg/m²	Age was similar in the different BMI groups
Dokras et al. (2006)[40]	1293 women < 38 years old undergoing first cycle of IVF, USA	Retrospective study	Women with BMI ≥ 40 kg/m² was associated with higher rates of cycle cancellation (25% compared with 11% in women with normal BMI) but no differences in clinical pregnancy rate or live birth rate	Adjustments made for age, year of treatment and PCOS. 25% had PCOS in the BMI < 25 kg/m² and 39% in women with a BMI > 40 kg/m²
Mitwally et al. (2006)[41]	180 women undergoing IVF, USA	Retrospective study	Women were less likely to conceive if their BMI was > 25 kg/m²	Abstract of oral presentation at the ASRM 2006
Stassart et al. (2006)[42]	370 women undergoing IVF, USA	Retrospective study	Declining pregnancy rates with increasing BMI	Abstract of oral presentation at the ASRM 2006
Woodford et al. (2006)[43]	205 women undergoing IVF, USA	Retrospective study	No effect on pregnancy rate with increasing BMI or waist:hip ratio	Abstract of oral presentation at the ASRM 2006
Gillett et al. (2006)[44]	504 women undergoing IVF, New Zealand	Prospective data	Women with BMI 18–32 kg/m² had 43% births compared with 29% for women with BMI ≥ 32 kg/m²	No adjustments for age
Ovulation induction with or without intrauterine insemination				
Hamilton-Fairley et al. (1992)[45]	100 women with clomifene-resistant PCOS undergoing ovulation induction with gonadotrophins	Retrospective	Women with BMI 25–27.9 kg/m² had similar clinical pregnancy rates to women with BMI 19–24.9 kg/m² but increased miscarriage rates (60% vs 27%; P < 0.05)	Adjusted for age

Study	Population	Study design	Association	Notes
Al-Azemi et al. (2004)[16]	270 women with PCOS undergoing ovulation induction with gonadotrophin or clomifene citrate	Prospective study	Women with BMI > 30 kg/m² had reduced live birth rates (64% vs 97%; P = 0.001) and increased miscarriage rates (22% vs 0%; P = 0.006) compared with women with normal BMI	Not adjusted for age but most women in the 20–39 year age group
Dodson et al. (2006)[46]	333 ovulatory women undergoing superovulation and intrauterine insemination, USA	Retrospective chart review	No impact of obesity on outcomes of intrauterine insemination but adjusted total gonadotrophin dose was greater in women with BMI ≥ 30 kg/m² (278 iu/cycle compared with 434 iu/cycle)	Adjusted for age, year and GnRH agonist or antagonist and multiple comparison testing
Balen et al. (2006)[17]	335 women with World Health Organization group II anovulatory infertility	Prospective study	No impact of increasing BMI on clinical pregnancy rate or miscarriage	Adjusted for potential confounding factors including age, total number of follicles and serum FSH
Donor oocytes				
Bellver et al. (2003)[47]	712 women undergoing ovum donation	Retrospective study	Women with BMI ≥ 30 kg/m² had increased miscarriage rates compared with women with normal BMI (38% vs 13%; P = 0.003) but no difference in the clinical pregnancy rate	No adjustments for age
Wattanakumtornkul et al. (2003)[48]	97 women undergoing embryo transfer after donor oocytes	Cohort study	No difference in live birth rate between women with BMI > 30 kg/m² (41.6%) and women with BMI < 25 kg/m² (42.3%)	No difference in age although the mean age was 39–41 years. Small study with only 12 women in the BMI > 30 kg/m² group
Styne-Gross et al. (2005)[49]	536 first cycle recipients of donor oocytes, USA	Retrospective chart review	Recipient BMI had no adverse impact on pregnancy outcomes	Adjusted for multiple statistical testing
Donor insemination				
Zaadstra et al. (1993)[50]	Fertility clinic in The Netherlands	Prospective cohort study of 500 women seeking donor insemination	Waist:hip ratio > 0.80 associated with 30% reduction in probability of conception per cycle	Adjusted for age, fatness, reasons for donor insemination, cycle length, smoking and parity

COH = controlled ovarian hyperstimulation; FSH = follicle stimulating hormone; GnRH = gonadotrophin-releasing hormone; ICSI = intracytoplasmic sperm injection; PCOS = polycystic ovary syndrome sperm injection (IVF/ICSI) cycles did not report an effect on clinical pregnancy rates. These studies were mostly smaller, older and had a low proportion of women with increased BMI,[18,20,22,23,25,37,39] with the exception of three larger more recent studies[30,32,40] that also did not show an impact of obesity on ART cycles. The remaining studies suggested an association with poorer pregnancy outcomes, including some studies that reported live birth rate.[26,27,31,33,34,36,38] Only one of the four studies of ovulation induction in women with PCOS reported a negative impact of obesity on the outcome of treatment[16,17,45,46] although two of them suggested an association with miscarriage.[16,45] Being overweight was consistently associated with greater gonadotrophin usage and increased cycle cancellation regardless of whether or not the women had PCOS.

The association between obesity and miscarriage following spontaneous conception is discussed in Chapter 11. However, miscarriage following ART cycles is briefly mentioned here. The impact of obesity on miscarriage following ART treatment is unclear. Several studies have reported an increase in early pregnancy loss following fertility treatments in women who were overweight.[16,17,29,35,45,49,50] In the three studies that considered the impact of BMI on miscarriage in women receiving ovum donation, two studies reported an effect[47,49] while a third one did not.[48] Winter[51] reported that women who were very obese had an increased risk of miscarriage although, after adjusting for other factors such as age, the effect was no longer present. In general, BMI is considered an independent risk factor and not directly related to fertility treatment.[52,53]

Why is there a difference between the population studies and the studies of women undergoing fertility treatments? One possible explanation for the difference between the two groups of studies is that the fertility treatments are able to overcome the barriers to conception by increasing the dosage of the gonadotrophins given. Other factors, such as the number of embryos transferred, need to be taken into consideration as well. There is some evidence to support this as women who had increased BMI also tended to require more gonadotrophins and a reduced number of oocytes.

Two studies were found that explored the impact of the male partner's BMI on fertility and semen parameters. One study only considered the impact of the BMI of 520 men on their semen parameters and a dose–response relationship was reported. In men with normal BMI, there were 18.6×10^6 per ml normal motile sperm cells, in men with BMI 26–29 kg/m², 3.6×10^6 per ml, and in men ≥ 30 kg/m², 0.7×10^6 per ml.[54] In the second study, the impact of BMI was considered only on infertility and men with a BMI 32–34 kg/m² were twice as likely to be infertile.[55] A dose–response relationship was found and the partner's BMI and age were controlled for. Further research on the impact of the male partner's BMI on both semen parameters and fertility should be undertaken.

Establishing causality: does being overweight reduce fertility?

In order to establish causality between pathology and symptoms, it has been suggested that certain criteria must exist.[56,57] The following questions have been suggested as a guide to establishing causality:

- Is there experimental evidence from human studies?
- Is the association between the proposed cause and effect strong?
- Is the association consistent from study to study?
- Is the temporal relationship correct?
- Is there a dose–response relationship?

- Is the association consistent with existing biological and environmental knowledge?
- Does the association make biological sense?
- Is the association specific?
- Is there a similar accepted link between an exposure and a disease?

Is there experimental evidence from human studies?

This question refers to the need for studies with an experimental design where the cause is removed or reduced and the disease rates are studied. Although this is often done in the context of a randomised controlled trial (RCT), it is not always possible. For example, in trying to establish the link between lung cancer and cigarette smoking, it was not feasible to do an RCT. However, in the example of obesity and infertility, it would help to establish whether obesity has a role in infertility by evaluating fertility rates following weight reduction with an RCT comparing weight reduction and lifestyle modification with expectant management. Unfortunately, only one small RCT of this intervention has been published. In this study, weight loss was associated with the resumption of ovulation in a group of 12 women who were previously obese, hyperandrogenic and anovulatory.[58] In the six women who reduced weight, four started to ovulate and there was a fall in androgen levels. One other RCT of women who are overweight and infertile, from South Australia, has commenced but the full results are not yet available.[59] Non-randomised studies of weight reduction support the concept that there is a relationship between obesity and fertility as weight loss is associated with the return of menstrual cycles and fertility in women who were previously overweight.[60–63] However, few of these studies are prospective or include a comparison or control group. All studies reported a return of regular menstrual cycles and fertility to some degree, even though the weight loss was only 10%.[64–66] Improvements in hyperandrogenism and hyperinsulinaemia were also seen with only 5–10% loss of initial body weight[63,67] and the spontaneous pregnancy rate can be improved with 10–15% weight loss.[68–71]

There are several possible mechanisms for the effect of reducing body weight on fertility. Weight loss in women who are obese leads to reduced insulin concentrations and free testosterone, and an increased concentration of SHBG.[60–62,68] High insulin concentrations (fasting or stimulated) have been associated with anovulation and the decrease in insulin concentration noted may be a factor in the resumption of ovulation. The response to fertility interventions has also been demonstrated as being affected by body weight, with the response to ovulation induction shown to be inversely related to BMI.[19]

Another approach to establishing causality in the absence of experimental human studies is to consider the impact of being overweight on treatment cycles, including IVF. A number of studies have shown a decrease in fertility rates in women who were overweight although at least ten of the 27 studies of IVF/ICSI in Table 8.2 did not show an association.

Is the association between the proposed cause and effect strong, and is the association consistent from study to study?

In relation to obesity and infertility, the association is both strong and consistent among the studies, which are mostly large case–control studies of women trying to conceive spontaneously. The relative risk of infertility with increased BMI was mostly at least doubled in the 11 epidemiological studies (Table 8.1). The odds ratio of conceiving following ART treatment was reduced by approximately 30–50% in those studies that showed an effect (Table 8.2). There is less consistency among the studies of women who had treatment cycles or ovulation induction as there are some dissenting studies.

Is the temporal relationship correct?

This question relates to the relationship between time and the onset of the condition. In this case, the question is whether or not the obesity preceded the onset of the infertility. In the Nurses' Health Study II, this was so, as the BMI at age 18 years was associated with later infertility at 33 years.[1] A certain bias exists, as being overweight is more likely in older women who may also be trying to conceive. This bias has to some extent been overcome by the use of multivariate analyses that take age into account.

Is there a dose–response relationship?

Do women who are morbidly obese have more problems conceiving than women who are only mildly obese? That is, does the extent of the obesity influence the infertility? Several studies were found that specifically addressed this question and they were consistent in supporting a dose–response relationship (Figure 8.1).

Is the association consistent with existing biological and environmental knowledge, and does the association make biological sense?

Regarding biological plausibility, there are a several possibilities. For example, it is accepted that women who are overweight are frequently anovulatory. It is known that, in women at both extremes of weight, that is with a BMI > 30 kg/m^2 or < 17 kg/m^2, abnormalities occur in the hypothalamic–pituitary–ovarian axis and, as a result, anovulation is common.[72] In the case of women with high BMI, the explanation is most likely because of the hypersecretion of insulin. The association does make biological sense in that pregnancy in women who are severely overweight often leads to complications for both the mother and infant and therefore a reduction in fertility is possibly protective.

Is the association specific?

Many women with obesity, even morbid obesity, do conceive and deliver without difficulty. Therefore, the association is not specific.

Is there a similar accepted link between an exposure and a disease?

One such example in the field of infertility is the role of tubal disease, where many of the above questions can be adequately answered from the literature. The association between fertility and tubal infertility is strong and consistent (although further well-designed studies are still needed), has an obvious temporal and dose–response relationship, is specific and makes both epidemiological and biological sense. In this way, it mirrors the causality criteria and supports the concept of obesity being associated with reduced fertility.

Overall, the evidence for the association of infertility and increased body weight is reasonably strong. This is summarised in Table 8.3.

Table 8.3. Summary of evidence for the association of obesity and infertility

Question	Explanation of question	Role of obesity in infertility
Is there experimental evidence from human studies?	What happens to fertility if weight loss occurs?	No data from randomised controlled trials but there is a large number of non-randomised studies that suggest a negative effect of BMI on fertility outcomes.
Is the association between the proposed cause and effect strong?	Is there a large effect size (relative risk) from well-designed studies?	There is a moderate effect size. The relative risk of infertility with increased BMI is mostly at least doubled from the 11 epidemiological studies. (Table 8.1). The odds ratio of conceiving following ART is reduced by approximately 30–50% in those studies that showed an effect (Table 8.2).
Is the association consistent from study to study?	Are there repeated observations by different studies?	There are consistent results for the population studies. Nine out of 11 studies agree that increased BMI is associated with reduced or delayed fertility. There were mixed results for the women undergoing fertility treatments. Ten out of 27 studies of IVF/ICSI and three out of four studies of ovulation induction did not report an association.
Is the temporal relationship correct?	Does the occurrence of the obesity precede the occurrence of the infertility?	Yes, as infertility is usually diagnosed sometime after the weight gain.
Is there a dose–response relationship?	Is infertility more likely with women who are morbidly obese?	Yes, as women with higher BMI are generally more infertile or require more fertility drugs to conceive or take longer to conceive.
Is the association consistent with existing biological and environmental knowledge?	Is there coherence of the evidence?	Yes, because of the anovulatory effect of being overweight and the negative impact of hyperinsulinaemia on fertility and the embryo.
Does the association make biological sense?	Is it likely that obesity could interfere with fertility?	Yes, because of anovulation. Treatment cycles may overcome the BMI impact on natural fertility.
Is the association specific?	Does obesity often lead to infertility?	Yes, although lean women with PCOS can also have ovulatory infertility and women who are overweight can conceive successfully.
Is there a similar accepted link between an exposure and a disease?	Is there another example of a cause for infertility that is analogous to obesity?	There is a strong and consistent association between infertility and tubal infertility.

Criteria for treatment

Some fertility services have chosen to set BMI thresholds for access to fertility treatment. In New Zealand, as obesity was considered to reduce a woman's chance of successful ART, access to publicly funded fertility treatment is restricted to women with a BMI range of 18–32 kg/m^2.[73] From 2000, women with a BMI outside this range were only accepted for publicly funded ART on the basis that they had undergone weight improvement to within the agreed range. Some clinics no longer accept referrals of women with a BMI > 35 kg/m^2, even for investigation.

Many fertility clinics in the UK have established their own criteria for treatment. In a survey published in 2006, 101 fertility clinics were asked for any specific weight criteria for women to access treatment.[74] Of the 86 clinics who returned the survey, 65% applied a specific limit for ovulation induction with anti-estrogens, 74% had a limit for treatment with gonadotrophins, 52% had a limit for artificial insemination, 65% had a limit for IVF and 57% had a limit for ovarian drilling. The BMI threshold for treatment differed considerably. Overall, the majority of centres had a BMI limit ≥ 35 kg/m^2 for most treatments. For the most expensive treatment of IVF, 40% of clinics treated up to a threshold of 30–35 kg/m^2 while the majority (57%) only treated up to a threshold of 25–30 kg/m^2.[74]

In the UK National Institute for Health and Clinical Excellence (NICE) fertility guideline published in 2004,[75] the following recommendations were made.

- Women with a BMI > 29 kg/m^2 should be informed that they are likely to take longer to conceive.
- Women with a BMI > 29 kg/m^2 and who are not ovulating should be informed that losing weight is likely to increase their chance of conceiving.
- Women should be informed that participating in a group programme involving exercise and dietary advice leads to more pregnancies than weight loss alone.

Prepregnancy advice

Women seeking fertility treatment have the opportunity to make some significant lifestyle changes not only to improve their chances of conceiving and their own health but also to improve the health of their offspring. The fertility specialist is in an ideal position to influence them regarding changes to lifestyle such as modifying dietary intake, increasing exercise, stopping smoking, reducing or stopping alcohol intake and reducing weight. Many of these recommendations are described in the NICE fertility guideline of 2004.[75]

Many women wish to know which dietary modification they should make. The most important determinant is energy balance. There are many diets available and few have been scientifically studied. Although low fat, high carbohydrate diets have been widely promoted, a modification of this approach to a low fat, moderate protein, lower carbohydrate diet is more consistent with a healthy diet.[76] A group environment that provides support for diet modifications and exercise is also advisable. There is only a minimal role for medication.[77] The use of insulin-sensitising agents has not been shown to result in weight reduction.[78]

Conclusion

By encouraging lifestyle changes such as weight loss, the message that obesity is a major health problem is reinforced. In addition, by reducing weight prior to pregnancy, the chances of obstetric complications and health problems for the offspring, as well as the costs of fertility treatment, can be reduced. Lifestyle changes such as weight reduction and exercise are firmly in the control of the woman. This is an important public health message for women and their families in their reproductive years and experience shows that some women will achieve these changes. Fertility services have an opportunity to promote this message during the pretreatment phase. Insisting on a BMI threshold for access to fertility treatments and investing in weight-reduction programmes before providing fertility treatment to women who are overweight makes sense and is surely good medicine.

References

1. Rich-Edwards JW, Goldman MB, Willett WC, Hunter DJ, Stampfer MJ, Colditz GA, et al. Adolescent body mass index and infertility caused by ovulatory disorder. *Am J Obstet Gynecol* 1994;171:171–7.
2. Rich-Edwards JW, Spiegelman D, Garland M, Hertzmark E, Hunter DJ, Colditz GA, et al. Physical activity, body mass index, and ovulatory disorder infertility. *Epidemiology* 2002;13:184–90.
3. Hassan MAM, Killick SR. Negative lifestyle is associated with a significant reduction in fecundity. *Fertil Steril* 2004;81:384–92.
4. Bolumar F, Olsen J, Rebagliato M, Saez-Lloret I, Bisanti L. Body mass index and delayed conception: a European Multicenter Study on Infertility and Subfecundity. *Am J Epidemiol* 2000;151:1072–9.
5. Lake JK, Power C, Cole TJ. Women's reproductive health: the role of body mass index in early and adult life. *Int J Obes Relat Metab Disord* 1997;21:432–8.
6. Grodstein F, Goldman MB, Cramer DW. Body mass index and ovulatory infertility. *Epidemiology* 1994;5:247–50.
7. Green BB, Weiss NS, Daling JR. Risk of ovulatory infertility in relation to body weight. *Fertil Steril* 1988;50:721–6.
8. Hartz AJ, Barboriak PN, Wong A, Katayama KP, Rimm AA. The association of obesity with infertility and related menstrual abnormalities in women. *Int J Obes* 1979;3:57–73.
9. Jensen TK, Scheike T, Keiding N, Schaumburg I, Grandjean P. Fecundability in relation to body mass and menstrual cycle patterns. *Epidemiology* 1999;10:422–8.
10. Howe G, Westhoff C, Vessey M, Yeates D. Effects of age, cigarette smoking, and other factors in fertility: findings in a large prospective study. *BMJ* 1985;290:1697–700.
11. Wilcox A, Weinberg C, Baird D. Caffeinated beverages and decreased fertility. *Lancet* 1988;2:1453–5.
12. Balen AH, Conway GS, Kaltsas G, Techatrasak K, Manning PJ, West C, et al. Polycystic ovary syndrome: the spectrum of the disorder in 1741 patients. *Hum Reprod* 1993;10:2107–11.
13. van der Spuy ZM, Dyer SJ. The pathogenesis of infertility and early pregnancy loss in polycystic ovary syndrome. *Best Pract Res Clin Obstet Gynaecol* 2004;18:755–71.
14. Mulders AG, Laven JS, Eijkemans MJ, Hughes EG, Fauser BC. Patient predictors for outcome of gonadotrophin ovulation induction in women with normogonadotrophic anovulatory infertility: a meta-analysis. *Hum Reprod Update* 2003;9:429–49.
15. Loh S, Wang JX, Matthews CD. The influence of body mass index, basal FSH and age on the response to gonadotrophin stimulation in non-polycystic ovarian syndrome patients. *Hum Reprod* 2002;17:1207–11.
16. Al-Azemi M, Omu FE, Omu AE. The effect of obesity on the outcome of infertility management in women with polycystic ovary syndrome. *Arch Gynecol Obstet* 2004;270:205–10.
17. Balen AH, Platteau P, Andersen AN, Devroey P, Sorensen P, Helmgaard L, Arce JC. The influence of body weight on response to ovulation induction with gonadotrophins in 335 women with World Health Organization group II anovulatory infertility. *BJOG* 2006;113:1195–202.
18. Lewis CG, Warnes GM, Wang X, Matthews CD. Failure of body mass index or body weight to influence markedly the response to ovarian hyperstimulation in normal cycling women. *Fertil Steril* 1990;53:1097–9.

19. Crosignani PG, Ragni G, Parazzini F, Wyssling H, Lombroso G, Perotti L. Anthropometric indicators and response to gonadotrophin for ovulation induction. *Hum Reprod* 1994;9:420–3.

20. Ramzy A-MI, Mansour RT, Serour GI, Elattar I, Amin Y, Aboulghar MA. Body weight and outcome of *in vitro* fertilization. *Middle East Fertil Soc J* 1996;1:72–7.

21. Wass P, Waldenström U, Rossner S, Hellberg D. An android body fat distribution in females impairs the pregnancy rate of IVF-embryo transfer. *Hum Reprod* 1997;2:2057–60.

22. Tinkanen H, Blauer M, Laippala P, Touhimaa P, Kujansuu E. Prognostic factors in controlled ovarian hyperstimulation. *Fertil Steril* 1999;72:932–6.

23. Lashen H, Ledger W, Bernal AL, Barlow D. Extremes of body mass do not adversely affect the outcome of superovulation and in-vitro fertilization. *Hum Reprod* 1999;14:712–5.

24. Jones KP, Hatasake HH, Peterson CM, Aoki V, Campbell B, Carrell DT. Body mass index (BMI) is inversely related to intrafolliclar hCG levesl and pregnancy rates of IVF patients. *Fertil Steril* 2000;74(3 Suppl 1):255.

25. Wittemer C, Ohl J, Bailly M, Bettahar-Lebugle K, Nisand I. Does body mass index of infertile women have an impact on IVF procedure and outcome? *J Assist Reprod Genet* 2000;17:547–52.

26. Wang JX, Davies M, Norman RJ. Body mass and probability of pregnancy during assisted reproduction treatment: retrospective study. *BMJ* 2000;321:1320–1.

27. Loveland JB, McClamrock HD, Malinow AM, Sharara FI. Increased body mass index has a deleterious effect on *in vitro* fertilization outcome. *J Assist Reprod Genet* 2001;18:382–6.

28. Salha O, Dada T, Sharma V. Influence of body mass index and self-administration of hCG on the outcome of IVF cycles: a prospective cohort study. *Hum Fertil (Camb)* 2001;4:37–42.

29. Wang JX, Davies MJ, Norman RJ. Obesity increases the risk of spontaneous abortion during infertility treatment. *Obes Res* 2002;10:551–4.

30. Engel JB, Ludwig M, Junge K, Howles CM, Diedrich K. No influence of body weight on pregnancy rate in patients treated with cetrorelix according to the single- and multiple-dose protocols. *Reprod Biomed Online* 2003;6:482–7.

31. Merryman DC, Yancey CA, Dalton KE, Houserman VL, Long CA, Honea KL. Regardless of oocyte source, body mass index is predictive of *in vitro* fertilization success. *Fertil Steril* 2003;S169.

32. Thum MY, Gafar A, Faris R, Wren M, Ogunyemi T, Abdalla H. The influence of body mass index on *in vitro* fertilization treatment outcome, risk of miscarriage, and pregnancy outcome. *Fertil Steril* 2003;S155.

33. Nichols JE, Crane MM, Higdon HL, Miller PB, Boone WR. Extremes of body mass index reduce *in vitro* fertilization pregnancy rates. *Fertil Steril* 2003;79:645–7.

34. Fedorcsak P, Dale PO, Storeng R, Ertzeid G, Bjercke S, Oldereid N, et al. Impact of overweight and underweight on assisted reproduction treatment. *Hum Reprod* 2004;19:2523–8.

35. Ferlitsch K, Sator MO, Gruber DM, Rucklinger E, Gruber CJ, Huber JC. Body mass index, follicle-stimulating hormone and their predictive value in *in vitro* fertilization. *J Assist Reprod Genet* 2004;21:431–6.

36. Ryley DA, Bayer SR, Eaton J, Zimon A, Klipstein S, Reindollar R. Influence of body mass index (BMI) on the outcome of 6,827 IVF cycles. *Fertil Steril* 2004;82 Suppl 2:S38.

37. Spandorfer SD, Kump L, Goldschlag D, Brodkin T, Davis OK, Rosenwaks Z. Obesity and *in vitro* fertilization: negative influences on outcome. *J Reprod Med* 2004;49:973–7.

38. Lintsen AM, Pasker-de Jong PC, de Boer EJ, Burger CW, Jansen CA, Braat DD, et al. Effects of subfertility cause, smoking and body weight on the success rate of IVF. *Hum Reprod* 2005;20:1867–75.

39. van Swieten EC, van der Leeuw-Harmsen L, Badings EA, van der Linden PJ. Obesity and Clomiphene Challenge Test as predictors of outcome of *in vitro* fertilization and intracytoplasmic sperm injection. *Gynecol Obstet Invest* 2005;59:220–4.

40. Dokras A, Baredziak L, Blaine J, Syrop C, VanVoorhis BJ, Sparks A. Obstetric outcomes after *in vitro* fertilization in obese and morbidly obese women. *Obstet Gynecol* 2006;108:61–9.

41. Mitwally MF, Leduc MM, Ogunleye O, Albuarki H, Diamond MP, Abuzeid M. The effect of body mass index (BMI) on the outcome of IVF and embryo transfer in women of different ethnic backgrounds. *Fertil Steril* 2006;86 Suppl 1:S68–9.

42. Stassart JP, Ball GD. The effect of body mass index on IVF outcome. *Fertil Steril* 2006;86 Suppl 1: S164–5.

43. Woodford DE, Grossman MP, Ku LT, Bohler HC, Makajima ST. Effect of body mass index (BMI) and/or weight distribution on IVF outcome. *Fertil Steril* 2006;86:S165.

44. Gillett WR, Putt T, Farquhar CM. Prioritising for fertility treatments – the effect of excluding women with a high body mass index. *BJOG* 2006;113:1218–21.

45. Hamilton-Fairley D, Kiddy D, Watson H, Paterson C, Franks S. Association of moderate obesity with a poor pregnancy outcome in women with polycystic ovary syndrome treated with low dose gonadotrophin. *Br J Obstet Gynaecol* 1992;99:128–31.

46. Dodson WC, Kunselman AR, Legro RS. Association of obesity with treatment outcomes in ovulatory infertile women undergoing superovulation and intrauterine insemination. *Fertil Steril* 2006;86:642–6.

47. Bellver J, Rossal LP, Bosch E, Zuniga A, Corona JT, Melendez F, *et al.* Obesity and the risk of spontaneous abortion after oocyte donation. *Fertil Steril* 2003;79:1136–40.

48. Wattanakumtornkul S, Damario MA, Stevens Hall SA, Thornhill AR, Tummon IS. Body mass index and uterine receptivity in the oocyte donation model. *Fertil Steril* 2003;80:336–40.

49. Styne-Gross A, Elkind-Hirsch KS, RT. Obesity does not impact implantation rates or pregnancy outcome in women attempting conception through oocyte donation. *Fertil Steril* 2005;83:1629–34.

50. Zaadstra BM, Seidell JC, Van Noord PA, te Velde ER, Habbema JD, Vrieswijk B, *et al.* Fat and female fecundity: prospective study of effect of body fat distribution on conception rates. *BMJ* 1993;306:484–7.

51. Winter E, Want J, Davies MJ, Norman R. Early pregnancy loss following assisted reproductive technology treatment. *Hum Reprod* 2003;17:3220–3.

52. Fedorcsak P, Storeng R, Dale PO, Tanbo T, Abyholm T. Obesity is a risk factor for early pregnancy loss after IVF or ICSI. *Acta Obstet Gynecol Scand* 2000;79:43–8.

53. Bellver J, Busso C, Pellicer A, Remohi J, Simon C. Obesity and assisted reproductive technology outcomes. *Reprod Biomed Online* 2006;12:562–8.

54. Kort HI, Massey JB, Elsner CW, Mitchell-Leaf D, Shapiro DB, Witt MA, *et al.* Impact of body mass index values on sperm quantity and quality. *J Androl* 2006;27:450–2.

55. Sallmen M, Sandler DP, Hoppin JA, Blair A, Baird DD. Reduced fertility among overweight and obese men. *Epidemiology* 2006;17:520–3.

56. Bradford Hill A. The environment and disease: association or causation? *Proc R Soc Med* 1965;58:295–300.

57. Rothman KJ. *Modern Epidemiology*. Boston: Little, Brown: 1996.

58. Guzick DS, Wing R, Smith D, Berga SL, Winters SJ. Endocrine consequences of weight loss in obese hyperandrogenic anovulatory women. *Fertil Steril* 1994;61:598–604.

59. Norman R, personal communication.

60. Bates GW, Whitworth NS. Effect of body weight reduction on plasma androgens in obese, infertile women. *Fertil Steril* 1982;38:406–9.

61. Harlass FE, Plymate SR, Fariss BL, Belts RP. Weight loss is associated with correction of gonadotropin and sex steroid abnormalities in the obese anovulatory female. *Fertil Steril* 1984;42:649–52.

62. Pasquali R, Antenucci D, Casimirri F, Venturoli S, Paradisi R, Fabbri R, *et al.* Clinical and hormonal characteristics of obese amenorrheic hyperandrogenic women before and after weight loss. *J Clin Endocrinol Metab* 1989;68:173–9.

63. Clark AM, Thornley B, Tomlinson L, Galletley C, Norman RJ. Weight loss in obese infertile women results in improvement in reproductive outcome for all forms of fertility treatment. *Hum Reprod* 1998;13:1502–5.

64. Falsetti L, Pasinetti E, Mazzani MD, Gastaldi A. Weight loss and menstrual cycle: clinical and endocrinological evaluation. *Gynecol Endocrinol* 1992;6:49–56.

65. Hollmann M, Runnebaum B, Gerhard I. Impact of waist-hip-ratio and body-mass-index on hormonal and metabolic parameters in young, obese women. *Int J Obes Relat Metab Disord* 1997;21:476–83.

66. Galletly C, Clark A, Tomlinson L, Blaney F. Improved pregnancy rates for obese, infertile women following a group treatment program. An open pilot study. *General Hosp Psychiatr* 1996;18:192–5.

67. Hamilton-Fairley D, Kiddy D, Anyaoku V, Koistinen R, Seppala M, Franks S. Response of sex hormone binding globulin and insulin-like growth factor binding protein-1 to an oral glucose

tolerance test in obese women with polycystic ovary syndrome before and after calorie restriction. *Clin Endocrinol* 1993;39:363–7.

68. Kiddy DS, Hamilton-Fairley D, Bush A, Short F, Anyaoku V, Reed MJ, *et al*. Improvement in endocrine and ovarian function during dietary treatment of obese women with polycystic ovary syndrome. *Clin Endocrinol* 1992;36:105–11.

69. Crave JC, Fimbel S, Lejeune H, Cugnardey N, Dechaud H, Pugeat M. Effects of diet and metformin administration on sex hormone-binding globulin, androgens, and insulin in hirsute and obese women. *J Clin Endocrinol Metab* 1995;80:2057–62.

70. Drezgic M, Penezic Z, Zarkovic M, Vujovic S, Ciric J, Trbojevic B, *et al*. Influence of three-week fasting on gonadotropin pulsatility in obese menstruating women. *Int J Obes Relat Metab Disord* 1996;20:608–12.

71. Crosignani PG, Colombo M, Vegetti W, Somigliana E, Gessati A, Ragni G. Overweight and obese anovulatory patients with polycystic ovaries: parallel improvements in anthropometric indices, ovarian physiology and fertility rate induced by diet. *Hum Reprod* 2003;18:1928–32.

72. Barbieri RL. The role of adipose tissue and hyperinsulinemia in the development of hyperandrogenism in women. In: Frisch R, editor. *Adipose Tissue and Reproduction*. Basel: Karger; 1990. p. 42–57.

73. Elective Services, The New Zealand Ministry of Health. *National Specialist Guidelines for Investigation of Infertility: Priority Criteria for Access to Public Funding of Infertility Treatment* [www.electiveservices.govt.nz/pdfs/gynaecology-infertility.pdf].

74. Zachariah M, Fleming R, Acharya U. Management of obese women in assisted conception units: a UK survey. *Hum Fertil* 2006;9:101–5.

75. National Institute for Clinical Excellence. *Fertility: Assessment and Treatment for People with Fertility Problems*. Clinical Guideline. London: RCOG Press; 2004 [guidance.nice.org.uk/CG11/guidance/pdf/English].

76. Norman RJ, Noakes M, Wu R, Davies MJ, Moran L, Wang JX. Improving reproductive performance in overweight/obese women with effective weight management. *Hum Reprod Update* 2004;10:267–80.

77. Pasquali R, Gambineri A. Metabolic effects of obesity on reproduction. *Reprod Biomed Online* 2006;12:542–51.

78. Lord JM, Flight IH, Norman RJ. Insulin-sensitising drugs (metformin, troglitazone, rosiglitazone, pioglitazone, D-chiro-inositol) for polycystic ovary syndrome. *Cochrane Database Syst Rev* 2003;(3): CD003053.

Chapter 9

Quality of life issues in gynaecology and women who are overweight

Georgina Jones

Introduction

It is well established that obesity (defined as a body mass index (BMI) exceeding 30 kg/m^2) has become a major public health concern because of the risks for health and the costs to health services. Although it is the physical consequences of obesity, in particular cardiovascular disease (coronary heart disease, hypertension and ischaemic stroke), diabetes mellitus and some cancers, that are the impetus for most public health campaigns and weight-loss interventions, there has been a growing body of literature which has identified that obesity is also a significant predictor for a poor psychological wellbeing and negative health-related quality of life, particularly in women.

In recent years it has also been found that gynaecological conditions (both benign and malignant) can have a negative impact upon a woman's daily wellbeing and functioning. However, what role does weight and obesity play in affecting quality of life? Considering quality of life issues for women with a gynaecological condition in the context of weight is particularly important as obesity can be a symptom of disease, such as polycystic ovary syndrome (PCOS), a risk factor for the development of a condition, such as endometrial cancer or miscarriage, a screening measure by which reproductive technologies are restricted and an impairment to the successful outcome of treatment, such as fertility treatment. As a result of this, the aims of this chapter are to:

1. provide a brief consideration of the literature on the psychological impact that obesity has in the general population and on women specifically

2. provide an overview of health-related quality of life measurement and the instruments available to measure obesity outcomes in gynaecology

3. review the health-related quality of life (HRQoL) literature in relation to gynaecology and obesity

4. give recommendations for future studies in this area.

Psychological consequences of obesity in the general population

The World Health Organization (WHO) has estimated that there are over 300 million adults worldwide who are clinically obese. Prevalence has increased particularly rapidly in the UK; a publication by the Department of Health[1] reported that, by 2004 compared with 1995, the proportion of men who were obese had risen by over 50%, while the proportion of women who were obese had risen by 36%. In addition, obesity now overshadows all other chronic illnesses in adolescents; between 1995 and 2004 the proportion of obese children rose by over 40%. Traditionally, the measurement of 'physical' parameters such as weight loss, with lifestyle interventions to support adults in managing or reducing their weight (e.g. through changes in diet content, reduced energy/calorie intake and increased physical activity) have been the outcomes of interest. However, there has also been an increasing interest in the psychosocial consequences of obesity.

One reason for this is because it is well documented that obesity is a stigmatised condition and is associated with negative attitudes and discrimination in many societies.[2] There is evidence that the negative 'fat is bad' stereotype is evident from early childhood. For example, it has been found that children as young as 6 years old characterise silhouettes of an overweight child as 'dirty', 'lazy', 'ugly' and 'stupid'[3] and that these negative perceptions of people who are obese continue into adolescence and adulthood.[4] Although there are numerous definitions of stigma, it is typically defined as the use of negative labels to identify a person. Individuals vary considerably in the way they respond to stigmatic labels but these can have a substantial and unavoidable impact on self-concept and can become the central factor in a person's identity to the exclusion of other attributes.[5]

One reason for these negative perceptions of people who are overweight or obese is the widespread belief in certain societies (and the UK is an example) that weight gain and loss are under personal control. Negative stereotypes about personal traits of laziness, lack of self-discipline and passivity, among others, have therefore become associated with the weight gain of obesity.[2] However, the relationship between obesity-related stigma is complex: children and adults who are obese have been found to have negative attitudes towards other obese individuals and healthcare professionals specialising in obesity have also shown evidence of this bias.[6] As well as interpersonal discrimination, people who are obese face difficulties in education and employment opportunities; these discriminatory behaviours are particularly evident for women who are obese in the workplace where, at all stages of employment, discrimination is evident.[7]

The role of gender on psychological wellbeing

Gender, and in particular female gender, has been identified as a potential risk factor for a poor psychological wellbeing. For example, the results from nationally representative samples of the US population have found that, compared with their normal weight counterparts, women, but not men, who are obese have a slightly higher rate of suicidal ideation and depression.[6,8] Although the definitive explanation for the gender differences is unknown, numerous hypotheses have been put forward. As mentioned earlier, discriminatory behaviours which in certain areas, such as the workplace, are more apparent may contribute to the poorer psychological wellbeing of women who are obese compared with their male counterparts. The gender difference may also be compounded by the different societal expectations that are evident regarding thinness. For example, it is been found that women report greater dissatisfaction with their body image and are teased more about their weight compared with men.[9]

In addition to the gender differences, differences in psychological wellbeing in women, between those who are obese and those who are not, have been identified. As reported by Fabricatore and Wadden,[6] two studies have found that, in the general population, women who were obese were 37% and 38%, respectively, more likely to be depressed than their peers with normal weight.[8,10] Similarly, more psychosocial problems in people who were obese were reported for women compared with men in a study which looked at psychosocial functioning before and after weight reduction.[11] The prevalent and stigmatised nature of the condition has meant that it has become important to understand the psychological consequences of obesity. However, as well as the psychological consequences, numerous studies have been carried out to measure the impact that being 'overweight' or 'obese' has upon HRQoL. Before discussing the outcomes of this research it is important to consider what quality of life measurement is and how it is measured.

What is meant by HRQoL?

The application of social science methods in the evaluation of medical care has been of growing importance in recent years. In particular, there is an increasing demand for the design, development and use of questionnaires that can assess people's experiences of health and illness or health-related quality of life. The past 20 years have witnessed a rise in interest, from both academics and professionals, in HRQoL and also attempts to measure it. However, because of this there are now a vast number of terms in the literature that are used to refer to the measurement of HRQoL and which have tried to define what is meant by this concept. Velikova et al.[12] maintains that HRQoL (or health status) refers to those areas of health which are affected by healthcare interventions; their definition is therefore more specific to clinical practice. However, Bullinger et al.[13] refers to HRQoL as the impact of a disease upon the ability to live a fulfilled life.

There is clearly no single definition that is universally accepted. The main problem is that the experience of quality of life is subjective and so, by its very nature, this concept is difficult to define.[14] In part the definition is dependent upon the condition or disease to be measured or the research questions that are being examined in the study.[15] Although there are numerous definitions, it is generally agreed that it is a multidimensional dynamic concept that encompasses physical, social and psychological aspects associated with a particular disease or its treatment.[16] Within these domains, typical items would include physical mobility, pain, personal and sexual relationships, sleep, ability to carry out work, leisure and social activities and domestic chores.[17]

Until recently, the measurement of health status was overlooked in the evaluation of medical care. Traditionally, medical care was evaluated using clinical measures of outcome, such as measures of mortality and other clinical diagnostic criteria that concentrated on the physical components of health and ignored the dimensions of wellbeing and functioning, which could have an impact on the health status of the individual.[18] However, in the latter half of the 20th century there was increasing awareness that health and illness are not purely dependent on physical wellbeing. In 1954, WHO emphasised this point in their definition of health as 'a state of complete physical mental and social well-being and not merely the absence of disease or infirmity'.[19]

As a result, there has been a growing demand to assess and evaluate the other dimensions of wellbeing that can impact on the health status of people and to develop measurement tools in the form of questionnaires and interview schedules that can evaluate systematically this subjective impact on wellbeing.[20] In the past, the evaluation of people's experiences of health and illness was primarily based on the objective judgements of clinicians. It has been suggested that these judgements were often based on intuition and personal experience.[21] Indeed, research has shown that clinical judgements are far from objective and show variations and low levels of agreement among doctors.[22] At the beginning of the 21st century, where there is much emphasis on evidence-based medicine and rigorous evaluations of care, there is a need and demand to quantify subjective wellbeing in a more reliable and systematic way.[21] It is increasingly being recognised that only with the accurate measurement of the experience of disease upon people's HRQoL can health care meet the demands and needs of those receiving it.

How is HRQoL measured?

HRQoL can be measured using either a qualitative or quantitative methodology. One way of collecting information on HRQoL using a qualitative methodology has been to conduct in-depth interviews with people with the condition of interest. The rationale behind this type of interviewing is that, compared with structured interviews in which all the questions are predetermined and most answers are fixed choices,[23] it allows subjects to describe their personal experiences in their own words.[24] For example, within gynaecology, this methodology has been used to collect information relating to HRQoL for endometriosis.[25] However, despite the rich data this generates, the limitations of qualitative methods mean that it is not suitable for large observational or randomised studies – those particularly favoured in medical research.

Consequently, quantitative methods have been more commonly adopted. In particular, there has been an increasing demand for the development of measurement tools in the form of questionnaires and interview schedules that can systematically assess and evaluate people's experiences of health and illness or health status.[26] They are principally designed to provide information on people's views of their own health.

Reliable assessment of quality of life depends on the psychometric properties of the questionnaire (i.e. the tests underlying the construction and evaluation of the questionnaire) and the statistical methods employed to analyse and interpret the data.[27] It is important therefore that any HRQoL questionnaire to be used is based on these psychometric properties. Although there are many tests that can be carried out to evaluate these properties, the general consensus is that they should be reliable, valid and sensitive to change or responsive.[28] A detailed discussion of these psychometric terms is outside the scope of this chapter; however, interested readers should refer to the aforementioned textbooks for more information.[27,28]

What instruments are available to measure obesity outcomes in women's reproductive health?

To measure obesity outcomes in gynaecology, a number of questionnaires can be chosen. These typically fall into three categories:

- generic – can be used to measure health status for any condition
- disease-specific – only used for the disease for which they have been developed
- condition-specific – developed to measure a particular condition, e.g. obesity or pain.

A number of disease-specific questionnaires have been developed specifically for use in both benign and malignant gynaecology and these have been documented in recent systematic reviews of the literature in these areas, respectively.[29,30] However, only one of the instruments, the polycystic ovary syndrome questionnaire (PCOSQ), contains items related specifically to weight issues.[31] In relation to generic instruments, the Short-Form 36 (SF-36) has been the most widely used measure with respect to obesity, quality of life and gynaecology. The dimensions of this instrument are well known, covering physical functioning and related role limitations, body pain, perceptions of general health and vitality, social functioning, mental and emotional health and related role limitations.[32] It is an established brief generic measure that usefully allows comparison between conditions. However, it does not contain any questions or domains that relate specifically to obesity. The consequences of this are considered later in the chapter.

A wide variety of obesity questionnaires are available; a review reporting the obesity-specific measures was undertaken in 2001.[33] Overall, these condition-specific measures do draw attention to a number of psychosocial dimensions of quality of life that are pertinent to people who are obese. This includes self-esteem, public distress, self-image and social activities. However, a number of these measures are not well validated or are really only indicated for use with intensive medical interventions such as surgery. The Impact of Weight on Quality of Life-Lite (IWQOL-Lite) questionnaire is the best-validated instrument and covers dimensions of physical functioning, self esteem, sexual life, public distress and work.[34] The Obesity and Weight-Loss Quality-of-Life (OWLQOL) questionnaire is also a relatively short, well-validated instrument covering a similar range of dimensions.[35] However, neither instrument includes dimensions of stigma sensitivity and related quality of life issues and thus this is an area in which there is a gap in available outcome measures.[2]

Obesity, gender and HRQoL

In the general population, it has been found that body weight is negatively associated with HRQoL. For example, an analysis of a recent population-based study carried out in the USA, the Medical Expenditure Survey,[36] revealed that SF-36 physical and mental component summary scores and the generic EuroQoL index and visual analogue scores were significantly lower in people who were severely obese (> 35 kg/m^2) compared with respondents of normal weight.[36] In addition, even after controlling for six chronic conditions (asthma, diabetes, hypertension, heart disease, stroke and emphysema), a negative HRQoL was evident in respondents whose weight exceeded the normal range (18.5–24.9 kg/m^2).

As mentioned earlier, in the general population obesity has been found to have a negative impact on psychological parameters: this has been found to be often more marked in women compared with men. Studies that have investigated gender differences in terms of HRQoL have also found a similar difference. A more impaired HRQoL has been found for women compared with men as measured on the Obesity-Related Well-being Scale (ORWELL).[37] Similarly, Kolotkin and Crosby[34] found that impaired HRQoL as measured on the IWQOL-Lite questionnaire was associated with a higher BMI in a sample of US individuals not in treatment for obesity; respondents with a BMI > 40 kg/m^2 showed a significantly worse HRQoL than the other BMI groups. In addition, gender differences were observed whereby women had a significantly greater impairment in HRQoL on the domains of physical function, self-esteem, sexual life and total score ($P < 0.001$) and work ($P < 0.004$) compared with their male counterparts; the largest difference being evident in the BMI category of 35–39.9 kg/m^2. This is similar to findings from other studies that have used the IWQOL-Lite, although a worse HRQoL in women compared with men was only observed on the domains of total score, sexual life and self-esteem.[38]

Gender differences in HRQoL between men and women has also been found with the SF-36 when administered to a sample of people with chronic psychiatric and medical conditions: lower scores were found for women who were obese or over-weight compared with their male counterparts.[39]

As weight appears to have a more negative impact on psychosocial parameters and HRQoL in women compared with men in the general population, what role does weight play in HRQoL in women with gynaecological conditions? As mentioned above, the role of weight plays an important part in gynaecological conditions. For example, in relation to endometrial cancer, it has been reported that most survivors of the disease are obese[40,41] and that obesity is also a risk factor for the development of the disease. Obesity is also a cardinal symptom of PCOS. As both adolescent and adult women with PCOS are more likely to be overweight, or experience difficulties maintaining their weight than their normative peers, frequent observation of reduced HRQoL due to the impact of weight problems may be expected within this population.

HRQoL and gynaecological conditions: the role of weight

Data from the general population have shown that, as BMI increases, HRQoL deteriorates. Similar trends have been found in relation to gynaecological conditions. For example, a recent study investigated associations between exercise, body weight and quality of life in a population-based sample of endometrial cancer survivors. BMI was classified according to WHO guidelines: underweight ($< 18.5 \ kg/m^2$), normal weight ($18.5–24.9 \ kg/m^2$), overweight ($25.0–29.9 \ kg/m^2$), moderately obese or class I ($30.0–34.9 \ kg/m^2$), severely obese or class II ($35.0–39.9 \ kg/m^2$) and very severely obese or class III ($\geq 40 \ kg/m^2$). As expected, the authors found that the best HRQoL, as measured on the Functional Assessment of Cancer Therapy – Anaemia (FACT-An) scale, was evident in the cancer survivors with normal weight compared with those who were very severely obese, who had the worst HRQoL. Overall, HRQoL worsened as BMI increased with the exception of the differences between the endometrial cancer survivors who were overweight and moderately obese: mean HRQoL scale scores were overall worse for the women who were overweight compared with those who were moderately obese.[42] This, and the findings mentioned above, would suggest that there is a negative correlation between elevated BMI and HRQoL. There is evidence that exposure to stigma is related to a higher BMI,[43] which may account for these findings. However, one gynaecological condition where the relationship between obesity and HRQoL is more complex is PCOS.

PCOS, obesity and HRQoL

Overall, the symptoms typically associated with PCOS, i.e. amenorrhoea, oligomenorrhoea, hirsutism, obesity, subfertility, anovulation and acne, have been shown to lead to a significant reduction in quality of life. For example, hirsutism has been shown to cause marked psychological stress[44] and infertility issues can cause tensions within the family, altered self-perception and problems at work.[45,46] However, in many of the cross-sectional studies that have been carried out in this area, it is weight which appears to be the worst area of HRQoL affected by PCOS.[47,48]

This is perhaps not surprising, given that the metabolic profile of the condition means that is very difficult for a woman with PCOS to lose weight. Indeed, with the exception of surgery, interventions to lose weight are often unsuccessful and associated with high rates of weight regain.[49] Thus many women with PCOS report frustration in losing weight and have low self-esteem and, consequently, a poor body image.[31] In relation to weight, a poor body image in women with PCOS may be compounded by cultural influences as it has been shown that android fat pattern, commonly associated with PCOS, is considered unattractive in many cultures.[50,51] However, other explanations as found in the general population regarding women, such as societal expectations of thinness, may also be responsible.

This is particularly evident in relation to adolescent girls with PCOS. Dramusic et al.[52] found that 87.5% of 50 adolescents with PCOS in Singapore reported being 'unhappy about their body weight'. High 'drive for thinness' and 'body dissatisfaction' scores were also observed in adolescents with PCOS compared with their normative counterparts. However, two studies that investigated the relationship between a clinical eating disorder, bulimia nervosa, and polycystic ovaries in a UK sample have reached different conclusions.[53,54] The psychological consequences of weight concerns for young women with PCOS is evident and suggests that more psychological support in this area is needed. There is no evidence at present on the existence of in-group discrimination between adolescents or women with PCOS who are obese, but again this would be important to explore in future studies.

The role that BMI plays in the quality of life of women with PCOS is complex. Some studies have shown that reductions in HRQoL are associated with an elevated BMI. For example, one study found a significant correlation ($P < 0.05$) between elevated BMI ($25–30$ 30 kg/m^2) and worse SF-36 Physical Sum Scale scores compared with women with PCOS with a normal BMI (< 25 kg/m^2) who reported higher Physical Sum Scale scores, thus indicating better quality of life.[55] Similarly, Elsenbruch et al.[56] also determined that BMI was a predictor of Physical Sum Scale scores on the SF-36. In addition, McCook et al.[57] found that BMI was significantly and negatively correlated with the weight domain of the PCOSQ ($P = 0.001$) and a simple linear regression established that weight scale scores were predicted by BMI. Trent et al.[58] concluded that elevated BMI contributed significantly to the differences in quality of life observed between adolescents with PCOS and age-matched controls, particularly on the domains of general health perceptions, physical functioning and family activities as measured on the Child Health Questionnaire (CHQ-CF87).

However, the results from other studies suggest no relationship between BMI status and HRQoL in women with PCOS. For example, even when significant differences in BMI exist between two ethnicities, HRQoL weight scores (as measured on the PCOSQ) have been found to be similar.[59] In addition, in studies that have controlled for BMI in their analysis of PCOSQ weight scores, it has been found that women with PCOS who have a 'normal weight' still report problems with their weight.[48] As also suggested by Coffey et al.,[48] the findings from this research suggest that all women with PCOS, regardless of their BMI measurement, have weight concerns, and therefore relying on this clinical measurement alone as an indicator of poor quality of life would overlook the difficulties experienced by women with PCOS who have a normal weight. One potential explanation for this is that women with PCOS with a normal BMI struggle to maintain their weight at this level although further research would be needed to explore this issue further.

The complex relationship between BMI measurement and self-reported quality of life weight scores is also evident in relation to other domains of HRQoL. For example, McCook et al.[57] found that although BMI was a predictor of weight domain scores, no such relationship existed between BMI and the other domain scores on the PCOSQ. However, Hashimoto et al.[59] reported a significant association between weight status and Body Hair scores on the PCOSQ in Brazilian participants. Finally, controlling for an elevated BMI has been found to have no impact on psychosocial wellbeing and sexual satisfaction, thus leading the authors to conclude that obesity is not the only determinant of a poor HRQoL.[60]

The lack of correlation between other clinical scores and HRQoL has been found for other areas of PCOS. For example, adolescents with PCOS who had a clinical severity score of moderate to severe, based upon a Ferriman Galley score > 8, a Global Acne rating of > 0 and a BMI > 30 kg/m^2, only rated their HRQoL mild.[61] There is also now considerable evidence that the assessments that people themselves make about their health status differ from the reports that healthcare professionals make.[19] In a study of menorrhagia,[62] symptoms were classed as severe by the individual, but the GP only rated the symptoms as moderate. Similarly, those who considered their symptoms to be only mild or moderate were rated as suffering from severe symptoms by their GP.

Similar problems have occurred in the measurement of HRQoL for other non-gynaecological diseases. The assessment of quality of life has been found to differ between the primary care givers of cardiac patients, i.e. their staff and families, and the individuals themselves.[63] Similarly, in relation to malignant disease, Present[64] found that estimates of quality of life given by people with cancer differ greatly from those given by their carers. These findings and the results from other areas of medicine have led to the view that HRQoL assessment is only reliable if given by the person themselves.[63,65]

Conclusion

The medical and social consequences of obesity often mean that it has a profound negative impact on the lives of women, both those in the normal population and those women with a gynaecological condition. It is evident that successfully helping to reduce bias and stigma may lead to improvements in the psychosocial wellbeing and quality of life for these women. A reduction in weight also appears to significantly improve HRQoL.[38] For example, treatment with metformin in a sample of women with PCOS led to an improvement in SF-36 HRQoL scores and these were significantly correlated with a reduction in weight.[55] Therefore, efforts to identify appropriate long-term weight-loss programmes/treatments would also be beneficial to women, particularly those with PCOS. However, the best ways of achieving this are unclear, particularly when obesity in women has been found to influence access to health care[66] and long-term weight-loss interventions are seldom successful.

The conflicting evidence found regarding the relationship between BMI and HRQoL needs to be investigated further. These results are not specific to studies in gynaecology. Indeed, research investigating the role of weight on HRQoL in other conditions, such as bariatric surgery, have found that an elevated BMI is not associated with a worse HRQoL.[67] In the aforementioned survey, one explanation may have been because only women with class II and class III obesity were studied (i.e. > 35 kg/m^2). It may be that, once above the threshold of severely obese, the impact of BMI is reduced. Another explanation may be that different samples have been the focus of investigation in these studies (i.e. comparisons are being made between people who are obese in the general population, a gynaecologically specific sample and those entering treatment programmes) and so it is not clear whether the findings reflect true differences. It is clear that more research is needed in this area before proper conclusions can be made on the role of BMI in quality of life. However, it is important for healthcare professionals to be aware that, although HRQoL may be worse in people with high BMI, even gynaecological patients with normal weight may be experiencing a poor HRQoL because of the problems associated with maintaining that weight and therefore may also need psychological support in this area.

Future research

As a result of the existing literature and research that has been concerned with investigating the role of obesity in HRQoL for women with gynaecological conditions, a number of recommendations can be made for future studies. Firstly, it is important to use standard guidelines to define obesity. With the exception of a few studies,[42] most studies which have been carried out in gynaecology have used cut-offs to illustrate obesity in their research which do not correspond to the WHO guidelines.[47] For example, Elsenbruch et al.[56,60] and Hahn et al.[55] reported a BMI ≥ 25 kg/m^2 to be associated with clinical obesity. Similarly, Trent et al.[58] classified BMI data in accordance with age and gender-specific recommendations from the Centers for Disease Control and Prevention (participants with a BMI between the 85th and 95th percentiles were classified as being at risk of overweight, and those with a BMI greater than the 95th percentile were classified as overweight).

Although reasons have been given for this, for example that the aim has been to catch the high end of overweight individuals including those who are obese, the heterogeneity in BMI definition may affect the comparative value of the results and conclusions reported, and thus should be viewed with caution. Recent publications have also stressed the need to take measurements other than BMI such as waist circumference, which is more directly proportional to total body fat and the amount of metabolically active visceral fat and is therefore a more accurate measure of metabolic risk.[68] Thus, in future studies of obesity in gynaecology, the relationship between this parameter and HRQoL outcomes may give a more accurate picture of the effect of weight on a woman's health status and help unravel some of the conflicting results that currently exist regarding BMI in this area.

Secondly, in any analysis it would be important to consider the potential impact of confounding variables on the interpretation of HRQoL scores, for example the existence of other chronic clinical conditions associated with obesity such as hypertension, heart disease and diabetes. This has seldom been carried out in studies of gynaecological patients and therefore may be affecting the true nature of the impact of weight on HRQoL.

Finally, consideration should be given to the instruments chosen to measure the effect of weight on HRQoL outcomes. In relation to PCOS, the results of a systematic review revealed that only four of the 12 studies used the disease-specific PCOSQ questionnaire to measure HRQoL. The remaining studies used one or a combination of generic instruments such as the SF-36 to perform assessments of HRQoL. Generic instruments are designed to gauge HRQoL over a broad spectrum of diseases, and thus may not be sensitive enough to measure HRQoL in specific illnesses.[20] For example, the domains of weight and infertility, observed as being significantly affected on the PCOSQ, would not be identified using only a generic questionnaire such as the SF-36 as there are no items pertaining to these dimensions. Questionnaires in which the items are patient generated hence designed specifically for people with a particular disease, should theoretically be more sensitive to changes in health status.

It has been suggested that, ideally, both a generic and disease-specific instrument should be applied in measuring HRQoL, thus enabling comparisons to be made at both a generic level and specifically to the disease of interest.[29,69] In relation to obesity, it would be beneficial to supplement a disease-specific questionnaire appropriate to the gynaecological condition of interest and then to supplement this with a generic obesity questionnaire such as the OWLQoL or IWQoL, as mentioned earlier. In the UK, a generic questionnaire such as the SF-36 could also be used should a comparison with normative data from the population be considered an important outcome of the study.

References

1. Department of Health. *Health Profile of England*. London: Department of Health; 2006.
2. Brown I, Thompson J, Todd A, Jones GL. Obesity, stigma and quality of life: a qualitative study. *Int J Interdisciplinary Soc Sci* 200;1:169–78.
3. Venes AM, Krupka LR, Gerad RJ. Overweight/obese patients: an overview. *Practitioner* 1982;226:1102–9.
4. Cramer P, Steinwert T. Thin is good, fat is bad: how early does it begin? *J Appl Dev Psychol* 1998;19:429–51.
5. Goffman E. *Stigma: Notes on the Management of Spoiled Identity*. Harmondsworth: Pelican Books; 1968.
6. Fabricatore AN, Wadden TA. Psychological aspects of obesity. *Clin Dermatol* 2004;22:332–7.
7. Roehling MV. Weight-based discrimination in employment: psychological and legal aspects. *Pers Psychol* 1999;52:969–1017.
8. Carpenter KM, Hasin DS, Allison DB, Faith MS. Relationship between obesity and DSM-IV major depressive disorder, suicide ideation and suicide attempts: Results from a general population study. *Am J Public Health* 2000;90:251–7.
9. Rodin J. Determinants of body fat and its implications for health. *Ann Behav Med* 1992;14:275–81.
10. Istvan J, Zavela K, Weidner G. Body weight and psychological distress in NHANES I. *Int J Obes Relat Metab Disord* 1992;16:999–1003.
11. Karlsson J, Taft C, Sjostrom L, Togererson JS, Sullivan M. Psychosocial functioning in the obese before and after weight reduction: construct validity and responsiveness of the obesity-related problems scale. *Int J Obes Relat Metab Disord* 2003;27:617–30.
12. Velikova G, Stark D, Selby P. Quality of life instruments in oncology. *Eur J Cancer* 1999;35:1571–80.
13. Bullinger M, Anderson R, Cella D. Developing and evaluating cross cultural instruments from minimum requirements to optimal models. *Qual Life Res* 1993;2:451–59.
14. Anderson B. Quality of life in progressive ovarian cancer. *Gynecol Oncol* 1994;55:S151–55.
15. Naughton MJ, McBee WL. Health-related quality of life after hysterectomy. *Clin Obstet Gynaecol* 1997;40:947–57.
16. Colwell H, Mathias SD, Pasta DJ, Henning JM, Steege JF. A health-related quality of life instrument for symptomatic patients with endometriosis: a validation study. *Am J Obstet Gynecol* 1998;179:47–55.
17. Seed P, Lloyd G. *Quality of Life*. London: Jessica Kingsley Publishers; 1997.
18. Albrecht GL. Subjective health assessment. In: Jenkinson C, editor. *Measuring and Medical Outcomes*. London: UCL Press; 1994. p. 7–26.
19. World Health Organization *The First Ten Years of the World Health Organization*. Geneva: World Health Organization; 1958.
20. Fitzpatrick R, Davey C, Buxton M, Jones DR. Patient-assessed outcome measures. In: Black N, Brazier J, Fitzpatrick R, Reeves B, editors. *Health Services Research Methods*. London: BMJ Publications; 1998. p. 13–22.
21. Jenkinson C. Assessment and evaluation of health and medical care: an introduction and overview. In: Jenkinson C, editor. *Assessment and Evaluation of Health and Medical Care: A Methods Text*. Buckingham: Open University Press; 1997. p. 1–5.
22. Wigton RS. Medical applications. In: Brehmer B, Joyce CRB, editors. *Human Judgement: the SJT View. Advances in Psychology*. Amsterdam: Elsevier; 1988. p. 227–45.
23. Britten N. Qualitative interviews in medical research. *BMJ* 1995;311:251–3.
24. Porter S. Qualitative research. In: Cormack DFS, editor. *The Research Process in Nursing*. Oxford: Blackwell Science; 1996. p. 113–22.
25. Jones GL, Jenkinson C, Kennedy SH. The impact of endometriosis upon quality of life: a qualitative analysis. *J Psychosom Obstet Gynaecol* 2004;25:123–33.
26. Fitzpatrick R. A pragmatic defence of health status measures. *Health Care Anal* 1996;4:265–72.
27. Fayers PM, Machin D. *Quality of Life: Assessment, Analysis and Interpretation*. Chichester: John Wiley & Sons; 2000.
28. Nunnally JC. *Psychometric Theory*. New Delhi: Tate McGraw-Hill; 1978.

29. Jones G, Kennedy S, Jenkinson C. Health-related quality of life measurement in women with common benign gynecological conditions: a systematic review. *Am J Obstet Gynecol* 2002;187:501–11.

30. Jones GL, Ledger WL, Bonnett TJ, Radley S, Parkinson N, Kennedy SH. The impact of treatment for gynaecological cancer upon health-related quality of life (HRQoL): a systematic review. *Am J Obstet Gynecol* 2006;194:26–42.

31. Cronin L, Guyatt G, Griffith L, Wong E, Azziz R, Futterweit W, *et al.* Development of a health-related quality-of-life questionnaire (PCOSQ) for women with polycystic ovary syndrome (PCOS). *J Clin Endocrinol Metab* 1998;83:1976–87.

32. Ware JE Jr, Sherbourne CD. The MOS 36-item short-form health survey (SF-36). I. Conceptual framework and item selection. *Med Care* 1992;30:473–83.

33. Kolotkin RL, Meter K, Williams GR. Quality of life and obesity. *Obes Rev* 2001 November;2:219–29.

34. Kolotkin RL, Crosby RD. Psychometric evaluation of the impact of weight on quality of life-lite questionnaire (IWQOL-Lite) in a community sample. *Qual Life Res* 2002;11:157–71.

35. Niero M, Martin M, Finger T, *et al.* Multi-cultural development of two new obesity-specific health-related quality of life and symptom measures: the OWLQOL (Obesity and Weight Loss Quality of Life) instrument and the WRSM (Weight-Related Symptom Measure). *Clin Ther* 2002;24:690–700.

36. Jia H, Lubetkin EI. The impact of obesity on health-related quality of life in the general US population. *J Public Health (Oxf)* 2005;27:156–64.

37. Mannucci E, Ricca V, Barciulli E, Di Bernardo M, Travaglini R, Cabras P, *et al.* Quality of life and overweight: the obesity related well-being (Orwell97) questionnaire. *Addict Behav* 1999;24:345–57.

38. Kolotkin RL, Crosby RD, Kosloski KD, Williams GR. Development of a brief measure to assess quality of life in obesity. *Obes Res* 2001;9:102–11.

39. Katz D, McHorney C, Atkinson R. Impact of obesity on health-related quality of life in patients with chronic illness. *J Gen Intern Med* 2000;15:789–96.

40. Anderson B, Connor JP, Andrews JI, Davis CS, Buller RE, Sorosky JI, *et al.* Obesity and prognosis in endometrial cancer. *Am J Obstet Gynecol* 1996;174:1171–8; discussion 1178–9.

41. von Gruenigen VE, Gil KM, Frasure HE, Jenison EL, Hopkins MP. The impact of obesity and age on quality of life in gynecologic surgery. *Am J Obstet Gynecol* 2005;193:1369–75.

42. Courneya KS, Karvinen KH, Campbell KL, Pearcey RG, Dundas G, Capstick V, Tonkin KS. Associations among exercise, body weight and quality of life in a population-based sample of endometrial cancer survivors. *Gynecol Oncol* 2005:422–30.

43. Puhl RM, Brownell KD. Confronting and coping with weight stigma: an investigation of overweight and obese adults. *Obesity (Silver Spring)* 2006;14:1802–15.

44. Sonino N, Fava GA, Mani E, Belluardo P, Boscaro M. Quality of life of hirsute women. *Postgrad Med J* 1993;69:186–9.

45. Paulson JD, Haarmann BS, Salerno RL, Asmar P. An investigation of the relationship between emotional maladjustment and infertility. *Fertil Steril* 1988;49:258–62.

46. Downey J, Yingling S, McKinney M, Husami N, Jewelewicz R, Maidman J. Mood disorders, psychiatric symptoms and distress in women presenting for infertility evaluation. *Fertil Steril* 1989;52:425–32.

47. Jones GL, Benes K, Clark TL, Denham R, Holder MG, Haynes TJ, *et al.* The polycystic ovary syndrome health-related quality of life questionnaire (PCOSQ): a validation. *Hum Reprod* 2004;19:371–7.

48. Coffey S, Bano G, Mason HD. Health-related quality of life in women with PCOS: A comparison with the general population using the PCOSQ and the SF-36. *Gynecol Endocrinol* 2006;22:80–6.

49. Hoeger KM. Role of lifestyle modification in the management of polycystic ovary syndrome. *Best Pract Res Clin Endocrinol Metab* 2006;20:293–310.

50. Brown PJ. Culture and evolution of obesity. *Hum Nat* 1991;2:31–57.

51. Deurenberg P, Deurenberg-Yap M, Guricci S. Asians are different from Caucasians and from each other in their body mass index/body fat per cent relationship. *Obes Rev* 2002;3:141–6.

52. Dramusic V, Rajan U, Chan P, Ratnam SS, Wong YC. Adolescent polycystic ovary syndrome. *Ann N Y Acad Sci* 1997;816:194–208.

53. Michelmore KF, Balen AH, Dunger DB. Polycystic ovaries and eating disorders: Are they related? *Hum Reprod* 2001;16:765–9.

54. Morgan JF, McCluskey SE, Brunton JN, Hubert Lacey J. Polycystic ovarian morphology and bulimia nervosa: a 9-year follow-up study. *Fertil Steril* 2002;77:928–31.

55. Hahn S, Janssen OE, Tan S, Pleger K, Mann K, Schedlowski M, *et al.* Clinical and psychological correlates of quality-of-life in polycystic ovary syndrome. *Eur J Endocrinol* 2005;153:853–60.

56. Elsenbruch S, Benson S, Hahn S, Tan S, Mann K, Pleger K, *et al.* Determinants of emotional distress in women with polycystic ovary syndrome. *Hum Reprod* 2006;21:1092–9.

57. McCook JG, Reame NE, Thatcher SS. Health-related quality of life issues in women with polycystic ovary syndrome. *J Obstet Gynecol Neonatal Nurs* 2005;34:12–20.

58. Trent M, Austin SB, Rich M, Gordon CM. Overweight status of adolescent girls with polycystic ovary syndrome: body mass index as mediator of quality of life. *Ambul Pediatr* 2005;5:107–11.

59. Hashimoto DM, Schmid J, Martins FM, Fonseca AM, Andrade LH, Kirchengast S, *et al.* The impact of the weight status on subjective symptomatology of the Polycystic Ovary Syndrome: a cross-cultural comparison between Brazilian and Austrian women. *Anthropol Anz* 2003;61:297–310.

60. Elsenbruch S, Hahn S, Kowalsky D, Offner AH, Schedlowski M, Mann K, *et al.* Quality of life, psychosocial well-being, and sexual satisfaction in women with polycystic ovary syndrome. *J Clin Endocrinol Metab* 2003;88:5801–7.

61. Trent ME, Rich M, Austin SB, Gordon CM. Quality of life in adolescent girls with polycystic ovary syndrome. *Arch Pediatr Adolesc Med* 2002;156:556–60.

62. Coulter A, Peto V, Jenkinson C. Quality of life and patient satisfaction following treatment for menorrhagia. *Fam Pract* 1994;11:394–401.

63. Woodend AK, Nair RC, Tang AS. Definition of life quality from a patient versus health care professional perspective. *Int J Rehabil Res* 1997;20:71–80. .

64. Present CA. Quality of life in cancer patients: who measures what? *Am J Clin Oncol* 1991;7:571–3.

65. Slevin ML, Plant H, Lynch D, Drinkwater J, Gregory WM. Who should measure quality of life, the doctor or the patient? *Br J Cancer* 1988;57:109–12.

66. Drury CA, Louis M. Exploring the association between bodyweight, stigma of obesity and health care avoidance. *J Am Acad Nurse Pract* 2002;14:554–61.

67. Sendi P, Brunotte R, Potoczna N, Branson R, Horber FF. Health-related quality of life in patients with class II and class III obesity. *Obes Surg* 2005;15:1070–6.

68. Haslam D, Sattar N, Lean M. ABC of obesity. Obesity – time to wake up. *BMJ* 2006;333:640–2.

69. Patrick DL, Bergner M. Measurement of health status in the 1990s. *Annu Rev Public Health* 1990;11:165–83.

Section 3

Pregnancy

Chapter 10

The epidemiology of obesity and pregnancy complications

Stephen Robinson and Christina KH Yu

Introduction

This chapter addresses the epidemiology of maternal obesity and its complications. The clinical management is not addressed. The prevalence of maternal obesity is described. Then the maternal, fetal and obstetric complications of maternal obesity are addressed before investigating the effect of maternal obesity on the long-term implications for maternal weight. Gestational diabetes and type 2 diabetes mellitus are addressed in a separate section, partly because they are also related to obesity, but also because they illustrate the four areas of medical complications of pregnancy.

Epidemiology of maternal obesity

Overweight and obesity are common in antenatal clinics in the UK.[1] The prevalence of women who are overweight is increasing. The definition of obesity in terms of risk of complications may vary between ethnic groups. Obesity can be defined in terms of weight related to height (body mass index (BMI) = weight/height^2) and in terms of regional adiposity (waist circumference) which is more related to insulin sensitivity. The importance of central, or omental, adiposity prior to pregnancy has been poorly studied but may be a risk factor for some but not all complications of overweight pregnancy.

Retrospective analysis of data from a validated maternity database system in Northwest Thames, in the early 1990s, was used to compare outcomes based on antenatal BMI measured at booking. In that study, 42% of women were primiparous and 72% were white (Figure 10.1).[2] Of the whole cohort, 28% of women were overweight and 11% were obese, defined by BMI measured at booking. Women who were obese were more likely to book late but this did not account for their increased BMI. A study performed at the same time in Washington in the USA demonstrated that, of 96 000 women, 52% were normal weight, 18% overweight and 10% obese.[3]

Pregnancy weight gain has been investigated in Finland, from the 1960s to 2000.[4] The proportion of normal BMI decreased from 66% in 1960 to 61% in 1985, to 53% in 2000, while those overweight or obese increased from 12–16% to 30% over those time frames. In a population of 22 000 women from California, ethnicity, BMI and risk of complications were studied.[5] The proportion of women with a BMI greater than 29 kg/m^2 was 8% in white women, 22% in African-American, 14% in Latina and 4% in Asian (oriental) women. The risk of complications varied among the different ethnicities. In a Swedish study involving 972 000 pregnancies, morbid obesity

(BMI > 40 kg/m²) was found in 0.35% of women and 1.3% had a BMI between 35 and 40 kg/m².[6]

A study in Glasgow comparing the weight of women at booking visits in 1990 and in 2002/2004 found a two-fold increase in women being identified as obese.[1] The number of women who were obese at booking increased from 9% to 19%. When adjusted for maternal age, parity, smoking status and deprivation status, the mean BMI increase was 1.37 kg/m².

A total of 36 821 women were studied in Middlesbrough over 14 years. The proportion of women who were obese increased from 9.9% to 16.0%; if the quadratic model of this increase continues, this will reach 22% by 2010. There was a significant association of maternal obesity with social deprivation.[7]

The recommended weight gain and the actual weight gain of pregnancy are increasing with time. Increasing weight gain has been associated with reduction in some abnormalities such as intrauterine growth restriction but increasing maternal weight gain in mothers who are overweight or obese is associated with an increased risk of adverse events.

The epidemiology of the complications of maternal obesity in pregnancy is divided into four groups. This chapter discusses the epidemiology and associations of maternal complications, fetal complications, complications to the pregnancy and finally the risk of maternal obesity after the pregnancy.

Epidemiology of maternal complications

There are considerable risks for maternal and fetal morbidity and mortality from maternal overweight and obesity. In the most recent Confidential Enquires into Maternal

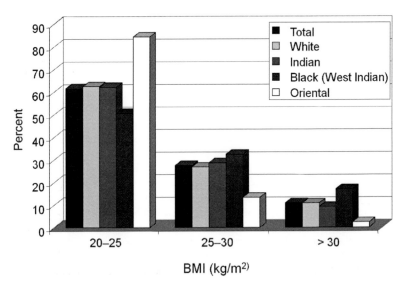

Figure 10.1. Prevalence of obesity by self-reported ethnicity in a study of 287 213 deliveries in Northwest Thames; women with a BMI < 20 kg/m² were not included; the proportions of each ethnic group were 72.3% white, 12.0% Indian, 2.8% black (West Indian) and 1.8% oriental; data from Sebire *et al.*[2]

Deaths in the UK report (2000–02),[8] 35% of all women (n = 78) who died were obese compared with 23% of the general maternal population, a dramatic rise from the 16% reported in 1993.

Hypertension

There is a well-described association of hypertension and adiposity outside pregnancy. However, not all studies have separated pregnancy-induced hypertension (PIH) and essential hypertension and studies vary in the definition and inclusion criteria. A systematic review on maternal BMI and risk of pre-eclampsia showed that the risk typically doubled with each 5–7 kg/m^2 increase in pregnancy BMI (Figure 10.2).[9] In the general population, increased waist circumference is associated with reduced insulin sensitivity and hypertension. Waist circumference measured at 16 weeks of gestation can predict PIH and pre-eclampsia, and a waist circumference greater than 80 cm gave an odds ratio of 1.8 (95% CI 1.1–2.9) for PIH and 2.7 (95% CI 1.1–6.8) for pre-eclampsia.[10]

Thromboembolism

In the Northwest Thames study, the prevalence of thromboembolism was 0.5% in women of normal weight, rising to 0.6% in those who were overweight and 0.12% in those who were obese (OR 1.60; 95% CI 1.01–2.56).[2]

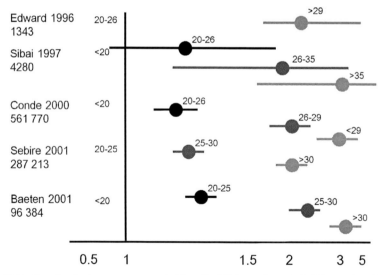

Figure 10.2. Hypertension in pregnancy, created from the O'Brien meta-analysis;[9] the number of women studied is indicated on the left for each study, followed by the comparator group; for some the reference group had a BMI < 20 kg/m², for others the reference group was a BMI of 20–25 kg/m²; overall, the risk of pre-eclampsia was 3.9% with a BMI of 20–25 or BMI < 30 kg/m² increasing to 13.5% in the BMI > 30 kg/m² group

Infections

Genital tract, wound and urinary tract infections are all significantly more common in women who are overweight or obese (Table 10.1).[2]

Epidemiology of fetal complications

Congenital malformations

There is conflicting evidence regarding the association between obesity and congenital malformations. One case–control study found that women with a BMI greater than 31 kg/m^2 had a significantly increased risk of delivering infants with a neural tube defect (NTD) and defects of the central nervous system, the great vessels in the heart and the ventral wall, and other intestinal defects.[11] The association between spina bifida and obesity was also demonstrated in another study, which concluded that, for every incremental unit increase (kg/m^2) in BMI, the risk of NTD is increased by 7%. There is also an increase in other malformations, such as omphalocele (three-fold), cardiac anomalies, especially septal defects (twofold), and multiple defects among the overweight and obese group.[12] However, other studies have not found this association of increased risk of congenital malformation and obesity.[13,14]

Table 10.1. Maternal complications according to each BMI category; in a study of 287 213 deliveries in Northwest Thames, the proportion of women with a complication and the odds ratio for that complication are given for women who were overweight or obese women; data from Sebire *et al.*[2]

	BMI (kg/m²)	Proportion (%)	OR (95% CI)
Chest infection	20–25	0.13	
	25–30	0.16	1.07 (0.81–1.41)
	> 30	0.28	1.34 (0.99–1.92)
Genital infection	20–25	0.66	
	25–30	0.73	1.24 (1.09–1.41)
	> 30	0.76	1.30 (1.07–1.56)
Wound infection	20–25	0.39	
	25–30	0.59	1.27 (1.09–1.48)
	> 30	1.34	2.24 (1.91–2.64)
Urinary tract infection	20–25	0.69	
	25–30	0.84	1.17 (1.04–1.33)
	> 30	1.10	1.39 (1.18–1.63)
Pyrexia of unknown origin	20–25	1.00	
	25–30	1.29	1.19 (1.08–1.32)
	> 30	1.54	1.29 (1.13–1.48)
Prolonged postnatal stay	20–25	20.35	
	25–30	21.08	1.00 (0.97–1.04)
	> 30	22.86	1.48 (0.82–2.69)

In a case–control surveillance program of birth defects, a daily folate intake of 400 μg of folate was protective against NTD in women with body weight less than 70 kg but not in more than 70 kg.[15] They concluded that the risk of NTD increases with maternal weight independent of folic acid intake.

Macrosomia

Several studies have shown that maternal obesity and excessive weight gain during pregnancy are associated with macrosomic babies.[2,6,16,17] Obesity and pre-gestational diabetes are independently associated with an increased risk of large-for-gestational-age infants and this impact of abnormal body habitus on birthweight increases with increasing BMI and is associated with significant obstetric morbidity.[18,19] Therefore the fetal macrosomia with maternal obesity is not merely a reflection of large mothers having larger babies. There have not been any randomised controlled studies; however, in a retrospective study of 245 526 singleton term deliveries in Sweden, women who gained the least weight in pregnancy were least likely to have large-for-gestational-age babies (OR 0.66; 95% CI 0.59–0.75).[20]

Antepartum stillbirth

Studies have suggested that obesity is associated with an increased risk of antepartum stillbirth. In a prospective population-based cohort study (n = 3480), a three-fold increase in antepartum stillbirth was found in the women who were morbidly obese compared with women with a normal BMI.[6]

In a large Swedish population-based cohort study (n = 167 750), the risk of late fetal death increased consistently with increasing prepregnancy BMI.[21] Among nulliparous women, the risk of late fetal death was approximately doubled among women with a normal BMI compared with lean women, tripled among those who were overweight and quadrupled among those who were obese. Among the parous women, the risk of late fetal death was significantly increased only among women who were obese. For early neonatal death, the risk was doubled in nulliparous women with a higher BMI but this was not true in parous women.

The Swedish Medical Birth Register was used to investigate the relationship between weight gain during pregnancy and antepartum stillbirth.[22] After controlling for multiple variables, women who were overweight (BMI 25–29.9 kg/m^2) or obese (BMI ≥ 30 kg/m^2) had a two-fold increase in the risk of term antepartum stillbirth. However, weight gain during pregnancy was not associated with an increased risk of antepartum stillbirth.

In a Danish study involving 24 505 singleton pregnancies, the overall rate of stillbirth was 4.6 per 1000 deliveries, and of neonatal death was 3.1 per 1000 live births. Maternal obesity was associated with a more than doubled risk of stillbirth (OR 2.8) and neonatal death (OR 2.6) compared with women with normal weight. No single cause of death explained the higher risk of stillbirth in babies of women who were obese. However, higher proportions of stillbirths caused by unexplained intrauterine death and feto-placental dysfunction were found in babies of women who were obese compared with those of women who were not obese (BMI < 30 kg/m^2). There were no apparent causes of neonatal death.[23]

Intrapartum and postpartum complications

The inability to obtain interpretable external fetal heart rates and uterine contraction patterns in women who are obese is frequent. Women with a BMI > 35 kg/m^2 are likely to have pre-existing medical conditions such as hypertension or diabetes which may further increase their anaesthetic risks. There are few data on the epidemiology of these associations.

Long-term implications for the fetus

Infants who are at the highest end of the distribution for weight or BMI or who grow rapidly during infancy have an increased risk of subsequent obesity.[24] Babies who were obese were nine times more likely than babies with normal weight to grow into adults who are obese, and infants who grew rapidly were five times more likely to become obese.

Epidemiology of obstetric complications

Infertility and miscarriage

Women who are obese have a higher prevalence of amenorrhoea and infertility. Obesity is common, occurring in 35–40% of women with polycystic ovary syndrome (PCOS).[25] Fifty percent of women who are overweight have polycystic ovaries or PCOS compared with 30% of lean women.[26] The risk of miscarriage before the first liveborn child is 25–37% higher in women who are obese.[27] Obesity has a negative impact on fertility treatment and, even if conception occurs, there is an increased risk of pregnancy loss. Three cohort studies have suggested that obesity is an independent risk factor for spontaneous miscarriage in women who undergo fertility treatment.[28–30] With ovulation induction using gonadotrophin-releasing hormone, there is a three-fold increase in the risk of pregnancy resulting in miscarriage, and with a donor oocyte, women with a BMI > 30 kg/m^2 have a four-fold increased risk of miscarriage. Therefore, women who are obese should be encouraged to lose weight prior to their fertility treatment as this can result in significant improvement in reproductive outcome for all fertility treatments.[31]

Delivery and surgical complications

Women who are obese have a higher induction of labour rate (25.5% for BMI 20–30 kg/m^2 and 36% for BMI > 30 kg/m^2, for which the OR is 1.6; 95% CI 1.3–1.9)[32] and a higher rate of failed induction (7.9% for BMI < 25 kg/m^2 versus 10.3% for BMI 25–30 kg/m^2 and 14.6% for BMI > 30 kg/m^2).[33] There is also a higher rate of operative vaginal delivery (8.4% versus 11.4% and 17.3% with increasing BMI; $P < 0.001$), shoulder dystocia (1% versus 1.8% and 1.9% with increasing BMI; $P < 0.021$) and third or fourth degree lacerations (26.3% versus 27.5% and 30.8% with increasing BMI; $P < 0.001$) compared with the normal BMI group.[33] In another study involving 126 080 deliveries, after excluding women with diabetes and hypertensive disease, there was a three-fold increase in risk of failure to progress in the first stage and a higher caesarean section rate of 27.8% versus 10.8% (OR 3.2) in women who were obese compared with women with normal weight.[34] The increase in emergency caesarean sections in women who are obese may be related to an increased number of large-for–gestational-age infants, suboptimal uterine contractions and increased fat disposition in the soft tissues of the pelvis leading to dystocia during labour.

The frequency of both elective (8.5% versus 4%) and emergency caesarean section (13.4% versus 7.8%) was almost twice as high for women with a BMI > 30 kg/m^2 compared with the normal BMI group.[2] Maternal obesity was found to influence the route of delivery independently of co-morbid conditions such as macrosomia, nulliparity, induction or diabetes, and women who were obese or overweight had a higher risk of caesarean section delivery compared with women with normal weight (13.8% and 10.4%, respectively, versus 7.7%; $P < 0.0001$).[35] Caesarean section rates were increased in nulliparous women (20.7% in the control group versus 33.8% in the obese group and 47.4% in the morbidly obese group; $P > 0.01$).[36] Caesarean section delivery has been found to be independently predicted by pregravid obesity and diabetes.[37]

A hospital-based perinatal database was used to identify women with a BMI > 35 kg/m^2 undergoing their first caesarean delivery. They reported an overall wound complication rate of 12.1% and those with a vertical skin incision were at greatest risk (34.6% versus 9.4%).[37] In the puerperium, endometritis, postpartum haemorrhage, prolonged hospitalisation and wound infections were more frequent in women who were obese (Table 10.1). The risk of postpartum haemorrhage rose with increasing BMI and was about 30% more frequent for women with moderately raised BMI and about 70% more frequent for women with very raised BMI compared with the normal BMI group.[2]

In a retrospective study of 245 526 singleton term deliveries in Sweden, women who gained least weight in pregnancy were least likely to have a range of adverse outcomes, including caesarean section (OR 0.81; 95% CI 0.73–0.90).[20]

Vaginal birth after caesarean section

In a study of 510 women attempting a trial of labour, the impact of maternal obesity and weight gain was investigated on the success of vaginal birth after caesarean section.[38] After adjusting for confounding factors such as ethnicity, labour induction, gestational age at delivery and infant birthweight, an increase in pregravid BMI and weight gain between pregnancies reduced the chance of having a vaginal birth after a single low transverse caesarean delivery (54.6% versus 70.5%; $P = 0.04$). In a study of 1213 women, the women who were obese were 50% less successful when attempting a trial of vaginal delivery after a caesarean section when compared with women who were underweight ($P = 0.043$).[39]

Breastfeeding

The fall in progesterone that occurs immediately postpartum is the trigger for the onset of copious milk secretion and the maintenance of the prolactin concentrations that are necessary for this trigger to be effective. Maternal obesity is associated with a reduction in breastfeeding frequency.[2,40,41] Although it is likely to be multifactorial in origin, simple mechanical difficulties of latching on and proper positioning of infant when the mother is obese can pose a problem for establishing breastfeeding. From an endocrine perspective, obesity is associated with reduced prolactin response to suckling.[42]

Long-term consequences for maternal obesity

For many of the complications described, there is dissociation between the optimal maternal weight gain for outcomes related to the fetus and outcomes related to the mother. Therefore a high pregnancy weight gain is associated with a statistically better fetal outcome but a worse outcome for maternal obesity. For all pregnant women, a weight gain of 10 kg is statistically associated with the best obstetric outcome. A weight gain of more than 9 kg in pregnancy is more likely to be retained after the pregnancy.[43] However, these data are based on the whole population and on obstetric outcome, not the weight gain associated with least chance of long-term weight retention. Gestational weight gain and postpartum behaviours associated with weight change from early pregnancy to 1 year postpartum have been investigated in 540 New York women.[44] At 1 year postpartum, the women were a mean of 1.5 ± 5.9 kg heavier, and 25% experienced a gain of 4.6 kg or more. Weight gain in excess of guidelines was three times more likely in low-income groups. Gestational weight gain, postpartum exercise and food intake were all associated with weight gain to 1 year postpartum.

In a randomised controlled trial of 120 women with normal weight, healthy eating and exercise were used to prevent excessive weight gain in pregnancy. The weight gain exceeded 15.9 kg in 33% of the intervention group compared with 58% of the untreated group. The postpartum retention of weight was proportional to weight gain in pregnancy.[45]

Maternal type 2 diabetes mellitus and gestational diabetes mellitus

Gestational diabetes mellitus (GDM) and type 2 diabetes mellitus lie on the same pathophysiological spectrum and illustrate the whole range of maternal, fetal, obstetric and long-term complications. GDM is glucose intolerance first recognised in pregnancy. Although not central to the diagnosis, glucose tolerance normally resolves following the pregnancy. However, it does predict risk of type 2 diabetes in later life: many women with gestational diabetes in fact have type 2 diabetes but it is first recognised in pregnancy. Obesity is more common in GDM and type 2 diabetes, although not universal. Obesity and diabetes are associated at a pathophysiological level and it is useful to consider them together. There is increasing awareness of the growing prevalence and complications of type 2 diabetes in pregnancy.

Women destined to develop type 2 diabetes are likely to develop GDM, rather than the GDM causing later type 2 diabetes.[46] The physiological insulin resistance of pregnancy can precipitate hyperglycaemia in a woman with a pre-existing insulin secretion deficit.[47] The return of her nonpregnant insulin resistance allows glucose tolerance to return to normal, but the insulin resistance and relative β-cell failure with increasing age can precipitate type 2 diabetes. Both GDM and type 2 diabetes are associated with obesity, in particular central obesity. The pathophysiology of type 2 diabetes and obesity are intimately related; obesity is not just a precipitant of type 2 diabetes. The increasing prevalence of obesity in society in general, including in teenage women, has been associated with an increased prevalence of women of reproductive age with type 2 diabetes. The prevalence of GDM reflects the prevalence of type 2 diabetes in an ethnic group, for example there is a high prevalence in south Asians,[48] who have increased risk of type 2 diabetes at a lower BMI than whites. Many have type 2 diabetes which is only diagnosed at the time of a screen for GDM.

Prevalence

Studies have shown a prevalence of type 2 diabetes in pregnancy between 3.2–6.3%.[49,50] In the USA, the prevalence of pre-existing diabetes increased from 0.2% to 0.5% from 1980 to 1995, and the percentage with type 2 diabetes increased from 26% to 65%.[51]

In a study of 16 102 women, the incidence of GDM was 2.3% in a controlled group, increasing to 6.3% in an obese group (OR 2.6) and 9.5% in a morbidly obese group (OR 4.0).[36] GDM may now affect 14% of pregnancies in the USA.[52] In the Northwest Thames study group, women with a BMI greater than 30 kg/m² had an OR of 3.6 for developing GDM compared with women with a normal BMI.[2] In a large Danish study consisting of 8000 women, the odds for developing GDM increased with BMI (BMI < 25 kg/m^2 OR 1; BMI 25–29 kg/m^2 OR 3.4; BMI > 30 kg/m^2 OR 15.3).[53]

Maternal risk

Of pregnant women with type 2 diabetes, 30.9% develop pre-eclampsia.[54] In a study of 201 Japanese women with type 2 diabetes, there was significant maternal risk in terms of retinopathy: 28% had non-proliferative retinopathy and 4.3% had proliferative retinopathy.[54] Nephropathy and hypertension were also risks for pregnant women who had type 2 diabetes.

Fetal risk

Pregnancy outcome was studied in type 1 diabetes, type 2 diabetes and a background Danish population.[55] Perinatal mortality was 6.6% in type 2 diabetes, four times that in type 1 diabetes, and nine times that in the non-diabetic population.

Congenital malformation is more common where the mother has pre-existing type 2 diabetes. In a study of 332 pregnancies in the USA, 11.7% had major congenital abnormalities.[56] In a study of 70 000 deliveries in Japan, no major abnormalities were found with type 1 diabetes, but there were 5.8% of deliveries with abnormalities when the mother had type 2 diabetes.[54] In the UK, an abnormality rate of 6.1% was found with type 1 diabetes, but 12.2% with type 2 diabetes.[57] In a regional database from Birmingham involving 182 women with type 2 diabetes, congenital malformations occurred in 9.9%.[58] In the Danish study, the rate of major abnormality was 6.7% in type 2 diabetes, double the rate with type 1 diabetes and in the background population.[55] In this study, glycated haemoglobin (HbA$_1$c) and type 2 diabetes were independently associated with serious fetal outcome, including major anomaly. There may be a small increase in malformation rate when a mother has GDM, suggesting that the mechanisms are not entirely related to hyperglycaemia.[59,60] Improved glycaemic control has not been shown to affect the risk of malformation when the mother has type 2 diabetes where the risk is significantly higher than background. Although glycaemia is certainly a risk factor for congenital malformation in type 1 and type 2 diabetes, other factors may be more important in type 2. These may include maternal age, unplanned pregnancy and endothelial dysfunction.

The original Pedersen hypothesis suggested that increased glucose concentrations in a diabetic mother leads to increased fetal growth. Obesity is associated with increased maternal insulin resistance and fetal hyperinsulinaemia even in the absence of maternal diabetes.[61] Insulin-resistant individuals have higher fasting plasma triglyceride levels and greater leucine turnover.[62,63] Amino acids are insulin secretogogues and an increased flux on amino acids could stimulate fetal hyperinsulinaemia. Triglycerides are energy rich and placental lipases can cleave triglycerides and transfer free fatty acids to the fetus across a haemochorial placenta.[64] The combination of an increased energy flux to the fetus and fetal hyperinsulinaemia may explain the increased frequency of large-for-gestational-age infants seen in women who are obese but not diabetic.

The risk of neonatal hypoglycaemia is more related to maternal diabetes, whereas fetal macrosomia is more related to maternal obesity.[64]

Obstetric implications

Women are less likely to address their type 2 diabetes compared with type 1 diabetes before pregnancy; possibly because they are not aware that they have it or because the pregnancy is unplanned.[65] In the Birmingham study, 53% of the women were delivered by caesarean section, of which 43% were elective and 57% were emergency. Of the caesarean section group, 22% were performed following induction of labour.[58]

Long-term outcomes

After delivery, maternal insulin resistance rapidly returns to a nonpregnant level. Type 2 diabetes that is controlled with insulin may require oral hypoglycaemic agents or control by diet alone. The glycaemic level in GDM usually returns to normal, but GDM is a major risk factor for later type 2 diabetes. The Boston study investigated women who were lean or obese with GDM, investigating their risk of later type 2 diabetes (Figure 10.3).[66] The risk of type 2 diabetes increases after a pregnancy complicated by GDM, the risk being greatest for women who are obese. The time from GDM to later type 2 diabetes depends on ethnic group, with the ethnic group with the highest background prevalence of type 2 diabetes having the shortest time from index GDM pregnancy to type 2 diabetes.[67] Progression from GDM to type 2 diabetes depends on ethnicity and studies are confounded by length of follow-up and cohort retention. The most rapid incidence of type 2 diabetes following GDM occurs in the first 5 years after delivery, after correcting for ethnicity.[68] Women with GDM should be counselled regarding the risk of later type 2 diabetes. The Diabetes Prevention Program[69] included some women who had had GDM and demonstrated that lifestyle interventions such as increased exercise and improved diet can significantly reduce the risk. Furthermore, women can be advised to have regular type 2 diabetes screening to diagnose the diabetes before complications arise.

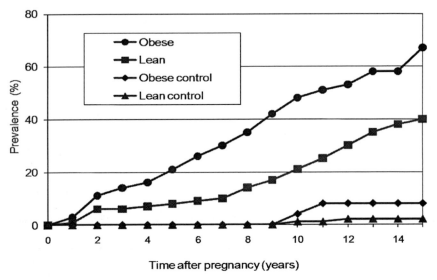

Figure 10.3. Prevalence of type 2 diabetes following gestational diabetes mellitus; women who were obese or lean, with and without GDM, were studied for 15 years following their pregnancy; few women without GDM went on to develop type 2 diabetes; for women with GDM, both those who were lean and those who were obese were more likely to progress to type 2 diabetes in later life; data from Donath and Amir[41]

Conclusion

The prevalence of maternal obesity, maternal gestational diabetes and type 2 diabetes are all increasing. All three are associated with adverse pregnancy outcomes. There are increased adverse outcomes for the mother, including hypertension, infection and thromboembolic disorders. Increased fetal risks include congenital malformation, macrosomia and increased perinatal mortality. For the mother who is obese, there are increased risks of operative delivery and long-term difficulties with obesity following her pregnancy.

Epidemiological studies, when considered with pathophysiological studies, have indicated that maternal weight and glycaemia, although related, are independent risk factors for adverse pregnancy outcomes. Glycaemia and regional adiposity may predict slightly different aspects of adverse outcome. Increased maternal age, increased weight, certain ethnicities and higher glucose and triglyceride concentrations are all associated with adverse outcomes. Maternal weight must be assessed at booking for every pregnancy and an individual pregnancy plan devised. More sophisticated predictors and screening tools for assessment of individual pregnancy risk need to be developed.

References

1. Kanagalingam MG, Forouhi NG, Greer IA, Sattar N. Changes in booking body mass index over a decade: retrospective analysis from a Glasgow Maternity Hospital. *BJOG* 2005;112:1431–3.

2. Sebire NJ, Jolly M, Harris JP, Wadsworth J, Joffe M, Beard RW, *et al.* Maternal obesity and pregnancy outcome: a study of 287,213 pregnancies in London. *Int J Obes Relat Metab Disord* 2001;25:1175–82.

3. Proceedings of the ASBS Consensus Conference on the State of Bariatric Surgery and Morbid Obesity: Health Implications for Patients, Health Professionals and Third-Party Payers, Washington, DC, USA, May 6–7, 2004. *Surg Obes Relat Dis* 2005;1:105–53.

4. Kinnunen TI, Luoto R, Gissler M, Hemminki E. Pregnancy weight gain from 1960s to 2000 in Finland. *Int J Obes Relat Metab Disord* 2003;27:1572–7.

5. Ramos GA, Caughey AB. The interrelationship between ethnicity and obesity on obstetric outcomes. *Am J Obstet Gynecol* 2005;193:1089–93.

6. Cedergren MI. Maternal morbid obesity and the risk of adverse pregnancy outcome. *Obstet Gynecol* 2004;103:219–24.

7. Heslehurst N, Ells LJ, Simpson H, Batterham A, Wilkinson J, Summerbell CD. Trends in maternal obesity incidence rates, demographic predictors, and health inequalities in 36,821 women over a 15-year period. *BJOG* 2007;114:187–94.

8. Confidential Enquiry into Maternal and Child Health. *Why Mothers Die 2000–2002. The Sixth Report of the Confidential Enquires Into Maternal Deaths in the United Kingdom*. London; RCOG Press; 2004. p. 2000–2.

9. O'Brien TE, Ray JG, Chan WS. Maternal body mass index and the risk of preeclampsia: a systematic overview. *Epidemiology* 2003;14:368–74.

10. Sattar N, Clark P, Holmes A, Lean ME, Walker I, Greer IA. Antenatal waist circumference and hypertension risk. *Obstet Gynecol* 2001;97:268–71.

11. Waller DK, Mills JL, Simpson JL, Cunningham GC, Conley MR, Lassman MR, *et al.* Are obese women at higher risk for producing malformed offspring? *Am J Obstet Gynecol* 1994;170:541–8.

12. Glazer NL, Hendrickson AF, Schellenbaum GD, Mueller BA. Weight change and the risk of gestational diabetes in obese women. *Epidemiology* 2004;15:733–7.

13. Moore LL, Singer MR, Bradlee ML, Rothman KJ, Milunsky A. A prospective study of the risk of congenital defects associated with maternal obesity and diabetes mellitus. *Epidemiology* 2000;11:689–94.

14. Feldman B, Yaron Y, Critchfield G, Leon J, O'Brien JE, Johnson MP, *et al*. Distribution of neural tube defects as a function of maternal weight: no apparent correlation. *Fetal Diagn Ther* 1999;14:185–9.

15. Werler MM, Louik C, Shapiro S, Mitchell AA. Prepregnant weight in relation to risk of neural tube defects. *JAMA* 1996;275:1089–92.

16. Weiss JL, Malone FD, Emig D, Ball RH, Nyberg DA, Comstock CH, *et al*. FASTER Research Consortium. Obesity, obstetric complications and cesarean delivery rate – a population-based screening study. *Am J Obstet Gynecol* 2004;190:1091–7.

17. Surkan PJ, Hsieh CC, Johansson ALV, Dickman PW, Cnattingius S. Reasons for increasing trends in large for gestational age births. *Am J Obstet Gynecol* 1994;104:720–6.

18. Jolly MC, Sebire NJ, Harris JP, Regan L, Robinson S. Risk factors for macrosomia and its clinical consequences: a study of 350,311 pregnancies. *Eur J Obstet Gynecol Reprod Biol* 2003;111:9–14.

19. Ehrenberg HM, Mercer BM, Catalano PM. The influence of obesity and diabetes on the prevalence of macrosomia. *Am J Obstet Gynecol* 2004;191:964–8.

20. Cedergren M. Effects of gestational weight gain and body mass index on obstetric outcome in Sweden. *Int J Gynecol Obstet* 2006;93:269–27.

21. Cnattingius S, Bergstrom R, Lipworth L, Kramer MS. Prepregnancy weight and the risk of adverse pregnancy outcomes. *N Engl J Med* 1998;338:147–52.

22. Stephansson O, Dickman PW, Johansson A, Cnattingius S. Maternal weight, pregnancy weight gain, and the risk of antepartum stillbirth. *Am J Obstet Gynecol* 2001;184:463–9.

23. Kristensen J, Vestergaard M, Wisborg K, Kesmodel U, Secher NJ. Pre-pregnancy weight and the risk of stillbirth and neonatal death. *BJOG* 2005;112:403–8.

24. Baird J, Fisher D, Lucas P, Kleijnen J, Roberts H, Law C. Being big or growing fast: systematic review of size and growth in infancy and later obesity. *BMJ* 2005;331:929.

25. Franks S. Polycystic ovary syndrome: a changing perspective. *Clin Endocrinol (Oxf)* 1989;31:87–120.

26. Hart R, Hickey M, Franks S. Definitions, prevalence and symptoms of polycystic ovaries and polycystic ovary syndrome. *Best Pract Res Clin Obstet Gynaecol* 2004;18:671–83.

27. Hamilton-Fairley D, Kiddy D, Watson H, Paterson C, Franks S. Association of moderate obesity with a poor pregnancy outcome in women with polycystic ovary syndrome treated with low dose gonadotrophin. *Br J Obstet Gynaecol* 1992;99:128–31.

28. Bellver J, Rossal LP, Bosch E, Zuniga A, Corona JT, Melendez F, *et al*. Obesity and the risk of spontaneous abortion after oocyte donation. *Fertil Steril* 2003;79:1136–40.

29. Wang JX, Davies MJ, Norman RJ. Polycystic ovarian syndrome and the risk of spontaneous abortion following assisted reproductive technology treatment. *Hum Reprod* 2001;16:2606–9.

30. Fedorcsak P, Storeng R, Dale PO, Tanbo T, Abyholm T. Obesity is a risk factor for early pregnancy loss after IVF or ICSI. *Acta Obstet Gynecol Scand* 2000;79:43–8.

31. Clark AM, Thornley B, Tomlinson L, Galletley C, Norman RJ. Weight loss in obese infertile women results in improvement in reproductive outcome for all forms of fertility treatment. *Hum Reprod* 1998;13:1502–5.

32. Usha Kiran TS, Hemmadi S, Bethel J, Evans J. Outcome of pregnancy in a woman with an increased body mass index. *BJOG* 2005;112:768–72.

33. Kabiru W, Raynor BD. Obstetric outcomes associated with increase in BMI category during pregnancy. *Am J Obstet Gynecol* 2004;191:928–32.

34. Sheiner E, Levy A, Menes TS, Silverberg D, Katz M, Mazor M. Maternal obesity as an independent risk factor for caesarean delivery. *Paediatr Perinat Epidemiol* 2004;18:196–201.

35. Ehrenberg HM, Durnwald CP, Catalano P, Mercer BM. The influence of obesity and diabetes on the risk of cesarean delivery. *Am J Obstet Gynecol* 2004;191:969–74.

36. Veille JC, Hanson R. Obesity, pregnancy, and left ventricular functioning during the third trimester. *Am J Obstet Gynecol* 1994;171:980–3.

37. Wall PD, Deucy EE, Glantz JC, Pressman EK. Vertical skin incisions and wound complications in the obese parturient. *Obstet Gynecol* 2003;102:952–6.

38. Durnwald CP, Ehrenberg HM, Mercer BM. The impact of maternal obesity and weight gain on vaginal birth after cesarean section success. *Am J Obstet Gynecol* 2004;191:954–7.

39. Juhasz G, Gyamfi C, Gyamfi P, Tocce K, Stone JL. Effect of body mass index and excessive weight gain on success of vaginal birth after cesarean delivery. *Obstet Gynecol* 2005;106:741–6.

40. Li R, Ogden C, Ballew C, Gillespie C, Grummer-Strawn L. Prevalence of exclusive breastfeeding among US infants: the Third National Health and Nutrition Examination Survey (Phase II, 1991–1994). *Am J Public Health* 2002;92:1107–10.

41. Donath SM, Amir LH. Does maternal obesity adversely affect breastfeeding initiation and duration? *Breastfeed Rev* 2000;8:29–33.

42. Rasmussen KM, Kjolhede CL. Prepregnant overweight and obesity diminish the prolactin response to suckling in the first week postpartum. *Pediatrics* 2004;113:e465–71.

43. Greene GW, Smiciklas-Wright H, Scholl TO, Karp RJ. Postpartum weight change: how much of the weight gained in pregnancy will be lost after delivery? *Obstet Gynecol* 1988;71:701–7.

44. Olsen M. Exercise during pregnancy. *Postgrad Med* 1988;83:36–8.

45. Polley BA, Wing RR, Sims CJ. Randomized controlled trial to prevent excessive weight gain in pregnant women. *Int J Obes Relat Metab Disord* 2002;26:1494–502.

46. O'Sullivan JB. Body weight and subsequent diabetes mellitus. *JAMA* 1982;248:949–52.

47. Buchanan TA, Metzger BE, Freinkel N, Bergman RN. Insulin sensitivity and B-cell responsiveness to glucose during late pregnancy in lean and moderately obese women with normal glucose tolerance or mild gestational diabetes. *Am J Obstet Gynecol* 1990;162:1008–14.

48. Department of Health. *National Service Framework for Diabetes: Standards.* London: The Stationery Office; 2001 [www.dh.gov.uk/PublicationsAndStatistics/Publications/PublicationsPolicyAndGuidance/PublicationsPolicyAndGuidanceArticle/fs/en?CONTENT_ID=4002951&chk=o9Kkz1].

49. Pettitt DJ, Knowler WC, Baird HR, Bennett PH. Gestational diabetes: infant and maternal complications of pregnancy in relation to third-trimester glucose tolerance in the Pima Indians. *Diabetes Care* 1980;3:458–64.

50. Livingston RC, Bachman-Carter K, Frank C, Mason WB. Diabetes mellitus in Tohon O'odham pregnancies. *Diabetes Care* 1993;16:318–21.

51. Engelgau MM, Herman WH, Smith PJ, German RR, Aubert RE. The epidemiology of diabetes and pregnancy in the U.S., 1988. *Diabetes Care* 1995;18:1029–33.

52. Jovanovic L, Pettitt DJ. Gestational diabetes mellitus. *JAMA* 2001;286:2516–8.

53. Rode L, Nilas L, Wøjdemann K, Tabor A. Obesity-related complications in Danish single cephalic term pregnancies. *Obstet Gynecol* 2005;105:537–42.

54. Omori Y, Minei S, Testuo T, Nemoto K, Shimizu M, Sanaka M. Current status of pregnancy in diabetic women. A comparison of pregnancy in IDDM and NIDDM mothers. *Diabetes Res Clin Pract* 1994;24 Suppl:S273–8.

55. Clausen TD, Mathiesen E, Ekbom P, Hellmuth E, Mandrup-Poulsen T, Damm P. Poor pregnancy outcome in women with type 2 diabetes. *Diabetes Care* 2005;28:323–8.

56. Towner D, Kjos SL, Leung B, Montoro MM, Xiang A, Mestman JH, Buchanan TA. Congenital malformations in pregnancies complicated by NIDDM. *Diabetes Care* 1995;18:1446–51.

57. Brydon P, Smith T, Proffitt M, Gee H, Holder R, Dunne F. Pregnancy outcome in women with type 2 diabetes mellitus needs to be addressed. *Int J Clin Pract* 2000;54:418–9.

58. Dunne F, Brydon P, Smith K, Gee H. Pregnancy in women with Type 2 diabetes: 12 years outcome data. *Diabet Med* 2003;20:734–8.

59. Sheffield JS, Butler-Koster EL, Casey BM, McIntire DD, Leveno KJ. Maternal diabetes mellitus and infant malformations. *Obstet Gynecol* 2002;100:925–30.

60. Farrell T, Neale L, Cundy T. Congenital anomalies in the offspring of women with type 1, type 2 and gestational diabetes. *Diabet Med* 2002;19:322–6.

61. Hoegsberg B, Gruppuso PA, Coustan DR. Hyperinsulinemia in macrosomic infants of nondiabetic mothers. *Diabetes Care* 1993;16:32–6.

62. Portman OW, Behrman RE, Soltys P. Transfer of free fatty acids across the primate placenta. *Am J Physiol* 1969;216:143–7.

63. Robinson S, Chan SP, Spacey S, Anyaoku V, Johnston DG, Franks S. Postprandial thermogenesis is reduced in polycystic ovary syndrome and is associated with increased insulin resistance. *Clin Endocrinol* 1992;36:537–43.

64. Thomas CR. Placental transfer of non-esterified fatty acids in normal and diabetic pregnancy. *Biol Neonate* 1987;51:94–101.

65. Boulot P, Chabbert-Buffet N, d'Ercole C, Floriot M, Fontaine P, Fournier A, *et al.*; Diabetes and Pregnancy Group, France. French multicentric survey of outcome of pregnancy in women with pregestational diabetes. *Diabetes Care* 2003;26:2990–3.

66. O'Sullivan JB. Body weight and subsequent diabetes mellitus. *JAMA* 1982;248:949–52.

67. Yue DK, Molyneaux LM, Ross GP, Constantino MI, Child AG, Turtle JR. Why does ethnicity affect prevalence of gestational diabetes? The underwater volcano theory. *Diabet Med* 1996;13:748–52.

68. Kim C, Newton KM, Knopp RH. Gestational diabetes and the incidence of type 2 diabetes: a systematic review. *Diabetes Care* 2002;25:1862–8.

69. Knowler WC, Barrett-Connor E, Fowler SE, Hamman RF, Lachin JM, Walker EA, et al. Diabetes Prevention Program Research Group. Reduction in the incidence of type 2 diabetes with lifestyle intervention or metformin. *NEJM* 2002;346:393–403.

Chapter 11

Antenatal complications of maternal obesity: miscarriage, fetal abnormalities, maternal gestational diabetes and pre-eclampsia

Eleanor Gate and Jane E Ramsay

Introduction

The effect of adiposity is manifest in nearly every aspect of female reproductive life, whether as a metabolic or reproductive complication or as a technical problem affecting clinical issues such as ultrasound scanning or surgery (Table 11.1). The 2002–04 Confidential Enquiry into Maternal Deaths in the UK has highlighted obesity as a significant risk for maternal death, with 35% of the women who died being obese; 50% more than in the general population.[1] In addition, the offspring of obese mothers also have a higher perinatal morbidity and long-term health problems.

Table 11.1. Potential effects of adiposity in pregnancy

	Medical complications	Technical complications
Maternal		
Prepregnancy	Menstrual disorders	
	Infertility	
Early-pregnancy	Miscarriage	Difficult ultrasound examination
	Fetal anomalies	
Antenatal	Pregnancy-induced hypertension	
	Pre-eclampsia	
	Gestational diabetes mellitus	
	Venous thromboembolic disease	
Intrapartum	Induction of labour	Operative issues
	Caesarean section	Anaesthetic issues
Postpartum	Haemorrhage	
	Infection	
	Venous thromboembolic disease	
Fetal	Macrosomia	Birth injury
	Fetal distress	
	Perinatal morbidity/mortality	

Such problems are of particular concern given recent evidence of doubling in the prevalence of obesity (now near one in five obese) in young women attending for antenatal care in UK maternity hospitals.[2] Figures released from the Department of Health (revised data from July 2006) have predicted that if the current trend in obesity continues there will be a further 1 230 573 women who are obese in 2010 compared with figures from 2003. In total there will be approximately six million women who are obese in England.[3]

Miscarriage

Amenorrhoea and infertility among women who are obese is more common than in their lean counterparts. Obesity itself is associated with poor pregnancy outcome and miscarriage in both women who are obese with polycystic ovary syndrome (PCOS) and in those with normal ovarian morphology. It is believed that up to 50% of women who are obese have polycystic ovaries or PCOS, compared with 30% of lean women.[4]

A meta-analysis of 13 studies examined patient predictors for outcome of gonado-trophin ovulation induction in women with normogonadotrophic anovulatory infer-tility. This work concluded that the most clinically useful predictors of poor outcome were obesity and insulin resistance.[5] The pooled odds ratio (OR) for women who were obese versus those who were not for the rate of spontaneous miscarriage was 3.05 (95% CI 1.45–6.44) (Table 11.2.). This association further emphasises the impor-tance of encouraging weight loss in order to maximise the chance of a successful preg-nancy outcome, prior to embarking on the management of anovulatory subfertility.

Most published studies have examined the rates of miscarriage in women with PCOS and in women who have received fertility treatment. Few studies have looked at identifying the risk of miscarriage within the obese general population. Lashen *et al.*[6] carried out a matched case–control study (parous women with one live child) that aimed to address this issue. A total of 1644 women who were obese (body mass index (BMI) > 30 kg/m^2) were paired with 3288 women of normal weight as controls (BMI 19–24.9 kg/m^2). The rates of spontaneous early (6–12 weeks), late (12–24 weeks) and recurrent (more than three) early miscarriage were observed. The women who were obese had a significantly higher incidence of early and recurrent early miscarriage when compared with the lean women in the control group (P = 0.04). The odds ratios for early and recurrent early miscarriage were 1.20 (95% CI 1.01–1.46) and 3.51 (95% CI 1.03–12.01), respectively.

Table 11.2. Risk of miscarriage in association with obesity; data from Mulders *et al.*[5], and Lashen *et al.*[6]

Study design	Risk of miscarriage
Meta-analysis of 13 studies in women with normogonadotrophic anovulatory infertility; examined patient predictors for outcome of ovulation induction with gonadotrophins: obese versus non-obese women	Rate of spontaneous miscarriage OR 3.05; 95% CI 1.45–6.44
Nested case–control study of women who were obese (BMI > 30 kg/m^2) compared with age-matched control group with normal BMI (19–24.9 kg/m^2).	Rate of early miscarriage (6–12 weeks) OR 1.20; 95% CI 1.01–1.46 Rate of recurrent miscarriage (greater than 3 successive) OR 3.51; 95% CI 1.03–12.01

OR = odds ratio; CI = confidence interval

One study suggested that a possible hypothesis for the observed increase in miscarriage in women who are obese could be an abnormality in the oocyte, but the authors emphasised that this had not been proven in previous studies.[7] The incidence of spontaneous miscarriage has been reported to increase with decreasing insulin sensitivity[8] and it has been suggested that insulin-sensitising agents, such as metformin, also reduce miscarriage rates.[9] One potential mechanism for this is increased production of inflammatory and pro-thrombotic agents produced by adipose tissue or released from endothelium secondary to stimulation by adipocyte-derived factors. Plasminogen activator inhibitor type 1 (PAI-1) has been suggested to be associated with increased rates of miscarriage in association with maternal obesity. Treatment with metformin appeared to reduce PAI-1 and miscarriage rates.[10,11] Another prospective study of pregnancy outcome examined 7332 women undergoing amniocentesis.[12] Of these women, 231 were subsequently diagnosed with gestational diabetes mellitus (GDM). Women with GDM were 7.7 times as likely (95% CI 2.8–21.1) to have an infant with a numeric sex chromosome defect as those without GDM, despite adjustment for age and BMI. These results suggest insulin resistance to be the primary association with the observed increased frequency of non-disjunction. This may suggest central or visceral obesity to be more important in the aetiology of miscarriage than 'overweight' alone.

Congenital abnormalities

Ultrasound imaging of the fetus in women who are grossly obese can be challenging. Adipose tissue can significantly attenuate the ultrasound signal by absorption of the associated energy. Therefore, a high-frequency, higher resolution signal would be more significantly absorbed at a lesser depth, necessitating sacrifice of image quality for depth of field. The first group to examine the efficacy of scanning the obese pregnant population was Wolfe et al. in 1990.[13] They showed that scans performed on women with a BMI greater than the 90th centile during the second and third trimester had a 14.5% reduction in visualisation of organs compared with lean women. This reduction was most marked when visualising the fetal heart, umbilical cord and spine. A study of routine ultrasound screening in pregnant women with diabetes identified the rate of major congenital anomalies among the women with diabetes to be 5.9-fold higher than controls (95% CI 2.9–11.9).[14] However, the detection rate was significantly lower for the women with diabetes compared with controls (30% versus 73%; $P < 0.01$) and this was related to the higher incidence of obesity. In an American retrospective cross-sectional study Hendler et al.[15] examined the rate of suboptimal ultrasonography visualisation in 11 019 pregnancies, of which 38.6% were in women who were obese (BMI $\geq$ 30 kg/m^2). This indicated that there was a 49.8% increase in the rate of suboptimal visualisation (SUV) of fetal cardiac anomalies and a 31% increase in SUV of craniospinal structures in women who were obese.

Studies have reported maternal obesity as an independent risk factor for fetal abnormalities including neural tube defects (NTDs) and other central nervous system anomalies (Table 11.3).[16] In 1994, a case–control study by Waller et al.[17] demonstrated that women with a BMI in excess of 31 kg/m^2 were also at risk of delivering a baby with NTDs (OR 1.8; 95% CI 1.1–3.0), especially spina bifida (OR 2.6; 95% CI 1.5–4.5). In addition, women who were obese had a significant risk of having a child with defects of the great vessels of the heart, ventral wall and intestinal tract.

A population-based study published in 2003 attempted to relate maternal obesity and overweight to several types of birth defect.[18] This case–control study examined major birth defects among approximately 40 000 births per year during the period 1993–97. This work confirmed findings from previous studies that women who were obese were around three times more likely than women of average weight to have an infant with either spina bifida or an omphalocoele. In addition, there was an increased incidence of rib defects, limb defects, holoprosencephaly, renal and urinary anomalies.

However, some further studies have not been able to reproduce these data. Feldman et al.[19] studied a large cohort (n = 72 915) of women based on biochemical screening and documented maternal weights and pregnancy outcomes. Their data concluded that there was no statistically significant difference in the incidence of NTDs between obese and non-obese patients.

Moore et al.[20] also concluded that there is no overall risk linking obesity and major congenital anomalies. This US prospective study (n = 22 951) examined the risk of non-chromosomal congenital anomalies associated with maternal obesity and diabetes. They concluded that there was no increased risk of NTDs, or other neurological, urogenital or cardiovascular anomalies in women who were obese. However, the adjusted relative risk (expressed as a prevalence risk (PR)) demonstrated a trend to

Table 11.3. Risks of fetal anomalies in association with obesity

Study	Study design	Risk of complication
Waller et al. (1994)[17]	Case–control study of NTDs and major birth defects in 1370 births during 1985–87	NTD: OR 1.8; 95% CI 1.1–3.0 Spina bifida: OR 2.6; 95% CI 1.5–4.5
Werler et al. (1996)[23]	Case–control surveillance programme of NTDs in 2355 births; relative risk for different maternal weights during 1988–94	Risk of NTDs: Maternal weight 80–89 kg: OR 1.9; 95% CI 1.2–2.9 Maternal weight 90–99 kg: OR 1.3; 95% CI 0.7–2.3 Maternal weight 100–109 kg: OR 3.1; 95% CI 1.4–7.0 Maternal weight ≥ 110 kg: OR 4.0; 95% CI 1.6–9.9
Feldman et al. (1999)[19]	Large cohort study of 72 915 consecutive cases of biochemical screening; five maternal weight ranges; data were analysed based on two groups, obese and non-obese (cut-off point 220 lbs)	Differences between maternal weight ranges were not statistically significant, $\chi^2 = 5.997$, $P = 0.19$, power = 0.99
Moore et al. (2000)[20]	Prospective study of birth defects associated with maternal obesity and diabetes mellitus in 22 951 births during 1984–87	Craniofacial defects: PR 2.2; 95% CI 0.9–5.4 Musculoskeletal defects: PR 1.5; 95% CI 0.7–3.4
Watkins et al. (2003)[18]	Case–control study of major birth defects among approximately 40 000 births per year during 1993–97	Spina bifida: OR 3.5; 95% CI 1.2–10.3 Omphalocele: OR 3.3; 95% CI 1.0–10.3 Heart defects: OR: 2.0; 95% CI 1.2–3.4
Anderson et al. (2005)[16]	Case–control study of major birth defects, maternal obesity and GDM in 974 births during 1997–2001	Anencephaly: OR 2.3; 95% CI 1.2–4.3 Spina bifida: OR 2.8; 95% CI 1.7–4.5 Isolated hydrocephaly: OR 2.7; 95% CI 1.5–5.0
	Case–control study of orofacial clefts among 988 171 births during1992–2001	Orofacial clefts: OR 1.30; 95% CI 1.11–1.53
Martinez-Frias et al. (2005)[22]	Case–control study and surveillance system of 61 000 births of mothers with GDM during 1976–2001	Obese and GDM: Overall risk of birth defects: OR 2.78; 95% CI 1.38–5.55 Cardiovascular defects: OR 2.82; 95% CI 1.31–7.04

CI = confidence interval; GDM = gestational diabetes mellitus; NTD = neural tube defect; OR = odds ratio; PR = prevalence ratio be higher for both craniofacial and musculoskeletal fetal abnormalities among the women who were obese (PR 2.2; 95% CI 0.91–5.4 and PR 1.5; 95% CI 0.69–3.4, respectively).

More specific congenital abnormalities have also been evaluated for an association with maternal obesity. A Swedish case–control study ($n = 988\ 171$) investigated whether women who were obese were more likely to have a child with orofacial cleft anomalies than women of normal weight.[21] A total of 1686 infants with orofacial cleft anomalies were identified and 84% of these defects were isolated. Cedergren et al.[21] found that women who were obese were at an increased risk of having a child with a cleft palate (adjusted OR 1.30; 95% CI 1.11–1.53), and that this risk was further increased when the clefts were associated with other malformations. This group hypothesised that these observations could be explained by the presence of undiagnosed type 2 diabetes in the obese population. In addition, the idea that poor nutrition could contribute was also postulated.

It is well recognised that maternal diabetes is a risk factor for the development of congenital abnormalities, including central nervous system defects. Research has also highlighted a multiplicative effect on the risk of central nervous system birth defects when maternal obesity and GDM exist contemporaneously. Anderson et al.[16] evaluated an American population in a case–control study ($n = 477$). After adjusting for maternal ethnicity, age, education, smoking, alcohol use and periconceptional vitamin use, women who were obese still had substantially increased risks of delivering offspring with anencephaly (OR 2.3; 95% CI 1.2–4.3), spina bifida (OR 2.8; 95% CI 1.7–4.5) and isolated hydrocephaly (OR 2.7; 95% CI 1.5–5.0). When GDM was examined in isolation, the only anomaly seen more frequently was holoprosencephaly. Also, mothers of infants with anencephaly were less likely to have GDM compared with the control group (OR 0.3; 95% CI 0.1–1.2). However, the authors commented that this disparity may be due to earlier termination rates for anencephaly compared with other defects. They concluded that the odds ratios for joint effects of GDM and maternal obesity were consistent with multiplicative interaction and these factors may operate through a shared causal mechanism.

Within a European population, Martinez-Frias et al.[22] investigated possible risk factors for the development of fetal anomalies in women with GDM. This hospital-based case–control study examined 61 000 women between 1976 and 2001. They did not study rates of NTDs. As seen in previous studies, their results were not entirely supportive of a link between obesity and congenital abnormalities. The data suggested that there was an increased risk of cardiovascular abnormalities in infants of women who had GDM, and that this relationship increased with an increase in pre-pregnancy BMI. However, in women who had normal glucose tolerance results, and who were also obese (prepregnancy BMI > 29.9 kg/m^2), there was no increased risk of the rate of congenital anomalies (OR 0.93; 95% CI 0.71–1.23) or congenital cardiac defects (OR 0.97; 95% CI 0.68–1.38). As suggested in the Swedish study, a possible hypothesis for the increased risk of anomalies in the obese GDM group could be the co-existence of undiagnosed pregestational type 2 diabetes.

The mechanisms involved in the association between obesity and congenital anomalies are not fully understood. Several possible hypotheses have been suggested. As highlighted already, the prevalence of undiagnosed type 2 diabetes or significant insulin resistance without frank glucose dysregulation may play more of a cardinal role than previously recognised. Epidemiological data from both the USA and Europe have suggested that 30–50% of adults with type 2 diabetes are undiagnosed. It has been concluded in some studies that prepregnancy diagnosis of diabetes may permit appropriate intervention prior to conception and that women who are obese and planning a pregnancy should be screened. One could postulate that weight reduction and tight glycaemic control may help reduce rates of congenital abnormalities in this high-risk group.

It has been observed that a contributing factor may be that women who are obese have increased nutritional requirements, or that nutritional deficiencies are the consequence of a poor-quality diet. Werler *et al.*[23] concluded that 400 µg of folic acid was protective against NTDs in women whose absolute body weight was less than 70 kg. This was not the case, however, in those greater than 70 kg. They also concluded that the risk of NTDs increases with maternal weight independent of folic acid intake.

Altered metabolic function has been documented in women who are obese. The role of hyperglycaemia, hyperinsulinaemia and elevated estrogen levels has been studied and hyperinsulinaemia has been noted to be an independent risk factor for NTDs.[24] In addition, the observed abnormal inflammatory and vascular profile displayed in the obese population may play a key role in this process.

Maternal obstetric complications

It is recognised that obesity is a risk factor for many maternal obstetric complications including pre-eclampsia and GDM. The mechanisms involved are complex but one possible unifying hypothesis encompasses a syndrome of insulin resistance, low-grade inflammation, dyslipidaemia and an alteration in systemic microvascular function. These different factors can all be described as part of the 'metabolic syndrome' and when manifest in pregnancy may predispose to placental vascular dysfunction. Links between obesity and the metabolic syndrome are well established and many of the clinical associations of the syndrome such as diabetes and hypertension may be observed in young pregnant women as GDM and pre-eclampsia (Figure 11.1).

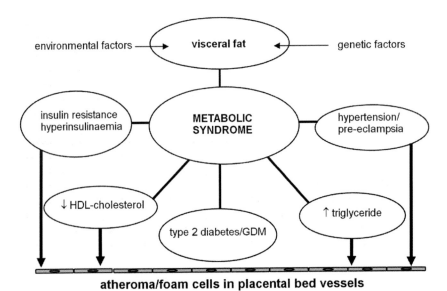

Figure 11.1. The metabolic syndrome and associations in pregnancy; HDL = high density lipoprotein; GDM = gestational diabetes mellitus

A plethora of data exists confirming the relationship between obesity and the development of pregnancy-induced hypertension and pre-eclampsia. In 1995, Sibai *et al.*[25] published a prospective multicentre study examining possible risk factors for pre-eclampsia. One variable included prepregnancy weight and they concluded that there was an increase of 20% in the occurrence of pre-eclampsia in women who were above their ideal weight. Sibai *et al.*[26] published further evidence based on the assessment of BMI in the early second trimester. This strongly predicted ($P < 0.0001$) the highest risk of pre-eclampsia being among women with BMI > 34 kg/m^2 (Figure 11.2).[12]

Most published work suggests between a two- and three-fold increase in risk of pre-eclampsia with a BMI of > 30 kg/m^2. However, waist circumference has also been reported to be a sensitive predictive marker of possible pregnancy hypertensive complications. In 2001, Sattar *et al.*[27] examined early pregnancy body composition data from 1142 pregnant women. Odds ratios were calculated for risk of hypertensive complications of pregnancy in association with a waist circumference > 80 cm at less than 16 weeks of gestation. The risk of pregnancy-induced hypertension was around two-fold greater (OR 1.8; 95% CI 1.1–2.9) and pre-eclampsia three-fold greater (OR 2.7; 95% CI 1.1–6.8) in association with central or visceral obesity.

In 2003, O'Brien *et al.*[28] carried out a systematic overview of 13 cohort studies including approximately 1.4 million women in order to assess the association between pre-eclampsia and maternal BMI. They observed that maternal obesity and insulin resistance are believed to be important risk factors in the development of placental endothelial dysfunction and pre-eclampsia. Their results indicated that there was an increase in the risk of pre-eclampsia as BMI rose, with the risk typically doubling for each 5–7 kg/m^2 increase in BMI.

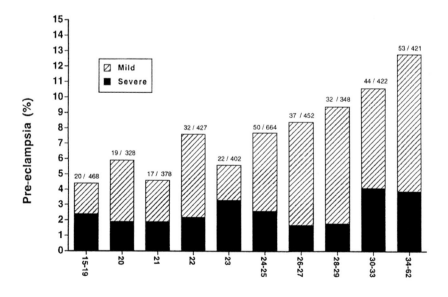

Figure 11.2. Linear elevation in risk of pre-eclampsia associated with BMI; reproduced with permission from Sibai *et al.*,[26] 1997 © Elsevier

Recent published data has aimed to quantify the independent relationship between the prepregnancy BMI and the risk of pre-eclampsia. In 2005, Bodnar et al.[29] examined a population of 1179 nulliparous women who were enrolled at 16 weeks of gestation. Results of this prospective study showed that the incidence of pre-eclampsia among women who were underweight, of normal weight, overweight or obese was 3.4%, 3.5% 8.0% and 6.4%, respectively. Blood pressure measurements were higher in the obese and overweight groups compared with the normal and underweight groups prior to 20 weeks of gestation. This difference, however, was not statistically significant. For unadjusted data, the relation between prepregnancy BMI and risk of pre-eclampsia was curvilinear. Adjusted results showed that the risk of pre-eclampsia doubled as the BMI rose from 21 to 26 kg/m^2 and nearly tripled at a BMI of 30 kg/m^2. It was observed that for a BMI of 30–35 kg/m^2 the risk remained relatively constant. At BMIs of greater than 35 kg/m^2 there was less information available and thus estimates became unreliable. However, Bodnar et al. repeated the multivariable analysis including nine women who had a BMI of greater than 46 kg/m^2 and found that the OR and the 95% confidence intervals for 35 and 40 kg/m^2 compared with a BMI of 21 kg/m^2 were 3.1 (1.6–5.9) and 3.0 (1.3–6.7), respectively. Based on these results one could conclude that at high BMI values the relationship between BMI and pre-eclampsia risk would be linear, but, as the study suggests, future data containing a larger sample size would be required to clarify the risk curve in women with very high BMI status.

Irrespective of this, the study suggests the possibility that women who are overweight could meaningfully lower their risk of pre-eclampsia with achievable reductions in body weight prior to pregnancy. If Bodnar's model is applied, then lowering of the prepregnancy BMI from 29.0 to 27.4 kg/m^2 (which would mean a weight loss of 4.5 kg or 10 lbs) in two women 1.65 m tall, would reduce the risk of developing pre-eclampsia by 50%. Such a modest reduction in weight is achievable and maintainable through lifestyle modification.

Interestingly and probably not surprisingly, a lot of data has been published in the USA and thus most of the available statistics are based on an American population model. However, rates of obesity have increased across Europe, including the UK. In Sweden the rates for obesity among fertile women doubled between 1980 and 1997. Cedergren et al.[30] observed that the numbers of women who were morbidly obese had markedly increased in Sweden over the past decade. They highlighted that although previous studies had shown that women who were morbidly obese had even more pregnancy complications and adverse outcomes, low patient numbers had often limited their statistical power. By assessing a large prospective data set, the Swedish group aimed to study the adverse obstetric and perinatal outcomes of a morbidly obese population. The study included 972 806 pregnancies in Sweden between 1992 and 2001. The subject group was further subdivided into women with BMI 35.1–40 kg/m^2 and women with BMI > 40 kg/m^2. The prevalence of a BMI between 35.1 and 40 kg/m^2 was 1.6% (12 698 of 805 275) and that of a BMI greater than 40 kg/m^2 was 0.4% (3480 of 805 275). The Scandinavian study showed that the risk of pre-eclampsia among women who were morbidly obese increased more than five-fold. The corresponding OR for women with BMIs between 35.1 and 40 kg/m^2 was 3.9 (95% CI 3.5–4.3). In the subgroup with a BMI of greater than 40 kg/m^2, the adjusted OR had further increased to 4.82 (95% CI 4.04–5.74). A merit of this study is that it examined a large European cohort. It supports previous evidence of the increased risk between pre-eclampsia and obesity. The authors further concluded that pregnancies among the morbidly obese population should be considered high risk and the women should receive appropriate antenatal care. The study highlighted the need for prepregnancy counselling and advice for this group of women. In addition, with appropriate weight management before and during pregnancy, postpartum weight gain may also be reduced and thus facilitate long-term behavioural changes with regard to nutrition and exercise.

Evidence of obesity among pregnant women as a worldwide concern was also examined in Australia by Callaway et al., in 2006.[31] They noted that 35% of Australian women between the ages of 25 and 35 years were overweight or obese but commented that the impact of obesity on the Australian obstetric population had not been assessed since 1981. They performed a retrospective review of data, and examined 11 252 singleton pregnancies delivered between January 1998 and December 2002. They divided their population into four subgroups based on their BMI. These groups were categorised according to their BMI as 'normal' (BMI 20.02–25 kg/m^2), 'overweight' (BMI 25.01–30 kg/m^2), 'obese' (BMI 30.01–40 kg/m^2), and 'morbidly obese' (BMI > 40 kg/m^2).

Using multiple logistic regression analysis, adjusted odds ratios were calculated for a number of variable outcomes. The risk of hypertensive disorders of pregnancy were increased in both the obese (OR 3.00; 95% CI 2.40–3.74) and morbidly obese (OR 4.87; 95% CI 3.27–7.24) in comparison with women of a normal BMI. In addition, the risk of development of GDM was also found to be increased in these subgroups, the OR for the obese subgroup was 2.95 (95% CI 2.05–4.25) and in the morbidly obese group OR was calculated as 7.44 (95% CI 4.42–12.54).

It is well documented that maternal obesity also increases the risk of GDM and that, along with pre-eclampsia, these complications can be categorised as part of the clinical manifestations of the metabolic syndrome as seen in pregnant women who are obese. GDM can be defined as carbohydrate intolerance of variable severity with onset or first recognition during pregnancy. Obesity is associated with marked hyperinsulinaemia (not necessarily with glucose dysregulation) and this has been demonstrated to persist to the third trimester of pregnancy.[32] GDM affects about 5% of all pregnancies.[33] Being overweight is a risk factor for carbohydrate intolerance both in the non-pregnant and pregnant state. Conversely, half of the women who develop GDM have no identifiable risk factor.[34]

In the Australian data,[31] the prevalence of pre-eclampsia and GDM were increased in their obese population. In 2004, Weiss et al.[35] carried out a large prospective study in the USA to determine the associations between obesity and obstetric complications. The authors examined a large multicentre database that included 16 102 women. Their results indicated that obesity and morbid obesity demonstrated a statistically significant association with gestational hypertension (OR 2.5 and 3.2, respectively), pre-eclampsia (OR 1.6 and 3.3, respectively) and GDM (OR 2.6 and 4.0, respectively). Interesting, Weiss et al. included overweight women in the control group (consisting of all women with a BMI < 30 kg/m^2), and thus concluded that their data may be more representative of the general US obstetric population.

Therefore evidence exists demonstrating an increased prevalence of pre-eclampsia and GDM in the obese population. Based on this evidence, can these conditions, if they were to co-exist in certain women, have an even greater impact on maternal obstetric complications? Previous studies have shown that in pregnant women with pre-existing diabetes, pre-eclampsia is associated with poor perinatal outcome, but hypertensive disorders are also increased in women diagnosed with GDM.[36] It has been documented that pregnancies that are complicated by pre-eclampsia have shown an exaggeration of the acquired third-trimester insulin resistance and hyperinsulinaemia which is seen in normal pregnancies.[37] Yogev et al.[36] studied the relationship between pre-eclampsia and the severity of GDM in a retrospective analysis of prospective data on 1813 patients diagnosed with GDM. Treatment categories were diet alone or diet and insulin therapy and were determined by the fasting glucose level from the oral glucose tolerance test (OGTT) (≤ 95 mg/dl). Although this study population did not consist of only women who were obese, the subgroup which developed pre-eclampsia (n = 174) had a 60% obesity rate, as opposed to those who did not develop pre-eclampsia (n = 1639), of whom 47% were obese. They found that those with more severe hyperglycaemia were significantly more likely to develop pre-eclampsia (OR 1.81; 95% CI 1.3–2.51). In addition, prepregnancy BMI and severity of GDM were independently and significantly associated with an increased rate of pre-eclampsia. They concluded that the rate of pre-eclampsia in GDM is associated with the severity of GDM and that optimising glycaemic control may help to reduce this risk.

Crowther et al.[38] conducted a randomised clinical trial to determine whether treatment of women with GDM reduced the risk of perinatal complications. The rate of serious perinatal complications was significantly lower among the infants of the women in the intervention group than among the infants of the women in the routine care group (1% versus 4%; P = 0.01). If GDM is diagnosed, tight metabolic control should be achieved through diet and, when indicated, insulin therapy. Insulin therapy is required more often in women who are obese with GDM than in lean women with the condition.[39]

In the long term, mothers with GDM have least a 50% greater chance of developing diabetes than the general population[40,41] and this risk may be greatest in obese women.[42] Therefore, in women who are obese with GDM it would seem that pregnancy offers an ideal opportunity for future lifestyle advice with regard to exercise and weight loss in order to reduce this potential for vascular disease in the long term.

As described previously, Sattar et al.[27] examined the relationship between waist circumference and the development of pre-eclampsia. In 2006, Cho et al.[43] investigated the association between waist circumference in women with a history of GDM as a risk factor for the development of diabetes in later life. A prospective study enrolled 909 women with a history of GDM. They were initially seen 6 weeks postpartum and then followed up annually. Assessment was based on 2 hour OGTT (75 g), including measured glucose, insulin, C-peptide, lipid profiles and lifestyle and dietary evaluation. The obesity parameters assessed were waist and hip circumference, subcutaneous fat thickness, percentage body fat and weight using bioelectrical impedance tests. Their results indicated that the diabetic incidence for 6 years was 12.8% and that all obesity parameters were increased in women who were either diabetic or displayed glucose intolerance (P < 0.001). Furthermore, when obesity indices for < 25th centile and > 75th centile were compared, an increased waist circumference presented the strongest data correlation (OR 5.8; 95% CI 2.8–11.8) and, after potential confounders were adjusted, this persisted (OR 3.86; 95% CI 1.8–8.2). They concluded that waist circumference, and thus central obesity, was a key risk factor for the development of diabetes in later life, in a population of women with a history of GDM.

So far the evidence of the associated risks of obesity has been studied almost exclusively within the pregnant adult population. But what of the risks associated in the adolescent population? Teenage pregnancy remains topical in the press and in 1999 the government published its Teenage Pregnancy Strategy to try to reduce teenage pregnancy rates.[44] The conception rate has declined (by 11.1% between 1998 and 2004), but current figures report 39 000 pregnancies per year in England in women aged under 18 years. It is accepted that an adolescent pregnancy has serious physical and mental health repercussions, as well as social and economic risks. However, little research had been conducted into the risks associated in the obese adolescent population. Sukalich et al.[45] published US data examining adverse obstetric outcomes in women under 19 years of age who were obese. Of the 93 605 deliveries observed between 1998 and 2003, 5851 were in women under 19 years (5361 women had documented height and prepregnancy weight). In a retrospective case–control study they found that 1498 were overweight or obese (BMI $\geq$ 25 kg/m^2), and that 3324 were of normal weight (BMI 18.5–24.9 kg/m^2). Women with a BMI of less than 18.5 kg/m^2 were excluded from the analysis (n = 539). This study illustrated that there was a step-wise increase in the risk of pre-eclampsia over all groups. Odds ratios for overweight, obese and morbidly obese were 1.6, 1.9 and 3.0, respectively (95% CI 1.2–1.4). The risk of GDM also increased in a linear manner across the overweight and obese groups and was statistically significant (OR 3.0; 95% CI 1.6–5.4). Perhaps the greatest concern is that this population group still has a long potential reproductive lifespan and yet at this stage they already demonstrate serious obstetric complications that may recur in future pregnancies.

When considering the risks associated with obesity and pregnancy, the importance of inter-pregnancy weight change must not be underestimated. Villamor et al.[46] published striking data that investigated this association, based on a large prospective-based study (n = 151 025) in Sweden (Table 11.4). They examined the links between inter-pregnancy BMI changes from first to second pregnancies and the risks of adverse outcomes in the second pregnancies. Maternal obstetric complications included pre-eclampsia and GDM. The relationship between adverse outcomes and weight gain was linear, even after adjustment for confounders. The risk of pre-eclampsia, gestational hypertension and GDM started to rise after the BMI rose by 1 kg/m^2 to less than 2 kg/m^2 and continued to increase progressively thereafter. It was noted that the risk of pre-eclampsia fell significantly in women who had lost more than one BMI unit between pregnancies when compared with the control group. To examine the effects of weight gain independently of obesity, a subset of 97 558 women whose BMI was less than 25 kg/m^2 was analysed. Surprisingly, the linear associations between gestational hypertension and GDM were significantly stronger in women whose BMI

Table 11.4. Adjusted odds ratios for obstetric complications in second pregnancy associated with changes in BMI since first pregnancy, by categories of BMI at first pregnancy: reproduced with permission from Villamor et al.,[46] 2006 © Elsevier

	Gestational hypertension				Gestational diabetes mellitus			
	First pregnancy BMI < 25 (n = 401)		First pregnancy BMI $\geq$ 25 (n = 300)		First pregnancy BMI < 25 (n = 417)		First pregnancy BMI $\geq$ 25 (n = 313)	
Change in BMI	Rate (%)	OR (95% CI)	Rate (%)	OR (95% CI)	Rate (%)	OR (95% CI)	Rate (%)	OR (95% CI)
< −1	0.3	1.09 (0.72–1.65)	0.8	0.98 (0.70–1.37)	0.3	0.89 (0.58–1.36)	0.7	0.96 (0.66–1.37)
−1 to < 1	0.3	1.00	0.8	1.00	0.3	1.00	0.7	1.00
1 to < 2	0.5	1.86 (1.45–2.38)	0.7	0.81 (0.56–1.16)	0.4	1.35 (1.04–1.74)	0.9	1.29 (0.93–1.81)
2 to < 3	0.5	1.94 (1.41–2.67)	0.9	1.02 (0.70–1.49)	0.5	1.95 (1.44–2.64)	1.0	1.36 (0.94–1.96)
$\geq$ 3	0.5	2.49 (1.79–3.47)	1.0	1.20 (0.87–1.67)	0.7	2.88 (2.15–3.88)	1.2	1.54 (1.11–2.13)
P, trend	< 0.0001	< 0.0001	0.22	0.32	< 0.0001	< 0.0001	0.0002	0.002
P, interaction	< 0.0001				0.0005			

was less than 25 kg/m² as compared with mothers who were overweight or obese. The data suggested that a gain of 1–2 kg/m² over an average of 2 years would increase the risk of development of gestational hypertension and GDM by 20–40% and a further linear increase in risk would follow further weight gain. More importantly, inter-pregnancy weight gain increases the risk of complications in women who were not overweight. Results indicated that even a modest increase in weight, resulting in a shift from healthy to overweight, could be enough to increase a woman's average risk of adverse pregnancy outcomes. In statistical terms, if a woman with a healthy BMI of 23 kg/m² gained 3 kg (1 BMI unit), between her first and second pregnancies, and even if she remained within a normal BMI, her risk for GDM would have increased by 30%. Had she become overweight (6 kg weight gain), her average risk would be increased by 100%, and if she became obese the average risk would rise by 200%.

Mechanisms

As described above, adipose tissue, particularly abdominal fat, is a source of free fatty acids and cytokines that contribute to dyslipidaemia, endothelial dysfunction and impaired insulin sensitivity. These mechanisms have been proposed to underlie coronary artery disease and similarly may explain the metabolic complications of pregnancy such as pre-eclampsia and GDM. However, whether such effects of adiposity are sustained during pregnancy has been sparsely investigated. Ramsay et al.[32] examined a detailed panel of metabolic and inflammatory parameters in lean and obese pregnant women during the third trimester. These data confirmed that as in non-pregnant obese individuals, obesity in pregnancy is associated with metabolic, inflammatory and vascular risk factors that may contribute to maternal complications in women who are obese. This has since been confirmed in a prospective study, by the same group.[47] (Table 11.5). In general, the women who were obese demonstrated a pro-inflammatory phenotype with impaired microvascular function from early in pregnancy. In lean women, inflammatory features were acquired in later pregnancy with an eventual apparent switch to a T_h2 system of inflammatory cytokines.

Despite this physiological effect, the women who were obese always demonstrated a more inflammatory process with consequent failure of pregnancy to achieve the normal increases in endothelial-dependent vasodilatation.[47] Levels of plasminogen activator inhibitor 2 (PAI-2) in women who were obese were also significantly less than in lean women in the first trimester, perhaps suggesting impaired placental function in women who are obese even at this early stage (Figure 11.3). This could provide more mechanistic evidence for the observed increased rate of miscarriage seen in women who are obese as discussed above.

In pre-eclamptic pregnancies the physiological hypertriglyceridaemia observed in healthy pregnancy is exaggerated. Fasting triglyceride concentrations are doubled compared with normal pregnancy and a three-fold increase in very low density lipoprotein (VLDL) and low density lipoprotein (LDL-III) concentrations are also observed.[48] Significantly, this hypertriglyceridaemia is observed well in advance of the clinical manifestations of the disease. As described above, these changes could contribute to endothelial damage and insulin resistance. It is also notable that the specific vascular lesion of pre-eclampsia 'acute atherosis with lipid-laden foam cells' as observed in the intima of the spiral arterioles of the placental bed, is similar to that seen in arteriosclerosis in non-pregnant women.[48] Pre-eclampsia is also believed to be a disease of inflammation and there is now substantial published evidence in this field (Redman et al.[49]). Granulocytes and monocytes are activated with increased

Table 11.5. Changes in plasma concentrations of soluble markers of inflammation and endothelial function with advancing gestation in lean and obese pregnant women; reproduced with permission from Stewart et al.,[47] 2007 © The Endocrine Society

Inflammatory marker	Plasma concentration (median and IQ range)		P value (lean vs obese)[a]
	Lean women	Obese women	
IL-6 (pg/ml)	P < 0.001[b]	P = 0.36[b]	
1st trimester	0.80 (0.50–0.93)	1.55 (1.10–2.65)	< 0.001
2nd trimester	1.00 (0.70–1.60)	1.80 (1.10–3.13)	0.001
3rd trimester	1.60 (1.10–2.00)	2.00 (1.38–3.05)	0.074
Postnatal	0.85 (0.60–1.38)	1.55 (1.05–3.18)	0.110
TNF-α (pg/ml)	P = 0.003[b]	P < 0.001[b]	
1st trimester	1.25 (1.00–1.80)	1.20 (0.98–1.60)	0.36
2nd trimester	1.50 (1.05–1.90)	1.20 (0.98–1.50)	0.39
3rd trimester	2.00 (1.38–2.48)	1.70 (1.40–2.48)	0.70
Postnatal	1.60 (1.10–2.40)	1.40 (1.20–2.00)	0.38
CRP (mg/l)	P < 0.001[b]	P < 0.001[b]	
1st trimester	3.25 (1.45–4.99)	8.43 (3.87–13.1)	0.001
2nd trimester	3.38 (1.47–5.61)	8.58 (4.23–12.6)	0.002
3rd trimester	3.11 (1.54–4.16)	4.80 (3.01–12.6)	0.028
Postnatal	1.02 (0.69–2.26)	4.76 (1.48–11.2)	0.003
IL-10 (pg/ml)	P = 0.51[b]	P = 0.33[b]	
1st trimester	1.10 (0.80–1.53)	1.00 (0.83–1.10)	0.19
2nd trimester	1.10 (0.90–1.45)	0.95 (0.83–1.20)	0.055
3rd trimester	1.10 (0.98–1.60)	1.00 (0.80–1.20)	0.86
Postnatal	1.20 (0.80–1.60)	1.10 (1.00–1.50)	0.69
sICAM-1 (ng/ml)	P < 0.001[b]	P = 0.029[b]	
1st trimester	147 (125–164)	176 (143–206)	0.003
2nd trimester	178 (151–228)	204 (175–244)	0.020
3rd trimester	170 (138–193)	174 (151–207)	0.20
Postnatal	159 (138–203)	205 (146–223)	0.085
sVCAM-1 (ng/ml)	P < 0.001[b]	P < 0.001[b]	
1st trimester	281 (230–314)	318 (260–354)	0.10
2nd trimester	347 (323–387)	355 (334–386)	0.54
3rd trimester	371 (342–394)	377 (334–428)	0.71
Postnatal	307 (253–381)	305 (262–354)	0.46
vWF (mU/ml)	P < 0.001[b]	P < 0.001[b]	
1st trimester	852 (658–1187)	769 (502–1319)	0.84
2nd trimester	1407 (854–1982)	1615 (1053–2012)	0.27
3rd trimester	2309 (1744–3009)	2497 (1877–3209)	0.79
Postnatal	667 (511–840)	602 (504–930)	0.82
PAI-1 (ng/ml)	P < 0.001[b]	P < 0.001[b]	
1st trimester	12.2 (8.5–17.6)	15.9 (13.1–17.3)	0.010
2nd trimester	36.9 (32.4–73.1)	34.5 (26.8–40.0)	0.15
3rd trimester	67.0 (52.3–103.1)	72.5 (51.3–123.6)	0.59
Postnatal	8.6 (6.0–10.1)	11.5 (6.218.3)	0.049
PAI-2 (ng/ml)	P < 0.001[b]	P < 0.001[b]	
1st trimester	36.5 (23.5–72.3)	18.5 (13.8–33.7)	0.001
2nd trimester	312 (232–417)	314 (269–445)	0.79
3rd trimester	491 (369–710)	450 (346–648)	0.48
Postnatal	1.6 (0.5–4.1)	1.0 (0.4–3.7)	0.65

[a] difference testing was carried out using two sample t-test on transformed data
[b] differences between time points was carried out on transformed data using repeated measures ANOVA in a general linear model
IQ range = interquartile range; IL-6 = interleukin 6; IL-10 = interleukin 10; TNF-α = tumour necrosis factor α; CRP = C-reactive protein; sICAM-1 = soluble intercellular adhesion molecule-1; sVCAM-1 = soluble vascular cell adhesion molecule-1; vWF = von Willebrand factor; PAI-1 = plasminogen activator inhibitor 1; PAI-2 = plasminogen activator inhibitor 2

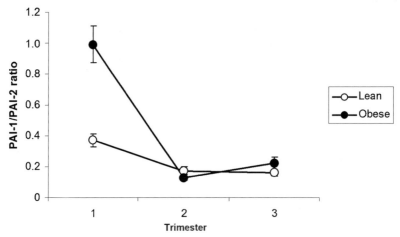

Figure 11.3. Plasminogen activator inhibitor 1/plasminogen activator inhibitor 2 ratio with advancing gestation; means with standard error are shown; ratios were significantly higher in women who were obese compared with lean women in the first trimester only; reproduced with permission from Stewart et al.,[47] 2007 © The Endocrine Society

release of pro-inflammatory cytokines such as tumour necrosis factor α (TNF-α) and interleukin 6 (IL-6). Increases in serum concentrations of the cell adhesion molecules VCAM-1 and ICAM-1 have also been demonstrated in women with pre-eclampsia. These metabolic and inflammatory stimuli that are suggested to promote microvascular dysfunction in pre-eclampsia are proposed to arise from the placenta. However, it seems reasonable to assume that the excess inflammatory burden as would be seen in pregnant women who are obese could potentially add fuel to this process, explaining some of the increased association of obesity with pre-eclampsia and GDM. Certainly, higher levels of fasting triglyceride concentrations and lower HDL-cholesterol have previously been demonstrated in the third trimester in pregnant women who are obese.[32]

Intervention and outcome

In women who are obese, the possibility must be considered for modification of risk factors in advance of, or early, in a pregnancy (Box 11.1). Weight loss through diet and exercise must be recommended and women informed of the potential for increased complications for both themselves and their offspring in the event of a pregnancy. Increased physical activity in women who are sedentary may result in a better pregnancy outcome for both mother and child. There are preliminary data to support this hypothesis and also some encouraging data on the effects of exercise in pregnancy on fetal development, with significantly higher birthweights and faster mid-trimester growth rates demonstrated[50,51]

Exercise in pregnancy may also reduce pregnancy complications such as GDM and does not appear to be harmful, with no association with premature labour or poor Apgar scores.[52]

Conclusion

Obesity in pregnancy is a significant health risk with linear associations observed between increasing BMI and complications such as GDM and pre-eclampsia. Women who are obese are at greater risk of miscarriage and fetal abnormalities and therefore addressing the exponentially increasing rates of this global epidemic are paramount for future health care.

Box 11.1.   Clinical suggestions for management of pregnancy in women who are obese (BMI > 35 kg/m²)

---

1. Prepregnancy counselling for women who are morbidly obese (subfertility/recurrent miscarriage/ diabetic clinics):
   - consider high doses of folic acid (5 mg)
   - importance of healthy diet and exercise in pregnancy: refer dietician, avoid excessive weight gain, consider screening for diabetes.
2. Early booking visit to plan pregnancy management:
   - low-dose aspirin in the presence of additional clinical risk factors for pre-eclampsia
   - consider antenatal thromboprophylaxis if additional clinical risk factors for venous thromboembolic disease (VTE).
3. Recommend detailed anomaly scan and serum screening for congenital abnormality.
4. Consider glucose tolerance testing at 28 weeks of gestation with potential for repeat in later pregnancy.

References

1. Confidential Enquiry into Maternal and Child Health. *Why Mothers Die 2000–2002. The Sixth Report of the Confidential Enquires Into Maternal Deaths in the United Kingdom.* London; RCOG Press; 2004.
2. Kanagalingam MG, Forouhi NG, Greer IA, Sattar N. Changes in booking body mass index over a decade: retrospective analysis from a Glasgow Maternity Hospital. *BJOG* 2005;112:1431–3.
3. Zaninotto P, Wardle H, Stamatakis E, Mindell J, Head J. *Forecasting Obesity to 2010.* London: National Centre for Social Research for Department of Health; 2006.
4. Hamilton-Fairley D, Kiddy D, Watson H, Paterson C, Franks S. Association of moderate obesity with a poor pregnancy outcome in women with polycystic ovary syndrome treated with low dose gonadotrophin. *Br J Obstet Gynaecol* 1992;99:128–31.
5. Mulders AG, Laven JS, Eijkemans MJ, Hughes EG, Fauser BC. Patient predictors for outcome of gonadotrophin ovulation induction in women with normogonadotrophic anovulatory infertility: a meta-analysis. *Hum Reprod Update* 2003;9:429–49.
6. Lashen H, Fear K, Sturdee DW. Obesity is associated with increased risk of first trimester and recurrent miscarriage: matched case–control study. *Hum Reprod* 2004;19:1644–6.
7. Bellver J, Rossal LP, Bosch E, Zuniga A, Corona JT, Melendez F, *et al.* Obesity and the risk of spontaneous abortion after oocyte donation. *Fertil Steril* 2003;79:1136–40.
8. Dale PO, Tanbo T, Haug E, Abyholm T. The impact of insulin resistance on the outcome of ovulation induction with low-dose follicle stimulating hormone in women with polycystic ovary syndrome. *Hum Reprod* 1998;13:567–70.
9. Glueck CJ, Phillips H, Cameron D, Sieve-Smith L, Wang P. Continuing metformin throughout pregnancy in women with polycystic ovary syndrome appears to safely reduce first-trimester spontaneous abortion: a pilot study. *Fertil Steril* 2001;75:46–52.
10. Glueck CJ, Wang P, Goldenberg N, Sieve L. Pregnancy loss, polycystic ovary syndrome, thrombophilia, hypofibrinolysis, enoxaparin, metformin. *Clin Appl Thromb Hemost* 2004;10:323–34.

11. Glueck CJ, Sieve L, Zhu B, Wang P. Plasminogen activator inhibitor activity, 4G5G polymorphism of the plasminogen activator inhibitor 1 gene, and first-trimester miscarriage in women with polycystic ovary syndrome. *Metabolism* 2006;55:345–52.

12. Moore LL, Bradlee ML, Singer MR, Rothman KJ, Milunsky A. Chromosomal anomalies among the offspring of women with gestational diabetes. *Am J Epidemiol* 2002;155:719–24.

13. Wolfe HM, Sokol RJ, Martier SM, Zador IE. Maternal obesity: a potential source of error in sonographic prenatal diagnosis. *Obstet Gynecol* 1990;76(3 Pt 1):339–42.

14. Wong SF, Chan FY, Cincotta RB, Oats JJ, McIntyre HD. Routine ultrasound screening in diabetic pregnancies. *Ultrasound Obstet Gynecol* 2002;19:171–6.

15. Hendler I, Blackwell SC, Bujold E, Treadwell MC, Wolfe HM, Sokol RJ, et al. The impact of maternal obesity on midtrimester sonographic visualization of fetal cardiac and craniospinal structures. *Int J Obes Relat Metab Disord* 2004;28:1607–11.

16. Anderson JL, Waller DK, Canfield MA, Shaw GM, Watkins ML, Werler MM. Maternal obesity, gestational diabetes, and central nervous system birth defects. *Epidemiology* 2005;16:87–92.

17. Waller DK, Mills JL, Simpson JL, Cunningham GC, Conley MR, Lassman MR, et al. Are obese women at higher risk for producing malformed offspring? *Am J Obstet Gynecol* 1994;170:541–8.

18. Watkins ML, Rasmussen SA, Honein MA, Botto LD, Moore CA. Maternal obesity and risk for birth defects. *Pediatrics* 2003;111(5 part 2):1152–8.

19. Feldman B, Yaron Y, Critchfield G, Leon J, O'Brien JE, Johnson MP, et al. Distribution of neural tube defects as a function of maternal weight: no apparent correlation. *Fetal Diagn Ther* 1999;14:185–9.

20. Moore LL, Singer MR, Bradlee ML, Rothman KJ, Milunsky A. A prospective study of the risk of congenital defects associated with maternal obesity and diabetes mellitus. *Epidemiology* 2000;11:689–94.

21. Cedergren M, Kallen B. Maternal obesity and the risk for orofacial clefts in the offspring. *Cleft Palate Craniofac J* 2005;42:367–71.

22. Martinez-Frias ML, Frias JP, Bermejo E, Rodriguez-Pinilla E, Prieto L, Frias JL. Pre-gestational maternal body mass index predicts an increased risk of congenital malformations in infants of mothers with gestational diabetes. *Diabet Med* 2005;22:775–81.

23. Werler MM, Louik C, Shapiro S, Mitchell AA. Prepregnant weight in relation to risk of neural tube defects. *JAMA* 1996;275:1089–92.

24. Yu CK, Teoh TG, Robinson S. Obesity in pregnancy. *BJOG* 2006;113:1117–25.

25. Sibai BM, Gordon T, Thom E, Caritis SN, Klebanoff M, McNellis D, et al. Risk factors for preeclampsia in healthy nulliparous women: a prospective multicenter study. The National Institute of Child Health and Human Development Network of Maternal-Fetal Medicine Units. *Am J Obstet Gynecol* 1995;172(2 Pt 1):642–8.

26. Sibai BM, Ewell M, Levine RJ, Klebanoff MA, Esterlitz J, Catalano PM, et al. Risk factors associated with preeclampsia in healthy nulliparous women. The Calcium for Preeclampsia Prevention (CPEP) Study Group. *Am J Obstet Gynecol* 1997;177:1003–10.

27. Sattar N, Clark P, Holmes A, Lean ME, Walker I, Greer IA. Antenatal waist circumference and hypertension risk. *Obstet Gynecol* 2001;97:268–71.

28. O'Brien TE TE, Ray JG, Chan WS. Maternal body mass index and the risk of preeclampsia: a systematic overview. *Epidemiology* 2003;14:368–74.

29. Bodnar LM, Ness RB, Markovic N, Roberts JM. The risk of preeclampsia rises with increasing prepregnancy body mass index. *Ann Epidemiol* 2005;15:475–82.

30. Cedergren MI. Maternal morbid obesity and the risk of adverse pregnancy outcome. *Obstet Gynecol* 2004;103:219–24.

31. Callaway LK, Prins JB, Chang AM, McIntyre HD. The prevalence and impact of overweight and obesity in an Australian obstetric population. *Med J Aust* 2006;184:56–9.

32. Ramsay JE, Ferrell WR, Crawford L, Wallace AM, Greer IA, Sattar N. Maternal obesity is associated with dysregulation of metabolic, vascular, and inflammatory pathways. *J Clin Endocrinol Metab* 2002;87:4231–7.

33. Ben-Haroush A, Yogev Y, Hod M. Epidemiology of gestational diabetes mellitus and its association with Type 2 diabetes. *Diabet Med* 2004;21:103–13.

34. Lavin JP Jr. Screening of high-risk and general populations for gestational diabetes. Clinical application and cost analysis. *Diabetes* 1985;2:24–7.

35. Weiss JL, Malone FD, Emig D, Ball RH, Nyberg DA, Comstock CH, *et al.* Obesity, obstetric complications and cesarean delivery rate – a population-based screening study. *Am J Obstet Gynecol* 2004;190:1091–7.

36. Yogev Y, Xenakis EM, Langer O. The association between preeclampsia and the severity of gestational diabetes: the impact of glycemic control. *Am J Obstet Gynecol* 2004;191:1655–60.

37. Seely EW, Solomon CG. Insulin resistance and its potential role in pregnancy-induced hypertension. *J Clin Endocrinol Metab* 2003;88:2393–8.

38. Crowther CA, Hiller JE, Moss JR, McPhee AJ, Jeffries WS, Robinson JS, *et al.* Effect of treatment of gestational diabetes mellitus on pregnancy outcomes. *N Engl J Med* 2005;352:2477–86.

39. Comtois R, Seguin MC, Aris-Jilwan N, Couturier M, Beauregard H. Comparison of obese and non-obese patients with gestational diabetes. *Int J Obes Relat Metab Disord* 1993;17:605–8.

40. Buchanan TA, Kjos SL. Gestational diabetes: risk or myth? *J Clin Endocrinol Metab* 1999;84:1854–7.

41. Linne Y, Barkeling B, Rossner S. Natural course of gestational diabetes mellitus: long term follow up of women in the SPAWN study. *BJOG* 2002;109:1227–31.

42. Schranz AG, Savona-Ventura C. Long-term significance of gestational carbohydrate intolerance: a longitudinal study. *Exp Clin Endocrinol Diabetes* 2002;110:219–22.

43. Cho NH, Jang HC, Park HK, Cho YW. Waist circumference is the key risk factor for diabetes in Korean women with history of gestational diabetes. *Diab Res Clin Pract* 2006;71:177–83.

44. DfES. *Teenage Pregnancy Next Steps: Guidance for Local Authorities and Primary Care Trusts on Effective Delivery of Local Strategies.* London: Department for Education and Skills; 2006.

45. Sukalich S, Mingione MJ, Glantz JC. Obstetric outcomes in overweight and obese adolescents. *Am J Obstet Gynecol* 2006;195:851–5.

46. Villamor E, Cnattingius S. Interpregnancy weight change and risk of adverse pregnancy outcomes: a population-based study. *Lancet* 2006;368:1164–70.

47. Stewart FM, Freeman DJ, Ramsay JE, Greer IA, Caslake M, Ferrell WR. Longitudinal assessment of maternal endothelial function and markers of inflammation and placental function throughout pregnancy in lean and obese mothers. *J Clin Endocrinol Metab* 2007;92:969–75.

48. Sattar N, Greer IA, Louden J, Lindsay G, McConnell M, Shepherd J, *et al.* Lipoprotein subfraction changes in normal pregnancy: threshold effect of plasma triglyceride on appearance of small, dense low density lipoprotein. *J Clin Endocrinol Metab* 1997;82:2483–91.

49. Redman CW, Sacks GP, Sargent IL. Preeclampsia: an excessive maternal inflammatory response to pregnancy. *Am J Obstet Gynecol* 1999;180(2 Pt 1):499–506.

50. Clapp JF 3rd, Kim H, Burciu B, Lopez B. Beginning regular exercise in early pregnancy: effect on fetoplacental growth. *Am J Obstet Gynecol* 2000;183:1484–8.

51. Campbell MK, Mottola MF. Recreational exercise and occupational activity during pregnancy and birth weight: a case–control study. *Am J Obstet Gynecol* 2001;184:403–8.

52. Carpenter MW. The role of exercise in pregnant women with diabetes mellitus. *Clin Obstet Gynaecol* 2000;43:56–64.

Chapter 12

Maternal obesity and adverse pregnancy outcomes: the role of nutrition and physical activity

Lisa Bodnar

Obesity is a substantial and escalating health problem worldwide. As thoroughly reviewed in Chapter 11, maternal obesity is linked to a host of perinatal problems that increase risk of pregnancy complications and adverse birth outcomes, including congenital anomalies, miscarriage, gestational diabetes and pre-eclampsia. As poor nutritional status and physical inactivity are common among women who are overweight, a logical question is whether such behaviours might contribute to these adverse outcomes. This information would be useful not only for understanding the mechanisms underlying the association between obesity and pregnancy outcomes, but also for targeting prenatal interventions for women who enter pregnancy when they are overweight or obese. Weight loss, even among women who are obese, is not recommended during pregnancy.[1] Healthcare professionals may, however, encourage pregnant women who are overweight to improve their diet quality and physical activity patterns as a potential means of preventing poor outcomes.

The objectives of this chapter are two-fold. First, it seeks to critically review the literature on the effect of dietary intake and leisure-time physical activity on congenital anomalies, miscarriage, diabetes and pre-eclampsia. The second goal is to relate these findings to obesity, and specifically to discuss the likelihood that improving diet and physical activity patterns could improve outcomes for women who enter pregnancy when they are overweight.

Literature review

Undoubtedly, the aetiologies of congenital malformations, miscarriage, gestational diabetes mellitus (GDM) and pre-eclampsia are multi-factorial. But for each of these adverse outcomes, there is evidence that behavioural or 'lifestyle' risk factors, including maternal nutritional status and leisure-time physical activity, may play an important role in their pathophysiology.

Congenital anomalies

Neural tube defects (NTDs) are major birth defects that have devastating consequences for families. The primary prevention of NTDs in the UK relies exclusively on folic acid supplementation in women of childbearing age,[2] while in the USA it hinges on both folic acid supplementation[3] and fortification of flour with folic acid.[4]

Nevertheless, improvements in folic acid nutriture do not eliminate all NTDs and scientists continue to search for modifiable risk factors for NTDs and other major birth defects, such as orofacial clefts and heart defects.

Folate and other B vitamins

The causal relation between periconceptional folate deficiency and NTD risk is the best known in all of perinatal health. The randomised trial of periconceptional folic acid conducted by the Medical Research Council Vitamin Study Group provided the most conclusive evidence of this effect. Supplementation with 4 mg/day of folic acid before and during early pregnancy among high-risk women reduced the recurrence rate of NTD by 71%.[5] Czeizel and colleagues[6,7] subsequently demonstrated that periconceptional folic acid prevents the first occurrence of NTDs and other major congenital abnormalities. Observational studies assessing dietary and/or supplemental folate intake have supported these data in relation to NTDs,[8,9] orofacial clefts,[10-12] and heart defects.[13]

Serum vitamin B_{12} concentrations measured in pregnancy or postpartum have been lower in mothers of malformed offspring in some studies[14-17] but not others.[18-20] Intakes of thiamine, niacin and pyridoxine at 14 months postpartum were found to be significantly lower in mothers of children with an orofacial cleft than control mothers.[21] These previous studies, however, collected blood or measured diet after the malformation was discovered and may not reflect nutritional status around the critical window of development.

Zinc

Investigation into the association between maternal zinc status and the risk of congenital malformations has been hampered by the difficulty in accurately assessing zinc nutriture.[22] In the most rigorous study to date, Velie et al.[23] found that women with high total preconceptional zinc intakes were 35% less likely to have an NTD-affected pregnancy than women with the lowest zinc intakes (OR 0.65; 95% CI 0.43–0.99), even after controlling for total folate intake and sociodemographic and lifestyle variables. Other studies of blood zinc concentrations, measured in pregnant women with a malformed fetus or postpartum women with a malformed offspring, have yielded conflicting results.[24-26] Ecological studies have found an increased incidence of NTDs in Egypt and the Middle East, where zinc intake is chronically low.[27] Additionally, women with acrodermatitis enteropathica, a very rare genetic disorder of zinc metabolism, are at increased risk of NTDs.[28] Although a Cochrane review of zinc supplementation trials failed to show a protective effect against congenital malformations,[29] the meta-analysis lacked sufficient sample size for reliable comparisons and supplementation was not commenced early enough in trials to address the outcome of interest. Preliminary data from an intervention study in Indonesia have found that mothers supplemented with zinc had a significantly lower incidence of cleft lip/palate in their offspring than children of mothers given placebo (1.2% versus 0%).[30] The final analysis of these data will clarify a number of unanswered questions about zinc nutriture and congenital malformations.

Antioxidants

Oxidative stress may contribute to congenital malformations, particularly in the setting of a diabetic pregnancy.[31] Selenium is an essential component of the antioxidant enzyme glutathione peroxidase. Mothers with NTD-affected pregnancies have been reported to have lower selenium concentrations in serum[24,32,33] and hair[32] than control mothers. Because selenium was determined in women who had already conceived a malformed fetus, altered selenium status may be a consequence rather than a contributor to disease risk. Vitamin C has received little attention in relation to malformations. Schorah et al.[34] measured preconceptional concentrations of leucocyte vitamin C in unsupplemented women who were at high risk of a recurrent NTD and reported that high-risk women were more likely than low-risk women to have inadequate vitamin C status. None of the aforementioned investigators studied women with diabetes. Periconceptional antioxidant therapy may confer some protective benefit against malformations in diabetic rat pregnancies[35-37] but its effect has not been studied in human pregnancy.

Diet patterns

Diet is a complex exposure and its complexity is often not captured by studying individual nutrients alone. The use of a composite score of diet quality has the advantage of being able to express many aspects of dietary intake concurrently. Carmichael et al.[38] developed a periconceptional diet quality index based on low (less than 10th percentile) intakes of folate, iron, vitamin B_6, vitamin A and calcium, and high (greater than 90th percentile) intakes of fat and sweets as percentages of total energy. Diet quality scores ranged from 0 to 14. The investigators observed that women who had a low score (< 4) on the index had an increased risk of an NTD-affected pregnancy (OR 1.6; 95% CI 1.0–2.6).

Diets that alter glycaemic control and insulin demand may cause markedly elevated glucose concentrations, which are thought to contribute to the development of congenital malformations.[39] A population-based case–control study in California[40] found that women with high periconceptional intakes of sucrose were 2.3 times as likely as low-sucrose consumers to have offspring with an NTD. Moreover, they observed that diets with a high glycaemic index (a classification of foods according to glycaemic response) were associated with a 1.9-fold increased risk of NTDs, even after excluding women with diabetes. This effect was strongest for women with prepregnancy obesity. Another report found that diets high in sweets are linked to NTDs,[41] although this study measured current diet in women 14 months after the delivery of their malformed child.

Dieting behaviours

Investigators have also explored the role of maternal dieting behaviours to restrict food intake on risk of NTD-affected offspring. An increased risk was found among women who reported dieting to lose weight (OR 2.1; 95% CI 1.1–4.1) and using fasting diets (OR 5.8; 95% CI 1.7–20.0) in the first trimester.[42] Adjustment for important confounders did not meaningfully change the results. The exact mechanism explaining these findings is unknown but could be due to reduced intake, absorption and metabolism of important micronutrients.

Physical activity

The effect of leisure-time physical activity on congenital malformations has been minimally studied but has strong biological plausibility. Exercise improves a number of physiological measures that are linked with malformations, most notably immune function, percentage body fat (independent of obesity), nutrient requirements, glucose metabolism, hormone concentrations and cardiovascular health.[43-47] Physical activity may promote relaxation and/or stress management in women, which may in turn cause physiological adaptive responses conducive to optimal fetal development.

This association was explored in a population-based case–control study of 538 mothers of malformed fetuses and 539 mothers of non-malformed controls.[48] Each woman's periconceptional physical activity level was assessed by in-home interview and summarised using an index reflecting reported frequency and exertion level for six activity groups. The effect of physical activity varied by periconceptional multivitamin use. Among non-users of periconceptional supplements, a dose–response relation was observed: the greater the physical activity frequency and exertion, the lower the risk of NTDs. A ten-unit increase in the physical activity index reduced risk of NTDs by about 50% (OR 0.52; 95% CI 0.31–0.89). In contrast, no significant association was observed among multivitamin users. The results, which were adjusted for known risk factors for NTDs, including obesity, race/ethnicity and education, suggested that the protective effect of physical activity may be limited to women who are at higher nutritional risk. No association was observed between physical activity and malformations in a cohort study of 158 well-conditioned recreational athletes and 90 less-active women,[49] but results were based only on six malformed infants.

Miscarriage

Between 12% and 16% of clinically recognised pregnancies end in miscarriage[50] and 1–2% of women of childbearing age experience recurrent miscarriage (three or more consecutive spontaneous miscarriages).[51] Identification of modifiable risk factors for miscarriage, such as maternal nutrition and physical activity, remains a public health priority.

Folate

The successful prevention of NTDs with folic acid and the knowledge that hyperhomocysteinaemia is a risk factor for miscarriage[52] led to the notion that folate might also prevent spontaneous miscarriage. Paradoxically, Hook and Czeizel[53] observed that folic acid supplementation increased the incidence of spontaneous miscarriage by 15–16%. These results were highly controversial,[54–58] with a sizable number of papers refuting these findings.[59–62] Indeed, limitations of Hook and Czeizel's work and many other observational studies studying folate deficiency and risk of miscarriage[63–65] included small sample sizes, highly selected populations, supplements containing nutrients other than folate, use of nonpregnant controls and lack of confounder adjustment.

Two prominent studies overcame these aforementioned limitations. Definitive evidence that periconceptional folic acid supplementation does not increase miscarriage rates came from a large-scale intervention study of over 23 000 women in China.[60] Miscarriage incidence was 9.0% among women who took 400 μg of folic acid alone and 9.3% for women who did not take folic acid early in pregnancy (RR 0.97; 95% CI 0.84–1.12). Additionally, in a well-designed observational study in Sweden, plasma folate in 468 cases and 921 controls at 6–12 weeks of gestation was related to miscarriage incidence. After controlling for age, smoking and previous miscarriages, women with low folate levels (≤ 4.9 nmol/l) were 1.5 times as likely as women with moderate folate levels (5.0–8.9 nmol/l) to have a spontaneous miscarriage. There was no increased risk at high folate concentrations. Other investigators have reported that a polymorphism in the methylenetetrahydrofolate reductase enzyme (a key enzyme in folate metabolism) that causes low plasma folate concentrations[66] increases the risk of recurrent spontaneous miscarriage.[67] Taken together, these results suggest that folate deficiency may be relevant for miscarriage.

Dietary antioxidants

Oxidative stress has been implicated in the pathogenesis of spontaneous and recurrent miscarriage[68,69] but dietary antioxidants have not been well studied in this area. Observational studies of vitamin C or vitamin E in relation to miscarriage had small sample sizes and did not control for known confounders.[69–72] Supplementation trials of vitamin C with or without multivitamins and vitamin E have found no association with miscarriage,[73–75] although none of the studies was designed to examine miscarriage as the primary outcome and therefore may not provide the most definitive data in this regard. Inadequate selenium status may[76–78] or may not[79] be more common in women who had either a first-trimester miscarriage or recurrent miscarriages compared with controls. If selenium is relevant, it may be due to its essential role in the antioxidant enzyme glutathione peroxidase[76,77,80] and/or its ability to modulate immune function.[81]

Multivitamins

A systematic review of randomised trials found no association between multivitamin supplementation and risk of either late or early miscarriage.[82] Because these studies were designed to study primary outcomes other than miscarriage, they may not be the most rigorous test of this question. Furthermore, the negative effect observed in these studies may be because supplements are most effective in populations with existing nutrient deficiencies. Supplements may also not adequately capture components of foods that are most relevant for miscarriage risk. For instance, Di Cintio and colleagues[83] studied women admitted for spontaneous miscarriage within the 12th gestational week and randomly selected controls with healthy term pregnancies. Intake of green vegetables, fruit, milk and fish was significantly less common and fat intake was significantly more common among the cases than the controls.[83] Therefore, poor diet quality, as measured with more global scales or scores, may be a more relevant nutritional determinant of miscarriage than individual nutrients.

Physical activity

There is a paucity of reports on the link between leisure-time physical activity and the risk of spontaneous miscarriage. In a small study of women who exercised intensely in early pregnancy and women who exercised only intermittently, there was no significant difference in the proportion of spontaneous miscarriages.[43] Latka *et al.*[84] found that any exercise during pregnancy protected against a chromosomally normal spontaneous miscarriage (OR 0.6; 95% CI 0.3–0.9). The protective effect remained after adjusting for education, age and prepregnancy body mass index (BMI). Contradictory findings came from an innovative study that examined peak activity levels at implantation, rather than averages across pregnancy.[85] Strenuous activity around the time of implantation had no relation to the risk of miscarriage close to implantation (RR 1.4; 95% CI 0.6–3.4), but had a strong association with miscarriage risk at 5 or more weeks of gestation (RR 4.8; 95% CI 2.0–11.4). While the study had a number of important strengths, some have questioned the internal consistency and biological plausibility of these findings.[86] As it was previously posited that regular exercise causes a blunting of hormonal changes that might protect against uterine contractions and pregnancy loss,[87] more research will be needed to elucidate the physiological response to strenuous activity in early pregnancy and how that relates to early pregnancy loss.

Gestational diabetes mellitus

Normal pregnancy is characterised by hyperglycaemia secondary to reduced insulin sensitivity in the peripheral tissues. As this insulin resistance increases across pregnancy, the inability to produce a sufficient amount of insulin causes impaired glucose tolerance (IGT), which may progress to gestational diabetes mellitus (GDM). Diet and physical activity have both been strongly linked to the development of IGT and GDM.

Macronutrients

A diet high in fat and low in complex carbohydrates is a strong risk factor for type 2 diabetes mellitus.[88–92] Diets low in complex carbohydrates or high in simple sugars also predispose to glucose intolerance in the nonpregnant state.[93–95] Much less attention has been given to these associations in pregnancy, and few studies have measured diet before the onset of GDM or IGT. In a small study of 35 women, high-fat diets were more common among women with a GDM recurrence in a subsequent pregnancy than those without a recurrence.[96] Wang *et al.*[97] studied a cohort of Chinese women consuming a traditional diet and found that a high intake of polyunsaturated fat in early pregnancy protected against IGT and GDM. Genetic or cultural factors may explain these contradictory findings. In an elegant analysis, Saldana and colleagues[98] untangled the effect of adding individual macronutrients, and hence energy (calories), to the diet from the effect of changing the diet's overall macronutrient composition on the risk of IGT and GDM. Results showed that when energy intake is held constant, increasing the percentage of energy from carbohydrate and simultaneously decreasing the percentage of energy from fat intake significantly decreased the risk of glucose intolerance. Similarly, in models not controlling for energy intake, increasing the absolute grams of carbohydrate without decreasing fat reduced the risk of IGT and GDM. Future analyses will lead to further understanding of the effect of dietary composition on IGT and GDM by separating subtypes of fat or carbohydrates.

Micronutrients

Vitamin C prevents abnormal insulin secretion attributable to pancreatic β-cell damage from oxidative stress,[99,100] inhibits hyperglycaemia-induced glycation of insulin in pancreatic β-cells[101] and improves insulin sensitivity and transport.[102,103] Maternal plasma ascorbic acid concentration at 13 weeks of gestation has been shown to be inversely associated with risk of GDM in a prospective cohort study of 755 women.[104] Furthermore, women in the lowest quartile of plasma ascorbate concentrations (< 55.9 μmol/l) were three times as likely as those in the highest quartile (≥ 74.6 μmol/l) to develop GDM. The same investigators conducted a case–control study and found that intrapartum plasma vitamin C concentrations were 31% lower in 67 women with GDM than in 260 controls.[105] While it is not known whether there are other studies that have rigorously assessed maternal dietary antioxidant status in relation to GDM or IGT, the strong association between dietary antioxidants and type 2 diabetes in nonpregnant individuals,[106] coupled with the similarity of GDM to type 2 diabetes,[107] suggests that this relationship could have significant biological relevance in pregnancy.

Other micronutrients have received less attention in relation to glucose tolerance in pregnancy. Dietary intakes of zinc and selenium have been reported to be significantly lower in women with gestational hyperglycaemia than controls, even after confounder adjustment.[108] Adjusted mean serum selenium concentrations have been shown to be lower in women with existing IGT and GDM[108,109] than in healthy pregnant controls, but have not been studied before the onset of disease.

Physical activity

In nonpregnant insulin-resistant individuals, recreational physical activity improves glucose tolerance and blunts the insulin response to a glucose load.[110,111] Indeed, in several small treatment studies, women with GDM randomised to a physical activity regimen had significantly improved glycaemic control – effects similar to those attained by traditional pharmacological therapies.[112–117] Preconceptional or early-pregnancy physical activity has just begun to attract investigators as a preventive factor for GDM. Prenatal exercise was found to reduce the incidence of GDM among women who were obese by 47% in one study.[118] In an observational study of 155 women with GDM and 386 normal pregnant controls interviewed at delivery, participation in any recreational prenatal physical activity before 20 weeks of gestation was associated with a significant 48% reduction in the odds of GDM.[119] Nevertheless, problems of recall and selection bias may have limited these findings.

Demsey and colleagues[120] improved upon past work with a prospective cohort study of 909 women who were pregnant and not diabetic, residing in Washington State and enrolled and interviewed early in pregnancy. They observed that women who reported participating in any recreational physical activity in the past year were about half as likely as women who were not active to develop GDM (RR 0.44; 95% CI 0.21–0.91). Furthermore, women who engaged in physical activity both before and during pregnancy had the lowest risk of GDM (RR 0.31; 95% CI 0.12–0.79). In the same population, Rudra *et al.*[121] reported on perceived exertion of recreational physical activity, a measure that captures women's perception of required effort rather than relying solely on absolute time and exertion. They found a direct inverse relation between perceived exertion and risk of GDM, even among women who did not meet the absolute time and exertion guidelines for physical activity during pregnancy. Research is needed in other populations to determine the generalisability of the findings.

Pre-eclampsia

Pre-eclampsia is a heterogeneous disorder that shares many pathophysiological changes and risk factors as cardiovascular disease.[122] Not surprisingly, maternal lifestyle variables have long been hypothesised to have a role in the aetiology of pre-eclampsia,[123] but only in the last decade has understanding of the disorder's pathogenesis risen to a level adequate to provide testable hypotheses.

Antioxidants

There has been lively debate on the role of antioxidants in pre-eclampsia prevention. Extensive evidence accumulated over the past 30 years supports a role for oxidative stress in the pathogenesis of pre-eclampsia.[124] Observational data have demonstrated that low intakes of vitamin C and/or vitamin E are predictors of pre-eclampsia.[105,125] However, the results of well-conducted randomised supplementation trials have been conflicting. In 1999, a small randomised trial of antioxidant supplementation, with 1000 mg vitamin C and 400 iu vitamin E or placebo initiated at 20 weeks of gestation among high-risk women, reported a 61% reduction in the risk of pre-eclampsia.[73] More recently, The Vitamins in Pre-eclampsia (VIP) trial, a randomised double-blind placebo-controlled trial of the same antioxidant therapy in a cohort of 2404 women with a range of clinical risk factors, found no difference in the incidence of pre-eclampsia between the treated and the placebo groups (15% versus 16%).[126] Moreover, the antioxidant group had a significantly higher incidence of perinatal complications, including low birthweight, fetal acidaemia, gestational hypertension and the need for medication therapies than the placebo group. Soon after, results of a randomised trial of the same antioxidant therapy or placebo conducted in low-risk nulliparous women were reported.[127] Again, no significant differences were observed between the vitamin and placebo groups for the risk of pre-eclampsia (6% versus 5%) or other primary outcomes. Certain adverse outcomes were more significantly common in the supplemented group. Continuing trials of antioxidant therapy for the prevention of pre-eclampsia (a US trial, a Brazil trial and a multicentre World Health Organization trial) will help to clarify the efficacy and safety of high-dose antioxidants in pregnancy.

Folate

A link between folate and pre-eclampsia has been suggested since serum homocysteine concentrations are slightly higher in women destined to develop pre-eclampsia and are markedly elevated in overt pre-eclampsia.[128] However, studies of serum or plasma folate concentrations before or after the clinical onset of pre-eclampsia have been inconsistent.[129–136] Similarly, folic acid supplementation has not conclusively been proven to have significant benefit for pre-eclampsia risk.[137,138]

Calcium

An inverse relation between calcium and pre-eclampsia has been documented in many epidemiological and clinical studies.[139–143] Low calcium intake was posited to be important for pre-eclampsia because of its ability to stimulate parathyroid hormone or renin release, thereby leading to vasoconstriction.[140] Although initial small calcium supplementation trials had promising results,[144] other more recent trials have had mixed findings.[145,146] The most recent meta-analysis from the Cochrane Library summarising supplementation trials of at least 1 g calcium for the prevention of pre-eclampsia reported a reduction in the risk of pre-eclampsia (12 trials, 15 206 women, RR 0.48; 95% CI 0.33–0.69).[147] The most striking effects were seen among women at high risk of developing pre-eclampsia (RR 0.22; 95% CI 0.12–0.42) and women with low baseline dietary calcium intakes (RR 0.36; 95% CI 0.18–0.70).

Multivitamins

Regular multivitamin use in the periconceptional period was found to reduce the risk of pre-eclampsia by 45% (RR 0.55; 95% CI 0.32–0.95), even after adjustment for sociodemographic and lifestyle variables.[148] These results are consistent with other observational studies of multivitamin use during pregnancy[149,150] and an uncontrolled trial of multivitamins provided at 20 weeks of gestation.[151] Past studies assessed typical multivitamins, which contain doses of nutrients around the daily recommended levels in pregnancy. While the leading evidence suggests that antioxidants or folate in the multivitamins may be the most relevant for this effect, many other micronutrients have been implicated and warrant further study.[152]

Omega-3 polyunsaturated fatty acids

Some studies have shown a protective effect of omega-3 polyunsaturated fatty acid (PUFAs) on pre-eclampsia occurrence[151,153,154] while others have found no association.[155–158] Confusing matters further are studies that found an increasing risk of pre-eclampsia in relation to high total PUFA intake (omega-3 and omega-6),[159,160] although these investigators did not separate the effects of omega-3 from omega-6 PUFAs. Olafsdottír and colleagues[161] reported a U-shaped relation between omega-3 PUFA intake and risk of 'hypertensive disorders of pregnancy' (i.e. gestational hypertension and pre-eclampsia), such that low and high intakes increased the risk of adverse outcome. The conflicting results are possibly due to differing times of exposure assessment, methods of assessing and classifying PUFA intake, and definitions of pre-eclampsia.

Physical activity

A number of investigations into the role of leisure-time physical activity in the pathogenesis of pre-eclampsia have recently been published, with promising benefits of exercise on disease risk. In a case–control study of 172 women with pre-eclampsia and 505 controls residing in Quebec City and Montreal, Marcoux and colleagues[162] found that women who reported performing regular recreational physical activity in the first half of pregnancy were less likely to develop pre-eclampsia, even after controlling for work activity and other confounders. There was a dose–response association observed, with decreasing risks as the average amount of time in exercise increased. Similar findings were reported in another case–control study conducted in Washington State.[163] Saftlas and colleagues[164] avoided the concerns about recall bias by conducting a prospective cohort study of 2638 pregnant women in New Haven, Connecticut who were interviewed at less than 16 weeks of gestation. Leisure-time physical activity had a protective effect on pre-eclampsia risk that was similar in magnitude to the aforementioned case–control studies. Others have observed that women who reported feeling very strenuous to maximal exertion during usual prepregnancy physical activity were 78% less likely to develop pre-eclampsia (OR 0.22; 95% CI 0.11–0.44) than women who reported negligible or minimal exertion.[165] Taken together, these results strongly suggest that a physical activity intervention may reduce the risk of pre-eclampsia.

Implications for pregnant women who are obese

Evidence suggests that enhancing maternal dietary intake and increasing recreational physical activity may reduce the risk of congenital malformations, miscarriage, GDM and pre-eclampsia. The relations are of variable strength but, overall, several associations are promising and warrant further exploration. The key question for clinicians caring for pregnant women who are obese and for researchers in this area is whether poor diet quality and physical inactivity mediate part of the association between obesity and adverse pregnancy outcomes. That is, will improving the diets and exercise patterns of women who are overweight prevent a proportion of negative events? At first glance, it may only seem logical that this would be the case: if lifestyle variables are strongly implicated in certain perinatal outcomes, why would these results not apply to pregnant women who are obese? However, it is very possible that the metabolic dysregulation observed in the setting of maternal obesity[166] is so vast that any positive changes in diet or exercise may be blunted or nullified.

Unfortunately, as far as is known, there are no controlled trials that have randomised women who are overweight or obese and pregnant or planning a pregnancy to an intervention aimed at modifying diet or exercise patterns and monitored pregnancy outcomes. This would be the definitive test of the hypothesis. Most previous intervention trials have studied only a small proportion of women who are obese and the results may not be applicable. So, in the absence of these data, any evidence has to come from studies where investigators have stratified their results by maternal overweight, which tests whether the effect of the nutrition or exercise exposure was heterogeneous among women who were lean or overweight. Although there are few studies that have presented data in this manner, those that did provide illuminating insights into potential effectiveness of a nutrition or exercise intervention on outcomes discussed here.

The most intriguing data come from studies of periconceptional nutrition and risk of congenital malformations. In a population-based case–control study, Werler et al.[8] found that at least 400 μg of folate reduced the risk of NTDs by 40% among women who weighed less than 70 kg but had no effect among women weighing 70 kg or more. Similarly, periconceptional multivitamin use was reported to be protective against isolated heart defects in the overall population, but after stratifying by prepregnancy BMI, there was no effect of multivitamin use on disease risk in women who were overweight or obese.[167] Compared with lean women, the OR and 95% CI for NTDs among women who were overweight in Canada was 1.4 (1.0–1.8) before mandatory folic acid fortification of wheat flour, and strengthened to 2.8 (1.2–6.6) post-fortification in 2000.[168] These results imply that folic acid fortification may have had little impact on NTD rates among women who are overweight in this region. Velie et al.[23] reported that total and dietary animal zinc intakes protected against NTDs in women with a BMI of 26 kg/m² or lower, while it conferred no effect in heavier women.

Fewer data are available for other outcomes. A prospective cohort study of pre-eclampsia demonstrated a 71% reduction in pre-eclampsia risk among periconceptional multivitamin users who were lean (OR 0.29; 95% CI 0.12–0.65) relative to lean non-users of multivitamins. There was no relation between multivitamin use and pre-eclampsia among women who were overweight (OR 1.08; 95% CI 0.52–2.25) compared with the same referent.[148] It is also noteworthy that, in one study, zinc supplementation during pregnancy increased birthweight and head circumference and reduced preterm delivery in mothers with a BMI < 26 kg/m² but had no effect on mothers whose BMI was ≥ 26 kg/m².[169] Although preterm birth is not common for women who are obese, these data also support a general trend seen in the literature: certain nutritional interventions aimed at enhancing micronutrient intake and subsequently improving outcomes may have substantially reduced efficacy among women who are overweight.

Conversely, some therapies may be more effective in women who are overweight rather than those who are lean. A high glycaemic index diet was a significantly stronger risk factor for NTDs in women whose prepregnancy BMI was more than 29 kg/m² than in leaner women.[40] Therefore, reducing or eliminating refined carbohydrates, for instance, may have little effect on glucose tolerance in women who are lean, but a powerful effect in women who are obese. Such an intervention could be important in reducing the risk of NTDs, GDM and pre-eclampsia. Enhanced effects of recreational physical activity may also be observed in pregnant women who are overweight. In a population-based birth registry in New York State, the risk of GDM was significantly reduced by 47% among women who were obese who exercised during pregnancy, but had no impact on women who were lean.[118] Furthermore, results from a randomised clinical trial of circuit-type resistance training in women with GDM to prevent insulin therapy found that the only differences in need for insulin were observed among women who were overweight.[170] Women with a high BMI in the diet-plus-exercise group were prescribed less insulin (P < 0.05) and showed a longer delay from GDM diagnosis to the initiation of insulin therapy (P < 0.05) compared with women who were overweight in the diet-alone group.

Conclusion

Currently, the mechanisms underlying the varying effects of nutrition and physical activity by overweight status can only be speculated upon. It is possible that the dose of nutrients assessed in past studies (most of which have been low doses, i.e. at the recommended dietary allowance) may not be adequate to overcome the metabolic disturbances characteristic of the obese state.[166] It is also possible that these metabolic or physiological factors might directly or indirectly alter the absorption, transport, or storage of nutrients in an obese individual. Women who are obese may have higher nutrient requirements than women who are lean. Conversely, exercise may be a more powerful modifier of metabolic risk factors, whereas changing one aspect of the diet (e.g. giving a multivitamin supplement) may have no impact if the global quality of the diet is poor. Future studies will be needed to test this hypothesis and others.

While normalising or reducing preconceptional weight would probably be the most ideal way for women who are overweight and planning a pregnancy to lower their risk of adverse birth outcomes, half of pregnancies are unplanned[171] and weight loss and maintenance is a challenging task for individuals living in obesogenic environments.[172] Because weight loss is discouraged during pregnancy,[1] the search must continue for modifiable risk factors for adverse outcomes among women who enter gestation when they are obese. Given the current evidence relating nutrition and recreational physical activity to NTDs, miscarriage, GDM and pre-eclampsia, it seems that improving these lifestyle variables provide promising starting points.

References

1. IOM. *Nutrition During Pregnancy*. Washington DC: National Academy Press; 1990.
2. Expert Advisory Group. *Folic Acid and the Prevention of Neural Tube Defects*. London: Department of Health; 1992.
3. US Public Health Service. Recommendations for the use of folic acid to reduce the number of cases of spina bifida and other neural tube defects. *MMWR Recomm Rep* 1992;41(RR-14):1–7.
4. Food and Drug Administration. Food standards: amendment of standards of identity for enriched grain products to require addition of folic acid. *Fed Regist* 1996;61:8781–807.
5. MRC Vitamin Study Research Group. Prevention of neural tube defects: results of the Medical Research Council vitamin study. *Lancet* 1991;338:131–7.
6. Czeizel AE, Dudas I. Prevention of the first occurrence of neural-tube defects by periconceptional vitamin supplementation. *N Engl J Med* 1992;327:1832–5.
7. Czeizel AE. Prevention of congenital abnormalities by periconceptional multivitamin supplementation. *BMJ* 1993;306:1645–8.
8. Werler MM, Louik C, Shapiro S, Mitchell AA. Prepregnant weight in relation to risk of neural tube defects. *JAMA* 1996;275:1089–92.
9. Shaw GM, Schaffer D, Velie EM, Morland K, Harris JA. Periconceptional vitamin use, dietary folate, and the occurrence of neural tube defects. *Epidemiology* 1995;6:219–26.
10. Wilcox AJ, Lie RT, Solvoll K, Taylor J, McConnaughey DR, Abyholm F, et al. Folic acid supplements and risk of facial clefts: national population based case–control study. *BMJ* 2007;334:464.
11. Shaw GM, Lammer EJ, Wasserman CR, O'Malley CD, Tolarova MM. Risks of orofacial clefts in children born to women using multivitamins containing folic acid periconceptionally. *Lancet* 1995;346:393–6.
12. van Rooij IA, Vermeij-Keers C, Kluijtmans LA, Ocké MC, Zielhuis GA, Goorhuis-Brouwer SM, et al. Does the interaction between maternal folate intake and the methylenetetrahydrofolate reductase polymorphisms affect the risk of cleft lip with or without cleft palate? *Am J Epidemiol* 2003;157:583–91.

13. Shaw GM, O'Malley CD, Wasserman CR, Tolarova MM, Lammer EJ. Maternal periconceptional use of multivitamins and reduced risk for conotruncal heart defects and limb deficiencies among offspring. *Am J Med Genet* 1995;59:536–45.

14. Suarez L, Hendricks K, Felkner M, Gunter E. Maternal serum B12 levels and risk for neural tube defects in a Texas-Mexico border population. *Ann Epidemiol* 2003;13:81–8.

15. Christensen B, Arbour L, Tran P, Leclerc D, Sabbaghian N, Platt R, *et al*. Genetic polymorphisms in methylenetetrahydrofolate reductase and methionine synthase, folate levels in red blood cells, and risk of neural tube defects. *Am J Med Genet* 1999;84:151–7.

16. Kirke PN, Molloy AM, Daly LE, Burke H, Weir DG, Scott JM. Maternal plasma folate and vitamin B12 are independent risk factors for neural tube defects. *Q J Med* 1993;86:703–8.

17. Wright ME. A case–control study of maternal nutrition and neural tube defects in Northern Ireland. *Midwifery* 1995;11:146–52.

18. Molloy AM, Kirke P, Hillary I, Weir DG, Scott JM. Maternal serum folate and vitamin B12 concentrations in pregnancies associated with neural tube defects. *Arch Dis Child* 1985;60:660–5.

19. Schorah CJ, Smithells RW, Scott J. Vitamin B12 and anencephaly. *Lancet* 1980;1:880.

20. Stoll C, Dott B, Alembik Y, Koehl C. Maternal trace elements, vitamin B12, vitamin A, folic acid, and fetal malformations. *Reprod Toxicol* 1999;13:53–7.

21. Krapels IP, van Rooij IA, Ocke MC, van Cleef BA, Kuijpers-Jagtman AM, Steegers-Theunissen RP. Maternal dietary B vitamin intake, other than folate, and the association with orofacial cleft in the offspring. *Eur J Nutr* 2004;43:7–14.

22. Tamura T, Goldenberg R. Zinc nutriture and pregnancy outcome. *Nutr Res* 1996;16:139–81.

23. Velie EM, Block G, Shaw GM, Samuels SJ, Schaffer DM, Kulldorff M. Maternal supplemental and dietary zinc intake and the occurrence of neural tube defects in California. *Am J Epidemiol* 1999;150:605–16.

24. Cengiz B, Soylemez F, Ozturk E, Cavdar AO. Serum zinc, selenium, copper, and lead levels in women with second-trimester induced abortion resulting from neural tube defects: a preliminary study. *Biol Trace Elem Res* 2004;97:225–35.

25. McMichael AJ, Dreosti IE, Ryan P, Robertson EF. Neural tube defects and maternal serum zinc and copper concentrations in mid-pregnancy: a case–control study. *Med J Aust* 1994;161:478–82.

26. Tamura T, Munger RG, Corcoran C, Bacayao JY, Nepomuceno B, Solon F. Plasma zinc concentrations of mothers and the risk of nonsyndromic oral clefts in their children: a case–control study in the Philippines. *Birth Defects Res A Clin Mol Teratol* 2005;73:612–16.

27. Sever LE. Zinc and human development: a review. *Hum Ecol* 1975;3:43–55.

28. Hambridge KM, Nelder KH, Walravens PA. Zinc, acrodermatitis enteropathica, and congenital malformations. *Lancet* 1975;1:577–8.

29. Mahomed K. Zinc supplementation in pregnancy. *Cochrane Database Syst Rev* 2000;(2):CD000230.

30. Osendarp SJ, West CE, Black RE. The need for maternal zinc supplementation in developing countries: an unresolved issue. *J Nutr* 2003;133:817S–27S.

31. Eriksson UJ, Borg LA. Diabetes and embryonic malformations. Role of substrate-induced free-oxygen radical production for dysmorphogenesis in cultured rat embryos. *Diabetes* 1993;42:411–9.

32. Guvenc H, Karatas F, Guvenc M, Kunc S, Aygun AD, Bektas S. Low levels of selenium in mothers and their newborns in pregnancies with a neural tube defect. *Pediatrics* 1995;95:879–82.

33. Martin I, Gibert MJ, Pintos C, Noguera A, Besalduch A, Obrador A. Oxidative stress in mothers who have conceived fetus with neural tube defects: the role of aminothiols and selenium. *Clin Nutr* 2004;23:507–14.

34. Schorah CJ, Wild J, Hartley R, Sheppard S, Smithells RW. The effect of periconceptional supplementation on blood vitamin concentrations in women at recurrence risk for neural tube defect. *Br J Nutr* 1983;49:203–11.

35. Cederberg J, Siman CM, Eriksson UJ. Combined treatment with vitamin E and vitamin C decreases oxidative stress and improves fetal outcome in experimental diabetic pregnancy. *Pediatr Res* 2001;49:755–62.

36. Siman CM, Eriksson UJ. Vitamin C supplementation of the maternal diet reduces the rate of malformation in the offspring of diabetic rats. *Diabetologia* 1997;40:1416–24.

37. Siman CM, Eriksson UJ. Vitamin E decreases the occurrence of malformations in the offspring of diabetic rats. *Diabetes* 1997;46:1054–61.

38. Carmichael SL, Shaw GM, Selvin S, Schaffer DM. Diet quality and risk of neural tube defects. *Med Hypotheses* 2003;60:351–5.

39. Jovanovic-Peterson L, Peterson CM. Abnormal metabolism and the risk for birth defects with emphasis on diabetes. *Ann N Y Acad Sci* 1993;678:228–43.

40. Shaw GM, Quach T, Nelson V, Carmichael SL, Schaffer DM, Selvin S, *et al*. Neural tube defects associated with maternal periconceptional dietary intake of simple sugars and glycemic index. *Am J Clin Nutr* 2003;78:972–8.

41. Friel JK, Frecker M, Fraser FC. Nutritional patterns of mothers of children with neural tube defects in Newfoundland. *Am J Med Genet* 1995;55:195–9.

42. Carmichael SL, Shaw GM, Schaffer DM, Laurent C, Selvin S. Dieting behaviors and risk of neural tube defects. *Am J Epidemiol* 2003;158:1127–31.

43. Clapp JF, Kiess W. Effects of pregnancy and exercise on concentrations of the metabolic markers tumor necrosis factor alpha and leptin. *Am J Obstet Gynecol* 2000;182:300–6.

44. Clapp JF, Rizk KH. Effect of recreational exercise on midtrimester placental growth. *Am J Obstet Gynecol* 1992;167:1518–21.

45. Hatch MC, Shu XO, McLean DE, Levin B, Begg M, Reuss L, *et al*. Maternal exercise during pregnancy, physical fitness, and fetal growth. *Am J Epidemiol* 1993;137:1105–14.

46. Schramm WF, Stockbauer JW, Hoffman HJ. Exercise, employment, other daily activities, and adverse pregnancy outcomes. *Am J Epidemiol* 1996;143:211–18.

47. Sternfeld B, Quesenberry CP, Husson G. Habitual physical activity and menopausal symptoms: a case–control study. *J Womens Health* 1999;8:115–23.

48. Carmichael SL, Shaw GM, Neri E, Schaffer DM, Selvin S. Physical activity and risk of neural tube defects. *Matern Child Health J* 2002;6:151–7.

49. Clapp JF. Exercise and fetal health. *J Dev Physiol* 1991;15:9–14.

50. Everett C. Incidence and outcome of bleeding before the 20th week of pregnancy: prospective study from general practice. *BMJ* 1997;315:32–4.

51. Coulam CB. Epidemiology of recurrent spontaneous abortion. *Am J Reprod Immunol* 1991;26:23–7.

52. Nelen WL, Blom HJ, Steegers EA, den Heijer M, Thomas CM, Eskes TK. Homocysteine and folate levels as risk factors for recurrent early pregnancy loss. *Obstet Gynecol* 2000;95:519–24.

53. Hook EB, Czeizel AE. Can terathanasia explain the protective effect of folic-acid supplementation on birth defects? *Lancet* 1997;350:513–15.

54. Czeizel AE. Miscarriage and use of multivitamins or folic acid. *Am J Med Genet* 2001;104:179–80.

55. Hall JG. Terathanasia, folic acid, and birth defects. *Lancet* 1997;350:1322; author reply 1323–4.

56. Hook EB. Folic acid: abortifacient or pseudoabortifacient? *Am J Med Genet* 2000;92:301–2.

57. Hook EB. Statistical and logical considerations in evaluating the association of prenatal folic-acid supplementation with pregnancy loss. *Am J Med Genet* 2001;104:181–2.

58. Schorah CJ, Smithells RW, Seller MJ, Terathanasia. Folic acid, and birth defects. *Lancet* 1997;350:1323; author reply 1323–4.

59. Burn J, Fisk NM. Terathanasia, folic acid, and birth defects. *Lancet* 1997;350:1322–3; author reply 1323–4.

60. Gindler J, Li Z, Berry RJ, Zheng J, Correa A, Sun X, Wong L, *et al*; Jiaxing City Collaborative Project on Neural Tube Defect Prevention. Folic acid supplements during pregnancy and risk of miscarriage. *Lancet* 2001;358:796–800.

61. Wald N, Hackshaw A. Folic acid and prevention of neural-tube defects. *Lancet* 1997;350:665.

62. Wald NJ, Hackshaw AK. Folic acid and miscarriage: an unjustified link. *Am J Med Genet* 2001;98:204.

63. Neiger R, Wise C, Contag SA, Tumber MB, Canick JA. First trimester bleeding and pregnancy outcome in gravidas with normal and low folate levels. *Am J Perinatol* 1993;10:460–2.

64. Streiff RR, Little AB. Folic acid deficiency in pregnancy. *N Engl J Med* 1967;276:776–9.

65. Wouters MG, Boers GH, Blom HJ, Trijbels FJ, Thomas CM, Borm GF, *et al*. Hyperhomocysteinemia: a risk factor in women with unexplained recurrent early pregnancy loss. *Fertil Steril* 1993;60:820–5.

66. Jacques PF, Bostom AG, Williams RR, Ellison RC, Eckfeldt JH, Rosenberg IH, *et al.* Relation between folate status, a common mutation in methylenetetrahydrofolate reductase, and plasma homocysteine concentrations. *Circulation* 1996;93:7–9.

67. Zetterberg H. Methylenetetrahydrofolate reductase and transcobalamin genetic polymorphisms in human spontaneous abortion: biological and clinical implications. *Reprod Biol Endocrinol* 2004;2:7.

68. Jauniaux E, Watson AL, Hempstock J, Bao YP, Skepper JN, Burton GJ. Onset of maternal arterial blood flow and placental oxidative stress. A possible factor in human early pregnancy failure. *Am J Pathol* 2000;157:2111–22.

69. Simsek M, Naziroglu M, Simsek H, Cay M, Aksakal M, Kumru S. Blood plasma levels of lipoperoxides, glutathione peroxidase, beta carotene, vitamin A and E in women with habitual abortion. *Cell Biochem Funct* 1998;16:227–31.

70. Nicotra M, Muttinelli C, Sbracia M, Rolfi G, Passi S. Blood levels of lipids, lipoperoxides, vitamin E and glutathione peroxidase in women with habitual abortion. *Gynecol Obstet Invest* 1994;38:223–6.

71. Vobecky JS, Vobecky J, Shapcott D, Blanchard R, Lafond R, Cloutier D, *et al.* Serum alpha-tocopherol in pregnancies with normal or pathological outcomes. *Can J Physiol Pharmacol* 1974;52:384–8.

72. Vobecky JS, Vobecky J, Shapcott D, Cloutier D, Lafond R, Blanchard R. Vitamins C and E in spontaneous abortion. *Int J Vitam Nutr Res* 1976;46:291–6.

73. Chappell LC, Seed PT, Briley AL, Kelly FJ, Lee R, Hunt BJ, *et al.* Effect of antioxidants on the occurrence of pre-eclampsia in women at increased risk: a randomised trial. *Lancet* 1999;354:810–6.

74. Henmi H, Endo T, Kitajima Y, Manase K, Hata H, Kudo R. Effects of ascorbic acid supplementation on serum progesterone levels in patients with a luteal phase defect. *Fertil Steril* 2003;80:459–61.

75. Steyn PS, Odendaal HJ, Schoeman J, Stander C, Fanie N, Grove D. A randomised, double-blind placebo-controlled trial of ascorbic acid supplementation for the prevention of preterm labour. *J Obstet Gynaecol* 2003;23:150–5.

76. Barrington JW, Lindsay P, James D, Smith S, Roberts A. Selenium deficiency and miscarriage: a possible link? *Br J Obstet Gynaecol* 1996;103:130–2.

77. Barrington JW, Taylor M, Smith S, Bowen-Simpkins P. Selenium and recurrent miscarriage. *J Obstet Gynaecol* 1997;17:199–200.

78. Al-Kunani AS, Knight R, Haswell SJ, Thompson JW, Lindow SW. The selenium status of women with a history of recurrent miscarriage. *BJOG* 2001;108:1094–7.

79. Nicoll AE, Norman J, Macpherson A, Acharya U. Association of reduced selenium status in the aetiology of recurrent miscarriage. *Br J Obstet Gynaecol* 1999;106:1188–91.

80. Zachara BA, Dobrzynski W, Trafikowska U, Szymanski W. Blood selenium and glutathione peroxidases in miscarriage. *BJOG* 2001;108:244–7.

81. Ferencik M, Ebringer L. Modulatory effects of selenium and zinc on the immune system. *Folia Microbiol* 2003;48:417–26.

82. Rumbold A, Middleton P, Crowther CA. Vitamin supplementation for preventing miscarriage. *Cochrane Database Syst Rev* 2005;(2):CD004073.

83. Di Cintio E, Parazzini F, Chatenoud L, Surace M, Benzi G, Zanconato G, *et al.* Dietary factors and risk of spontaneous abortion. *Eur J Obstet Gynecol Reprod Biol* 2001;95:132–6.

84. Latka M, Kline J, Hatch M. Exercise and spontaneous abortion of known karyotype. *Epidemiology* 1999;10:73–5.

85. Hjollund NH, Jensen TK, Bonde JP, Henriksen TB, Andersson AM, Kolstad HA, *et al.* Spontaneous abortion and physical strain around implantation: a follow-up study of first-pregnancy planners. *Epidemiology* 2000;11:18–23.

86. Hatch M. Physical activity before you know you are pregnant. *Epidemiology* 2000;11:4–5.

87. Artal R, Artal-Mittelmark R, Wiswell A. *Exercise in Pregnancy*. Baltimore: Williams & Williams; 1986.

88. The Diabetes Prevention Program. Design and methods for a clinical trial in the prevention of type 2 diabetes. *Diabetes Care* 1999;22:623–34.

89. Feskens EJ, Virtanen SM, Räsänen L, Tuomilehto J, Stengård J, Pekkanen J, et al. Dietary factors determining diabetes and impaired glucose tolerance. A 20-year follow-up of the Finnish and Dutch cohorts of the Seven Countries Study. Diabetes Care 1995;18:1104–12.

90. Gittelsohn J, Wolever TM, Harris SB, Harris-Giraldo R, Hanley AJ, Zinman B. Specific patterns of food consumption and preparation are associated with diabetes and obesity in a Native Canadian community. J Nutr 1998;128:541–7.

91. Marshall JA, Hoag S, Shetterly S, Hamman RF. Dietary fat predicts conversion from impaired glucose tolerance to NIDDM. The San Luis Valley Diabetes Study. Diabetes Care 1994;17:50–6.

92. Tuomilehto J, Lindström J, Eriksson JG, Valle TT, Hämäläinen H, Ilanne-Parikka P, et al. Finnish Diabetes Prevention Study Group. Prevention of type 2 diabetes mellitus by changes in lifestyle among subjects with impaired glucose tolerance. N Engl J Med 2001;344:1343–50.

93. Garg A, Bantle JP, Henry RR, Coulston AM, Griver KA, Raatz SK, et al. Effects of varying carbohydrate content of diet in patients with non-insulin-dependent diabetes mellitus. JAMA 1994;271:1421–8.

94. Nuttall FQ. Dietary fiber in the management of diabetes. Diabetes 1993;42:503–8.

95. Vinik AI, Jenkins DJ. Dietary fiber in management of diabetes. Diabetes Care 1988;11:160–73.

96. Moses RG, Shand JL, Tapsell LC. The recurrence of gestational diabetes: could dietary differences in fat intake be an explanation? Diabetes Care 1997;20:1647–50.

97. Wang Y, Storlien LH, Jenkins AB, Tapsell LC, Jin Y, Pan JF, et al. Dietary variables and glucose tolerance in pregnancy. Diabetes Care 2000;23:460–4.

98. Saldana TM, Siega-Riz AM, Adair LS. Effect of macronutrient intake on the development of glucose intolerance during pregnancy. Am J Clin Nutr 2004;79:479–86.

99. Dou C, Xu DP, Wells WW. Studies on the essential role of ascorbic acid in the energy dependent release of insulin from pancreatic islets. Biochem Biophys Res Commun 1997;231:820–2.

100. Wells WW, Dou CZ, Dybas LN, Jung CH, Kalbach HL, Xu DP. Ascorbic acid is essential for the release of insulin from scorbutic guinea pig pancreatic islets. Proc Natl Acad Sci U S A 1995;92:11869–73.

101. Abdel-Wahab YH, O'Harte FP, Mooney MH, Barnett CR, Flatt PR. Vitamin C supplementation decreases insulin glycation and improves glucose homeostasis in obese hyperglycemic (ob/ob) mice. Metabolism 2002;51:514–7.

102. Paolisso G, D'Amore A, Volpe C, Balbi V, Saccomanno F, Galzerano D, et al. Evidence for a relationship between oxidative stress and insulin action in non-insulin-dependent (type II) diabetic patients. Metabolism 1994;43:1426–9.

103. Paolisso G, Giugliano D. Oxidative stress and insulin action: is there a relationship? Diabetologia 1996;39:357–63.

104. Zhang C, Williams MA, Sorensen TK, King IB, Kestin MM, Thompson ML, et al. Maternal plasma ascorbic Acid (vitamin C) and risk of gestational diabetes mellitus. Epidemiology 2004;15:597–604.

105. Zhang C, Williams MA, Frederick IO, King IB, Sorensen TK, Kestin MM, et al. Vitamin C and the risk of gestational diabetes mellitus: a case–control study. J Reprod Med 2004;49:257–66.

106. Will JC, Ford ES, Bowman BA. Serum vitamin C concentrations and diabetes: findings from the Third National Health and Nutrition Examination Survey, 1988–1994. Am J Clin Nutr 1999;70:49–52.

107. Pendergrass M, Fazioni E, Defronzo RA. Non-insulin-dependent diabetes mellitus and gestational diabetes mellitus: same disease, another name? Diabetes Rev 1995;3:566–83.

108. Bo S, Lezo A, Menato G, Gallo ML, Bardelli C, Signorile A, et al. Gestational hyperglycemia, zinc, selenium, and antioxidant vitamins. Nutrition 2005;21:186–91.

109. Tan M, Sheng L, Qian Y, Ge Y, Wang Y, Zhang H, et al. Changes of serum selenium in pregnant women with gestational diabetes mellitus. Biol Trace Elem Res 2001;83:231–7.

110. Yki-Jarvinen H, Koivisto VA. Effects of body composition on insulin sensitivity. Diabetes 1983;32:965–9.

111. Young JC, Enslin J, Kuca B. Exercise intensity and glucose tolerance in trained and nontrained subjects. J Appl Physiol 1989;67:39–43.

112. Avery MD, Leon AS, Kopher RA. Effects of a partially home-based exercise program for women with gestational diabetes. Obstet Gynecol 1997;89:10–15.

113. Avery MD, Walker AJ. Acute effect of exercise on blood glucose and insulin levels in women with gestational diabetes. *J Matern Fetal Med* 2001;10:52–8.

114. Bung P, Artal R, Khodiguian N, Kjos S. Exercise in gestational diabetes. An optional therapeutic approach? *Diabetes* 1991;40 Suppl 2:182–5.

115. Garcia-Patterson A, Martin E, Ubeda J, Maria MA, de Leiva A, Corcoy R. Evaluation of light exercise in the treatment of gestational diabetes. *Diabetes Care* 2001;24:2006–7.

116. Jovanovic-Peterson L, Durak EP, Peterson CM. Randomized trial of diet versus diet plus cardiovascular conditioning on glucose levels in gestational diabetes. *Am J Obstet Gynecol* 1989;161:415–19.

117. Lesser KB, Gruppuso PA, Terry RB, Carpenter MW. Exercise fails to improve postprandial glycemic excursion in women with gestational diabetes. *J Matern Fetal Med* 1996;5:211–17.

118. Dye TD, Knox KL, Artal R, Aubry RH, Wojtowycz MA. Physical activity, obesity, and diabetes in pregnancy. *Am J Epidemiol* 1997;146:961–5.

119. Dempsey JC, Butler CL, Sorensen TK, Lee IM, Thompson ML, Miller RS, et al. A case–control study of maternal recreational physical activity and risk of gestational diabetes mellitus. *Diabetes Res Clin Pract* 2004;66:203–15.

120. Dempsey JC, Sorensen TK, Williams MA, Lee IM, Miller RS, Dashow EE, et al. Prospective study of gestational diabetes mellitus risk in relation to maternal recreational physical activity before and during pregnancy. *Am J Epidemiol* 2004;159:663–70.

121. Rudra CB, Williams MA, Lee IM, Miller RS, Sorensen TK. Perceived exertion in physical activity and risk of gestational diabetes mellitus. *Epidemiology* 2006;17:31–7.

122. Roberts JM. Pregnancy related hypertension. In: Creasy RK, Resnik R, editors. *Maternal Fetal Medicine*. Philadelphia: W.B. Saunders; 1998.

123. Chesley LC. *Hypertensive Disorders of Pregnancy*. New York: Appleton-Century-Crofts; 1978.

124. Hubel CA. Oxidative stress and preeclampsia. *Fetal Matern Med Rev* 1997;9:73–101.

125. Rumbold AR, Maats FH, Crowther CA. Dietary intake of vitamin C and vitamin E and the development of hypertensive disorders of pregnancy. *Eur J Obstet Gynecol Reprod Biol* 2005;119:67–71.

126. Poston L, Briley AL, Seed PT, Kelly FJ, Shennan AH. Vitamin C and vitamin E in pregnant women at risk for pre-eclampsia (VIP trial): randomised placebo-controlled trial. *Lancet* 2006;367:1145–54.

127. Rumbold AR, Crowther CA, Haslam RR, Dekker GA, Robinson JS; ACTS Study Group. Vitamins C and E and the risks of preeclampsia and perinatal complications. *N Engl J Med* 2006;354:1796–806.

128. Mignini LE, Latthe PM, Villar J, Kilby MD, Carroli G, Khan KS. Mapping the theories of preeclampsia: the role of homocysteine. *Obstet Gynecol* 2005;105:411–25.

129. Powers RW, Evans RW, Majors AK, Ojimba JI, Ness RB, Crombleholme WR, et al. Plasma homocysteine concentration is increased in preeclampsia and is associated with evidence of endothelial activation. *Am J Obstet Gynecol* 1998;179:1605–11.

130. Rajkovic A, Catalano PM, Malinow MR. Elevated homocyst(e)ine levels with preeclampsia. *Obstet Gynecol* 1997;90:168–71.

131. Rajkovic A, Mahomed K, Malinow MR, Sorenson TK, Woelk GB, Williams MA. Plasma homocyst(e)ine concentrations in eclamptic and preeclamptic African women postpartum. *Obstet Gynecol* 1999;94:355–60.

132. Ray JG, Laskin CA. Folic acid and homocyst(e)ine metabolic defects and the risk of placental abruption, pre-eclampsia and spontaneous pregnancy loss: A systematic review. *Placenta* 1999;20:519–29.

133. Sanchez SE, Zhang C, Malinow MR, Ware-Jauregui S, Larrabaure G, Williams MA. Plasma folate, vitamin B12, and homocyst(e)ine concentrations in preeclamptic and normotensive Peruvian women. *Am J Epidemiol* 2001;153:474–80.

134. Cotter AM, Molloy AM, Scott JM, Daly SF. Elevated plasma homocysteine in early pregnancy: a risk factor for the development of severe preeclampsia. *Am J Obstet Gynecol* 2001;185:781–5.

135. Cotter AM, Molloy AM, Scott JM, Daly SF. Elevated plasma homocysteine in early pregnancy: a risk factor for the development of nonsevere preeclampsia. *Am J Obstet Gynecol* 2003;189:391–4; Discussion 394–6.

136. Hogg BB, Tamura T, Johnston KE, Dubard MB, Goldenberg RL. Second-trimester plasma homocysteine levels and pregnancy-induced hypertension, preeclampsia, and intrauterine growth restriction. *Am J Obstet Gynecol* 2000;183:805–9.

137. Mahomed K. Folate supplementation in pregnancy. *Cochrane Database Syst Rev* 2000;(2): CD000183.

138. Charles DH, Ness AR, Campbell D, Smith GD, Whitley E, Hall MH. Folic acid supplements in pregnancy and birth outcome: re-analysis of a large randomised controlled trial and update of Cochrane review. *Paediatr Perinat Epidemiol* 2005;19:112–24.

139. Belizan JM, Villar J. The relationship between calcium intake and edema-, proteinuria-, and hypertension-getosis: an hypothesis. *Am J Clin Nutr* 1980;33:2202–10.

140. Belizan JM, Villar J, Repke J. The relationship between calcium intake and pregnancy-induced hypertension: up-to-date evidence. *Am J Obstet Gynecol* 1988;158:898–902.

141. Hamlin RH. The prevention of eclampsia and pre-eclampsia. *Lancet* 1952;1:64–8.

142. Repke JT, Villar J. Pregnancy-induced hypertension and low birth weight: the role of calcium. *Am J Clin Nutr* 1991;54:237S–41S.

143. Villar J, Belizan JM, Fischer PJ. Epidemiologic observations on the relationship between calcium intake and eclampsia. *Int J Gynaecol Obstet* 1983;21:271–8.

144. Bucher HC, Guyatt GH, Cook RJ, Hatala R, Cook DJ, Lang JD, et al. Effect of calcium supplementation on pregnancy-induced hypertension and preeclampsia: a meta-analysis of randomized controlled trials. *JAMA* 1996;275:1113–17.

145. Levine RJ, Hauth JC, Curet LB, Sibai BM, Catalano PM, Morris CD, et al. Trial of calcium to prevent preeclampsia. *N Engl J Med* 1997;337:69–76.

146. Villar J, Abdel-Aleem H, Merialdi M, Mathai M, Ali MM, Zavaleta N, et al; World Health Organization Calcium Supplementation for the Prevention of Preeclampsia Trial Group. World Health Organization randomized trial of calcium supplementation among low calcium intake pregnant women. *Am J Obstet Gynecol* 2006;194:639–49.

147. Hofmeyr GJ, Atallah AN, Duley L. Calcium supplementation during pregnancy for preventing hypertensive disorders and related problems. *Cochrane Database Syst Rev* 2006;3:CD001059.

148. Bodnar LM, Tang G, Ness RB, Harger G, Roberts JM. Periconceptional multivitamin use reduces the risk of preeclampsia. *Am J Epidemiol* 2006;164:470–7.

149. Hernandez-Diaz S, Werler MM, Louik C, Mitchell AA. Risk of gestational hypertension in relation to folic acid supplementation during pregnancy. *Am J Epidemiol* 2002;156:806–12.

150. Merchant AT, Msamanga G, Villamor E, Saathoff E, O'Brien M, Hertzmark E, et al. Multivitamin supplementation of HIV-positive women during pregnancy reduces hypertension. *J Nutr* 2005;135:1776–81.

151. Olsen SF, Secher NJ. A possible preventive effect of low-dose fish oil on early delivery and pre-eclampsia: indications from a 50-year-old controlled trial. *Br J Nutr* 1990;64:599–609.

152. Roberts JM, Balk JL, Bodnar LM, Belizan JM, Bergel E, Martinez A. Nutrient involvement in preeclampsia. *J Nutr* 2003;133:1684S–92S.

153. Anonymous. Pre-eclampsia and prostaglandins [letter]. *Lancet* 1985;1:1267–8.

154. Williams MA, Zingheim RW, King IB, Zebelman AM. Omega-3 fatty acids in maternal erythrocytes and risk of preeclampsia. *Epidemiology* 1995;6:232–7.

155. Bulstra-Ramakers MT, Huisjes HJ, Visser GH. The effects of 3g eicosapentaenoic acid daily on recurrence of intrauterine growth retardation and pregnancy induced hypertension. *Br J Obstet Gynaecol* 1995;102:123–6.

156. Salvig JD, Olsen SF, Secher NJ. Effects of fish oil supplementation in late pregnancy on blood pressure: a randomised controlled trial. *Br J Obstet Gynaecol* 1996;103:529–33.

157. Kesmodel U, Olsen SF, Salvig JD. Marine n-3 fatty acid and calcium intake in relation to pregnancy induced hypertension, intrauterine growth retardation, and preterm delivery. A case–control study. *Acta Obstet Gynecol Scand* 1997;76:38–44.

158. Olsen SF, Secher NJ, Tabor A, Weber T, Walker JJ, Gluud C. Randomised clinical trials of fish oil supplementation in high risk pregnancies. Fish Oil Trials In Pregnancy (FOTIP) Team. *Br J Obstet Gynaecol* 2000;107:382–95.

159. Clausen T, Slott M, Solvoll K, Drevon CA, Vollset SE, Henriksen T. High intake of energy, sucrose, and polyunsaturated fatty acids is associated with increased risk of preeclampsia. *Am J Obstet Gynecol* 2001;185:451–8.

160. Scholl TO, Leskiw M, Chen X, Sims M, Stein TP. Oxidative stress, diet, and the etiology of preeclampsia. *Am J Clin Nutr* 2005;81:1390–6.

161. Olafsdottir AS, Magnusardottir AR, Thorgeirsdottir H, Hauksson A, Skuladottir GV, Steingrimsdottir L. Relationship between dietary intake of cod liver oil in early pregnancy and birthweight. *BJOG* 2005;112:424–9.

162. Marcoux S, Brisson J, Fabia J. The effect of leisure time physical activity on the risk of pre-eclampsia and gestational hypertension. *J Epidemiol Community Health* 1989;43:147–52.

163. Sorensen TK, Williams MA, Lee IM, Dashow EE, Thompson ML, Luthy DA. Recreational physical activity during pregnancy and risk of preeclampsia. *Hypertension* 2003;41:1273–80.

164. Saftlas AF, Logsden-Sackett N, Wang W, Woolson R, Bracken MB. Work, leisure-time physical activity, and risk of preeclampsia and gestational hypertension. *Am J Epidemiol* 2004;160:758–65.

165. Rudra CB, Williams MA, Lee IM, Miller RS, Sorensen TK. Perceived exertion during prepregnancy physical activity and preeclampsia risk. *Med Sci Sports Exerc* 2005;37:1836–41.

166. Ramsay JE, Ferrell WR, Crawford L, Wallace AM, Greer IA, Sattar N. Maternal obesity is associated with dysregulation of metabolic, vascular, and inflammatory pathways. *J Clin Endocrinol Metab* 2002;87:4231–7.

167. Watkins ML, Botto LD. Maternal prepregnancy weight and congenital heart defects in offspring. *Epidemiology* 2001;12:439–46.

168. Ray JG, Wyatt PR, Vermeulen MJ, Meier C, Cole DE. Greater maternal weight and the ongoing risk of neural tube defects after folic acid flour fortification. *Obstet Gynecol* 2005;105:261–5.

169. Goldenberg RL, Tamura T, Neggers Y, Copper RL, Johnston KE, DuBard MB, et al. The effect of zinc supplementation on pregnancy outcome. *JAMA* 1995;274:463–8.

170. Brankston GN, Mitchell BF, Ryan EA, Okun NB. Resistance exercise decreases the need for insulin in overweight women with gestational diabetes mellitus. *Am J Obstet Gynecol* 2004;190:188–93.

171. Finer LB, Henshaw SK. Disparities in rates of unintended pregnancy in the United States, 1994 and 2001. *Perspect Sex Reprod Health* 2006;38:90–6.

172. Lowe MR. Self-regulation of energy intake in the prevention and treatment of obesity: is it feasible? *Obes Res* 2003;11 Suppl: 44S–59S.

Chapter 13

Obesity in pregnancy and the legacy for the next generation: what can we learn from animal models?

Lucilla Poston and Paul Taylor

Introduction

Obesity is estimated to affect 15–20% of the global population[1] and is prevalent among all age groups, including women of reproductive age. In the USA, the latest National Health and Nutrition Examination Survey (NHANES), for 1999–2002, reported that 29% of women aged 20–39 years were clinically obese (defined as a body mass index (BMI) > 29.9 kg/m^2).[2] Once less prevalent, obesity in the UK is now approaching the levels in the USA, and recent statistics suggest that women in the UK are now the most obese in Europe.[3,4] Figures from the Department of Health based on the Health Survey for England 2003 predict that, by 2010, one in three adults will be obese, while 27% of girls aged 11–15 years will be obese, just as they are approaching childbearing age.[5] In the USA, not only are more women entering pregnancy with a high BMI[6] but many are exceeding the recommended gestational weight gain.[7,8] In a survey of 36 821 women attending a north-eastern UK maternity clinic between 1990 and 2004, 16% of the pregnant women were obese in 2004 and the number is accelerating towards an estimated 22% in 2010.[9]

Obesity in any age group of either sex is deleterious to health and the increasing concern over the effects of obesity on maternal and neonatal outcomes is reflected in a growing literature, including several excellent reviews in this book. Less obvious, and certainly far less appreciated, is the potential for maternal obesity and its biochemical consequences to permanently influence the developing child in a way that increases predisposition to obesity and diabetes in later life.

Developmental programming of adulthood disease

The 'developmental programming' concept was largely inspired by reports from Barker and his colleagues[10] in the 1980s, describing an association between risk of cardiovascular disease and low birthweight in cohorts of middle-aged men and women in the UK for whom detailed birth records were available. Similarly, Singhal and Lucas[11] had proposed that detrimental influences in early life may increase risk for later disease. The early papers from Barker and colleagues were followed by others showing that low birthweight was not only associated with increased risk of death from cardiovascular disease but also insulin resistance and obesity, i.e. each of the criteria which define the metabolic syndrome. Subsequent studies from geographically diverse populations have given strength to this hypothesis and have included the observation that premature children of low birthweight for gestational age also have heightened risk, as well as those born small at term.[12] Later developments have extended the hypothesis to include associations between low birthweight and rapid catch-up growth in infancy with adulthood risk of disease.[11,13,14]

Although it is generally considered that maternal obesity is associated with more large-for-gestational-age (LGA) than small-for-gestational-age (SGA) deliveries, a report of 187 290 Scottish women has documented a high rate of elective preterm deliveries and associated low birthweight among nulliparous women who were obese, whereas multiparous women who were obese had far fewer preterm deliveries.[15] This was considered to be the result of the higher rate of pre-eclampsia in the nulliparous women. A high rate of preterm delivery and low birthweight among nulliparous women with a BMI > 30 kg/m^2 has also recently been observed.[16] Surprisingly therefore, some offspring of women who are obese may have a heightened risk of cardiovascular disease through being born small or preterm. However, among the obese obstetric population, the risk of higher birthweight predominates and the rising incidence of LGA deliveries in some sizeable population studies in Europe has been attributed to the gradual increase over recent years in maternal obesity.[17] Inter-pregnancy weight gain between first and second deliveries has also been linked to an increased risk of an LGA delivery in the second pregnancy, even among women who are not obese. Even moderate weight gain between successive pregnancies resulted in significant increase in adverse pregnancy outcomes including LGA birth.[18] In terms of the developmental programming of adulthood cardiovascular and metabolic risk, the possible consequences of being born large are far less well documented. Higher birthweight in normoglycaemic pregnancies is generally associated with raised adult-hood BMI, and larger babies tend to become heavier adults; but detailed investigation of the relative contribution of lean and fat mass suggests that this association can reflect increased lean body mass rather than fat mass.[19] Chapter 16 provides a detailed summary of the literature, which suggests persistence of fat, rather than muscle, in the offspring of mothers who are obese or those who develop gestational diabetes mellitus (GDM), and has given rise to the 'fetal overnutrition' hypothesis.[20–22] Supporting evidence includes associations between maternal prepregnancy and childhood weight after adjustment for potential lifestyle confounding variables[23] and the demonstration that maternal rather than paternal adiposity is a major determinant of neonatal or adolescent adiposity.[24–26] Children of women who had diabetes when pregnant are also more likely to develop insulin resistance in later life and to become overweight.[27] While this may represent in part a genetically inherited disorder, studies of sib-pairs discordant for maternal diabetes show that this relationship holds only in offspring prenatally exposed to diabetes, strongly suggesting a developmentally acquired trait that is environmental rather than genetic in origin.[28,29]

Also, independent of birthweight, infants of mothers with GDM have a greater neonatal fat mass[30] as do infants of mothers who were obese and normoglycaemic,[31] and another report documents a high rate of childhood metabolic syndrome (central adiposity, insulin resistance and hypertension) in LGA babies born to mothers with GDM[32] compared with babies average for gestational age (AGA). Importantly, in the same study, the risk of metabolic syndrome was also present, but to a lesser extent, in LGA babies from mothers who were normoglycaemic. As a caveat to the human studies reported here, there has been mounting awareness of the potentially confounding inaccuracy of using BMI and birthweight as indices of 'fatness' in mother and baby, respectively. To address these issues, attention is increasingly focused on the more specific measurement of adiposity in parents and children, and there is a need for more and larger prospective studies incorporating preferred methods for assessment of body composition.[21]

Animal models of developmental programming

While studies in cohorts of women and children provide convincing evidence for the fetal 'overnutrition' hypothesis, it is inevitably difficult to correct for associations between maternal obesity and offspring phenotype given the many potential confounding variables within diverse human populations, such as childhood diet and activity and the genetic traits associated with obesity. In this regard, animal models are likely to prove useful and, importantly, provide insight into the underlying mechanisms of developmental programming.

Experimental protocols in rodents dominate the literature, largely for reasons of their rapid development to adulthood, but have the disadvantage that rats and mice are altricial animals, being born at a much earlier stage of development than man. However, while this may have implications for extrapolation to humans, the maturation of many homeostatic processes, such as the sympathetic nervous system, occurs over a broad perinatal period,[33] being relevant to both altricial and precocial mammals. Some experimenters have investigated sheep and a few have studied non-human primates, both having the advantage of greater maturity at birth, but these are long-term investigations requiring patience and considerable cost as several years must elapse before offspring can be investigated as mature adults.

Developmental programming of obesity by maternal undernutrition

In common with the epidemiological focus on the consequences of fetal and neonatal undernutrition, the literature in experimental animals is largely centred upon fetal nutrient deprivation and influence upon the adult metabolic and cardiovascular phenotype. Many studies have supported the concept that maternal undernutrition during critical periods can 'programme' offspring obesity, especially when the offspring are challenged postnatally with a hypercalorific diet.[34-37] Protein restriction *in utero*, commonly employed to induce fetal nutrient restriction in rats and mice, leads to susceptibility to obesity in adulthood.[38,39] In the more severe models of nutrient deprivation in which animals are subjected to as much as a 70% reduction in food intake, stress may be as great an influence as diet since, for example, prenatal stress in mice can also lead to increased body weight in adult offspring.[40] Offspring of nutrient-restricted dams often show rapid 'catch-up' growth when the dam is allowed free access to a normal diet postpartum, and therefore experience a high calorific intake in this period, as do the developing offspring of overfed dams where the enriched diet is often continued postpartum and suckling neonates are exposed to a richer milk supply. It could be argued, therefore, that mechanisms leading to adult obesity in the two opposing nutritional states may not be as different as supposed, should the postpartum period be a 'critical' window of vulnerability. Moreover, while overnutrition in pregnancy is associated with GDM, hyperglycaemia and hyperinsulinaemia, undernutrition followed by re-feeding is associated with the condition of 'starvation diabetes', which is characterised by impaired insulin secretion and action.[41] Hence, semi-starvation models of programming may also induce a degree of maternal hyperglycaemia on re-feeding in late pregnancy, thereby providing another potential common pathway between apparently disparate models. In both models, maternal hyperglycaemia would be freely transmitted to the fetus and can lead to overstimulation of the fetal pancreas with subsequent fetal hyperinsulinaemia, frequently implicated as a vector of fetal programming.[42]

Developmental programming of obesity by maternal overnutrition

The potential for maternal overnutrition to have persistent effects on offspring health and cardiovascular risk status has attracted fewer investigations, but these are generally supportive of the hypernutritional programming of obesity.[43] In 1986, Lewis and colleagues[44] recognised that overfeeding in the pre-weaning period in baboons increased adiposity through fat cell hypertrophy; this was gender dependent as only females were affected. In the rat, Guo and Jen[45] reported increases in body weight and adiposity in weaned offspring fed a 40% fat (by weight) diet during pregnancy. Increased body weights and a two-fold increase in the weight of the visceral fat depot have been reported in adult offspring of mildly overweight fat-fed dams (24% fat by weight: lard) that were weaned on to a normal chow diet,[46–48] and higher weight gain was also observed by Zhang and colleagues[49] in offspring of mice fed a lard- and protein-enriched diet. Increases in offspring body weight and/or adiposity compared with controls have also been reported in weanlings of dams fed 10% fish oil supplemented with gamma-linolenic acid[50] or of obese rats fed a 'highly palatable diet' rich in sugar and fats.[51] Adult offspring adiposity or increased weight have also been reported in normally fed offspring of dams fed a diet supplemented with 2% conjugated linoleic acid,[52] soy bean oil (a diet with a high n-6:n-3 fatty acid ratio)[53] or safflower oil (a diet rich in n-6 fatty acids).[54]

Others have addressed the hypothesis using obese genetically modified mice. Two reports have clearly shown developmentally induced adiposity in wild type offspring of obese mice in which hyperphagia and obesity in the dams is induced by partial knock out of the leptin receptor. Thus, wild type offspring (+/+) of obese heterozygous leptin-deficient mice (Lepr db/+) have been shown to develop increased fat mass in adulthood, so supporting transfer of a non-genetic obesogenic trait from mother to offspring.[55,56]

Developmental programming of insulin resistance by maternal hypernutrition

As might be expected, abnormal glucose homeostasis has been reported to accompany developmentally 'programmed' adiposity, but not invariably. Some authors have investigated insulin sensitivity using glucose tolerance tests and have addressed mechanisms by evaluating expression of insulin signalling proteins. Determination of pancreatic β-cell function has also provided interesting insight.

The first-phase insulin secretion in response to a glucose load, considered to be the most vulnerable phase of insulin secretion, is enhanced in 3-month-old offspring of rats fed a safflower oil-enriched diet[54] and could, as suggested in man, be a prodrome for development of later type 2 diabetes mellitus. The offspring of these fat-fed dams had significantly elevated liver triglyceride content and raised expression of insulin signalling proteins, consistent with reduced hepatic insulin sensitivity, but increased quadriceps insulin sensitivity. Also, pups fed a carbohydrate-enriched milk formula from birth developed lifelong hyperinsulinaemia despite being weaned onto a normal diet.[57,58] Insulin signalling in the liver of the adult wild type progeny of Lepr db/+ mice is also abnormal as shown by decreased insulin stimulated phosphorylation of Akt, a key intermediate in insulin signalling.[55] Interestingly, weanling offspring of obese dams fed a highly palatable diet have reduced muscle mass and increased deposition of fat in the muscle, which could contribute to later insulin resistance.[51] In our laboratory, we have found that 1-year-old offspring of dams fed a lard-rich diet are insulin resistant as well as being hypertensive and fatter than controls. Moreover, these animals demonstrate associated pancreatic β-cell morphology indicative of β-cell exhaustion and insulin depletion, with reduced glucose-stimulated insulin release in isolated islets.[48] Evidence that maternal fat feeding reduces neonatal β-cell number and volume[59] may suggest that the developing pancreas is particularly vulnerable to the influence of a maternal hypercalorific diet rich in fats. This may be especially true in the early postnatal period when the pancreas undergoes a high degree of remodelling through apoptosis and proliferation during what is a critical developmental window.

Interesting insight into similar critical windows of development, which are susceptible to a maternal hypercalorific diet and/or obesity, and into potential mechanisms has already been gained from animal models, and will now be briefly reviewed.

The suckling period as a critical window of development in programming of obesity

The suckling period appears to be particularly critical in programming of obesity arising from a hypernutritional environment. The strongest evidence is derived from studies in which postnatal overfeeding in normal rat pups has been induced by reducing the litter size after delivery so that each pup receives more milk than a pup in a litter of normal size. These pups develop into fatter adult animal.[42,60-65] Adverse influence of a maternal obesogenic environment has also been studied in a strain of obesity-prone rats. Cross-fostering litters of obesity-resistant pups to dams of the obesity-prone strain has been shown to result in greater susceptibility to diet-induced adiposity in later life in the genetically normal offspring.[66] In another approach to address the potentially critical role of the suckling period, Srinivasan et al.[57] artificially reared newborn pups from normally fed dams on a high-carbohydrate milk substitute and found this to lead to increased adiposity and insulin resistance in later life, and that this phenotype is transmittable to the next generation. Maternal diabetes in rats also programmes offspring obesity,[67] as has been proposed from cohort studies of offspring from women affected by diabetes in pregnancy, and Plagemann and colleagues[68] have shown that transient neonatal hyperinsulinaemia during critical postnatal periods is likely to play a role in the programming of the obese phenotype. Yura and colleagues[69] have, however, implicated leptin, since leptin injection into mouse pups postpartum led to obesity in the offspring, but evidence from studies in rats is not entirely supportive.[63,70] Having been implicated as programming vectors, the question remains as to how insulin or leptin, or both, may permanently affect offspring metabolism so that the animal becomes obese as it grows into adulthood.

Extrapolation to the human situation must be exercised with care; rats and mice are born more immature compared with the human child. However, there is a substantial literature favouring breastfeeding over formula feeding in relation to prevention of obesity in children and, together with the evidence that formula-fed infants exhibiting rapid catch-up growth are at risk of obesity, could also indicate an important role for postnatal hypernutrition in the developmental programming of obesity in humans.[13,21,71,72]

Developmental programming of obesity: mechanistic insights

Obesity arises from an imbalance between energy intake and energy expenditure; therefore programmed animals may become obese because of altered appetite regulation or altered energy expenditure via physical activity or tissue metabolism.

Increased appetite

The hypothalamus plays a central role in coordination of appetite regulatory pathways. In the arcuate nucleus (ARC), neuropeptide Y (NPY) and agouti-related protein (AgRP) neurons are the major site of the appetite stimulating (orexigenic) drive while pro-opiomelanocortin (POMC) and cocaine- and amphetamine-regulated transcript (CART)-secreting neurons provide the inhibitory anorexigenic drive. It is now proposed that the hypothalamic control of appetite may be developmentally regulated by exposure to a hypercalorific diet.[73–76] In rodents, development is mostly postnatal and therefore more amenable and relevant to experimental manipulation. Extensive neuronal development is likely to occur in the suckling period in humans and primates and therefore may also have relevance to the human situation.[33]

Overfeeding of neonatal rat pups produced by reducing litter size results in offspring hyperphagia and adiposity hyperleptinaemia, hyperinsulinaemia, and resistance to leptin feedback on the ARC.[6,63–65] Kozak et al.[77] have also directly implicated the hypothalamus by showing that the increase in feeding in response to NPY injection into the lateral ventricle of the brain is exaggerated in 6-month-old offspring of mothers fed a heavily fat-enriched diet (margarine), and another study has shown that weaning pups of dams fed a high-fat diet demonstrate upregulation of appetite stimulatory galanin and orexin mRNA expression in the paraventricular nucleus (PVN) and lateral hypothalamus, respectively.[78] Overfeeding of ewes during pregnancy appears to alter anorexigenic mechanisms, at least in the early postnatal period, through alteration of the appetite-inhibiting CART-expressing neurones.[75,79,80] The recent demonstration that exogenous leptin can alter neuronal outgrowth from the ARC to the PVN of the rodent brain, as shown in early postnatal life in the leptin-deficient (ob/ob) mice, has led to the important proposal that dietary-induced surges in leptin in the developing fetal or neonatal brain could permanently 'hard wire' appetite regulatory systems.[81,82] Several studies in mice and rats in which leptin has been injected into rodent pups have led to equivocal results in relation to phenotype but have shown clear effects on fat mass.[69,70] These studies have attracted much attention in this field because an early and irreversible effect on appetite regulatory centres in the developing brain presents an attractive hypothesis, and one that is testable.

Locomotor activity

There have been few attempts to determine physical activity in offspring prenatally exposed to maternal obesity or to a hypernutritional environment during development. A maternal diet rich in saturated fats has been shown to reduce offspring locomotor activity as assessed by a swim test,[83] whereas it has been found that offspring of lard-fed dams are less active when investigated by remote radio-telemetric recording.[46] Studies from weaning to adulthood are required to determine whether this precedes development of adiposity or whether reduced locomotor activity may be a determining factor.

Metabolism

As far as is known, no study has been published in which metabolic rate has been determined in offspring of obese dams or dams fed a hypercalorific diet. There is, however, some evidence to suggest that adipose tissue metabolism may be altered in a manner that might contribute to increased fat deposition. Unlike many tissues, adipose tissue has the potential for unlimited growth and diet-induced increases in fat cell number may also be irreversible. Adipocyte hypertrophy occurs in weanling progeny of obese rats fed a highly palatable diet[51] and direct infusion of glucose into the ovine fetus is accompanied by a parallel increase in fat mass[84] but it is not known whether these changes persist to adulthood. Muhlhausler *et al.*[85] have shown an increase in expression of peroxisome proliferator-activated receptor γ (PPARγ), lipoprotein lipase, adiponectin and leptin mRNA expression in the fetal perirenal fat of lambs whose mothers were fed a diet that was 55% above energy-maintenance requirements. The data suggests a proliferative increase in signalling pathways that could contribute to obesity in later life. Further evidence for effects on adipocyte metabolism comes from a study of white and brown adipose tissue from 8-week-old wild type offspring of Lepr db/+ dams, which showed that the increased adipose mass was due to adipose cell hypertrophy and was associated with increased leptin and apelin mRNA expression, overexpression of which has been linked to obesity.[56]

Conclusion

Protocols in experimental animals have lent considerable strength to the 'fetal hypernutrition' hypothesis but suggest that the fetal and neonatal periods should be considered as equally susceptible to a hypernutritional environment. The various animal models, including genetically modified mice, provide the means to interrogate the mechanisms underlying developmental programming of obesity and aberrant glucose homeostasis. While it is understood that the hypothalamic control of appetite regulatory centres and adipocyte metabolism are likely to be involved, the exact molecular mechanisms are yet to be defined. Models of maternal undernutrition that have implicated altered methylation status of genes intimately involved in metabolism clearly suggest that the methylation status of candidate genes should be investigated in the hypernutritional models of programming.[86] It is clear from the differing protocols used to study effects of maternal overnutrition that dietary composition as well as maternal obesity *per se* could play an equally important role, but the relative contributions of starch, sugars, different fats and protein require better definition and are open to further more detailed interrogation. This is particularly relevant to the human situation in which, if an optimal diet were defined for prevention of offspring obesity and insulin resistance, one could anticipate optimising the maternal diet among pregnant women who are obese with a view to reducing the long-term risk of ill health in the offspring.

References

1. World Health Organization. *Global Strategy on Diet, Physical Activity and Health.* WHO; 2003.
2. Hedley AA, Ogden CL, Johnson CL, Carroll MD, Curtin LR, Flegal KM. Prevalence of overweight and obesity among US children, adolescents, and adults, 1999–2002. *JAMA* 2004;291:2847–50.
3. European Commission. Eurostat 2007 [epp.eurostat.ec.europa. eu/portal/page?_pageid=1090,30070682,1090_33076576&_dad=portal&_schema=PORTAL].
4. American College of Obstetricians and Gynecologists. ACOG Committee Opinion number 315, September 2005. Obesity in pregnancy. *Obstet Gynecol* 2005;106:671–5.
5. Department of Health. *Forecasting Obesity to 2010.* London: DH; 2006 [www.dh.gov.uk/assetRoot/04/13/86/29/04138629.pdf].
6. Yen J, Shelton J. Increasing prepregnancy body mass index: Analysis of trends and contributing variables. *Obstet Gynecol* 2005;193:1994–8.
7. Olson CM, Strawderman MS, Hinton PS, Pearson TA. Gestational weight gain and postpartum behaviors associated with weight change from early pregnancy to 1 y postpartum. *Int J Obes Relat Metab Disord* 2003;27:117–27.

8. Institute of Medicine. *Nutrition during Pregnancy. Part I. Weight Gain.* Washington, DC: National Academy Press; 1990.

9. Heslehurst N, Ells LJ, Simpson H, Batterham A, Wilkinson J, Summerbell CD. Trends in maternal obesity incidence rates, demographic predictors, and health inequalities in 36,821 women over a 15-year period. *BJOG* 2007;114:187–94.

10. Barker DJ, Osmond C. Childhood respiratory infection and adult chronic bronchitis in England and Wales. *Br Med J (Clin Res Ed)* 1986;293:1271–5.

11. Singhal A, Lucas A. Early origins of cardiovascular disease: is there a unifying hypothesis? *Lancet* 2004;363:1642–5.

12. Johansson S, Iliadou A, Bergvall N, Tuvemo T, Norman M, Cnattingius S. Risk of high blood pressure among young men increases with the degree of immaturity at birth. *Circulation* 2005;112:3430–6.

13. Stettler N, Stallings VA, Troxel AB, Zhao J, Schinnar R, Nelson SE, *et al.* Weight gain in the first week of life and overweight in adulthood: a cohort study of European American subjects fed infant formula. *Circulation* 2005;111:1897–903.

14. Barker DJ, Osmond C, Forsen TJ, Kajantie E, Eriksson JG. Trajectories of growth among children who have coronary events as adults. *N Engl J Med* 2005;353:1802–9.

15. Smith GC, Shah I, Pell JP, Crossley JA, Dobbie R. Maternal obesity in early pregnancy and risk of spontaneous and elective preterm deliveries: a retrospective cohort study. *Am J Public Health* 2007;97:157–62.

16. Poston L, Seed P, Rajasingham D, Briley A, Shennan A. Pregnancy outcome in obese primiparous pregnant women recruited to the Vitamins in Pre-eclampsia trial. *Reprod Sci* 2007;23:240A.

17. Surkan PJ, Hsieh CC, Johansson AL, Dickman PW, Cnattingius S. Reasons for increasing trends in large for gestational age births. *Obstet Gynecol* 2004;104:720–6.

18. Villamor E, Cnattingius S. Interpregnancy weight change and risk of adverse pregnancy outcomes: a population-based study. *Lancet* 2006;368:1164–70.

19. Singhal A, Wells J, Cole TJ, Fewtrell M, Lucas A. Programming of lean body mass: a link between birth weight, obesity, and cardiovascular disease? *Am J Clin Nutr* 2003;77:726–30.

20. Ebbeling CB, Pawlak DB, Ludwig DS. Childhood obesity: public-health crisis, common sense cure. *Lancet* 2002;360:473–82.

21. Oken E, Gillman MW. Fetal origins of obesity. *Obes Res* 2003;11:496–506.

22. Lawlor DA, Chaturvedi N. Treatment and prevention of obesity – are there critical periods for intervention? *Int J Epidemiol* 2006;35:3–9.

23. Salsberry PJ, Reagan PB. Dynamics of early childhood overweight. *Pediatrics* 2005;116:1329–38.

24. Lawlor DA, Smith GD, O'Callaghan M, Alati R, Mamun AA, Williams GM, *et al.* Epidemiologic evidence for the fetal overnutrition hypothesis: findings from the mater-university study of pregnancy and its outcomes. *Am J Epidemiol* 2007;165:418–24.

25. Shields BM, Knight BA, Powell RJ, Hattersley AT, Wright DE. Assessing newborn body composition using principal components analysis: differences in the determinants of fat and skeletal size. *BMC Pediatr* 2006;6:24.

26. Harvey NC, Poole JR, Javaid MK, Dennison EM, Robinson S, Inskip HM, *et al.* Parental determinants of neonatal body composition. *J Clin Endocrinol Metab* 2007;92:523–6.

27. Dorner G, Plagemann A. Perinatal hyperinsulinism as possible predisposing factor for diabetes mellitus, obesity and enhanced cardiovascular risk in later life. *Horm Metab Res* 1994;26:213–21.

28. Dabelea D, Hanson RL, Lindsay RS, Pettitt DJ, Imperatore G, Gabir MM, *et al.* Intrauterine exposure to diabetes conveys risks for type 2 diabetes and obesity: a study of discordant sibships. *Diabetes* 2000;49:2208–11.

29. Dabelea D, Pettitt DJ. Intrauterine diabetic environment confers risks for type 2 diabetes mellitus and obesity in the offspring, in addition to genetic susceptibility. *J Pediatr Endocrinol Metab* 2001;14:1085–91.

30. Catalano PM, Thomas A, Huston-Presley L, Amini SB. Increased fetal adiposity: a very sensitive marker of abnormal *in utero* development; *Am J Obstet Gynecol* 2003;189:1698–704.

31. Sewell MF, Huston-Presley L, Super DM, Catalano P. Increased neonatal fat mass, not lean body mass, is associated with maternal obesity. *Am J Obstet Gynecol* 2006;195:1100–3.

32. Boney CM, Verma A, Tucker R, Vohr BR. Metabolic syndrome in childhood: association with birth weight, maternal obesity, and gestational diabetes mellitus. *Pediatrics* 2005;115:e290–6.

33. Grove KL, Grayson BE, Glavas MM, Xiao XQ, Smith MS. Development of metabolic systems. *Physiol Behav* 2005;86:646–60.

34. Bispham J, Gardner DS, Gnanalingham MG, Stephenson T, Symonds ME, Budge H. Maternal nutritional programming of fetal adipose tissue development: differential effects on messenger ribonucleic acid abundance and peroxisome proliferator-activated and prolactin receptors. *Endocrinology* 2005;146:3943–9.

35. Budge H, Gnanalingham MG, Gardner DS, Mostyn A, Stephenson T, Symonds ME. Maternal nutritional programming of fetal adipose tissue development: long-term consequences for later obesity. *Birth Defects Res C Embryo Today* 2005;75:193–9.

36. Stocker CJ, Arch JR, Cawthorne MA. Fetal origins of insulin resistance and obesity. *Proc Nutr Soc* 2005;64:143–51.

37. Vickers MH, Breier BH, Cutfield WS, Hofman PL, Gluckman PD. Fetal origins of hyperphagia, obesity, and hypertension and postnatal amplification by hypercaloric nutrition. *Am J Physiol Endocrinol Metab* 2000;279:E83–7.

38. Ozanne SE, Lewis R, Jennings BJ, Hales CN. Early programming of weight gain in mice prevents the induction of obesity by a highly palatable diet. *Clin Sci (Lond)* 2004;106:141–5.

39. Zambrano E, Bautista CJ, Deas M, Martinez-Samayoa PM, Gonzalez-Zamorano M, Ledesma H, *et al.* A low maternal protein diet during pregnancy and lactation has sex- and window of exposure-specific effects on offspring growth and food intake, glucose metabolism and serum leptin in the rat. *J Physiol* 2006;571:221–30.

40. Mueller BR, Bale TL. Impact of prenatal stress on long term body weight is dependent on timing and maternal sensitivity. *Physiol Behav* 2006;88:605–14.

41. Zawalich WS, Dye ES, Pagliara AS, Rognstad R, Matschinsky FM. Starvation diabetes in the rat: onset, recovery, and specificity of reduced responsiveness of pancreatic beta-cells. *Endocrinology* 1979;104:1344–51.

42. Plagemann A. Perinatal programming and functional teratogenesis: Impact on body weight regulation and obesity. *Physiol Behav* 2005;86:661–8.

43. Armitage JA, Khan IY, Taylor PD, Nathanielsz PW, Poston L. Developmental programming of the metabolic syndrome by maternal nutritional imbalance: how strong is the evidence from experimental models in mammals? *J Physiol* 2004;561:355–77.

44. Lewis DS, Bertrand HA, McMahan CA, McGill HC Jr, Carey KD, Masoro EJ. Preweaning food intake influences the adiposity of young adult baboons. *J Clin Invest* 1986;78:899–905.

45. Guo F, Jen KL. High-fat feeding during pregnancy and lactation affects offspring metabolism in rats. *Physiol Behav* 1995;57:681–6.

46. Khan IY, Taylor PD, Dekou V, Seed PT, Lakasing L, Graham D, *et al.* Gender-linked hypertension in offspring of lard-fed pregnant rats. *Hypertension* 2003;41:168–75.

47. Khan IY, Dekou V, Hanson M, Poston L, Taylor PD. Predictive adaptive responses to maternal high fat diet prevent endothelial dysfunction but not hypertension in adult rat offspring. *Circulation* 2004;110:1097–102.

48. Taylor PD, McConnell J, Khan IY, Holemans K, Lawrence KM, Asare-Anane H, *et al.* Impaired glucose homeostasis and mitochondrial abnormalities in offspring of rats fed a fat-rich diet in pregnancy. *Am J Physiol Regul Integr Comp Physiol* 2005;288:R134–9.

49. Zhang J, Wang C, Terroni PL, Cagampang FR, Hanson M, Byrne CD. High-unsaturated-fat, high-protein, and low-carbohydrate diet during pregnancy and lactation modulates hepatic lipid metabolism in female adult offspring. *Am J Physiol Regul Integr Comp Physiol* 2005;288:R112–18.

50. Amusquivar E, Ruperez FJ, Barbas C, Herrera E. Low arachidonic acid rather than alpha-tocopherol is responsible for the delayed postnatal development in offspring of rats fed fish oil instead of olive oil during pregnancy and lactation. *J Nutr* 2000;130:2855–65.

51. Bayol SA, Simbi BH, Stickland NC. A maternal cafeteria diet during gestation and lactation promotes adiposity and impairs skeletal muscle development and metabolism in rat offspring at weaning. *J Physiol* 2005;567:951–61.

52. Bee G. Dietary conjugated linoleic acid consumption during pregnancy and lactation influences growth and tissue composition in weaned pigs. *J Nutr* 2000;130:2981–9.

53. Korotkova M, Gabrielsson BG, Holmang A, Larsson BM, Hanson LA, Strandvik B. Gender-related long-term effects in adult rats by perinatal dietary ratio of n-6/n-3 fatty acids. *Am J Physiol Regul Integr Comp Physiol* 2005;288:R575–9.

54. Buckley AJ, Keseru B, Briody J, Thompson M, Ozanne SE, Thompson CH. Altered body composition and metabolism in the male offspring of high fat-fed rats. *Metabolism* 2005;54:500–7.

55. Yamashita H, Shao J, Qiao L, Pagliassotti M, Friedman JE. Effect of spontaneous gestational diabetes on fetal and postnatal hepatic insulin resistance in Lepr(db/+) mice. *Pediatr Res* 2003;53:411–18.

56. Lambin S, van Bree R, Caluwaerts S, Vercruysse L, Vergote I, Verhaeghe J. Adipose tissue in offspring of Lepr(db/+) mice: early-life environment vs. genotype. *Am J Physiol Endocrinol Metab* 2007;292:E262–71.

57. Srinivasan M, Laychock SG, Hill DJ, Patel MS. Neonatal nutrition: metabolic programming of pancreatic islets and obesity. *Exp Biol Med (Maywood)* 2003;228:15–23.

58. Mitrani P, Srinivasan M, Dodds C, Patel MS. Autonomic involvement in the permanent metabolic programming of hyperinsulinemia in the high-carbohydrate rat model. *Am J Physiol Endocrinol Metab* 2007;292:E1364–77.

59. Cerf ME, Williams K, Nkomo XI, Muller CJ, Du Toit DF, Louw J, et al. Islet cell response in the neonatal rat after exposure to a high-fat diet during pregnancy. *Am J Physiol Regul Integr Comp Physiol* 2005;288:R1122–8.

60. Plagemann A, Harder T, Melchior K, Rake A, Rohde W, Dorner G. Elevation of hypothalamic neuropeptide Y-neurons in adult offspring of diabetic mother rats. *Neuroreport* 1999;10:3211–16.

61. Bassett DR, Craig BW. Influence of early nutrition on growth and adipose tissue characteristics in male and female rats. *J Appl Physiol* 1988;64:1249–56.

62. Plagemann A, Harder T, Rake A, Waas T, Melchior K, Ziska T, et al. Observations on the orexigenic hypothalamic neuropeptide Y-system in neonatally overfed weanling rats. *J Neuroendocrinol* 1999;11:541–6.

63. Schmidt I, Fritz A, Scholch C, Schneider D, Simon E, Plagemann A. The effect of leptin treatment on the development of obesity in overfed suckling Wistar rats. *Int J Obes Relat Metab Disord* 2001;25:1168–74.

64. Davidowa H, Plagemann A. Hypothalamic neurons of postnatally overfed, overweight rats respond differentially to corticotropin-releasing hormones. *Neurosci Lett* 2004;371:64–8.

65. Velkoska E, Cole TJ, Morris MJ. Early dietary intervention: long-term effects on blood pressure, brain neuropeptide Y, and adiposity markers. *Am J Physiol Endocrinol Metab* 2005;288:E1236–43.

66. Gorski JN, Dunn-Meynell AA, Hartman TG, Levin BE. Postnatal environment overrides genetic and prenatal factors influencing offspring obesity and insulin resistance. *Am J Physiol Regul Integr Comp Physiol* 2006;291:R768–78.

67. Plagemann A. Perinatal nutrition and hormone-dependent programming of food intake. *Horm Res* 2006;65 Suppl 3:83–9.

68. Harder T, Rake A, Rohde W, Doerner G, Plagemann A. Overweight and increased diabetes susceptibility in neonatally insulin-treated adult rats. *Endocr Regul* 1999;33:25–31.

69. Yura S, Itoh H, Sagawa N, Yamamoto H, Masuzaki H, Nakao K, et al. Role of premature leptin surge in obesity resulting from intrauterine undernutrition. *Cell Metab* 2005;1:371–8.

70. Vickers MH, Gluckman PD, Coveny AH, Hofman PL, Cutfield WS, Gertler A, et al. Neonatal leptin treatment reverses developmental programming. *Endocrinology* 2005;146:4211–16.

71. Gillman MW, Rifas-Shiman SL, Camargo CA Jr, Berkey CS, Frazier AL, Rockett HR, et al. Risk of overweight among adolescents who were breastfed as infants. *JAMA* 2001;285:2461–7.

72. Owen CG, Martin RM, Whincup PH, Smith GD, Cook DG. Effect of infant feeding on the risk of obesity across the life course: a quantitative review of published evidence. *Pediatrics* 2005;115:1367–77.

73. Cripps RL, Martin-Gronert MS, Ozanne SE. Fetal and perinatal programming of appetite. *Clin Sci (Lond)* 2005;109:1–11.

74. McMillen IC, Adam CL, Muhlhausler BS. Early origins of obesity: programming the appetite regulatory system. *J Physiol* 2005;565(Pt 1):9–17.

75. Muhlhausler BS, Adam CL, Marrocco EM, Findlay PA, Roberts CT, McFarlane JR, et al. Impact of glucose infusion on the structural and functional characteristics of adipose tissue and on

hypothalamic gene expression for appetite regulatory neuropeptides in the sheep fetus during late gestation. *J Physiol* 2005;565(Pt 1):185–95.

76. Plagemann A, Davidowa H, Harder T, Dudenhausen JW. Developmental programming of the hypothalamus: a matter of insulin. A comment on: Horvath, T. L., Bruning, J. C.: Developmental programming of the hypothalamus: a matter of fat. Nat. Med. (2006) 12: 52–53. *Neuro Endocrinol Lett* 2006;27:70–2.

77. Kozak R, Burlet A, Burlet C, Beck B. Dietary composition during fetal and neonatal life affects neuropeptide Y functioning in adult offspring. *Brain Res Dev Brain Res* 2000;125:75–82.

78. Beck B, Kozak R, Moar KM, Mercer JG. Hypothalamic orexigenic peptides are overexpressed in young Long-Evans rats after early life exposure to fat-rich diets. *Biochem Biophys Res Commun* 2006;342:452–8.

79. Muhlhausler BS, Adam CL, Findlay PA, Duffield JA, McMillen IC. Increased maternal nutrition alters development of the appetite-regulating network in the brain. *FASEB J* 2006;20:1257–9.

80. Muhlhausler BS. Programming of the appetite-regulating neural network: a link between maternal overnutrition and the programming of obesity? *J Neuroendocrinol* 2007;19:67–72.

81. Bouret SG, Draper SJ, Simerly RB. Trophic action of leptin on hypothalamic neurons that regulate feeding. *Science* 2004;304:108–10.

82. Horvath TL, Bruning JC. Developmental programming of the hypothalamus: a matter of fat. *Nat Med* 2006;12:52–3; Discussion 53.

83. Raygada M, Cho E, Hilakivi-Clarke L. High maternal intake of polyunsaturated fatty acids during pregnancy in mice alters offsprings' aggressive behavior, immobility in the swim test, locomotor activity and brain protein kinase C activity. *J Nutr* 1998;128:2505–11.

84. Stevens D, Alexander G, Bell AW. Effect of prolonged glucose infusion into fetal sheep on body growth, fat deposition and gestation length. *J Dev Physiol* 1990;13:277–81.

85. Muhlhausler BS, Duffield JA, McMillen IC. Increased maternal nutrition stimulates peroxisome proliferator activated receptor-gamma, adiponectin, and leptin messenger ribonucleic acid expression in adipose tissue before birth. *Endocrinology* 2007;148:878–85.

86. Lillycrop KA, Phillips ES, Jackson AA, Hanson MA, Burdge GC. Dietary protein restriction of pregnant rats induces and folic acid supplementation prevents epigenetic modification of hepatic gene expression in the offspring. *J Nutr* 2005;135:1382–6.

Chapter 14
Obesity and anaesthesia

Martin Dresner

Introduction

Given that the incidence of a number of surgical conditions is increased in women who are obese, and that the complications of pregnancy that require surgical intervention are also increased, it follows that these women are more likely to require anaesthesia at some time than their peers who are of normal weight. It is also the case that obesity predisposes to medical conditions that increase anaesthetic risk, such as ischaemic heart disease and obstructive sleep apnoea. Not only this, but certain complications of anaesthesia are more common in obese people, such as problems with intubation. This introduction can therefore be summarised with the statement that *obesity increases the need for and the risk from anaesthesia*. The Association of Anaesthetists of Great Britain and Northern Ireland (AAGBI) has produced guidelines for the anaesthetic management of people who are obese, which will be published in 2007.

Measuring and describing obesity

Body mass index (BMI) has become the established method of measuring and describing obesity. However, just as for surgeons, BMI has its limitations in conveying the problems posed by obesity for anaesthetists. This is because of the physical and metabolic heterogeneity that exists among individuals with the same BMI. An example of this is that central or abdominal obesity produces more risk of cardiac disease than obesity distributed more to the hips and bottom. A waist measurement greater than 88 cm in women is associated with a high incidence of morbidity and mortality,[1] even if BMI is normal. Whatever a woman's BMI, the likelihood of anaesthetic problems can only be adequately assessed by physical examination and clinical investigations performed in the preoperative or antenatal period.

Preoperative and antenatal anaesthetic assessment

Anaesthetists assess most women requiring surgery at the time of admission to hospital. UK anaesthetists are increasingly embracing the culture of clinic-based assessment of people deemed to be at increased risk. This process is designed to reduce patient risk and preoperative cancellations, so it is in the interests of gynaecologists and obstetricians to support the development of this service within their trusts.

BMI is the usual obesity criterion used to trigger referral by surgeons and pre-assessment nurses to the anaesthetic clinic, but in the absence of clear evidence the precise threshold figure can be agreed locally. A BMI of 40 kg/m^2 may be appropriate for younger women but a lower value might be advisable for older women who are more likely to have developed obesity-related systemic morbidity such as ischaemic heart disease. It is useful for obstetricians and gynaecologists to appreciate the key physical features of obesity that are of concern to anaesthetists so that they can refer women who may fall outside of the BMI referral trigger. These include:

■ obesity in the hands, arms and neck that may that may cause difficulties with vascular access

■ obesity affecting the neck and tongue and a history of snoring and obstructive sleep apnoea, all of which may cause problems with airway management and intubation

■ obesity affecting the lumbar and thoracic spine, which may severely hamper spinal and epidural techniques (the most common forms of regional anaesthesia used in obstetrics and gynaecology).

Subsequent anaesthetic management may demand specialist equipment, senior personnel with specific skill sets, prolonged post-anaesthetic care and possibly high-dependency or intensive care. Planning of the date, location and duration of surgery must clearly be a multidisciplinary process that includes anaesthetists. It must not be assumed that the required skills and equipment are always available without prior planning.

Anaesthetic assessment also provides the opportunity to counsel patients about the procedures and risks. The AAGBI guidelines allow anaesthetists to be mindful of the psychological as well as physical needs of people who are obese, which is vital if rapport and trust are to be gained. Fear of causing offence should not deter anaesthetists from pointing out the problems of obesity, but this must be performed in a non-pejorative and sympathetic manner.

General considerations

Hospitals that have a bariatric surgical programme may already have the organisational commitment, protocols, expertise and staff training required for the safe anaesthetic management of obese patients. Other units may need to address these issues afresh, and AAGBI guidelines propose that one or more consultant anaesthetists be named as part of the multidisciplinary team charged with establishing this culture. This must, of course, consider the fact that not all surgery on women who are obese will take place on an elective basis and provision must be made for the availability of appropriate equipment and personnel on an emergency basis. In order to achieve this level of organisation, it is necessary to consider the following points:

■ staff training

■ risk reduction

■ specialised equipment.

Staff training

The basic training of surgeons, anaesthetists, nurses, technicians and porters does not necessarily include adequate consideration of the problems of managing people who are obese. An example of this is lifting and handling training, which, although mandatory, does not routinely include the use of specialised lifting equipment. This is important for the safety of patients, who are at increased risk of injury to skin, muscle and nerves from pressure when immobilised by anaesthesia, and from falling during transfer between trolleys and operating tables. Staff are at significant risk of back injury during the movement of people who are obese. Lifting, handling and pressure area care are therefore keys areas for staff training. An anaesthetist should join other key members of a multidisciplinary theatre team in organising appropriate training for staff through internal or external training sessions, possibly with secondments to units with established bariatric services. Consideration should also be given to documentation and updating of this training.

As well as adequate training, it must also be appreciated that staff numbers may need to be increased during the care of people who are obese. A policy may be required to determine from where such additional staff can be obtained in both elective and emergency situations.

Risk reduction

It would seem logical to assume that weight loss immediately before surgery would reduce the risk of perioperative morbidity and mortality. However, some studies refute this assumption[2,3] and rapid weight loss might actually increase risk through dehydration and malnutrition. Despite being overweight, some individuals are already in a poor nutritional state. Weight loss, therefore, only has value if a significant delay before surgery is possible, and then it should probably be directed by a trained dietician. The same argument is probably true for smoking.

Despite these points, surgeons and anaesthetists can still reduce perioperative risk by considering the following factors.

Aspiration prophylaxis

Obstetricians are well aware of the risk of aspiration during anaesthesia in pregnancy. Many of the physical causes of gastro-oesophageal reflux also apply to the obese, so it is wise to assume that women who are obese are also at increased risk of aspiration of stomach contents during and after general anaesthesia. Strict adherence to fasting guidelines and the prescription of drugs to reduce the volume and acidity of gastric secretions are important precautions. Anaesthetic techniques are modified to take account of this risk, using techniques such as rapid sequence induction, cricoid pressure, and induction in the reversed Trendelenberg position.

Thromboprophylaxis

Although the responsibility for thromboprophylaxis could be considered to rest primarily with surgeons, it should be planned in discussion with anaesthetists. Epidural or spinal anaesthesia is considered to be contraindicated within 12 hours of a patient receiving prophylactic low molecular weight heparin. If these regional anaesthetic techniques were deemed to be critical components of the planned anaesthesia, the untimely administration of heparin might lead to postponement of surgery. The removal of epidural catheters must also be performed in an appropriate window between anticoagulant doses, so this must be performed in consultation with the anaesthetic team.

Sensible surgical scheduling

Surgery should be scheduled only when appropriately experienced surgeons and anaesthetists are available. Clinicians who feel inadequately experienced for these cases must be encouraged to seek the assistance of senior colleagues without fear of loss of reputation.

It is possible that tension may arise if the safest time for surgery conflicts with waiting time targets, and clinicians must be prepared to make a robust case for delaying surgery when it is in the patient's best interests.

On the day of surgery, it makes sense for patients who are obese to be scheduled early in a session to allow adequate time for postoperative monitoring before consultant staff leave the hospital.

Postoperative care

Women who are obese should be nursed in an area with adequate numbers of trained staff, with the appropriate equipment. This, in itself, may preclude the usual surgical ward, and a period in a high-dependency ward may be appropriate. Of course, obesity-related co-morbidity and the complexity of the surgery undertaken may also justify some time in a high-dependency or intensive care ward.

Patients with obstructive sleep apnoea may require non-invasive respiratory support devices in the postoperative period. A chest physician or intensive care anaesthetist with the appropriate experience should be contacted before surgery to provide advice and contribute to postoperative care.

Postoperative physiotherapy should be planned to reduce the risks of post-anaesthetic respiratory insufficiency, and early mobilisation in and out of bed will contribute to thromboprophylaxis.

Risk management

In its proactive form, risk management should include the formation of the multidisciplinary obesity team and the development of specific guidelines and protocols. The AAGBI recommends that an individual senior clinician takes responsibility for liaising with managers about the provision of adequate resources, and works in direct communication with the hospital's clinical governance lead. There are some advantages in this individual being a consultant anaesthetist, because obesity is a problem not confined to a single sex or surgical specialty. This individual should also collate and manage the review of adverse incident reports, ensuring that these contribute to the development and improvement of the care of women who are obese.

Special equipment

The multidisciplinary group set up to consider the care of people who are obese should examine patient journeys carefully to identify areas where special equipment may be needed. This will prevent certain items being forgotten because they fall between the natural areas of interest of each of the individual contributing practitioners. The list should certainly include:

- large patient gowns
- large thromboembolic deterrent stockings
- large blood pressure cuffs: standard cuffs, if they work at all, may overestimate blood pressure readings. In some patients, invasive arterial monitoring with an arterial line is necessary. In most hospitals, care of a patient needing an arterial line is confined to high-dependency and intensive care units. This issue has particular relevance in the care of women in labour who are obese and have pre-eclampsia.
- patient-lifting equipment
- aids for transferring people between beds

▓ operating tables: each operating table has a maximum weight tolerance. This tolerance may be different when the lithotomy position is used. Modern operating tables have been designed for people who are morbidly obese, with width extensions, electrically controlled positioning and excellent table mobility. As surgeons, anaesthetists and anaesthetic assistants all have differing requirements, choice for purchase should involve all these professionals.

▓ pressure area care tools, such as pressure-reducing mattresses and gel pads

▓ a high weight tolerance critical care bed

▓ a high weight tolerance maternity bed.

Specific anaesthetic problems

Specific anaesthetic problems are discussed in some detail in the guidance of the AAGBI, and are alluded to in the preceding paragraphs. To reiterate, the practical problems facing the anaesthetist include:

▓ difficulty securing peripheral and central vascular access

▓ difficult and inaccurate blood pressure measurement

▓ challenging, and therefore slow, regional analgesia and anaesthesia

▓ increased risk of difficult and failed intubation and other methods of airway management

▓ increased risk of regurgitation of gastric contents during general anaesthesia

▓ equipment problems, such as operating tables and ventilators

▓ moving the anaesthetised patient

▓ postoperative care.

Conclusion

Obesity threatens the health of women with surgical disease, as well as those in labour and their babies. It also poses significant challenges for all medical and ancillary staff. While safer childbirth, surgery and anaesthesia can be worked towards, it is incumbent on others to tackle the problem of obesity itself. Politically correct dogma that discourages the open discussion of an individual's obesity must give way to clear information about the dangers of excessive weight gain. While significant weight loss before surgery is rarely practical, guidance to minimise weight gain during pregnancy and to achieve weight loss after delivery should be delivered with urgency.

References

1. Després J, Lemieux I, Prud'Homme D. Treatment of obesity: need to focus on high risk abdominally obese patients. *Br Med J* 2001;322:716–20.

2. Fasol R, Schindler M, Schumacher B, Schlaudraff K, Hannes W, Seitelberger R, *et al.* The influence of obesity on perioperative morbidity: retrospective study of 502 aortocoronary bypass operations. *Thorac Cardiovasc Surg* 1992;40:126–9.

3. Shenkman Z, Shir Y, Brodsky JB. Perioperative management of the obese patient. *Br J Anaesth* 1993;70:349–59.

Chapter 15
Anti-obesity surgery for women planning pregnancy

John G Kral, Frederic-Simon Hould, Simon Marceau, Margaret Eckert-Norton, Simon Biron and Picard Marceau

Introduction

The 'nature versus nurture' debate has prevailed for 150 years among the scientifically educated, whereas deism, creationism or intelligent design have endured for millennia through clerics exploiting the ignorance and 'spiritual needs' of the masses. In parallel with biomedical advances and the information explosion of the 20th century, there has been a rapid increase in global obesity affecting all age groups. It has been convenient to blame the obese for their sins of gluttony and sloth, a practice that persists even in these 'enlightened' times. This chapter advocates humane compassion toward people who are obese as it proposes early, pre-gestational treatment of overnutrition to prevent transmission of obesity to the next generation. Surprisingly, evidence is presented here demonstrating that such 'nurture' can overrule the DNA of 'nature'.

Obesity and pregnancy

Obesity in girls and young women deserves much more attention than in males; the numbers and weights of women who are obese have steadily been increasing. The populations with the highest prevalences of obesity have the highest birth rates although obesity *per se* is associated with involuntary infertility. Girls who are obese have earlier menarche, are more socio-economically and educationally challenged (owing to increased truancy and earlier drop-out), and are more likely to give birth earlier and have more children than those who are not obese. The sharpest increase in childhood obesity among girls is in the age interval 9–12 years, from which time it is likely to persist into adulthood.[1] No realistic remedies are expected within the next half-century and, even if extraordinary measures were available and implemented in 2008, they would not decrease the size of obese populations during this time.

The reason for paying more attention to obesity in women than in men, however, is neither the increased prevalence nor the maternal risks during pregnancy. Maternal obesity and accelerated gestational weight gain are significant risk factors for offspring obesity, which propagates into adolescence and adulthood, feeding into a vicious cycle of exponential growth. This fact has been neglected in the current discussions of the burgeoning epidemic of obesity.

Severe obesity

'Severe obesity' denotes a magnitude of relative weight level, expressed by the body mass index (BMI), and is associated with significantly increased mortality and presence of chronic severe fatal disease (e.g. type 2 diabetes mellitus, hypertension, cardiopulmonary failure) compared with the general population. The prevalence of severe ('morbid'), extreme obesity and 'super-obesity' has been increasing at a more rapid rate than moderate or milder forms.[2,3] This trend is important to recognise for three reasons.

1. Having a severely obese family member is associated with a six-fold increased likelihood of the presence of genetic obesity within the family.[4,5] A severely obese fertile woman poses a greater genetic risk than an obese man.

2. Severe obesity is a marker of binge-eating disorder (BED), which is refractory to conventional non-operative treatment of obesity and is associated with the most prevalent known form of monogenic obesity (about 5–7% of people who are obese).[6]

3. The only effective treatment of severe obesity is surgical.

Anti-obesity surgery

Surgical treatment of obesity was introduced in the middle of the 20th century to treat and palliate people with severe obesity who were largely proven to be unresponsive to other treatment. As surgery and anaesthesia became safer, and the severity of obesity was increasingly recognised among the lay public and the medical community to be associated with numerous chronic diseases, such as diabetes, hypertension, congestive cardiac and pulmonary failure, asthma, thromboembolism, cancers and many other conditions, the practice of anti-obesity surgery spread. With advances in laparoscopic surgery, which is especially well suited to people who are obese, and increasingly powerful epidemiological studies demonstrating the risks of obesity and the disappointing results of non-surgical treatments, the numbers of people undergoing surgery have also increased exponentially.[7] This has led to the broadening of the indications to include people with less severe obesity and of the age range for eligibility. More women who have undergone anti-obesity surgery are becoming pregnant, or are contemplating pregnancy. All need counselling.

The following is a description of anti-obesity operations as they have evolved since the 1950s, with explanations of the mechanisms, effects and adverse effects as they relate to nutritional sufficiency. It is also a review of outcomes of pregnancies after anti-obesity surgery with comparisons with outcomes before the mothers had had surgery. Remarkably, gastrointestinal surgery can have primary preventive capacity with the potential for curbing the obesity epidemic.

Operations for obesity

Methods

Two generic types of operation, malabsorptive and restrictive, and a hybrid have dominated the field since 1950, when three women in Sweden had small bowel resections to achieve malabsorption as a treatment for intractable severe obesity. Owing to reluctance to excise significant lengths of bowel in the USA, Linner and colleagues introduced intestinal bypass operations, which retain all of the small bowel, most of which is bypassed, leaving approximately 50 cm of varying proportions of jejunum and ileum in continuity. Jejuno–ileal bypass dominated anti-obesity surgery from 1960 to 1980, although Mason introduced a gastric bypass operation in 1963.

Gastric bypass

As more and more complications after jejuno–ileal bypass surfaced, and gastric bypass was perfected, gastric bypass increased in popularity. After several modifications, the Roux-en-Y gastric bypass (RYGB) operation, now adapted for laparoscopy, became the most common obesity operation performed in the USA since early 1990. It consists of a minute (< 20 ml) proximal pouch at the cardia, attached via a gastrojejunostomy to a 75–100 cm limb of distal jejunum into which the bypassed stomach, duodenum and approximately 50 cm of proximal jejunum are anastomosed in Roux-en-Y fashion (Figure 15.1). Modifications of the traditional RYGB, bypassing significantly longer limbs of small bowel ('long-limb' and 'long-long' gastric bypass), were introduced to increase malabsorption in the RYGB for use in heavier patients.

Biliopancreatic diversion

In order to avoid the blind loop of intestinal bypass operations, susceptible to bacterial overgrowth, and to achieve greater weight loss, Scopinaro introduced biliopancreatic

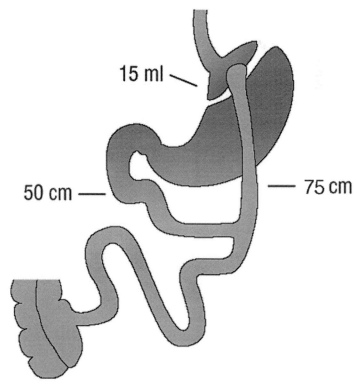

Figure 15.1. Roux-en-Y gastric bypass: an isolated proximal gastric pouch attached to a 75 cm limb of jejunum, bypassing the stomach, duodenum and 50 cm of proximal jejunum

bypass or diversion (BPD) in the mid 1970s. It consists of gastrectomy, gastro-ileos-tomy, duodenal stump closure and a biliopancreatic jejunal–ileal limb anastomosed to the terminal ileum, effectively limiting gastric capacity and causing maldigestion and malabsorption: in essence a hybrid operation. This is by far the most complex operation, with the greatest potential for causing malnutrition. BPD has been modi-fied by exchanging the conventional two-thirds gastrectomy for a sleeve gastrectomy retaining the intact pylorus yet excluding the duodenum: a duodenal switch(DS) (Figure 15.2). BPD has also been adapted for laparoscopy and is considered by many to be the most technically demanding of all laparoscopic gastrointestinal operations.

Gastric restriction

Because Mason was convinced that the chief mechanism responsible for weight loss after gastric bypass was restriction caused by the small proximal stomach left in con-tinuity, he developed a purely restrictive gastric operation, a vertical banded gas-troplasty in 1980, leaving the normal gastrointestinal continuity intact. The gastro-plasty consisted of a stapled 30 ml proximal gastric compartment connected via a narrow banded fixed opening (circumference approximately 5 cm) into the remaining stomach. Gastric restriction (or obstruction) was taken to a new level through the

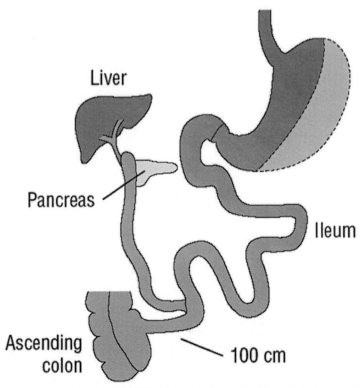

Figure 15.2. Biliopancreatic diversion (BPD) with duodenal switch (DS): two-thirds sleeve gastrectomy with post-pyloric attachment to ileum, bypassing the duodenum and jejunum, which are drained into ileum 100 cm before the ileo-caecal valve

ingenuity of Kuzmak, who created an inflatable, and thus adjustable, circumgastric band not requiring stapling. Such bands can easily and safely be placed laparoscopically. Laparoscopic adjustable gastric banding (LAGB) has completely replaced stapled gastroplasties and non-adjustable bands, which have virtually disappeared since 2000 (Figure 15.3).

Mechanisms

Obstruction

Gastric restriction works by limiting the amount of solid food that can be ingested at any one time and by slowing the rate at which food enters the main part of the stomach. Liquids and melting foods such as ice cream, chocolate and potato chips are not limited unless the stomach pouch opening is blocked by solid food (or pills and tablets). If the patient does not chew well and pay attention to what she swallows, there is a risk of vomiting, as there is whenever pouch capacity is exceeded. Purely gastric restrictive operations cause weight loss mainly through nimiety, an unpleasant sense of fullness, rather than satiety, although there are claims that the mere presence of a band, even when uninflated, causes 'satiety'.[8] Gastric bypass causes gastric restriction during the first 12–18 months postoperative until the pouch and anastomosis between pouch and jejunum have stretched.

Diversion

When the restrictive component has diminished, other anorectic mechanisms take over. The small gastric pouch has very limited digestive capacity, and in the absence

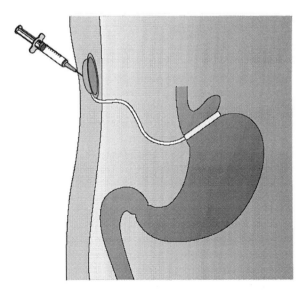

Figure 15.3. Adjustable gastric band: attached to a subcutaneous injectable port, the circumgastric band creates a 20 ml pouch

of a pylorus to meter the passage of poorly digested nutrients into the small bowel, stretch- and chemoreceptors and counter-regulatory gut hormones are inappropriately activated and send anorexigenic neuro-humoral signals to the brain. These signals may either be aversive or satiating, probably depending on the rate of delivery and composition of nutrients appearing in the small bowel. Interestingly similar mechanisms operate after purely malabsorptive operations and after orad transposition of distal limbs of small bowel, both of which expose the lower gut to undigested nutrients. These mechanisms account for the greater efficacy and durability of hybrid and malabsorptive operations.[9]

Surgical morbidity and mortality

Obese people are prone to usual surgical complications such as wound infections, pneumonia and atelectasis, thromboembolism, hernias and anastomotic leaks. Competent bariatric surgeons routinely employ effective preventative measures, anaesthesia has improved and the laparoscopic approach has further contributed to reducing surgical morbidity among the obese. Abdominal hernias and wound infections have virtually disappeared.

Anti-obesity surgery, as with all surgery, is undertaken on the premise that the operation is less hazardous than the condition being treated. Much of the controversy over anti-obesity surgery through the years has not solely been based on strong anti-obesity biases, but also on ignorance of the substantially elevated risk of death among obese people. Surgical mortality rates must be stratified for sex, age, smoking status and number and severity of co-morbidities and their control. As with most technically demanding surgery, higher volumes are required for better perioperative outcomes.

Women with reproductive capacity have the lowest risk of dying from anti-obesity surgery in the hands of a competent surgeon: rates are less than 1%, essentially similar to the rate associated with undergoing anaesthesia. Younger women have significantly lower risk, keeping in mind that extremely severe obesity takes many years to develop, is associated with infertility and increases with increasing parity.

Complications and side effects

It is evident from the functional consequences of the changes caused by the various operations that there are risks of excessive vomiting and of diarrhoea. Both may cause nutritional deficiencies that are easily treated, and both are preventable through behavioural adaptation, although behavioural modification alone is mostly unsuccessful in treating obesity. Vomiting from gastric restriction and inability to adapt eating behaviour may cause structural changes to the already vulnerable distal oesophagus of a person who is obese. Data are insufficient to allow conclusions about the magnitude of this problem. The crucial prerequisite for undertaking anti-obesity surgery is that there are sufficient resources for educating and monitoring patients and for providing supplements to prevent deficiencies of vitamins and minerals.

It is exceedingly rare for people to lose too much weight; when this occurs, it is often attributable to mental problems. The more common problem is weight regain, especially in people who have had purely gastric restrictive operations. The adjustable band, however, motivates patients to make frequent visits to the doctor, a strategy known to improve weight loss by non-surgical treatment methods as well.

Candidates for surgery

Indications

Weight

Traditional indications for anti-obesity surgery were based on weight ('excess' weight of more than 45 kg or twice actuarial weight-for-height standards), but have since been modified to include the existence of serious reversible co-morbidity in people with BMI between 35 and 40 kg/m^2 or 40 kg/m^2 and above without co-morbidity, although it is highly unlikely for someone with a BMI of 40 kg/m^2 to lack co-morbidity. Mean weights are generally higher in published surgical series in the USA. The large, nationwide Swedish Obese Subjects (SOS) study that started in the late 1980s has used the inclusion criterion of a BMI of 37 kg/m^2 for women and 34 kg/m^2 for men, with no requirement of co-morbidity.[10] Two studies of people with BMI of 30–35 kg/m^2 have appeared since 2004 (one Italian,[11] the other Australian[12]). It is likely this trend toward lower BMI will continue owing to the safety of simple laparoscopic operations and the absence of non-surgical alternatives with comparable durability of weight loss.

Age

An age range of 25–65 years was initially recommended for people to undergo anti-obesity surgery; mean ages are 37–40 years in large series of data. Here, too, there has been a widening trend: younger and older people are more commonly having anti-obesity operations.[13] Owing to the extreme rise in paediatric and adolescent obesity and realisation of the dire consequences of obesity in the young, surgical treatment is increasingly being performed at younger ages. When all other treatments have failed to normalise the weight trajectory of girls by the time they have attained reproductive capacity, and in the absence of effective contraception, it may be warranted to perform anti-obesity surgery rather than to risk an obese pregnancy.[14] This raises the issue of eligibility for undergoing anti-obesity surgery.

Eligibility

Third-party payers in the USA for many years refused to reimburse any form of obesity treatment since obesity was not considered to be a disease. When these biases were finally overcome, insurance companies made access to anti-obesity surgery especially difficult by creating numerous obstacles in the approval process, several of which remain. From a strictly medical point of view, there are eligibility criteria that have face validity but lack supportive hard evidence, while others meet 'reasonability' standards in spite of evidence demonstrating the absence of value. A common 'requirement' has been that the person must have undergone prior 'serious' or 'medically supervised' weight loss. In practice, the majority of candidates have undergone five to seven prior episodes of weight loss, typically short lived, before even contemplating or being referred for surgical treatment of obesity.

Since anti-obesity surgery has exceptionally large behavioural consequences, the consent process must be 'educated' rather than 'informed'. Thus, an eligibility requirement states that the person must be able to cooperate with treatment plans and comprehend the reasons for being operated, the behavioural consequences of various treatment options and the requirements of follow-up. For this reason, it is often advised to exclude people with drug or alcohol 'problems'. This is not the place to debate the appropriateness or feasibility of such a practice. Remarkably, psychiatric consultation is rarely warranted and routinely has no proven benefit. However, 'comprehension' does have serious implications when considering surgical candidacy of young people who are obese, placing extraordinary demands on parents and caregivers. Although not studied, psychiatric evaluation of patient and family should be mandated for young people.

The risk of developing deficiencies is the bane of effective anti-obesity surgery. There are no realistic mechanisms for ensuring follow-up to monitor adherence to taking recommended supplements but, before the operation, efforts must be made to ascertain whether the person has the means and ability to cooperate with follow-up. Obviously, this is especially important in young women.

Benefits of surgery

Weight loss

In keeping with weight-based indications, most outcomes are presented as weight loss, usually expressed either as percentage of initial weight or percentage of 'excess' weight lost (PEWL). 'Excess' is defined as weight exceeding 'ideal' or 'desirable' weight for height corresponding to actuarial minimum mortality. With adoption of BMI as a weight unit, 'desirable' is set at BMI 18–24 kg/m². Typically, weight loss amounts to one-third of preoperative weight maintained for 5 years in the majority of patients. Data on the largest numbers of case series, followed for the longest periods of time, emanate from gastric bypass performed in the USA. Historically, all purely gastric restrictive operations provide lower magnitude – typically one-quarter of preoperative weight – and less durable weight loss in lower proportions of patients. As yet, there are too few and too limited studies of adjustable gastric banding followed for 5 years or more to allow conclusions about efficacy or comparisons with gastric bypass. It is not feasible ethically to randomise between operations with very different effects on eating behaviour.[15]

Improved morbidity and mortality

Although the majority of women measure postoperative satisfaction in terms of weight loss, medically and probably socio-economically weight loss is less important than reduction of co-morbidity or improvement in health-related quality-adjusted life years.

It is in the durability of weight loss for treatment and secondary prevention of co-morbidity that surgical treatment substantially outperforms all other forms of treatment. The vast majority of co-morbidities are either cured or ameliorated by surgically induced voluntary weight loss, even those with structural changes such as osteoarthritis, myocardial hypertrophy, venous hypostasis ulcers and liver cirrhosis.[16,17] Compilation of 10 year mortality data from the Swedish SOS study has convincingly demonstrated decreased post-surgical mortality compared with the best available, community standard treatment in a country known for its socialised medicine and virtually unlimited access to care.[18] The study supports earlier registry data[19,20] and earlier[21] and contemporaneous case series.[22–24]

Population outcomes that have greatest relevance to women who are severely obese and planning pregnancy are the cure or improvement of:

- infertility
- impaired glucose tolerance and type 2 diabetes

- hypertension
- dyslipidaemia (high very low density lipoprotein (VLDL) cholesterol and low high density lipoprotein (HDL) cholesterol)
- urinary incontinence.

Fuel-mediated teratogenesis

Importance of maternal over- and undernutrition for pregnancy outcomes

Consistent reports of adverse effects of overweight and obesity,[25] of weight gain, whether it precedes conception[26] or occurs during gestation,[27] and of co-morbidities such as gestational diabetes mellitus (GDM),[28] type 1 or 2 diabetes,[29] pre-eclampsia or the insulin resistance syndrome continue to raise questions about the causal relationship between obesity and perinatal outcomes.[30] Maternal obesity was demonstrated to be an independent risk factor for caesarean delivery in an Israeli study of 126 080 deliveries excluding cases with hypertensive disorders and diabetes mellitus.[31] Remarkably, the prevalence of obesity (BMI $\geq$ 30 kg/m^2) was only 1.4% during the period 1988–2002, probably owing to the predominantly white population. Caesarean rates were 28% among women who were obese versus a relatively low rate of 11% in their general population (OR 3.2; $P < 0.001$).

Numerous reports link the intrauterine environment to early and late morbidity in the offspring, fuelling speculation over mechanisms for 'imprinting' or precursors of adult disease.[32–34] Fetal undernutrition is a recognised risk factor for developmental arrest, fetal death and malformations, and a harbinger of childhood and ultimately adult disease. Such concerns underlie public health recommendations for optimal gestational weight gain in the general population, exemplified by those published by the Institute of Medicine (IOM) in the USA.[35] Although these recommendations do adjust for 'obesity', they pertain to BMI > 30 kg/m^2 with no specifications for higher levels, probably owing to a dearth of data. A study of LAGB modified the IOM criteria by not setting any minimum weight gain for mothers with BMI > 35 kg/m^2.[36] Interestingly, according to some studies, more than 75% of women who are severely obese report losing weight during pregnancy even without having had anti-obesity surgery.

Most literature on gestational food restriction emanates from catastrophic famine,[32,37,38] which cannot discriminate between effects of maternal stress and involuntary undernutrition. Furthermore, results are confounded by the compensatory behaviour of the mothers and by catch-up growth when food becomes available. Anti-obesity surgery is unique in providing both voluntarily reduced body weight and decreased gestational weight gain in the absence of dieting, a known stressor.[39]

The most serious concern for post-surgical pregnancies is the risk of fetal undernutrition. In the following section, outcomes of pregnancies conceived after maternal anti-obesity surgery are reviewed, focusing on other aspects than vitamin and mineral deficiencies since these are easily preventable by effective monitoring and supplementation.

Effects of anti-obesity surgery on subsequent gestation

There is sufficient information from the era of intestinal bypass operations, albeit from small case series, that can be translated to and compiled with more modern malabsorptive surgical methods in order to evaluate risks and benefits of surgically induced weight loss for pregnancy outcomes. With respect to purely gastric restrictive operations, i.e. vertical banded gastroplasty, circumgastric banding and adjustable gastric banding, overall results of pregnancies are similar among the operations, although it is important to keep in mind that there are very few data on pregnancy outcomes many years after restrictive operations, when significant maternal weight regain may have occurred. Post-gastric bypass pregnancies have been reported since 1982, revealing consistent findings over the years:[40–43] regardless of method, post-surgical pregnancy outcomes are significantly better than before maternal surgery. Although of no importance for subsequent pregnancy, there is one study comparing pregnancy outcomes after unspecified bariatric operations performed via laparoscopic versus open approaches. As expected there are no statistically significant differences between the two.[44]

Offspring outcomes after malabsorptive surgery (BPD)

Pregnancy outcomes have been studied in a relatively large cohort of women who had undergone BPD or BPD with DS,[45] the most effective obesity operation and consequently the one with the greatest potential for causing intrauterine undernutrition. The study compared 45 children, aged 2–18 years, born to unoperated women who were severely obese (mean BMI 48 ± 8 kg/m^2), with 172 same-age siblings born after maternal surgery at mean BMI 31 ± 9 kg/m^2, with respect to prevalences of obesity/overweight, underweight and psychosocial development, and also comparing with community standards.[46] Offspring obesity after maternal surgery was 52% lower and severe obesity was 45% lower than among siblings (P = 0.006) reaching obesity levels in the general population, while there was no increase in the prevalence of underweight or small-for-gestational-age (SGA) infants. Developmentally, 'postsurgical' offspring performed scholastically at the same levels as their peers in the community at large.

A subgroup of 35 women with mean preoperative BMI of 57.1 ± 8.5 kg/m^2 subsequently underwent malabsorptive surgery and later conceived when their BMI had reached 41.4 ± 2.8 kg/m^2. Offspring outcomes among these primigravidae were matched with those of 17 unoperated (preoperative) primigravidae with BMI 42.2 ± 2.6 kg/m^2. The offspring prevalence of obesity in women who were not operated upon was 70% (12 of 17), compared with a prevalence of 35% (13 of 35) among those born after maternal surgery (P = 0.037.)

Together, these results imply that both genetic and environmental adverse influences on the offspring can be nullified by preventing intrauterine overnutrition.

Maternal outcomes after BPD

Among 568 mothers who were severely obese prior to surgery, there were 1236 term pregnancies, 16.7% of which were premature. The miscarriage rate was 21.6%. After surgery, among 109 women, the miscarriage rate was 26% while the prevalence of prematurity was 13.6%. Before surgery, caesarean section rates among primigravidae were 34%, compared with 20.3% after maternal surgery,[45] which was the same as the prevalence in the local general population.

Pregnancy complications such as GDM, pre-eclampsia, pregnancy hypertension and even fetal loss are all conditions with high rates of recurrence, independent of obesity. In the sibling-matched cohort, 47% (21 of 45) of pregnancies before surgery were complicated, requiring hospitalisation in 36%. Type 2 diabetes was present in 18%, GDM in 16%, hypertension in 22% and pre-eclampsia in 11%. These numbers are commonly encountered in severely obese populations and exceed community standards. After maternal surgery, there were no cases of type 2 diabetes or GDM, hypertension or pre-eclampsia (all $P < 0.01$), indicating that there were neither recurrences nor *de novo* cases during pregnancies after maternal weight-loss surgery.

These results imply that interconceptional weight loss cures GDM, pre-eclampsia and pregnancy hypertension.

Timing of postoperative pregnancy

Although operated women are advised to avoid pregnancy postoperatively during the early rapid weight-loss phase (which usually lasts 6–12 months after purely restrictive procedures and 12–18 months after malabsorptive and hybrid operations), obesity-related anovulation reverses very early during weight loss and pregnancies do occur. This uncontrolled 'experiment' theoretically represents a 'worst case' fetal nutrition scenario. Certainly, one might reason that the risks of deficiencies and fetal undernutrition would be the greatest during this period unless there was diligent monitoring and supplementation.

Two studies have compared results during such early pregnancies with those occurring later after maternal surgery.[43,45] Among 46 pregnancies with deliveries within 2 years of maternal BPD, the miscarriage rate (10 of 46; 21.7%) was similar to that during delayed pregnancies. Furthermore, the birthweights of 'early' infants did not differ from those born more than 2 years after maternal surgery.[45] In a paper specifically comparing 21 pregnancies conceived during the first year after maternal gastric bypass with 13 conceived later, there were no differences in fetal weight, term pregnancy rates or complications.[43] In the BPD series, the 'early' mothers stopped losing weight, although not gaining, during the pregnancy, only to resume weight loss after delivery. In the gastric bypass series, the 'early' average weight gain was 2 kg with a wide range (32 kg loss to 20 kg gain), while average gain in the late group was 15 kg (range 5.5–35 kg). Thus, it can be concluded that there is no evidence to support the seemingly reasonable recommendation to avoid pregnancy early after anti-obesity surgery. Furthermore, there is evidence that absence of weight gain during this period does not pose an increased risk.

Comparison of outcomes

Overall, regardless of surgical method and time period, whether intestinal bypass in the 1960–70s, gastroplasty in the 1980s, gastric bypass from 1980s to 2007 or adjustable banding from mid 1990s to 2007, post-surgical pregnancy outcomes are similar. Although there are relatively few case reports of adverse pregnancy outcomes, which are likely to be under-reported owing to negative ascertainment bias, the preponderance of case series and population studies unequivocally demonstrates similar trends: the increased overall complication rates associated with obese pregnancies are lower after anti-obesity surgery (Table 15.1). Although bariatric surgeons generally are strongly biased towards the operations they perform, and are too willing to proclaim a 'gold standard', there is no evidence that favours one procedure over another with respect to postoperative pregnancies. Indeed, as has been the case throughout the history of anti-obesity surgery, the evaluation of trade-offs is ultimately subjective and can be best made by the individual patient given sufficient information.

Mechanisms of beneficial effects

It is not surprising that weight loss improves the outcomes of pregnancies of women who are obese[47] although the majority of papers on weight loss and pregnancy con-

Table 15.1. Pregnancy outcome changes after maternal obesity surgery compared with before maternal surgery compiled from the literature; all post-surgery outcomes equal to general population standards except those marked *

Outcome	Change
Fetal	
Malformations*	±
Loss/miscarriage	±
Intrauterine growth restriction	±
Apgar scores	±
Macrosomia/LGA	↓
Mean birthweight	↑
SGA*	↑
Delivery	
Weeks of gestation	±
Premature membrane rupture	(↓)
Labour induction	↓
Failed induction	↓
Caesarean section	↓
Full term births	±
Preterm births*	± (↓)
Stillbirths	± (↓)

LGA = large for gestational age; SGA = small for gestational age
Key: ↓ = significant decrease; ↑ = significant increase; (↓) = decreasing trend; ± = no change

cern fecundity rather than gestational complications. Anti–obesity surgery effectively achieves what other treatment modalities do not: sustained, medically significant weight loss, correcting the co-morbidities of obesity,[10,12] including but not limited to the metabolic syndrome.[16] Remaining to be determined are the mechanisms of the beneficial effects of weight loss and whether there are optimal amounts of maternal weight loss.

It is neither feasible nor necessary to disentangle the effects of obesity from those of dyslipidaemia and/or impaired glucose metabolism manifested as impaired fasting glucose (IFG) or impaired glucose tolerance (IGT) or disposal, which measure varying degrees of insulin resistance. The 'fetal overnutrition hypothesis'[48,49] is no longer hypothetical, since it has been shown that pre- or interconceptional weight loss and limitation of gestational nutrient availability effectively abrogate the maternal transmission of obesity to the offspring.[46] The malabsorptive BPD operation effectively reduces metabolisable intrauterine energy levels to 'normal'.[50] Furthermore, all anti–obesity operations improve glucose metabolism immediately postoperative, before occurrence of any weight loss.[51] Together with similar normalisation of lipid metabolism, both 'lipotoxic' and 'glucotoxic' effects on the fetus are prevented, thus ending fuel-mediated teratogenesis[49] and the 'never-ending cycle of obesity'[52] as was recently proposed.[53]

Conclusion

Pregnancy outcomes after maternal anti-obesity surgery are significantly improved regardless of the type of operation. The mechanisms include normalisation of maternal glucose and lipid metabolism and abrogation of fetal overnutrition. The prevalence of obesity in offspring followed for 18 years after maternal anti-obesity surgery corresponds to levels in the general population. Recommendations for optimal gestational weight management are needed in women who are severely obese with BMI ≥ 35 kg/m^2.

References

1. Thompson DR, Obarzanek E, Franko DL, Barton BA, Morrison J, Biro FM, *et al.* Childhood overweight and cardiovascular disease risk factors: the National Heart, Lung, and Blood Institute Growth and Health Study. *J Pediatr* 2007;150:18–25.
2. Freedman DS, Khan LK, Serdula MK, Galuska DA, Dietz WH. Trends and correlates of class 3 obesity in the United States from 1990 through 2000. *JAMA* 2002;288:1758–61.
3. Sturm R. Increases in clinically severe obesity in the United States, 1986–2000. *Arch Intern Med* 2003;163:2146–8.
4. Lee JH, Reed DR, Price RA. Familial risk ratios for extreme obesity: implications for mapping human obesity genes. *Int J Obes* 1997;21:935–40.
5. Silventoinen K, Kapria J, Lahelma E, Viken RJ, Rose RJ. Assortative mating by body height and BMI: Finnish twins and their spouses. *Am J Hum Biol* 2003;15:620–940.
6. Branson R, Potoczna N, Kral JG, Lentes KU, Hoehe MR, Horber FF. Binge eating is a major phenotype of melanocortin 4 receptor gene mutations. *N Engl J Med* 2003;348:1096–103.
7. Steinbrook R. Surgery for severe obesity. *N Engl J Med* 2004;350:1075–9.
8. Dixon AF, Dixon JB, O'Brien PE. Laparoscopic adjustable gastric banding induces prolonged satiety: a randomized blind crossover study. *J Clin Endocrinol Metab* 2005;90:211–37.
9. Naslund E, Kral JG. Patient selection and the physiology of gastrointestinal antiobesity operations. In: Livingston EH, Martin RF, editors. *Surg Clin North Am* 2005;85(6):725–40.
10. Sjöström L, Lindroos AK, Peltonen M, Torgerson J, Bouchard C, Carlsson B, *et al.* Lifestyle, diabetes, and cardiovascular risk factors 10 years after bariatric surgery. *N Engl J Med* 2004;351:2683–93.
11. Angrisani L, Favretti F, Furbetta F, Iuppa A, Doldi SB, Paganelli M, *et al.* Group for Lap-Band System: results of multicenter study on patients with BMI < or + 35 kg/m2. *Obes Surg* 2004;14:415–18.
12. O'Brien PE, Dixon JB, Laurie C, Skinner S, Proietto J, McNeil J, *et al.* Treatment of mild to moderate obesity with laparoscopic adjustable gastric banding or an intensive medical program. *Ann Intern Med* 2006;144:625–33.
13. Fatima J, Houghton SG, Iqbal CW, Thompson GB, Que FL, Kendrick ML, *et al.* Bariatric surgery at the extremes of age. *J Gastrointest Surg* 2006;10:1392–6.
14. Kral JG. A stitch in time versus a life in misery. *Surg Obes Relat Dis* 2007;3:2–5.
15. Kral JG, Dixon JB, Horber FF, Rössner S, Stiles S, Torgerson JS, *et al.* Flaws in evidence-based medicine methodologies may adversely affect public health directives. *Surgery* 2005;137:279–84.
16. Kral JG, Thung SN, Biron S, Hould FS, Lebel S, Marceau S, *et al.* Effects of surgical treatment of the metabolic syndrome on liver fibrosis and cirrhosis. *Surgery* 2004;135:48–58.
17. Sugerman HJ, Kral JG. Evidence-based medicine reports on bariatric surgery: a critique. *Int J Obes* 2005;29:735–45.
18. Sjöström L. Soft and hard endpoints over 5 to 18 years in the intervention trial Swedish Obese Subjects. *Obes Rev* 2006;7(Suppl 2):27.
19. Christou NV, Sampalis JS, Liberman M, Look D, Auger S, McLean AP, *et al.* Surgery decreases long-term mortality, morbidity, and health care use in morbidly obese patients. *Ann Surg* 2004;240:416–23.

20. Flum DR, Dellinger EP. Impact of gastric bypass operation on survival: a population-based analysis. *J Am Coll Surg* 2004;199:543–51.

21. MacDonald KG Jr, Long SD, Swanson MS, Brown BM, Morris P, Dohm GL, *et al*. The gastric bypass operation reduces the progression and mortality of non-insulin-dependent diabetes mellitus. *J Gastrointest Surg* 1997;1:213–20.

22. Peeters A, O'Brien P, Laurie C, Anderson M, Dixon J, English D, *et al*. Does weight loss improve survival? Comparison of a bariatric surgical cohort with a community based control group. *Obes Rev* 2006;7(Suppl 2):95.

23. Adams T, Gress R, Smith S, Halverson C, Rosamond W, Simpser S, *et al*. Long-term mortality following gastric bypass surgery. *Obes Rev* 2006;7(Suppl 2):94.

24. Busetto L, Mazza M, Miribelli D, Petroni ML, Segato G, Chiusolo M, *et al*. Total mortality in morbid obese patients treated with laparoscopic adjustable gastric banding: a case–control study. *Obes Rev* 2006;7(Suppl 2):95.

25. Rosenberg TJ, Garbers S, Chavkin W, Chiasson MA. Prepregnancy weight and adverse perinatal outcomes in an ethnically diverse population. *Obstet Gynecol* 2003;102(5 Pt 1):1022–7.

26. Villamor E, Cnattingius S. Interpregnancy weight change and risk of adverse pregnancy outcomes: a population-based study. *Lancet* 2006;368:1164–70.

27. Stephansson O, Dickman PW, Johansson A, Cnattingius S. Maternal weight, pregnancy weight gain, and the risk of antepartum stillbirth. *Am J Obstet Gynecol* 2001;184:463–9.

28. Crowther CA, Hiller JE, Moss JR, McPhee AJ, Jeffries WS, Robinson JS; Australian Carbohydrate Intolerance Study in Pregnant Women (ACHOIS) Trial Group. Effect of treatment of gestational diabetes mellitus on pregnancy outcomes. *N Engl J Med* 2006;352:2477–86.

29. Macintosh MCM, Fleming KM, Bailey JA, Doyle P, Modder J, Acolet D, *et al*. Perinatal mortality and congenital anomalies in babies of women with type 1 or type 2 diabetes in England, Wales, and Northern Ireland: population based study. *BMJ* 2006;333:177–80.

30. Caughey AB. Obesity, weight loss, and pregnancy outcomes. *Lancet* 2006;368:1164–70.

31. Sheiner E, Levy A, Menes TS, Silverberg D, Katz M, Mazor M. Maternal obesity as an independent risk factor for caesarean delivery. *Paediatr Perinat Epidemiol* 2004;18:196–201.

32. Ravelli GP, Stein ZA, Susser MW. Obesity in young men after famine exposure *in utero* and early infancy. *N Engl J Med* 1976;295:349–53.

33. Waterland RA, Garza C. Potential mechanisms of metabolic imprinting that lead to chronic disease. *Am J Clin Nutr* 1999;69:179–97.

34. Levin BE. The obesity epidemic: metabolic imprinting on genetically susceptible neural circuits. *Obes Res* 2000;8:342–7.

35. Institute of Medicine (Subcommittees on Nutritional Status and Weight Gain During Pregnancy, Committee on Nutritional Status During Pregnancy and Lactation, Food and Nutrition Board). *Nutrition During Pregnancy. Part I, Weight Gain*. Washington, DC: National Academy Press; 1990.

36. Dixon JB, Dixon ME, O'Brien PE. Birth outcomes in obese women after laparoscopic adjustable gastric banding. *Obstet Gynecol* 2005;106(5 Pt 1):965–72.

37. Stanner SA, Yudkin JS. Fetal programming and the Leningrad Siege study. *Twin Res* 2001;4:287–92.

38. Ross MG, Desai M. Gestational programming: population survival effects of drought and famine during pregnancy. *Am J Physiol Regul Integr Comp Physiol* 2005;288:R33.

39. McLean JA, Barr SI, Prior JC. Cognitive dietary restraint is associated with higher urinary cortisol excretion in healthy premenopausal women. *Am J Clin Nutr* 2001;73:7–12.

40. Printen KJ, Scott D. Pregnancy following gastric bypass for the treatment of morbid obesity. *Am Surg* 1982;48:363–5.

41. Richards DS, Miller DK, Goodman GN. Pregnancy after gastric bypass for morbid obesity. *J Reprod Med* 1987;32:172–5.

42. Wittgrove AC, Jester L, Wittgrove P, Clark GW. Pregnancy following gastric bypass for morbid obesity. *Obes Surg* 1998;8:461–4.

43. Dao T, Kuhn J, Ehmer D, Fisher T, McCarty T. Pregnancy outcomes after gastric-bypass surgery. *Am J Surg* 2006;192:762–6.

44. Sheiner E, Levy A, Silverberg D, Menes TS, Levy I, Katz M, Mazor M. Pregnancy after bariatric surgery is not associated with adverse perinatal outcome. *Am J Obstet Gynecol* 2004;190:1335–40.

45. Marceau P, Kaufman D, Biron S, Hould F-S, Lebel S, Marceau S, Kral JG. Outcome of pregnancies after biliopancreatic diversion. *Obes Surg* 2004;14:318–24.

46. Kral JG, Biron S, Simard S, Hould FS, Lebel S, Marceau S, Marceau P. Large maternal weight loss from obesity surgery prevents transmission of obesity to children followed 2–18 years. *Pediatrics* 2006;118:e1644–9.

47. Hall LF, Neubert AG. Obesity and pregnancy. *Obstet Gynecol Surv* 2005;60:253–60.

48. Lawlor DA, Smith GD, O'Callaghan M, Alati R, Mamun AA, Williams GM, *et al.* Epidemiologic evidence for the fetal overnutrition hypothesis: findings from the mater-university study of pregnancy and its outcomes. *Am J Epidemiol* 2007;165:418–24.

49. Freinkel N. Banting Lecture 1980. Of pregnancy and progeny. *Diabetes* 1980;29:1023–35.

50. Tataranni PA, Mingrone G, Raguso CA, De Gaetano A, Tacchino RM, Castagneto M, *et al.* Twenty-four-hour energy and nutrient balance in weight stable postobese patients after biliopancreatic diversion. *Nutrition* 1996;12:239–44.

51. Pories WJ, MacDonald KG, Morgan EJ, Sinha MK, Dohm GL, Swanson MS, *et al.* Surgical treatment of obesity and its effect on diabetes: 10-y follow-up. *Am J Clin Nutr* 1992;55(2 Suppl):582S–585S.

52. Foreyt JP, Poston WS. Obesity: a never-ending cycle? *Int J Fertil Womens Med* 1998;43:111–16.

53. Kral JG. Preventing and treating obesity in girls and young women to curb the epidemic. *Obes Res* 2004;12:1539–46.

Chapter 16

Maternal obesity and gestational diabetes: consequences for the offspring

Patrick Catalano

Maternal and paternal factors associated with fetal growth

Maternal diabetes and the increased population risk of obesity is becoming a greater problem not only in the developed areas of the world but also in developing countries with large populations and high birth rates. Because the increased risks of diabetes and obesity are now becoming manifest in adolescents and even children as young as 2–5 years old,[1] the concept of *in utero* fetal programming assumes even more importance. Fetal programming is the effect of the *in utero* environment on events that have a permanent effect on the physiology or metabolism of the organism. This chapter will consider normal fetal growth, fetal growth in infants of women with diabetes and fetal growth in infants of women who are obese.

Based on the studies of Hytten,[2] more than two-thirds of fetal growth occurs in the third trimester, with the fetus increasing weight from approximately 1000 g to 3400 g. Multiple factors contribute to the variability in fetal growth. These include ethnic, geographic and socio-economic factors. In the early 1960s, the World Health Organization reported that birthweight in various Indian populations was affected by socio-economic status, with neonates of women in lower socio-economic classes having smaller offspring than their more affluent counterparts.[3] Relative to geographic issues, altitude has long been recognised as a factor resulting in decreasing birthweights as compared with those infants born at sea level, with the decrease in oxygen tension at higher altitudes being the most ready explanation for the decreased birthweight.[4] Lastly, differences in various ethnic groups accounts for much of the variation in birthweight, with Asian and African women having lighter babies in comparison with their white counterparts.[4]

Within the aforementioned parameters, however, the maternal environment during pregnancy has profound effects on *in utero* fetal growth. There is a strong correlation between maternal height and weight and fetal growth. In general, the taller and heavier a woman is prior to conception, the more her infant will weigh at birth.[5] These correlations are more robust in nulliparous than in multiparous women.[6] Similarly, there are also significant increases in birthweight related to maternal weight gain during gestation.[6] The interaction of maternal pregravid weight and weight gain on fetal growth are interesting relative to the underlying physiology of fetal growth. Based on the studies of Abrams and Laros,[7] women who are lean or underweight will need to have a significant increase in weight gain in pregnancy in order to have a normally grown fetus. In contrast, women who are overweight or obese will more likely have a larger baby, even with little or no weight gain. Maternal parity also has an effect on fetal growth. Increasing parity results in an increase of approximately 100 g with each successive pregnancy.[8] The effect appears to plateau after the fifth pregnancy. This may be related to increased maternal weight retention after successive pregnancies but does not appear to be related to maternal age, once adjusted for other co-variables.

The issue of maternal nutrition and fetal growth has been addressed in many animal studies, mostly addressing the issue of fetal programming in growth-restricted models, although more recent work has focused on the problem of maternal obesity and obesogenic diets. In the human, the studies of Barker[9] have addressed the issue of fetal programming in the human intrauterine growth restriction (IUGR) model. The Barker hypothesis notes that poor nutrition *in utero* leads to fetal adaptations that produce permanent changes in insulin and glucose metabolism. For example, IUGR followed by increased availability of food and/or decreased activity result in dysregulation such as the metabolic syndrome.[10] Lucas *et al.*,[11] however, suggested that 'size in early life is related to health outcomes only after adjustment for current size, it is probably the change in size between these points rather than fetal biology that is implicated'.[11] For example, in the Early Bird Study,[12] 300 British children were followed longitudinally. Insulin resistance was the same in children who had high birthweight and remained at an elevated birthweight centile through age 5 years, compared with those who had a lower birthweight but attained a similar centile. In fact the IUGR model for the fetal programming hypothesis is more robust relative to aspects of the metabolic syndrome such as hypertension rather than obesity.[13]

Unfortunately, the human studies addressing the issue of maternal undernutrition in pregnancy mostly relate to starvation conditions during wartime. The best documented of these are the studies of the Dutch famine of 1944–5.[14] Starvation conditions had specific dates of onset and liberation-specific dates for the relief of starvation conditions. Nutritional developments in early pregnancy followed by increased access to food in later pregnancy results in babies being heavier at birth compared with babies born either before or after the famine. This may represent *in utero* catch-up growth. In contrast, if the famine occurred during late gestation, the babies weighed less and were thinner at birth, with no change in length. Nutritional supplementation can improve birthweight. Based on the Guatemalan studies, the type of supplementation, i.e. protein or carbohydrate, may not make a difference in the increase in birthweight, assuming minimum protein requirements are achieved.[15]

Relative to maternal factors, paternal anthropometric factors have limited impact on fetal growth. Morton[16] reported that, in half-siblings where the mother was the common parent, the correlation of birthweight between the half-siblings was $r = 0.58$. In contrast, the correlation of birthweights between half-siblings where the father was the common parent was only $r = 0.19$. Animal cross-breeding studies support these findings. Walton and Hammond[17] cross-bred Shetland ponies with Shire horses. The size of the foals was approximately the same size as the foals of the maternal pure breed. Thus, maternal regulation was more important in determining intrauterine growth than paternal factors. Finally, Klebanoff *et al.*,[18] using a Danish population registry, reported that paternal birthweight, adult height and weight together explained approximately 3% of the variance in birthweight, compared with 9% for the corresponding maternal factors. In summary, maternal factors, most importantly maternal pregravid weight, have the strongest correlation with birthweight.

Genetic factors associated with fetal growth

Approximately 25% of fetal growth is presumed to be related to genetic factors. The most obvious example is that the average male newborn weighs 150 g more at birth in comparison with females, adjusted for any potential co-variables. In 1998, Hattersley et al.[19] reported on the various phenotypic permutations associated with the single-gene mutations in the glucokinase gene. Glucokinase phosphorylates glucose to glucose-6-phosphate in the pancreas and liver. A heterozygous glucokinase mutation results in hyperglycaemia, usually with a mildly elevated fasting glucose and an abnormal oral glucose tolerance test. This is due to both a defect in the sensing of glucose by the β-cell, resulting in decreased insulin release, and, to a lesser degree, from reduced hepatic glycogen synthesis. If the heterozygous mutation is present in the fetus, then the altered glucose sensing by the fetal pancreas will result in a decrease in insulin secretion. Because in the fetus insulin is a primary stimulus for growth, any defect in fetal insulin secretion will result in decreased fetal growth and possible growth restriction. Hence, depending on whether mother, fetus or both have this gene defect in the glucokinase gene, the phenotype of the infant can vary from IUGR, through normal fetal growth and on` to macrosomia.

In contrast, genetic imprinting may result in the offspring having the phenotype of an infant of a mother with gestational diabetes mellitus (GDM) when the mother has normal glucose tolerance. Genetic imprinting is defined as the expression of either a maternal or paternal gene, the parent of origin of which determines the expression of a single allele of a gene. An example of genetic imprinting which results in the offspring having the phenotype of a GDM mother is the Beckwith–Wiedemann syndrome.[20] At birth, these infants present with macrosomia, defined as an average birthweight of 4 kg with increased subcutaneous tissue and muscle mass. Other findings include neonatal polycythaemia and hypoglycaemia. The hypoglycaemia may be related to increased insulin-like growth factor-II (IGF-II) expression, resulting in neonatal hyperinsulinaemia. The most common situation is when the maternal copy of the gene (11p15.5) is inactivated. The only active copy of the gene is then the paternal copy. Hence, at birth, the infant with Beckwith–Wiedemann syndrome may have the phenotype of an infant of a mother with GDM based on macrosomia, hypoglycaemia and polycythaemia, whereas the mother may have completely normal glucose tolerance. The interaction of genes and the environment then have the potential to produce a myriad of phenotypes in the infant of a mother with GDM, although fetal macrosomia still represents the most common phenotype.

Birthweight criteria for normal fetal growth

The criteria for normal fetal growth are population specific, based on issues reviewed earlier. Therefore, most reports describe fetal growth in relationship to population percentiles, most usually less than 10th centile as small for gestational age (SGA), 10th–90th centile as appropriate or average for gestational age (AGA), and greater than 90th centile as large for gestational age (LGA). These may be further delineated for gender and race. IUGR usually refers to a neonate that is SGA and in addition has evidence of decreased intrauterine growth such as an increased head to abdominal ratio (asymmetric IUGR) or physiological hypoglycaemia at birth. At the other end of the birthweight spectrum, infants are often classified as macrosomic or overgrown if fetal weight is greater than 4000 g, although some define macrosomic if birthweight is greater than 4500 g. However, it has become apparent in recent years that these criteria used to classify birthweight are not stable but rather represent a moving target.

In Canada and the USA, there was a significant decrease in term SGA neonates (11–27%) and increase in term LGA infants (5–24%) from 1985 to 1998. This increase was observed in both whites and African-Americans.[21] In Denmark, there was a significant (16.7–20%) increase in macrosomic neonates, defined as birthweight greater than 4000 g, during the period 1990–99.[22] Similarly in Sweden, there was a 23% increase in LGA newborns during the same period.[23] In the Cleveland population, a mean 116 g increase in term birthweight was observed from 1975 to 2004.[24] This increase in birthweight was observed not just for the upper centiles but for the lower 5th and 10th centiles as well. Thus, the increase in birthweight represents an entire population shift, not just an increase at the upper end of the birthweight scale. Although there were significant changes in the ethnic distribution of the population, the increase in birthweight over time remained significant once adjusted for significant co-variables. Lastly, when a stepwise regression analysis was performed, the 20 lb (9 kg) increase in maternal weight that was observed in the population at term, from 1987 to 2004, had the strongest correlation with the observed increased birthweight.[24]

Body composition in the assessment of fetal growth

In an effort to improve understanding of fetal growth, studies have concentrated on measures of body composition, i.e. fat and fat-free or lean body mass. The rationale for this approach stems from as far back as 1923 from the work of Moulton,[25] who described that the variability in weight within mammalian species was accounted for more by the fat mass than the fat-free or lean body mass. This concept was again examined by Sparks[26] assessing body composition among 169 stillbirths. He described a relatively comparable accretion of lean body mass in SGA, AGA and LGA fetuses, but considerable variation in the amounts of adipose tissue. The amount of fat in the SGA fetus was significantly less than the AGA fetus, which was less than that observed in the LGA fetus. Furthermore, relative to body composition, the human neonate is vastly different in comparison with other mammalian species. The term human fetus has the greatest percentage of body fat at birth (approximately 12–14%) in comparison with other common mammalian animal research models. For example, rodents have only approximately 1–3% body fat at birth. For these reasons, fetal growth is assessed in the research protocols using measures of neonatal body composition. The employed methodologies include anthropometric, stable isotope and total body electrical conductivity (TOBEC). These methods have been previously described.[27–29]

The utility of using body composition in understanding fetal growth is exemplified by a previous study by our group evaluating the proportion of the variance in birthweight explained by body composition analysis of neonates, i.e. fat and fat-free mass. The mean birthweight of the population was 3553 ± 462 g and the mean percentage body fat was 13.7% ± 4.2%. Fat-free mass accounted for about 86% of mean birthweight and for 83% of the variance in birthweight. In contrast, body fat accounted for only about 14% of birthweight and for 46% of the variance in birthweight.[30] Measures of body composition can also help to explain some of the variations in birthweight observed in a normal non-diabetic population. For example, it is well recognised that, at term, male neonates weigh on average 150 g more than females. Based on studies by our group and others, male infants have greater fat-free mass but similar fat mass as compared with females.[31] Therefore, although the percentage of body fat of females is greater than that of males, this is secondary to the decrease in fat-free mass rather than an increase in female fat mass. It is also well recognised that infants of women who smoke during pregnancy have neonates that are lighter (approximately 200 g) compared with women who do not smoke, and are at increased risk of being SGA. Lindsay et al.[32] showed that the infants of women who smoked during pregnancy had significantly less fat-free mass (2799 ± 292 g versus 2965 ± 359 g; $P = 0.02$) but not fat mass (343 ± 164 g versus 387 ± 216 g; $P = 0.32$). The decrease in fat-free mass was most apparent in the length of the long bones in the distal arms and legs. In summary, neonatal body composition measurements at term can assist in explaining some of the variation in birthweight observed in a normal population and provide a rationale for possible mechanisms.

Infants of women with gestational diabetes

There is an increased risk of fetal overgrowth or macrosomia in infants of women with GDM. The percentage of infants of women with GDM who fall within the normal birthweight centiles is often used as a positive outcome measure of glucose control and obstetrical management. We have recently published a series of studies[33] comparing the body composition analysis of infants of women with normal glucose tolerance (NGT) and GDM within 48 hours of birth (Figure 16.1). Although there was no significant difference in birthweight or fat-free mass between the groups, there was a significant increase in fat mass and percentage body fat in the infants of the mothers with GDM. The TOBEC body composition analyses were confirmed by the anthropometric/skinfold measurements. These data were adjusted for potential confounding variables such as parity and gestational age without any significant change in results.

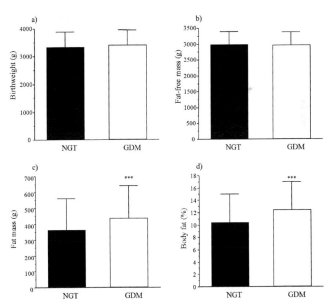

Figure 16.1. Neonatal body composition in infants of women with normal glucose tolerance (NGT) and gestational diabetes mellitus (GDM); a) birthweight $P = 0.26$, b) fat-free mass $P = 0.74$, c) fat mass $P = 0.0002$, d) percentage body fat $P = 0.0001$ (mean + standard deviation); adapted with permission from Catalano et al.[33]

We further analysed the data after stratification of the group into birthweight sub-sets, AGA[33] and LGA.[34] As shown in Table 16.1, there are no significant differences in birthweights between the AGA infants of mothers with GDM or NGT. However, there was again a significant increase in fat mass, percentage body fat and skinfold measures in the infants of the GDM mothers compared with the NGT group. Interestingly, the fat-free mass in the infants of the GDM mothers was significantly less compared with the infants in the NGT group. Similar results were obtained when we limited the analysis to LGA neonates only (Table 16.2). This relative increase in fat mass but not body weight may have obstetric implications, such as the increased incidence of shoulder dystocia in GDM compared with NGT neonates in similar birthweight categories. Based on these results, we conclude that birthweight alone may not be a sensitive enough measure to recognise subtle difference in fetal growth in infants of mothers with GDM.

Because many women with GDM are overweight or obese, we elected to perform a stepwise logistic regression analysis on the 220 infants of mothers with NGT and 195 term infants of mothers with GDM, previously described (Table 16.3).[35] Not surprisingly, gestational age at term was the independent variable with the strongest correlation with both birthweight and fat-free mass. Maternal smoking had a negative correlation with both birthweight and fat-free mass and paternal weight had a weak correlation with only fat-free mass. In contrast, maternal pregravid body mass index (BMI) had the strongest correlation with fat mass ($r^2 = 0.066$) and percentage body fat ($r^2 = 0.072$), therefore explaining approximately 7% of the variance in both fat mass

Table 16.1. Neonatal body composition and anthropometrics in average-for-gestational-age (AGA) infants of women with gestational diabetes mellitus (GDM) or normal glucose tolerance (NGT); data from Catalano et al.[33]

Neonatal anthropometrics	Women with GDM ($n = 132$)	Women with NGT ($n = 175$)	P value
Weight (g)	3202 ± 357	3249 ± 372	0.27
Fat-free mass (g)	2832 ± 286	2919 ± 287	0.008
Fat mass (g)	371 ± 163	329 ± 150	0.02
Body fat (%)	11.4 ± 4.6	9.9 ± 4.0	0.002
Triceps (mm)	4.5 ± 0.9	4.1 ± 0.8	0.0002
Subscapular (mm)	5.1 ± 1.1	4.5 ± 1.0	0.0001
Flank (mm)	4.0 ± 1.2	3.7 ± 0.8	0.007
Thigh (mm)	5.7 ± 1.2	5.2 ± 1.3	0.002
Abdomen (mm)	3.3 ± 0.9	3.0 ± 0.8	0.002

Table 16.2. Neonatal body composition in large-for-gestational-age (LGA) infants of women with gestational diabetes (GDM) or normal glucose tolerance (NGT); data from Durnwald et al.[34]

Neonatal anthropometrics	Women with GDM ($n = 50$)	Women with NGT ($n = 52$)	P value
Weight (g)	4060 ± 380	4120 ± 351	0.13
Fat-free mass (g)	3400 ± 312	3564 ± 310	0.0009
Fat mass (g)	662 ± 163	563 ± 206	0.02
Body fat (%)	16.2 ± 3.3	13.5 ± 4.5	0.002

and percentage body fat. Although approximately 50% of the women had GDM, only 2% of the variance (r^2 = 0.016) in fat mass in this population was explained by a mother having GDM. Furthermore, Ehrenberg *et al.*[36] reported that, although the risk of having an LGA neonate was greatest for women with a history of diabetes (OR 4.4) when compared with maternal obesity (OR 1.6), there was a four-fold greater number of LGA babies born to women who were obese than to women with diabetes. This was because the prevalence of overweight/obesity and diabetes was 47% and 5%, respectively. Therefore, at least in our population, maternal obesity and not diabetes appears to be the more important factor contributing to the population's increase in mean birthweight.

Table 16.3. Stepwise regression analysis of factors relating to fetal growth and body composition in infants of women with gestational diabetes mellitus (GDM) (n = 195) and normal glucose tolerance (NGT) (n = 220); pregravid maternal obesity has the strongest correlation with neonatal measures of fat mass and % body fat in contrast to lean body mass; reproduced with permission from Catalano and Ehrenberg[35]

Factor	r^2	Δr^2	P value
Birthweight			
Estimated gestational age	0.114	–	
Pregravid weight	0.162	0.048	
Weight gain	0.210	0.048	
Smoking (–)	0.227	0.017	
Parity	0.239	0.012	$P = 0.0001$
Lean body mass			
Estimated gestational age	0.122	–	
Smoking (–)	0.153	0.03 1	
Pregravid weight	0.179	0.026	
Weight gain	0.2 12	0.033	
Parity	0.225	0.013	
Maternal height	0.241	0.016	
Paternal weight	0.250	0.009	$P = 0.0001$
Fat mass			
Pregravid body mass index	0.066	–	
Estimated gestational age	0.136	0.070	
Weight gain	0.171	0.035	
Group (GDM)	0.187	0.016	$P = 0.0001$
Percentage body fat			
Pregravid body mass index	0.072	–	
Estimated gestational age	0.116	0.044	
Weight gain	0.147	0.031	
Group (GDM)	0.166	0.019	$P = 0.0001$

Infants of women who are overweight or obese

If infants of women with GDM have increased body fat rather than fat-free mass, what then is the difference, if any, in body composition between pregravid women who are overweight or obese compared with women who are lean or of average weight? Sewell et al.[37] evaluated 76 singleton neonates of women who were overweight or obese and 144 neonates of women who were lean or of average weight, again using anthropometric and TOBEC measurements of body composition. None of these women had GDM. There were no significant differences in gestational age between the groups. Additionally, there were no significant differences in maternal age, parity, use of tobacco, or obstetric or maternal medical problems between the groups. However, 14% of the infants of the mothers who were overweight or obese were macrosomic (birthweight greater than 4000 g) compared with only 5% in the neonates of the women who were lean or of average weight ($P < 0.04$), while weight gain in the overweight/obese group was actually less (13.8 ± 7.5 kg versus 15.2 ± 5.3 kg; $P < 0.001$) than in the lean/average weight group. The differences in neonatal body composition are depicted in Figure 16.2. As was observed in the infants of women with GDM, the infants of the women who were overweight or obese were significantly heavier because of an increase in fat mass ($P = 0.008$) and not fat-free mass ($P = 0.22$). In this study, weight gain in women who were overweight or obese (BMI ≥ 25 kg/m^2) had the strongest correlation with percentage body fat ($r^2 = 0.13$; $P = 002$), whereas weight gain was not significantly related to fat mass in the women who were lean or of average weight. In summary, the increased birthweight observed for infants of women who are obese or overweight is similar to that observed for infants of women with GDM, i.e. an increase in fat mass rather than fat-free mass.

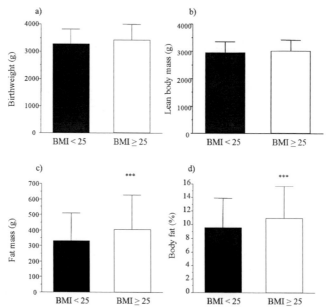

Figure 16.2. Neonatal body composition in infants of women with pregravid BMI < 25 kg/m² and BMI > 25 kg/m²; a) birthweight $P = 0.051$, b) fat-free mass $P = 0.22$, c) fat mass $P = 0.008$, d) percentage body fat $P = 0.006$ (mean + standard deviation); adapted with permission from Sewell et al.[37]

Since there is an independent effect of maternal pregravid weight and GDM on birthweight, Langer et al.[38] evaluated the effect of obesity on fetal growth for women with GDM. They reported that, in women with GDM controlled well on diet alone, the odds of fetal macrosomia, defined as birthweight greater than 4000 g, was significantly increased (OR 2.12) in GDM women who were obese compared with GDM women having a normal BMI. Similar results were found in women who were lean or obese with GDM that was poorly controlled on diet or insulin. In contrast, with well-controlled GDM, irrespective of whether the woman was lean or obese, as long as it was managed with diet plus insulin, there was no significant increased risk of macrosomia with increasing pregravid BMI. Hence only in a well-controlled GDM woman on diet plus insulin was there no difference in the rate of fetal macrosomia in obese as compared with lean women. The effect of insulin on metabolites other than glucose may explain these observations.

In a similar study, Schaefer-Graf et al.[39] reported in 2003 on the independent predictors of fetal macrosomia in utero, defined as an ultrasound abdominal circumference greater than the 90th centile for gestational age, and at the time of delivery, defined as birthweight greater than the 90th centile in local German population standards. The independent predictors which were examined included maternal age, parity, history of previous LGA infant or maternal GDM, prepregnancy BMI, weight gain during the index pregnancy, smoking, hypertension, glucose values from the diagnostic oral glucose tolerance, HbA_{1c}, daily glucose profiles and the use of insulin. Using successive multivariate logistic regression, the results were as follows:

- at entry, only the history of an LGA baby in a previous pregnancy and maternal BMI $\geq$ 30 kg/m^2 were predictive for a fetal abdominal circumference greater than the 90th centile
- at 24 weeks of gestation, only a history of an LGA baby was predictive of the abdominal circumference greater than the 90th centile
- at 28 weeks of gestation, only maternal BMI $\geq$ 30 kg/m^2 and a history of an LGA baby were predictive of an abdominal circumference greater than the 90th centile

It is of note that only at 32 and 36 weeks of gestation was the fasting glucose a better predictor of ultrasound macrosomia than a history of a prior LGA infant and maternal obesity. At birth, only maternal pregravid BMI $\geq$ 30 kg/m^2 and a history of an LGA baby were predictive of having an LGA baby. Therefore, maternal pregravid obesity rather than other factors including glucose values were better predictors of fetal overgrowth in a population of women with GDM.

Long-term risks for the offspring

In women with pregravid obesity and/or GDM there may be long-term risks of obesity and glucose intolerance for the offspring. Whitaker[40] reported on a retrospective cohort study of over 8000 low-income children whose mothers were followed from the first trimester of pregnancy until 24–59 months of infant age. The prevalence of childhood obesity defined as BMI $\geq$ 95th percentile for age and gender was 14.8% in children at 4 years of age. The prevalence was 24.1% if the mothers were obese in the first trimester in comparison with 9.0% of children whose mothers had had normal weight at the same gestational age. The relative risk of childhood obesity associated with maternal obesity in the first trimester was significant at 2.3 at 4 years of age. Dabelea et al.[41] reported that the mean adolescent BMI was 2.6 kg/m^2 greater in sibling offspring of diabetic pregnancies compared with siblings born to the same women when they had normal glucose tolerance previously. The risk of developing the metabolic syndrome in adolescents of mothers with GDM was addressed by Boney et al.[42] in a longitudinal cohort study of infants of women with GDM and normal glucose tolerance. The authors defined the metabolic syndrome as the presence of two or more of the following: obesity, hypertension, glucose intolerance and dyslipidaemia. Maternal obesity was defined as a pregravid BMI > 27.3 kg/m². Children who were LGA at birth had a significant increased hazard ratio for the metabolic syndrome (HR 2.19) by 11 years of age, as did the offspring of women who were obese (HR 1.81). Maternal GDM was not independently significant, but the risk of the development of the metabolic syndrome was significantly greater in the LGA as compared with the AGA offspring of GDM mothers (HR 3.6). Therefore, both maternal pregravid obesity and GDM may independently affect the risk of adolescent obesity and components of the metabolic syndrome.

Conclusion

There is a great variability in fetal growth in the human, based on both genetic and environmental factors. Although humans cannot control their genes (with the possible exception of epigenetic phenomena), they may be able to affect fetal growth through alterations in the maternal environment. Based on these data, the maternal pregravid environment or factors in very early gestation may result in alterations in growth that have long-term implications, i.e. fetal programming. Much as the prevention of congenital anomalies in women with pre-gestational diabetes can be improved by tight glucose control prior to conception, and so too may the more subtle effects of fuel-mediated teratogenesis on fetal growth, as described by Freinkel,[43] be improved by pre-conception issues related to diet and weight regulation. Therefore, a better understanding of the underlying genetic predispositions, physiology and mechanisms relating to maternal and feto-placental interactions as they relate to fetal growth is necessary.

References

1. Ogden CL, Flegal KM, Carroll MD, Johnson CL. Prevalence and trends in overweight among US children and adolescents, 1999–2000. *JAMA* 2002;288:1728–32.
2. Hytten FD. Weight gain in pregnancy. In: Hytten FE, Chamberlain G, editors. *Clinical Physiology in Obstetrics.* Oxford: Blackwell Scientific Publications; 1991. p. 173–203.
3. Lawrence W, Miller DG, Isaacs M, *et al. Nutrition in Pregnancy and Lactation.* Report of a WHO Expert Committee. Vol. 302. WHO Expert Committee on Nutrition, Pregnancy and Lactation; 1965. p. 1–54.
4. Ounsted M, Ounsted C. *On Fetal Growth Rate (Its Variations and Their Consequences).* (Clinics in Developmental Medicine No. 46). Suffolk: Lavenham Press; 1973.
5. Love EJ, Kinch RAH. Factors influencing the birth weight in normal pregnancy. *Am J Obstet Gynecol* 1965;91:342–9.
6. Humphreys RC. An analysis of the maternal and foetal weight factors in normal pregnancy. *J Obstet Gynaecol Br Emp* 1954;61: 764–71.
7. Abrams BF, Laros RK. Prepregnancy weight, weight gain and birth weight. *Am J Obstet Gynecol* 1986;4:503–9.
8. Thompson AM, Billewicz WZ, Hytten FE. The assessment of fetal growth. *J Obstet Gynecol* 1968;5:903–16.
9. Barker DJ. Fetal and infant origins of adult disease. *BMJ* 1990;301:1111.

10. Armitage JA, Khan IY, Taylor PD, Nathanielsz PW, Poston L. Developmental programming of the metabolic syndrome by maternal nutritional imbalance: how strong is the evidence from experimental models in mammals? *J Physiol* 2004;561(Pt 2):355–77.

11. Lucas A, Fentrell MS, Cule TJ. Fetal origins of adult disease – the hypothesis revisited. *BMJ* 1999;319:245–9.

12. Wilkin TJ, Metcalf BS, Murphy MJ, Kirkby J, Jeffery AN, Voss LD. The relative contribution of birth weight, weight change and current weight to insulin resistance in contemporary 5 year olds, the EarlyBird Study. *Diabetes* 2002;51:3468–72.

13. Hypponen E, Power C, Davey-Smith G. Perinatal growth, BMI and risk of type 2 diabetes by early midlife. *Diabetes Care* 2003;26:2512–17.

14. Ravelli ACJ. Body size of newborn babies after prenatal exposure to the Dutch famine of 1944–1945. In: *Prenatal Exposure to the Dutch Famine and Glucose Tolerance and Obesity at Age 50*. Thesis. Amsterdam: University of Amsterdam; 1999. p. 51–62.

15. Lechtig A, Habicht JP, Delgado H, Klein RE, Yarbrough C, Martorell R. Effect of food supplementation during pregnancy on birthweight. *Pediatrics* 1975;56:508–20.

16. Morton NE. The inheritance of human birth weight. *Ann Hum Genet* 1955;20:125–34.

17. Walton A, Hammond S. Maternal effects on growth and conformation in Shire horse-Shetland pony crosses; *Proc R Society Lond B Biol Sci* 1938;125B:311–35.

18. Klebanoff MA, Mednick BR, Schulsinger C, Secher NJ, Shiono PH. Father's effect on infant birth weight. *Am J Obstet Gynecol* 1998;178:1022–6.

19. Hattersley AT, Beards F, Ballantyne E, Appleton M, Harvey R, Ellard S. Mutations in the glucokinase gene of the fetus result in reduced birth weight. *Nat Genet* 1998;19:268–70.

20. Beckwith–Wiedemann syndrome. In: Jones KL, editor. *Smith's Recognizable Patterns of Human Malformations*. 6th ed. London: W.B. Saunders; 1997. p. 174–7.

21. Ananth CV, Wen SW. Trends in fetal growth among singleton gestations in the United States and Canada, 1985 through 1998. *Semin Perinatol* 2002;26:260–7.

22. Surkan PJ, Hsieh CC, Johansson AL, Dickman PW, Cnattingius S. Reasons for increasing trends in large for gestational age births. *Obstet Gynecol* 2004;104:720–6.

23. Orskou J, Kesmodel U, Henrikson TB, Secker NJ. An increasing proportion of infants weigh more than 4000 grams at birth. *Acta Obstet Gynecol Scand* 2001;80:931–6.

24. Catalano PM. Management of obesity in pregnancy. *Obstet Gynecol* 2007;109(2 Pt 1):419–33.

25. Moulton CR. Age and chemical development in mammals. *J Biol Chem* 1923;57:79–97.

26. Sparks JW. Human intrauterine growth and nutrient accretion. *Semin Perinatol* 1984;8:74–93.

27. Fiorotto MC, Klish WJ. Total body electrical conductivity measurements in the neonate. *Clin Perinatol* 1991;18:611–27.

28. Catalano PM, Thomas AJ, Avallone DA, Amini SB. Anthropometric estimation of neonatal body composition. *Am J Obstet Gynecol* 1995;173:1176–81.

29. Fiorotto ML, Cochran WJ, Funk RC, Sheng HP, Klish WJ. Total body electrical conductivity measurements: effects of body composition and geometry. *Am J Physiol* 1987;252(4 Pt 2): R794–800.

30. Catalano PM, Tyzbir ED, Allen SR, McBean JH, McAuliffe TL. Evaluation of fetal growth by estimation of body composition. *Obstet Gynecol* 1992 (Vol. 79).

31. Catalano PM, Drago NM, Amini SB. Factors affecting fetal growth and body composition. *Am J Obstet Gynecol* 1995;172:1459–63.

32. Lindsay CA, Thomas AJ, Catalano PM. The effect of smoking tobacco on neonatal body composition. *Am J Obstet Gynecol* 1997;172:1124–8.

33. Catalano PM, Thomas A, Huston-Presley L, Amini SB. Increased fetal adiposity: A very sensitive marker of abnormal *in utero* development. *Am J Obstet Gynecol* 2003;189:1698–704.

34. Durnwald C, Huston-Presley L, Amini S, Catalano P. Evaluation of body composition of large-for-gestational-age infants of women with gestational diabetes mellitus compared with women with normal glucose tolerance levels. *Am J Obstet Gynecol* 2004;191:804–8.

35. Catalano PM, Ehrenberg HM. The short- and long-term implications of maternal obesity on the mother and her offspring. *BJOG* 2006;113:1126–33.

36. Ehrenberg HM, Mercer BM, Catalano PM. The influence of obesity and diabetes on the prevalence of macrosomia. *Am J Obstet Gynecol* 2004;191:964–8.

37.   Sewell MF, Huston-Presley L, Super DM, Catalano P. Increased neonatal fat mass and not lean body mass is associated with maternal obesity. *Am J Obstet Gynecol* 2006;195:1100–3.

38.   Langer O, Yogev Y, Xenakis EM, Brustman L. Overweight and obese in gestational diabetes: the impact on pregnancy outcome. *Am J Obstet Gynecol* 2005;192:1768–76.

39.   Schaefer-Graf UM, Kjos SL, Kilavuz O, Plagemann A, Brauer M, Dudenhausen JW, *et al.* Determinants of fetal growth at different periods of pregnancies complicated by gestational diabetes mellitus or impaired glucose tolerance. *Diabetes Care* 2003;26:193–8. Erratum in: *Diabetes Care* 2003;26:1329.

40.   Whitaker RC. Predicting preschool obesity at birth: The role of maternal obesity in early pregnancy. *Pediatrics* 2004;114:E29–36.

41.   Dabelea D, Hanson RL, Lindsay RS, Pettitt DJ, Imperatore G, Gabir MM, *et al.* Intrauterine exposure to diabetes conveys risks for type 2 diabetes and obesity: A study of discordant sibships. *Diabetes* 2000;49:2208–11.

42.   Boney CM, Verma A, Tucker R, Vohr BR. Metabolic syndrome in childhood: Association with birth weight, maternal obesity and gestational diabetes mellitus. *Pediatrics* 2005;115:290–6.

43.   Freinkel N. Diabetic embryopathy and fuel-mediated organ teratogenesis: Lessons from animal models. *Horm Metab Res* 1988;20:463–75.

Section 4

Long-term health

Chapter 17
Obesity in urogynaecology and laparoscopy

Anthony Smith and Sharif Ismail

Introduction

Obesity is associated with an increased abdominal girth and raised intra-abdominal pressure. These factors contribute to a mechanical influence on the urogynaecological conditions of urinary incontinence and prolapse. Laparoscopy and laparoscopic surgery are influenced by obesity both from the additional challenges of anaesthesia (see Chapter 14) and surgery, and the additional difficulties because of the distortion of anatomy by the increased abdominal girth and adipose tissue. The metabolic aspects of obesity are not a primary concern in urogynaecology and laparoscopy.

Obesity may be measured in various ways and is most commonly defined by the ratio between weight and squared height, the body mass index (BMI). Some studies have shown that women with a higher BMI have a higher intra-abdominal pressure.[1,2] Other studies have demonstrated that the antero-posterior diameter of the abdomen, another index of obesity, correlates much more closely with raised intra-abdominal pressure.[3] However, virtually all the literature on obesity in urogynaecology and laparoscopy employs BMI to define obesity and the influence of obesity may be underestimated in these areas.

Epidemiology

Incontinence

There is no evidence that abnormal detrusor function is more prevalent in women who are obese (abnormal detrusor function is seen in women with poorly controlled type 2 diabetes mellitus secondary to glycosuria or neuropathy). There is evidence that stress incontinence is more common in women who are obese.[4] It has always been assumed, although not proven, that this is secondary to the raised intra-abdominal pressures generated by obesity. Obesity is not as strong an influence on the prevalence of stress incontinence as age and parity.

Prolapse

Most studies suggest that prolapse is more common in women who are obese[5] but this is not confirmed in all studies.[6] It is possible that these apparent differences are due to the way that the studies were performed and the definitions used. Symptoms of prolapse may not be the most reliable index of whether prolapse is present[6] and many symptoms commonly associated with prolapse are also described by women with good pelvic floor support. In a study of nearly 400 women in Manchester, advancing age and parity were closely correlated with the finding of prolapse on examination and the development of prolapse symptoms. Women with prolapse were not found to have a higher BMI. However, women who had no symptoms of prolapse but were found to have prolapse on examination had a higher BMI, suggesting that BMI may be a modifiable risk factor for the development of prolapse.[7]

There is some evidence that women who are obese have more symptoms of pelvic floor dysfunction. Kapoor et al.[8] found that a group of women who were obese awaiting gastric bypass surgery had more urinary incontinence affecting lifestyle and more difficulty with defecation than a group of age-matched controls. However, sexual function was not impaired in the obese group.

Investigation

There is no evidence that obesity influences the results of investigations used in urogynaecology. Cough tests and the Valsalva manoeuvre are employed by some clinicians and one would expect the raised intra-abdominal pressure found in women who are obese to influence the result. Standardisation of the Valsalva pressure has been researched[9] but has not been widely employed.

Obesity and treatment for urogynaecological problems

There are two issues with treatment: firstly, does weight loss (as a treatment) influence the symptoms; and, secondly, does being obese influence the outcome of other treatments?

Weight loss as a treatment

Incontinence

The clinical guideline published in 2006 by the National Institute for Health and Clinical Excellence (NICE) on management of urinary incontinence in women[10] advises clinicians to 'encourage overweight women to lose weight in the treatment of all types of incontinence'. Although this sounds sensible and is widely practised by clinicians, there is very little evidence that weight loss will result in improvement of incontinence whether produced by detrusor overactivity, urethral sphincter weakness or a combination of both. In a series of nine women, all of the six women with a weight loss of more than 5% achieved a reduction in incontinence episodes of more than 50%.[11] This research group conducted a prospective randomised controlled study of women on the waiting list for surgery for stress incontinence. Weight loss of 5–10% produced a significant improvement in the frequency of stress and urge incontinence episodes, similar to that produced by other non-surgical treatments, when compared with controls.[12] Lifestyle changes (weight loss, exercise, diet, etc.) are commonly encouraged as part of the package provided during a course of pelvic floor physiotherapy. This has made it difficult to define which part of the package – physiotherapy or lifestyle changes – is contributing to any improvement.

Prolapse

No robust studies have been published on the influence of pelvic floor physiotherapy on prolapse. Furthermore, there have been no studies to determine whether lifestyle changes, including weight loss, influence prolapse or prolapse symptoms. The

PROSPER study, a prospective randomised trial of physiotherapy for prolapse, will commence shortly and is designed to address these influences.

Does obesity influence outcome from treatment?

Incontinence

There is no Level 1 evidence on the influence of obesity on the outcome of surgical treatment for stress incontinence. Several studies have examined whether women who are obese within a cohort undergoing treatment have fared less well.

There are no prospective randomised trials that suggest superiority of one surgical technique over another in the obese population. Studies have suggested increased failure rates among women who are obese undergoing needle bladder neck suspensions[13] or retropubic suspensions.[14] In contrast, a retrospective study of anti-incontinence surgery in 198 women demonstrated that overall continence did not correlate with obesity in women undergoing anterior colporrhaphy, anterior colporrhaphy with needle bladder neck suspension or Burch colposuspension, although cure rates were markedly better in those in the Burch colposuspension cohort overall.[15]

Studies have demonstrated satisfactory efficacy for transvaginal tape (TVT) for women who are obese comparable with those who are not.[16,17] The former study,[16] a prospective cohort study, examined the outcome at 6 months after TVT in women with a BMI < 25 kg/m^2, 25–29 kg/m^2 and ≥ 30 kg/m^2, and found no difference in cure rate. The authors reported two failures in the cohort of 242 women, who both had a BMI < 25 kg/m^2. It is unclear whether women who are obese have a higher risk of recurrence with time, as might be expected with higher intra-abdominal pressures. A longer term (minimum 52 months) retrospective study of 81 women demonstrated no difference in the rate of complications in women who were obese but a trend towards higher failure rate.[18] The authors suggested that low BMI may be a risk factor for failure. One study suggested an increased incidence of postoperative urge incontinence in women with a high BMI, greater than 30 kg/m^2, undergoing TVT, but no difference in subjective or objective cure rates.[17]

It is generally accepted that, although obesity may be associated with other factors (coronary artery disease, ventilatory/airway problems, thromboembolic phenomena, etc.) that may place the patient at a somewhat higher surgical risk overall, it is unclear whether obesity alone is an independent predictor for surgical risk or morbidity specifically in stress incontinence surgery.

There are no studies, prospective or retrospective, that have suggested obesity has a positive or favourable influence on outcome in stress incontinence surgery.

Prolapse

There is no literature on the influence of obesity on the outcome of treatment for prolapse.

Obesity and laparoscopy

Until 1990, the laparoscope was very much the tool of the gynaecologist, who used it for diagnosis, minor adhesiolysis and tubal occlusion. Since then there has been a dramatic increase in the use of the laparoscope, primarily for assistance with surgical procedures, and for many procedures (e.g. ectopic pregnancy and cholecystectomy) it has become the method of choice. Ironically, the number of laparoscopic tubal occlusions now performed annually in the UK has fallen markedly (Hospital Episode Statistics data). Since 1990, there have been many advances in the equipment available, both with regard to the camera systems and to the instrumentation. This section will discuss:

1. the additional risks of laparoscopy and laparoscopic surgery for women who are obese
2. the advantages of laparoscopic surgery for women who are obese
3. surgical procedures in which obesity is more common.

Additional risks of laparoscopy and laparoscopic surgery in the obese patient

The main risk areas in laparoscopy and laparoscopic surgery are with:

- anaesthesia
- first port entry
- additional port entry
- carbon dioxide insufflation
- the surgical procedure.

Anaesthesia

People who are obese may have additional medical problems that make them at risk of operative complications, include anaesthetic ones.[19] These additional problems include diabetes mellitus, hypertension, hypoventilation, sleep apnoea,[20] angina and chronic obstructive pulmonary disease.[21] In addition, there is an increased risk of thromboembolic disease.[19] This is discussed in more detail in Chapter 14.

First port entry

The debate about the optimal entry technique continues. There is no robust evidence to support the use of open entry as a means of reducing the risk of bowel injury, but it may have some advantage in reducing the risk of major vascular injury. The increased depth of the anterior abdominal wall in women who are obese might be expected to increase the risk.

Two prospective multicentre studies, involving 9475 and 3500 women undergoing interval laparoscopic tubal sterilisation, found obesity to be associated with a higher incidence of complications.[22,23] Jamieson *et al.*[22] found that obesity is an independent risk factor for complications (OR 1.7; 95% CI 1.2–2.6).

Direct trocar insertion is associated with more complications in women who are obese.[24] A panniculus causes caudal deviation in the vertical axis of the umbilicus[25] and can make Veress needle and trocar entry difficult.[26] Assessing for such caudal deviation and its correction, by manual displacement of the umbilicus in a cranial direction to ensure a minimum distance of 8 cm between the umbilicus and anterior superior iliac spines, followed by open laparoscopy was found to have a low incidence of entry problems, such as preperitoneal insufflation, subcutaneous emphysema, visceral and vascular injury and penetration of an overlying skin fold.[27] Insertion through the base, rather than the lower margin, of the umbilicus was also found to reduce the incidence of preperitoneal insufflation.[26] The angle of insertion may have to be increased to 90°, from the usual of 40° used with people who are not obese.[28] Other alternatives include Veress needle insertion through the uterus[29] and the use of optical trocars (VISIPORT™; Tyco Healthcare).[30]

Additional port entry

The avoidance of injury to major anterior abdominal wall vessels during placement of additional ports requires visualisation of the vessels by direct view and trans-illumination. Both of these techniques are more difficult in women who are obese and therefore more likely to fail.

Carbon dioxide insufflation

There are no studies on the influence of obesity on carbon dioxide insufflation during laparoscopic surgery. The higher pressures used by some surgeons, particularly during first port entry, might be expected to produce additional challenges with ventilation.

Surgical procedure

A retrospective study found no significant difference in the incidence of intraoperative and postoperative complications during laparoscopic management of tubal ectopic pregnancy in 27 women who were obese (BMI > 30 kg/m^2) when compared with 90 who were not (BMI ≤ 30 kg/m^2).[31] On the other hand, a prospective study found a higher incidence of major operative complications during laparoscopic hysterectomy in 30 women who were obese (BMI > 30 kg/m^2) when compared with 217 who were not (BMI < 30 kg/m^2).[32]

A retrospective study compared total laparoscopic hysterectomy in women who were and were not obese.[33] It included 270 patients and showed total laparoscopic hysterectomy to be associated with a three-fold increase in blood loss exceeding 500 ml.

The incidence of lung atelectasis was found to be significantly higher in people who were morbidly obese than those who were not obese when compared using computed tomography (CT) scans prior to induction of general anaesthesia for laparoscopic procedures, after extubation as well as 24 hours later.[34] Before induction of general anaesthesia, lung atelectasis was encountered in 2.1% of people who were morbidly obese, in comparison with 1.0% of those who were not obese($P < 0.01$). After extubation, the incidence was 7.6% for those who were morbidly obese and 2.8% for those who were not obese ($P < 0.05$). The incidence 24 hours after anaes-thesia was 9.7% for people who were morbidly obese and 1.9% for those who were not obese ($P < 0.01$).

Most studies report that laparoscopic surgery takes longer than open surgery. In the COLPO trial comparing open and laparoscopic colposuspension, the laparoscopic procedure, by experienced laparoscopic surgeons, took an additional 15 minutes to perform.[35] A retrospective study compared total laparoscopic hysterectomy in women who were and were not obese.[33] It included 270 women and showed total laparo-scopic hysterectomy required at least 2 hours to complete in those who were obese (RR 1.6; 95% CI 1.2–2.0).

Conversion from laparoscopic to open surgery may be an additional risk for people who are obese. A retrospective study showed those with BMI ≥ 30 kg/m^2) to be 14 times more likely than those with BMI < 30 kg/m^2 to require conversion to laparot-omy during laparoscopic management of benign adnexal masses (OR 13.78; 95% CI 1.76–29.1).[36] They also had significantly longer operating time (143 ± 87 minutes versus 114 ± 41 minutes; $P = 0.04$) and longer hospital stay (1.07 ± 1.87 days versus 0.51 ± 1.06 days; $P = 0.04$). Another retrospective study showed higher BMI to be associated with significantly higher conversion to laparotomy rate and average blood loss in attempted laparoscopically assisted vaginal hysterectomy (LAVH).[37] The study included 670 women: 162 with BMI > 25 kg/m^2 and 508 with BMI ≤ 25 kg/m^2. Similarly, another retrospective study looked at the conversion rate in 55 women with endometrial carcinoma undergoing laparoscopic lymph node dissection.[38] The rate was significantly higher in those with a Quetelet Index greater than 35 (82.1% versus 44.4%; P = 0.004). Likewise, a third retrospective study showed obesity to be the most common reason for conversion in 67 attempted laparoscopic hysterectomies for early-stage endometrial cancer in elderly women (≥ 65 years old).[39] The same pattern was confirmed in a fourth retrospective study that included 103 attempted laparoscopic lymph node dissections in women with endometrial (95) and ovarian (8) cancer.[40] It remains to be seen whether robotic surgery might reduce such conversion rates.

Advantages of laparoscopic surgery in the obese patient

Laparoscopic surgery is believed by many to produce the advantages of less intra-operative morbidity and reduced postoperative pain and morbidity, leading to a shorter convalescence. The cosmetic value of smaller wounds is also valued by patients. The literature does not wholly support the perceived advantages, although there are few robust studies to assess the key indicators of intra- and postoperative events.

In the COLPO trial, a prospective randomised trial comparing laparoscopic and open colposuspension, women who had the laparoscopic procedure used less post-operative analgesia and had less infective morbidity, including wound infections, after surgery.[35] Women who are obese are probably more likely to develop wound infections after surgery and may therefore gain more from smaller wounds. Early mobilisation after surgery is encouraged after all types of surgery but the reduction in pain and wound morbidity will aid the mobility of women who are obese, which may in turn reduce the risk of other problems such as thromboembolism.

In weighing up whether surgery in women who are obese is better performed by an open or laparoscopic technique, the additional risks of laparoscopic surgery need to be placed against the potential benefits.

Surgical procedures in which obesity is more common

There are a number of gynaecological conditions in which obesity is more common and where laparoscopic surgery may be required.

Polycystic ovary syndrome

Obesity is a feature of polycystic ovary syndrome (PCOS),[41] which may be managed by laparoscopic ovarian diathermy. However, morbid obesity (BMI ≥ 35 kg/m^2) is associated with a low rate of ovulation following laparoscopic ovarian diathermy in anovulation.[42] A large series reported lower ovulation rates following ovarian diathermy for PCOS in women who were morbidly obese.[43] The rate fell from 96% in women who were slim or moderately obese to 70% in women who were morbidly obese.

Endometriosis

Obesity was found to be a risk factor for endometriosis in a retrospective study involving 1079 infertile women who underwent diagnostic laparoscopy.[44] A 10 year observational study found an inverse relationship between the incidence of endometriosis and BMI at the age 18 years (OR 0.8; 95% CI 0.6–1.1). An inverse relationship with BMI at the time of laparoscopy was only detected in those who were infertile.[45]

Endometrial carcinoma

Obesity is a risk factor for endometrial carcinoma (see Chapter 18). Laparoscopic treatment is now favoured by some surgeons and a small audit in a UK tertiary referral oncology unit recently demonstrated similar operating times and shorter postoperative hospital stays (11.5 versus 4 days) after the laparoscopic procedure.[46] In a larger, prospective series in the USA women with BMI ranging from 28 to 60 kg/m² were treated for stage 1 endometrial cancer and, although the operating time was longer, more lymph nodes were removed and a smaller drop in haematocrit, together with a shorter convalescence, were demonstrated in the laparoscopic group, compared with those women who had surgery performed by laparotomy.[47] A third study retrospectively compared total laparoscopic hysterectomy with total abdominal hysterectomy in 78 women who were morbidly obese with endometrial cancer.[48] The women who had laparoscopic hysterectomy were heavier and had higher ASA (American Society of Anesthesiologists) scores. Nonetheless, the laparoscopic group had a shorter hospital stay (4.4 ± 3.9 days versus 7.9 ± 3.0 days; $P < 0.001$) and lower incidence of wound infections (2.1% versus 48.4%).

Alternatives to laparoscopy in people who are obese

Although laparoscopy and laparoscopic surgery may be safely performed on women who are obese, there are additional risks and alternatives should always be considered. Diagnostic laparoscopy and dye testing for tubal occlusion is commonly performed in routine gynaecological practice. The use of other tubal patency tests should be considered, particularly when the chance of finding pelvic pathology is low.

Transvaginal aspiration of ovarian cysts under ultrasound guidance has been advocated in women who are obese as an alternative to surgery, to reduce associated risks.[49] The approach, however, risks recurrence, which may necessitate repeat aspiration.

References

1. Noblett KL, Jensen JK, Ostergard DR. The relationship of body mass index to intra-abdominal pressure as measured by multi-channel cystometry. *Int Urogynecol J Pelvic Floor Dysfunct* 1997;8:323–6.

2. Bai SW, Kang JY, Rha KH, Lee MS, Kim JY, Park KH. Relationship of urodynamic parameters and obesity in women with stress urinary incontinence. *J Reprod Med* 2002;47:559–63.

3. Sugerman H, Windsor A, Bessosm WL. Intra-abdominal pressure, sagittal abdominal diameter and obesity comorbidity. *J Intern Med* 1997 January;241:71–9.

4. Dwyer PL, Lee ET, Hay DM. Obesity and urinary incontinence in women. *Br J Obstet Gynaecol* 1988;95:91–6.

5. Progetto Menopausa Italia Study Group. Risk factors for genital prolapse in non-hysterectomized women around menopause. Results from a large cross-sectional study in menopausal clinics in Italy. *Eur J Obstet Gynecol Reprod Biol* 2000;93:135–40.

6. Uustall Fornell E, Wingren G, Kjolhede P. Factors associated with pelvic floor dysfunction with emphasis on urinary and faecal incontinence and genital prolapse: an epidemiological study. *Acta Obstet Gynaecol Scand* 2004;83:383–9.

7. N Ali, personal communication.

8. Kapoor DS, Davila GW, Rosenthal RJ, Ghoneim GM. Pelvic floor dysfunction in morbidly obese women: pilot study. *Obes Res* 2004;12:1104–7.

9. Greenland HP, Hosker GL, Smith AR. A valsalvometer can be effective in standardising the Valsalva manoeuvre. *Int Urogynecol J Pelvic Floor Dysfunct* 2007;18:499–502.

10. National Collaborating Centre for Women and Children's Health, National Institute for Health and Clinical Excellence. *Urinary Incontinence: the Management of Urinary Incontinence in Women.* Clinical Guideline. London: RCOG Press; 2006.

11. Subak L, Johnson C, Whitcomb E, Boban D, Saxton J, Brown J. Does weight loss improve incontinence in moderately obese women? *Int Urogynecol J* 2002;13:40–3.

12. Subak LL, Whitcomb E, Shen H, Saxton J, Vittinghoff E, Brown JS. Weight loss: a novel and effective treatment for urinary incontinence. *J Urol* 2005 July;154:190–5.

13. O'Sullivan DC, Chilton CP, Munson KW. Should Stamey colposuspension be our primary surgery for stress incontinence? *Br J Urol* 1995;75:457–60.

14. Alcalay M, Monga A, Stanton SL. Burch colposuspension: a10–20 year follow up. *Br J Obstet Gynaecol* 1995;102:740–5.

15. Zivkovic F, Tamussino K, Pieber D, Haas J. Body mass index and outcome of incontinence surgery. *Obstet Gynecol* 1999;93(5 Pt 1):753–6.

16. Mukherjee K, Constantine G. Urinary stress incontinence in obese women: tension-free vaginal tape is the answer. *BJU Int* 2001;88:881–3.

17. Rafii A, Daraï E, Haab F, Samain E, Levardon M, Deval B. Body mass index and outcome of tension-free vaginal tape. *Eur Urol* 2003;43:288–92.

18. Tsivian A, Neuman M, Kessler O, Mogutin B, Korczak D, Levin S, *et al.* Does patient weight influence the outcome of the tension free vaginal tape procedure? *Gynecol Surg* 2006;3:195–8.

19. Sugerman HJ, Sugerman EL, Wolfe L, Kellum JM Jr, Schweitzer MA, DeMaria EJ. Risks and benefits of gastric bypass in morbidly obese patients with severe venous stasis disease. *Ann Surg* 2001;234:41–6.

20. Lara MD, Kothari SN, Sugerman HJ. Surgical management of obesity; A review of the evidence relating to the health benefits and risks. *Treatments Endocrinol* 2005;4:55–64.

21. Lamvu G, Zolnoun D, Boggess J, Steege JF. Obesity: physiologic changes and challenges during laparoscopy. *Am J Obstet Gynecol* 2004;191:669–74.

22. Jamieson DJ, Hillis SD, Duerr A, Marchbanks PA, Costello C, Peterson HB. Complications of interval laparoscopic tubal sterilisation: Findings from the United States Collaborative Review of Sterilisation. *Obstet Gynecol* 2000;96:997–1002.

23. Destefano F, Greenspan JR, Dicker RC, Peterson HB, Strauss LT, Rubin GL. Complications of interval laparoscopic tubal sterilisation. *Obstet Gynecol* 1983;61:153–8.

24. Byron JW, Fujiyoshi CA, Miyazawa K. Evaluation of the direct trocar insertion technique at laparoscopy. *Obstet Gynecol* 1989;74(3 Pt 1):423–5.

25. Hurd WW, Bude RO, DeLancey JO, Pearl ML. The relationship of the umbilicus to the aortic bifurcation: Implications for laparoscopic techniques. *Obstet Gynecol* 1992;80:48–51.

26. Hurd WH, Bude RO, DeLancey JO, Gauvin JM, Aisen AM. Abdominal wall characterization with magnetic resonance imaging and computed tomography: The effect of obesity on the laparoscopic approach. *J Reprod Med* 1991;36:473–6.

27. Pelosi MA 3rd, Pelosi MA. Alignment of the umbilical axis; An effective maneuver for laparoscopic entry in the obese patient. *Obstet Gynecol* 1998;92:869–72.

28. Poindexter AN, Ritter M, Fahim A, Humphrey H. Trocar introduction performed during laparoscopy for the obese patient. *Surg Gynecol Obstet* 1987;165:57–9.

29. Awadalla SG. Transuterine insertion of Veress needle in laparoscopy. *Obstet Gynecol* 1990;76:314–5.

30. Wolf JS Jr. Laparoscopic access with a visualising trocar. *Tech Urol* 1997;3:34–7.

31. Hsu S, Mitwally MF, Aly A, Al-Saleh M, Batt RE, Yeh J. Laparoscopic management of tubal ectopic pregnancy in obese women. *Fertil Steril* 2004;81:198–202.

32. Holub Z, Jaber A, Kliment L, Fischlova D, Wagnerova M. Laparoscopic hysterectomy I obese women; A clinical prospective study. *Eur J Obstet Gynecol Reprod Biol* 2001;98:77–82.

33. Heinberg EM, Crawford BL 3rd, Weitzen SH, Bonilla DJ. Total laparoscopic hysterectomy in obese versus nonobese patients. *Obstet Gynecol* 2004;103:674–80.

34. Eichenberger A, Proietti S, Wicky S, Frascarolo P, Suter M, Spahn DR, *et al.* Morbid obesity and post-operative pulmonary atelectasis; An underestimated problem. *Anesth Analg* 2002;95:1788–92.

35. Kitchener HC, Dunn G, Lawton V, Reid F, Nelson L, Smith AR; COLPO Study Group. Laparoscopic versus open colposuspension – results of a prospective randomised controlled trial. *BJOG* 2006;113:1007–13.

36. Thomas D, Ikeda M, Deepika K, Medina C, Takacs P. Laparoscopic management of benign adnexal mass in obese women. *J Minim Invasive Gynecol* 2006;13:311–14.

37. Shen CC, Hsu TY, Huang FJ, Huang EY, Huang HW, Chang CY, *et al*. Laparoscopic-assisted vaginal hysterectomy in women of all weights and the effect of weight on complications. *J Am Assoc Gynecol Laparosc* 2002;9:468–73.

38. Scribner DR Jr, Walker JL, Johnson GA, McMeekin DS, Gold MA, Mannel RS. Laparoscopic pelvic and paraaortic lymph node dissection in the obese. *Gynecol Oncol* 2002;84:426–30.

39. Scribner DR Jr, Walker JL, Johnson GA, McMeekin SD, Gold MA, Mannel RS. Surgical management of early-stage endometrial cancer in the elderly: is laparoscopy feasible? *Gynecol Oncol* 2001;83:563–8.

40. Scribner DR Jr, Walker JL, Johnson GA, McMeekin SD, Gold MA, Mannel RS. Laparoscopic pelvic and paraaortic lymph node dissection: analysis of the first 100 cases. *Gynecol Oncol* 2001;82:498–503.

41. Eden JA, Place J, Carter GD, Jones J, Alaghband-Zadeh J, Pawson ME. The diagnosis of polycystic ovaries in subfertile women. *Br J Obstet Gynaecol* 1989;96:809–15.

42. Amer SA, Li TC, Ledger WL. Ovulation induction using laparoscopic ovarian drilling in women with polycystic ovarian syndrome: Predictors of success. *Hum Reprod* 2004;19:1719–24.

43. Gjonnaess H. Ovarian electrocautery in the treatment of women with polycystic ovary syndrome (PCOS). Factors affecting the results. *Acta Obstet Gynecol Scand* 1994;73:407–12.

44. Calhaz-Jorge C, Mol BW, Nunes J, Costa AP. Clinical predictive factors for endometriosis in a Portuguese infertile population. *Hum Reprod* 2004;19:2126–31.

45. Missmer SA, Hankinson SE, Spiegelman D, Barbieri RL, Marshall LM, Hunter DJ. Incidence of laparoscopically confirmed endometriosis by demographic, anthropometric and lifestyle factors. *Am J Epidemiol* 2004;160:784–96.

46. Yu CK, Cutner A, Mould T, Olaitan A. Total laparoscopic hysterectomy as a primary surgical treatment for endometrial cancer in morbidly obese women. *BJOG* 2005;112:115–17.

47. Eltabbakh GH, Shamonki MI, Moody JM, Garafano LL. Hysterectomy for obese women with endometrial cancer: Laparoscopy or laparotomy? *Gynecol Oncol* 2000;78(3 Pt 1):329–35.

48. Obermair A, Manolitsas TP, Leung Y, Hammond IG, McCrtney AJ. Total laparoscopic hysterectomy versus total abdominal hysterectomy for obese women with endometrial cancer. *Int J Gynecol Cancer* 2005;15:319–24.

49. Duke D, Colville J, Keeling A, Broe D, Fotheringham T, Lee MJ. Transvaginal aspiration of ovarian cysts; Long-term follow up. *Cardiovasc Intervent Radiol* 2006;29:401–5.

Chapter 18
Obesity and female malignancies

Sean Kehoe

Introduction

The relationship between obesity and an increased relative risk of certain cancers has been recognised for some years but interest in the relationship has increased in recent times with the rise in obesity rates. The contribution of obesity to cancer incidence is difficult to determine accurately but a recent analysis of cancers across Europe suggested that 70 000 cases (of 3.5 million) were attributable to obesity.[1] Not only does obesity seem to be related to incidence but also mortality rates when a malignancy develops, with a large study on a US population reporting a relative risk of death from malignancy at 1.62 for the heaviest as compared with women with normal weight.[2] Indeed, studies on potential prevention of cancer list lifestyle factors that, if altered, could reduce the incidence of cancer by up to 50%, and obesity is considered to be one of the important rectifiable factors.[3,4]

Although obesity is deemed to be an important contributor to cancer risk from many epidemiological studies, specific research into the molecular mechanisms by which obesity increases cancer risk are somewhat sparse and, for specific malignancies, are non-existent. Nevertheless, some findings can be related to gynaecological cancers.

Aetiology

Obesity results in an increase in serum adipocytokines, namely adiponectin and leptin. Other members of this family include vistafin, resistin and more recently retinol binding protein 4 (RBP4). The roles of the more recently discovered cytokines have not been investigated in cancer aetiology. These cytokines have a wide spectrum of actions, influencing satiety, inflammation, production of other cytokines, such as tumour necrosis factor (TNF) and vascular endothelial growth factor (VEGF) and T-cell function, the last two being particularly pertinent to malignant processes.[5,6] While serum levels of certain adipocytokines are altered in some cancers, the actual causal relationship has yet to be elucidated (Table 18.1).

Table 18.1. Obesity-related factors and diagnosed cancers

Cancer type	Serum/plasma findings
Endometrial	↑ C-peptide
	↓ adiponectin
Breast	↓ adiponectin (post-menopausal women only)
	↑ IGF-I (premenopausal women only)
	↓ IGFBP-3
Ovarian	↑ IGFBP-2

IGF = insulin-like growth factor; IGFBP = insulin-like growth factor binding protein

Recent research has focused on adiponectin, whereby its activity through a variety of receptors has been shown to promote apoptosis in both breast and prostate cell lines.[7,8] An elevated serum leptin concentration has been noted in some breast cancers, and an increased presence of leptin receptor in breast cancer tumours related to poorer survival patterns.[9] Leptins have also been implicated in animal models to enhance production of VEGF, an important growth factor in malignant neoplasia as indicated by the introduction of anti-VEGF therapies for some cancers, including ovarian cancer.[10] Leptin has a proliferative action on breast cancer cell lines and, as with many of the adipocytokines, the actual pathways involved in the association require further research.[11] Activity via the insulin-like growth factor receptors are interesting in that this translates to the clinical situation found in some gynaecological cancers, particularly endometrial cancer.[12,13]

Impact on screening

Methods of screening are used to prevent cervical carcinoma and to detect breast cancer at an early stage, and, in endometrial cancer, transvaginal ultrasound is employed to triage women with postmenopausal bleeding. When comparing women with body mass index (BMI) < 25 kg/m^2 with women with BMI greater than this, mammography has been shown to have a 20% increase in false positive rate.[14] Transvaginal ultrasonography for detecting endometrial thickness for postmenopausal bleeding revealed, in a cohort of 594 women, that the area under the receiver operating characteristic (ROC) curve was 0.87 but that this fell to 0.75 in women who were obese.[15]

Besides the increased inaccuracy of screening methods due to obesity, research has also revealed that women who are obese tend to delay or not access relevant screening programmes at all, owing to either embarrassment or discomfort caused by the screening, such as a cervical smear. This further confounds matters relating to the relationship between obesity and cancer because prevention or early detection is impeded by virtue of a high BMI.[16–18]

Ovarian cancer

Ovarian cancer is the most lethal of all the gynaecological cancers, accounting for about 4700 deaths per year in the UK.[19] As with many of the other cancers, the relationship between obesity and ovarian cancer is primarily based on epidemiological series, and the findings are contradictory. Both BMI and waist:hip ratio (WHR) have been investigated. Most series are case-controlled, although not all influencing variables are included in many of the studies (Table 18.2).

In one study, the Quetelet Index was employed and, comparing the highest with lower values, the odds ratio was 1.7 (95% CI 1.1–2.7).[20] Interestingly, this study noted a higher risk of serous and endometrioid tumours, which was confined to premenopausal women. The study by Kuper et al.,[21] on a population-based cohort of over 500 women with ovarian cancer, also noted the association with serous malignancies, particularly in premenopausal women, but these were borderline rather than frankly invasive tumours. A further study also noted a increased incidence of endometrioid and clear cell tumours in women with a BMI > 30 kg/m^2 and another epidemiologically based series from Norway noted an association with height, endometrioid ovarian cancers and women younger than 60 years of age.[22,23]

The Iowa Women's Health Study monitored over 31 000 women over a 15 year period and, following appropriate exclusions, 223 women were diagnosed with

Table 18.2. Conclusions of studies investigating ovarian cancer and obesity

Study	Study type	Main conclusions
Farrow et al. (1989)[20]	Case–control	↑ risk with ↑ Quetelet Index ↑ serous/endometrioid cancer in premenopause
Kuper et al. (2002)[21]	Case–control	↑ risk with ↑ weight/BMI in premenopause ↑ serous borderline in premenopause
Peterson et al. (2006)[34]	Case–control	No association with BMI
Hoyo et al. (2005)[35]	Case–control	↑ risk with high BMI at 18 years ↑ risk with high WHR, weight/BMI 1 year prediagnosis
Zhang et al. (2005)[37]	Case–control, hospital-based	↑ risk with high BMI 5 year prediagnosis NOT at diagnosis or aged 21 years
Riman et al. (2004)[22]	Case–control	↑ risk with BMI > 30 kg/m² ↑ in mucinous and clear cell tumours ↓ risk with ↑ physical activity aged 18–30 years
Fairfield et al. (2002)[26]	Nurses' Health Study	No association overall ↑ risk with BMI > 25 kg/m² at 18 years
Engeland et al. (2003)[23]	Cohort	↑ risk if obese in younger life ↑ in endometrioid cancer, in < 60 years age group, with ↑ height
Purdie et al. (2001)[36]	Case–control	↑ risk with ↑ BMI and ↑ effect is less with physical activity
Anderson et al. (2004)[24]	Prospective, Iowa, population-based	↑ risk with BMI > 30 kg/m² at 18 years ↑ risk with high WHR ↑ risk with vigorous exercise ↑ serous tumours with ↑ height
Lacey et al. (2006)[25]	Prospective ACO/NCI, population-based	No association with height/BMI or weight
Lukanova et al. (2002)[28]	Case–control	↓ risk with ↑ BMI

ACO = American Cancer Society; BMI = body mass index; NCI = National Cancer Institute; WHR = waist:height ratio.

cancer.[24] During the period BMI, WHR and physical activity were self-reported. A positive association was noted between height (RR 1.86; 95% CI 1.06–3.29) for highest versus lowest quartiles, and a BMI > 30 kg/m² at age 18 years carried a relative risk of 1.83 compared with BMI < 25 kg/m². Interestingly, vigorous exercise was found to be associated with a greater incidence of ovarian cancer (RR 2.23; 95% CI 1.29–4.38). The study by Riman et al.[22] also assessed physical activity and noted a reduced risk of epithelial ovarian cancer when the highest physical activity was compared with the lowest active group within the age bracket of 18–30 years. A further US cohort study, by the American Cancer Society and the National Cancer Institute, prospectively collected data from over 46 026 women, with a total of 346 ovarian cancers diagnosed.[25] As with the Iowa study, data relating to anthropometric measurements were by phone/mail contact. In this study, there was no significant finding relating to the woman's weight, although with severe obesity (BMI > 35 kg/m²) there was a non-significant elevated relative risk. No relationship was found between these parameters and histological subtype. The Nurses' Health Study concurs with these findings. During a 20 year follow-up, 402 cases of ovarian carcinoma were detected and, controlling for age, combined oral contraceptive use, parity menarche, tubal ligation, no association between recent BMI and ovarian cancer was found. However, in this study there was a two-fold increase at 18 years of age in premenopausal ovarian cancer risk comparing BMI $\geq$ 25 kg/m^2 with BMI < 20 kg/m^2.[26]

A study reported by Greer et al.[27] on 762 women with ovarian cancer, incorporating influencing factors such as hormonal use, found that, compared with the control population, the women with cancer were taller and heavier at age 18 years. However, when parity was taken into account, the higher anthropometric measurements were associated with increased ovarian cancer risk only in nulliparous women. Lukanova et al.[28] reported on a multicentre study of 122 women from a combined US and European study and found an inverse relationship between obesity and ovarian cancer, and when those with a BMI > 30 kg/m^2 were compared with $\leq$ 23 kg/m^2, the low odds ratio suggested a protective effect (OR 0.38; 95% 0.17–0.85). Regarding height, some association was noted but primarily in premenopausal women. The issue of BMI or weight at age 18 years is a common parameter to measure in obesity and cancer risk, and, in Lubin's study on this topic, a 42% increased risk was noted in those with BMI > 30/kg/m^2, from a large cohort of over 1000 cases.[29]

Outcome and obesity

Regarding mortality and obesity, there are three recent reports. The prospective study by Rodriguez et al.[30] examined BMI, height and risk of mortality in over 300 000 postmenopausal women. The study group comprised 1511 women and ovarian cancer mortality was highest in those with a BMI > 30 kg/m^2 (RR 1.26; 95% CI 1.07–1.48) but, interestingly, limited to women who were never-users of hormone replacement therapy (HRT). Height was also related to mortality risk. A second study supports these findings in that a reduced survival was noted in women with a BMI > 25 kg/m^2 (hazard ratio (HR) 2.33; 95% CI 1.12–4.87) when compared with those with a BMI < 20 kg/m^2.[31] The third study compared patients who were obese (BMI > 30 kg/m^2) with those who were not and noted a higher incidence of early-stage disease, but that obesity was independently associated with a poorer overall disease-free interval and survival time in women diagnosed with advanced ovarian cancer.[32]

While a diversity of findings exist in relation to ovarian cancer and obesity, the accumulated evidence seems to be in favour of an increased risk with a high BMI and increased associated mortality.[33–37]

Endometrial cancer

The relationship between obesity and endometrial cancer has been known for many years. Increased risk of endometrial cancer is noted in diabetes, polycystic ovary syndrome (PCOS) and hypertension, all of which have relevance to increased BMI.[38,39] Importantly, this is one malignancy that has increased in incidence, from 13 to 17 per 100 000 of population over the past 30 years.[19] The explanations are manifold but could include increased longevity in women, the increasing numbers of women with obesity or the continued reduction in hysterectomy rates.

There are two main types of endometrial cancer: type I (around 80%), mostly endometrioid carcinomas, considered more estrogen-dependent and associated with endometrial hyperplasia, hyperlipidaemia, obesity and with a good clinical outcome; and type II tumours, primarily serous and clear cell tumours, associated more with elderly women and which are more aggressive disease types.

A large 1 million women study from Norway with long-term follow-up identified 9227 women who developed endometrial cancer.[40] When compared with women with normal BMI, those who were overweight (BMI > 25 kg/m^2) or obese (> 30 kg/m^2), had a relative risk of 1.36 (95% CI 1.29–1.42) and 2.51 (95% CI 2.38–2.66), respectively. When stratified according to type I or II disease, the effect was mainly noted for type I tumours, although an effect remained for the type II disease. However, in this study, certain variables such as hormonal use, parity and diabetes were unknown. A case–control study of women with serous and endometrioid carcinomas supported these findings, in that a high BMI increased by three-fold the risk of endometrioid although not serous type carcinomas.[41] Another large series, on over 62 000 women with 226 endometrial cancers, noted an association with height (175 cm or more: RR 2.57; 95% CI 1.32–4.99; compared with heights of 160 cm or less), and a four-fold increase with a BMI > 30 kg/m^2 compared with a normal BMI.[42] The study also reported that low physical activity conferred a higher risk and supporting this association was the finding that the risk was indeed reduced in those who undertook 90 minutes of non-occupational physical activity each day (RR 0.54; 95% CI 0.34–0.85).

The relationship between changing body weight during a lifetime seems to have some but seemingly minor effects. Weiderpass et al.,[43] with a cohort of 709 women, did not find an association with obesity at 18 years, although, inevitably, data may not always be recalled correctly. Xu et al.[44] noted that weight at puberty did not confer an increased risk, but increasing weight during adulthood did. Gaining more than 5 kg between the ages of 40 and 50 years increased the risk (OR 2.5; 95% CI 1.4–3.9) even in women with BMI < 25 kg/m^2. In both these studies, the weight near diagnosis carried the most risk relevance.

Accepting that obesity does confer increased risk of endometrial cancer, weight reduction should therefore have a protective effect. One study has reported on this in a group of 740 women with diagnosed endometrial cancer and a control population of over 2000 women. The relationship with increasing weight was noted but those who reduced their weight and maintained this reduction had an OR of 0.7 (95% CI 0.6–0.9).[45]

Outcome and obesity

Few papers are available on the impact of obesity on mortality. The US Gynecologic Oncology Group reported on a cohort of 380 women within a randomised controlled trial on adjuvant therapy versus observation. In 53% of women, the BMI was > 30 kg/m^2. The main conclusions were that a high BMI was associated with greater adverse effects from cutaneous radiation and, while mortality was higher, this was due to non-endometrial cancer factors.[46] Recurrence rates were not influenced by an individual's BMI. One interesting study on exercise in women treated for endometrial cancer noted an improved quality of life with increased physical activity, although not impacting on overall survival.[47]

Cervical cancer

There is very sparse information on obesity and cervical cancer. The main impact may well be on the effects of screening as discussed previously.[16–18] Lacey et al.[48] undertook a case–control study of 124 women with cervical adenocarcinomas, 139 with squamous carcinomas and a control group of 304 women. BMI, WHR and human papilloma virus (HPV) testing were undertaken and height, weight and BMI were positively associated with adenocarcinomas (BMI > 30 kg/m^2: RR 2.1; 95% CI

1.1–3.8). No such association was noted with squamous carcinomas. From another study, serum levels of leptin, after correction for BMI, were not altered in women with cervical cancer compared with controls.[49] The only other relevant information pertains to survival outcome and obesity, whereby one study on 229 women with stage 1B tumours showed a poorer survival rate in women with a low BMI, while in another study a poorer survival outcome was associated with a high BMI.[50,51]

Breast cancer

Breast cancer affects over 43 000 women each year in the UK, with an associated mortality rate of over 12 000.[19] As one of the most common cancers affecting women, it is not surprising that large epidemiological studies are available to ascertain the impact of obesity in this condition. The Iowa Women's Health Study is one such series, with prospective data on over 33 000 women. After 15 years of follow-up, 1987 women had developed breast cancer. Weight changes during the periods 18–30 years of age, 30 years to menopause, and after the menopause were collated. Women with increasing weight over time had the highest risk of developing breast cancer. Women who maintained weight or lost weight during the 30 years to menopause time period had a relative risk of 0.36 (95% CI 0.22–0.60). In any category, the association with reduced risk was noted in women who, at some stage, lost weight they had gained during any period.[52] An even larger prospective study, the Nurses' Health Study, provides supportive evidence for these findings.[53] In a 24 year follow-up period, nearly 4500 women had developed breast cancer. Compared with those who maintained a somewhat stable weight, an increase of 25 kg from the age of 18 years increased the relative risk to 1.45 (95% CI 1.27–1.66) and an increase of 10 kg increased the relative risk to 1.18 (95% CI 1.03–1.35). A previous report from the same study had revealed the possible protective effect of a high BMI at 18 years for premenopausal breast cancer, and the adverse association between BMI > 30 kg/m^2 and postmenopausal breast cancer in non-HRT users.[54] The Women's Health Initiative (WHI) study monitored postmenopausal breast cancer in a cohort of over 85 000 women, of whom 1030 had the disease. For HRT users, anthropometric measurements did not confer any difference to breast cancer risk, but for non-HRT users, those with a BMI > 31 kg/m^2 had a relative risk of 2.52 (95% CI 1.62–3.93).[55] These findings are supported by the large European Prospective Investigation into Cancer and Nutrition (EPIC) study, which involved 73 000 premenopausal and over 100 000 postmenopausal women. During a 5 year period, 1879 women developed breast cancers. In postmenopausal non-HRT users, BMI was associated with an increased risk (BMI > 30 kg/m^2 had a 31% increased risk compared with those with BMI < 25 kg/m^2), whereas this did not exist in HRT users, although the adverse HRT effect was noted in women who were lean. In premenopausal women, weight and higher BMI showed an inverse relationship with breast cancer risk.[56]

Outcome and obesity

A study on 1254 women aged 20–54 years with breast cancer involved anthropometric assessment and recall of weight at the age of 20 years. During a 10 year follow-up from diagnosis, mortality was associated with a higher BMI (HR 1.48; 95% CI 1.09–2.01), and also with a high BMI when aged 20 years.[57] Another study did not find any association with weight and recurrence rates, but an increased risk (HR 1.62) in developing a contra-lateral breast cancer in those with high BMI.[58] There is consistency within the studies of a poorer outcome in women who are obese after primary treatment, and this finding remains even when age, menopausal status and tumour estrogen-receptor status are taken into account.[59-62] Height is also a variable that, in one study, was associated with outcome.[62] The causal relationship must presumably be with adipocytokines and their actions in these women.

Conclusion

Throughout the Western world, obesity has been recognised as a major health problem. The association with the increased risk of cancer development is also noted and, as can been seen from epidemiological studies, women's cancers are not immune to this. The overall consensus for endometrial, ovarian and breast cancer is that obesity increases the chances of developing these diseases, impacts the accuracy of screening and, indeed, adversely affects survival patterns. The most important area requiring investigation is the molecular pathways associated with malignancy and obesity cytokines, which may yield novel therapeutic targets.

References

1. McMillan DC, Sattar N, McArdle CS. ABC of obesity. Obesity and cancer. *BMJ* 2006;333:1109–11.
2. Calle EE, Rodriguez C, Walker-Thurmond K, Thun MJ. Overweight, obesity, and mortality in a prospectively studied cohort of US adults. *N Engl J Med* 2003;348:1625–38.
3. Soerjomataram I, de Vries E, Pukkala E, Coebergh JW. Excess of cancers in Europe: A study of eleven major cancers amenable to lifestyle change. *Int J Cancer* 2007;120:1336–43.
4. Danaei G, Vander Hoorn S, Lopez AD, Murray CJ, Ezzati M; Comparative Risk Assessment collaborating group (Cancers). Causes of cancer in the world: comparative risk assessment of nine behavioural and environmental risk factors. *Lancet* 2005;366:1784–93.
5. Tilg H, Moschen AR. Adipocytokines: mediators linking adipose tissue, inflammation and immunity. *Nat Rev Immunol* 2006;6:772–83.
6. Housa D, Housova J, Vernerova Z, Haluzik M. Adipocytokines and cancer. *Physiol Res* 2006;55:233–44.
7. Dieudonne MN, Bussiere M, Dos Santos E, Leneveu MC, Giudicelli Y, Pecquery R. Adiponectin mediates antiproliferative and apoptotic responses in human MCF7 breast cancer cells. *Biochem Biophys Res Commun* 2006;345:271–9.
8. Bub JD, Miyazaki T, Iwamoto Y. Adiponectin as a growth inhibitor in prostate cancer cells. *Biochem Biophys Res Commun* 2006;340:1158–66.
9. Sulkowska M, Golaszewska J, Winchwicz A, Koda M, Baltaziak M, Sulkowska S. Leptin – from regulation of fat metabolism to stimulation of breast cancer growth. *Path Oncol Res* 2006;12:69–72.
10. Gonzalez RR, Cherfils S, Escobar M, Yoo JH, Carino C, Styer AK, *et al.* Leptin signaling promotes the growth of mammary tumors and increases the expression of vascular endothelial growth factor (VEGF) and its receptor type two (VEGF-R2). *J Biol Chem* 2006;281:26320–8.
11. Garofalo C, Surmacz E. Leptins and cancer. *J Cell Physiol* 2006;207:12–22.
12. Rose DP, Komninou D, Stephenson GD. Obesity, adipocytokines, and insulin resistance in breast cancer. *Obes Rev* 2004;5:153–65.
13. Renehan AG, Frystyk J, Flyvbjerg A. Obesity and cancer risk: the role of the insulin-IGF axis. *Trends Endocrinol Metab* 2006;17:328–36.
14. Elmore JG, Carney PA, Abraham LA, Barlow WE, Egger JR, Fosse JS, *et al.* The association between obesity and screening mammography accuracy. *Arch Intern Med* 2004;164:1140–7.
15. van Doorn LC, Dijkhuizen FP, Kruitwagen RF, Heintz AP, Kooi GS, Mol BW. DUPOMEB (Dutch Study in Postmenopausal Bleeding). Accuracy of transvaginal ultrasonography in diabetic or obese women with postmenopausal bleeding. *Obstet Gynecol* 2004;104:571–8.
16. Wee CC, McCarthy EP, Davis RB, Phillips RS. Screening for cervical and breast cancer: is obesity an unrecognized barrier to preventive care? *Ann Intern Med* 2000;132:697–704.
17. Fontaine KR, Heo M, Allison DB. Body weight and cancer screening among women. *J Womens Health Gend Based Med* 2001;10:463–70.

18. Ferrante JM, Chen PH, Jacobs A. Breast and cervical cancer screening in obese minority women. *J Womens Health (Larchmt)*; 2006;15:531–41.

19. Cancer Research UK [info.cancerresearchuk.org/cancerstats/].

20. Farrow DC, Weiss NS, Lyon JL, Daling JR. Association of obesity and ovarian cancer in a case–control study. *Am J Epidemiol* 1989;129:1300–4.

21. Kuper H, Cramer DW, Titus-Ernstoff L. Risk of ovarian cancer in the United States in relation to anthropometric measures: does the association depend on menopausal status? *Cancer Causes Cont* 2002;13:455–63.

22. Riman T, Dickman PW, Nilsson S, Nordlinder H, Magnusson CM, Persson IR. Some life-style factors and the risk of invasive epithelial ovarian cancer in Swedish women. *Eur J Epidemiol* 2004;19:1011–19.

23. Engeland A, Tretli S, Bjorge T. Height, body mass index, and ovarian cancer: a follow-up of 1.1 million Norwegian women. *J Natl Cancer Inst* 2003;95:1244–8.

24. Anderson JP, Ross JA, Folsom AR. Anthropometric variables, physical activity, and incidence of ovarian cancer: The Iowa Women's Health Study. *Cancer* 2004;100:1515–21.

25. Lacey JV Jr, Leitzmann M, Brinton LA, Lubin JH, Sherman ME, Schatzkin A, *et al*. Weight, height and body mass index and ovarian cancer in a cohort study. *Ann Epidemiol* 2006;16:869–76.

26. Fairfield KM, Willett WC, Rosner BA, Manson JE, Speizer FE, Hankinson SE. Obesity, weight gain, and ovarian cancer. *Obstet Gynecol* 2002;100:288–96.

27. Greer JB, Modugno F, Ness RB, Allen GO. Anthropometry and the risk of epithelial ovarian cancer. *Cancer* 2006;106:2247–57.

28. Lukanova A, Toniolo P, Lundin E, Micheli A, Akhmedkhanov A, Muti P, *et al*. Body mass index in relation to ovarian cancer: a multi-centre nested case–control study. *Int J Cancer* 2002;99:603–8.

29. Lubin F, Chetrit A, Freedman LS, Alfandary E, Fishler Y, Nitzan H, *et al*. Body mass index at age 18 years and during adult life and ovarian cancer risk. *Am J Epidemiol* 2003;157:113–20.

30. Rodriguez C, Calle EE, Fakhrabadi-Shokoohi D, Jacobs EJ, Thun MJ. Body mass index, height, and the risk of ovarian cancer mortality in a prospective cohort of postmenopausal women. *Cancer Epidemiol Biomarkers Prev* 2002;11:822–8.

31. Zhang M, Xie X, Lee AH, Binns CW, Holman CD. Body mass index in relation to ovarian cancer survival. *Cancer Epidemiol Biomarkers Prev* 2005;14:1307–10.

32. Pavelka JC, Brown RS, Karlan BY, Cass I, Leuchter RS, Lagasse LD, *et al*. Effect of obesity on survival in epithelial ovarian cancer. *Cancer* 2006;107:1520–4.

33. Olsen CM, Green AC, Whiteman DC, Sadeghi S, Kolahdooz F, Webb PM. Obesity and the risk of epithelial ovarian cancer: a systematic review and meta-analysis. *Eur J Cancer* 2007;43:690–709.

34. Peterson NB, Trentham-Dietz A, Newcomb PA, Chen Z, Gebretsadik T, Hampton JM, *et al*. Relation of anthropometric measurements to ovarian cancer risk in a population-based case–control study (United States). *Cancer Causes Cont* 2006;17:459–67.

35. Hoyo C, Berchuck A, Halabi S, Bentley RC, Moorman P, Calingaert B, *et al*. Anthropometric measurements and epithelial ovarian cancer risk in African-American and White women. *Cancer Causes Cont* 2005;16:955–63.

36. Purdie DM, Bain CJ, Webb PM, Whiteman DC, Pirozzo S, Green AC. Body size and ovarian cancer: case–control study and systematic review (Australia). *Cancer Causes Cont* 2001;12:855–63.

37. Zhang M, Xie X, Holman CD. Body weight and body mass index and ovarian cancer risk: a case–control study in China. *Gynecol Oncol* 2005;98:228–34.

38. Akhmedkhanov A, Zeleniuch-Jacquotte A, Toniolo P. Role of exogenous and endogenous hormones in endometrial cancer: review of the evidence and research perspectives. *Ann N Y Acad Sci* 2001;943:296–315.

39. Giudice LC. Endometrium in PCOS: Implantation and predisposition to endocrine CA. *Best Pract Res Clin Endocrinol Metab* 2006;20:235–44.

40. Bjorge T, Engeland A, Tretli S, Weiderpass E. Body size in relation to cancer of the uterine corpus in 1 million Norwegian women. *Int J Cancer* 2006;120:378–83.

41. Sherman ME, Sturgeon S, Brinton LA, Potischman N, Kurman RJ, Berman ML, *et al*. Risk factors and hormone levels in patients with serous and endometrioid uterine carcinomas. *Mod Pathol* 1997;10:963–8.

42. Schouten LJ, Goldbohm RA, van den Brandt PA. Anthropometry, physical activity, and endometrial cancer risk: results from the Netherlands cohort study. *Int J Gynecol Cancer* 2006;16 Suppl 2:492.

43. Weiderpass E, Persson I, Adami HO, Magnusson C, Lindgren A, Baron JA. Body size in different periods of life, diabetes mellitus, hypertension, and risk of postmenopausal endometrial cancer (Sweden). *Cancer Causes Cont* 2000;11:185–92.

44. Xu WH, Xiang YB, Zheng W, Zhang X, Ruan ZX, Cheng JR, et al. Weight history and the risk of endometrial cancer among Chinese women. *Int J Epidemiol* 2006;35:159–66.

45. Trentham-Dietz A, Nichols HB, Hampton JM, Newcomb PA. Weight change and risk of endometrial cancer. *Int J Epidemiol* 2006;35:151–8.

46. von Gruenigen VE, Tian C, Frasure H, Waggoner S, Keys H, Barakat RR. Treatment effects, disease recurrence, and survival in obese women with early endometrial carcinoma: a Gynecologic Oncology Group study. *Cancer* 2006 15;107:2786–91.

47. Courneya KS, Karvinen KH, Campbell KL, Pearcey RG, Dundas G, Capstick V, et al. Exercise, body weight and quality of life in a population-based sample of endometrial cancer survivors. *Gynecol Oncol* 2005;97:422–30.

48. Lacey JV Jr, Swanson CA, Brinton LA, Altekruse SF, Barnes WA, Gravitt PE, et al. Obesity as a potential risk factor for adenocarcinomas and squamous cell carcinomas of the uterine cervix. *Cancer* 2003 15;98:814–21.

49. Lebrecht A, Ludwig E, Huber A, Klein M, Schneeberger C, Tempfer C, et al. Serum vascular endothelial growth factor and serum leptin in patients with cervical cancer. *Gynecol Oncol* 2002;85:32–5.

50. Finan MA, Hoffman MS, Chambers, R, Fiorica JV, DeCesare S, Kline RC, et al. Body mass predicts the survival of patients with new International Federation of Gynecology and Obstetrics Stage IB1 and IB2 cervical carcinoma treated with radical hysterectomy. *Cancer* 1998;83:98–102.

51. Guo WD, Hsing AW, Li JY, Chen JS, Chow WH, Blot WJ. Correlation of cervical cancer mortality with reproductive and dietary factors, and serum markers in China. *Int J Epidemiol* 1994;23:1127–32.

52. Harvie M, Howell A, Vierkant RA, Kumar N, Cerhan JR, Kelemen LE, et al. Association of gain and loss of weight before and after menopause with risk of postmenopausal breast cancer in the Iowa women's health study. *Cancer Epidemiol Biomarkers Prev* 2005;14:656–61.

53. Eliassen AH, Colditz GA, Rosner B, Willett WC, Hankinson SE. Adult weight change and risk of postmenopausal breast cancer. *JAMA* 2006;296:193–201.

54. Huang Z, Hankinson SE, Colditz GA, Stampfer MJ, Hunter DJ, Manson JE, et al. Dual effects of weight and weight gain on breast cancer risk. *JAMA* 1997;278:1407–11.

55. Morimoto LM, White E, Chen Z, Chlebowski RT, Hays J, Kuller L, et al. Obesity, body size, and risk of postmenopausal breast cancer: the Women's Health Initiative (United States). *Cancer Causes Cont* 2002;13:741–51.

56. Lahmann PH, Hoffmann K, Allen N, van Gils CH, Khaw KT, Tehard B, et al. Body size and breast cancer risk: findings from the European Prospective Investigation into Cancer and Nutrition (EPIC). *Int J Cancer* 2004 20;111:762–71.

57. Abrahamson PE, Gammon MD, Lund MJ, Flagg EW, Porter PL, Stevens J, et al. General and abdominal obesity and survival among young women with breast cancer. *Cancer Epidemiol Biomarkers Prev* 2006;15:1871–7.

58. Dignam JJ, Wieand K, Johnson KA, Fisher B, Xu L, Mamounas EP. Obesity, tamoxifen use, and outcomes in women with estrogen receptor-positive early-stage breast cancer. *J Natl Cancer Inst* 2003;95:1467–76.

59. Whiteman MK, Hillis SD, Curtis KM, McDonald JA, Wingo PA, Marchbanks PA. Body mass and mortality after breast cancer diagnosis. *Cancer Epidemiol Biomarkers Prev* 2005;14:2009–14.

60. Enger SM, Greif JM, Polikoff J, Press M. Body weight correlates with mortality in early-stage breast cancer. *Arch Surg* 2004;139:954–58.

61. Loi S, Milne RL, Friedlander ML, McCredie MR, Giles GG, et al. Obesity and outcomes in premenopausal and postmenopausal breast cancer. *Cancer Epidemiol Biomarkers Prev* 2005;14:1686–91.

62. Petrelli JM, Calle EE, Rodriguez C, Thun MJ. Body mass index, height, and postmenopausal breast cancer mortality in a prospective cohort of US women. *Cancer Causes Cont* 2002;13:325–32.

Chapter 19
Menopause and hormone replacement therapy

Margaret CP Rees, Eugene J Kongnyuy, Ingrid Flight and Robert Norman

Introduction

Worldwide, women's life expectancy is increasing.[1] Currently, female life expectancy at birth in the UK is 81 years and it is estimated to reach 85 years by 2031.[2] British women can thus expect more than 30 years of postmenopausal life. Women gain weight at mid life, which is of concern since cardiovascular disease is the leading cause of death. Hormone replacement therapy (HRT) is commonly prescribed to treat menopausal symptoms and to prevent postmenopausal bone loss.[3] However, many women are concerned that HRT will result in weight gain and this is an important reason for discontinuation.[4]

This chapter will examine weight changes at the menopause and the evidence regarding HRT on weight and body fat distribution that has been re-evaluated in a Cochrane systematic review.[5]

Weight change at midlife

Women gain weight with age, and this tends to begin at or near menopause.[6] Population studies undertaken in Australia and the USA show that weight gain is in the region of 2 kg.[7–9] The 5 year Australian study of 233 women found a mean weight gain of 2.1 ± 5.1 kg. The US study of 485 middle-aged women found an average weight gain of 2.25 ± 4.19 kg over 3 years.[8] Furthermore, weight gain was significantly associated with increases in blood pressure and levels of total cholesterol, low density lipoprotein cholesterol, triglycerides and fasting insulin, all recognised risk factors for coronary heart disease. The US observational Study of Women's Health Across the Nation (SWAN) of 3064 women across the menopause transition found a mean weight increase of 2.1 kg.

Body fat distribution also changes independently of weight gain, again starting around the time of the menopause. There is an increase in body fat as a percentage of body weight and a redistribution of body fat, with a relative increase in the proportion of abdominal fat.[10] This centralised abdominal (android) fat distribution is a recognised risk factor for cardiovascular disease.[11]

The reasons why women gain weight are disputed. They include age, menopausal status and lifestyle. Psychological factors such as anxiety and depression have been implicated.[12] The SWAN study found that change in menopausal status was not associated with weight gain or significantly associated with increases in waist circumference.[9] However, regular physical activity may help to mitigate the tendency for weight gain and adverse changes in body composition and fat distribution that accompany ageing and the menopausal transition.[13]

Hormone replacement therapy types and use

Hormone replacement therapy consists of an estrogen combined with a progestogen for women who have not had a hysterectomy.[3] Progestogens are added to reduce the risk of endometrial cancer found with unopposed estrogen. They are given cyclically or continuously with the estrogen. Various routes of administration are employed: oral, transdermal, subcutaneous, intranasal and vaginal.

Estrogens

Two types of estrogen are available: synthetic and natural. Synthetic estrogens, such as ethinylestradiol, are generally considered to be unsuitable for HRT because of their greater metabolic impact. Natural estrogens include estradiol, estrone and estriol, which, although synthesised from soya beans or yams, are chemically identical to the native human hormone. Conjugated equine estrogens contain about 50–65% estrone sulphate, and the remainder consists of equine estrogens.

Progestogens

Most progestogens used in HRT are synthetic. Currently, they are mainly given orally, although norethisterone and levonorgestrel are available in transdermal patches combined with estradiol, and levonorgestrel can be delivered directly to the uterus. Progesterone is formulated as a 4% vaginal gel but its availability varies worldwide. Most synthetic progestogens used in HRT are 17-hydroxyprogesterone and 19-nortestosterone derivatives. The 17-hydroxyprogesterone derivatives are dydrogesterone and medroxyprogesterone acetate. The 19-nortestosterone derivatives include norethisterone and levonorgestrel. Several new progestogens have been synthesised and one of these, drospirenone, is used in HRT. Drospirenone has antimineralocorticoid and anti-androgenic properties.

Tibolone

Tibolone is a synthetic steroid compound that can be considered to be a prodrug since it has no inherent pharmacological activity but is converted *in vivo* to metabolites with estrogenic, progestogenic and androgenic properties. It is classified as HRT in the *British National Formulary*.

HRT use

HRT is used to treat menopausal symptoms such as hot flushes and to conserve bone mass.[3] Treatment for vasomotor symptoms is the most common indication for HRT and women in their 50s usually use it for up to 5 years. However, although menopausal symptoms usually resolve within 2–5 years, some women experience symptoms for many years – even into their 70s and 80s.

With regard to osteoporosis, treatment needs to be continued for life as bone mineral density falls when treatment is stopped. Use of HRT for 5–10 years after the menopause had been assumed to delay the peak incidence of hip fracture by a corresponding amount. Most epidemiological studies, however, suggest that 5–10 years of HRT soon after the menopause does not give any significant reduction in the risk of hip fracture 30 years later. Although some women will be happy to take HRT for life, others may view treatment as a continuum of options and will wish to change to other agents such as raloxifene, a bisphosphonate or strontium ranelate because of the small but measurable increase in risk of breast cancer associated with the long-term use of combined HRT.

Women with a premature menopause are usually advised to continue with HRT until the average age of the natural menopause, which in the UK is 52 years, and thus may have to take it for several decades. It is of note that a US study has shown that women below the age of 45 years who are not given HRT following bilateral oophorectomy are at increased risk of mortality compared with age-matched women with intact ovaries.[14]

HRT, body weight and fat distribution

The effect of estrogen- and progestogen-based HRT has been re-evaluated in a Cochrane systematic review.[5] However, there are little data regarding tibolone.[15]

The Cochrane review searched the Cochrane Menstrual Disorders and Subfertility Group trials register, MEDLINE, EMBASE, Current Contents, Biological Abstracts and CINAHL. Attempts were made to identify trials from citation lists of review articles and from relevant papers already obtained. In most cases, the first authors of each eligible trial were contacted for additional information. All those trials that had been located as at July 2005 were examined for eligibility. The large Women's Health Initiative randomised trials were thus included.[16,17]

All randomised controlled trials (RCTs) that detailed the effect of HRT on weight or body fat distribution, including studies where HRT was combined with other therapy such as diet, supplements or exercise, were examined. Studies were considered eligible even though the main focus of the trial may have been on another aspect of HRT. Previous HRT use should have ceased at least 1 month (in the case of patches, cream or gel) or 3 months (for oral preparations or subcutaneous pellets) before commencement of the study. The participant inclusion criteria were:

- women of any ethnicity who were either perimenopausal or postmenopausal
- perimenopausal women were defined as those aged 45 years or older or who had elevated follicle stimulating hormone concentrations, and who had menstruated intermittently within the previous 12 months
- postmenopausal women were defined as those aged 45 years or older and who had not menstruated for more than 12 months
- women of any age who had menopause artificially induced by bilateral oophorectomy and whose oophorectomy took place at least 1 month before entry into a trial.

Studies of women with pre-existing major disease were excluded. The reviewers analysed only those randomised studies that compared treatments with placebo or no treatment. There was no differentiation made between continuous therapy and cyclical estrogen plus progestogen therapy.

Unopposed estrogen

Nine RCTs of estrogen versus placebo or no therapy, with a total of 12 221 women, were included in the review. The largest of these trials (Women's Health Initiative

2004) provided follow-up for up to 9 years, but only data recorded up to 4 years were included because of the high proportion of missing data after this time.[17–25] While seven trials used oral estrogens, one used a gel and another a cream.[18,19]

Sufficient data were available to enable a meta-analysis of studies concerning the effect of unopposed estrogen on body weight and body mass index (BMI). Use of unopposed estrogen had no significant effect on weight gain compared with that in non-users (0.03 kg; 95% CI −0.61 to 0.67 kg). Similarly, there was no significant difference in BMI between women using unopposed estrogen and non-users (−0.14 kg/m^2; 95% CI −0.40 to 0.12 kg/m^2). Insufficient data were available for meta-analysis of waist:hip ratio (WHR), and no data were available for analysis of fat mass or skinfold thickness.

Nine RCTs with a total of 10 194 participants provided weight data (Figure 19.1). All studies included in this meta-analysis showed that women using estrogen gained an average of 0.03 kg more compared with non-users but this was not statistically significant. However, in the only study using ethinylestradiol, Speroff et al.[20] found that this regimen caused an average of 2.02 kg weight gain more than those not taking HRT.

Two studies reported on the effect of HRT on BMI (Figure 19.2).[17,21] Meta-analysis showed no significant change. Only one study examined estrogen and WHR, and found no effect.[21]

Combined estrogen plus progestogen trials

Twenty RCTs of combined HRT versus placebo or no therapy were included in the review.[16,18,20,22,23,26–40] Women's Health Initiative 2002 was the largest trial included and alone contributed 13 204 participants.[16] Although the study started with 16 608 participants, data on body weight and BMI were only available for 431 women by the end of the trial 8 years later. Thus, data after the fourth year, when figures on 13 204 participants were available, were analysed. The second largest trial contributed 2763 participants.[31] Use of combined HRT had no significant effect on mean weight gain compared with those women not taking it (Figure 19.3). Also combined HRT had no significant effect on mean BMI increase compared with non-users (Figure 19.4). Only one study measured the WHR and one measured abdominal skinfold thickness.[28,34] Neither study found any statistically significant difference between HRT users and non-users.

Tibolone

The data with regard to tibolone are limited. A 2 year RCT was undertaken in 139 postmenopausal women (mean age 55 years, range 54–58 years) of tibolone 1.25 mg/day (n = 52), tibolone 2.5 mg/day (n = 39) or estradiol 2 mg/day plus norethisterone 1 mg/day (n = 48).[15] It found that body weight increased significantly (P < 0.001) during the 24 month period by a similar extent in all treatment groups (mean ± standard deviation: 1.5 ± 2.4 kg; 2.0 ± 2.4 kg; 1.5 ± 3.6 kg; P = 0.62 in the tibolone 1.25 mg/day, tibolone 2.5 mg/day and estradiol/norethisterone groups, respectively).

Does weight loss improve postmenopausal health?

A Health Technology Assessment review of obesity treatments modelled the impact of weight reduction on risk factor change.[41] Women with obesity-related diseases, who had intentional weight loss, had an associated reduced risk of death, cardiovascular disease death, cancer and diabetes-related death. Long-term weight loss was associated with reduced risk of developing type 2 diabetes and with improved glucose tolerance. Regression analysis demonstrated that a weight loss of 10 kg (about 5%) was associated with a fall in total cholesterol of 0.25 mmol/l and a weight loss of 10% was associated with a reduction in systolic blood pressure of 6.1 mmHg. However it is not known whether weight loss improves health outcomes in postmenopausal women since most studies are short, about 12 months in duration.[42]

Conclusion

Women gain weight at midlife but this may be prevented by regular physical activity. Systematic review has found that HRT has no effect on body weight and cannot prevent weight gain at the menopause. While weight loss should be beneficial to the health of postmenopausal women, most studies are short and do not have data on clinical endpoints such as myocardial infarction and stroke.

Review: Oestrogen and progestogen hormone replacement therapy for peri-menopausal and post-menopausal women: weight and body fat distribution
Comparison: 01 Oestrogen (any dose) versus placebo or no treatment
Outcome: 01 Weight (kg)

Study	HRT N	Mean(SD)	control N	Mean(SD)	Weighted Mean Difference (Fixed) 95% CI	Weight (%)	Weighted Mean Difference (Fixed) 95% CI
01 Subcategory							
Armstrong 1996	7	65.40 (6.30)	55	68.60 (9.50)		1.5	-3.20 [-8.50, 2.10]
Espeland 1997	170	70.90 (12.90)	166	72.00 (14.60)		4.7	-1.10 [-4.05, 1.85]
Gallagher 1991	16	72.15 (13.35)	13	67.54 (12.22)		0.5	4.61 [-4.71, 13.93]
Good 1996	182	69.60 (11.10)	91	68.60 (10.00)		6.0	1.00 [-1.61, 3.61]
Limpaphayom 1996	19	56.31 (9.26)	42	61.35 (16.66)		1.0	-5.04 [-11.58, 1.50]
Lindheim 1994	28	65.50 (5.29)	20	63.70 (11.18)		1.5	1.80 [-3.48, 7.08]
Speroff 1996	552	66.92 (9.79)	136	64.90 (10.97)		10.1	2.02 [0.00, 4.04]
Jensen 1987d	20	61.50 (8.80)	25	61.10 (7.60)		1.7	0.40 [-4.47, 5.27]
WHI 2004	4288	78.80 (17.60)	4364	79.00 (18.00)		73.0	-0.20 [-0.95, 0.55]
Total (95% CI)	5282		4912			100.0	0.03 [-0.61, 0.67]

Test for heterogeneity chi-square=10.32 df=8 p=0.24 I²=22.5%
Test for overall effect z=0.08 p=0.9

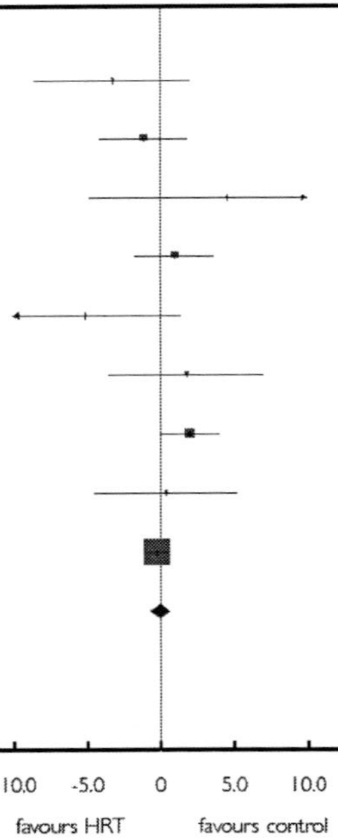

-10.0 -5.0 0 5.0 10.0
favours HRT   favours control

Figure 19.1. Estrogen (any dose) versus placebo or no treatment; outcome = weight; reproduced with permission from Kongnyuy et al.,[5] © Cochrane Collaboration

Review: Oestrogen and progestogen hormone replacement therapy for peri-menopausal and post-menopausal women: weight and body fat distribution

Comparison: 01 Oestrogen (any dose) versus placebo or no treatment

Outcome: 02 BMI

Study	HRT		control		Weighted Mean Difference (Fixed)	Weight	Weighted Mean Difference (Fixed)
	N	Mean(SD)	N	Mean(SD)	95% CI	(%)	95% CI
Espeland 1997	170	26.40 (4.50)	166	27.10 (5.00)		6.4	-0.70 [-1.72, 0.32]
WHI 2004	4260	30.30 (6.20)	4337	30.40 (6.40)		93.6	-0.10 [-0.37, 0.17]
Total (95% CI)	4430		4503			100.0	-0.14 [-0.40, 0.12]

Test for heterogeneity chi-square=1.25 df=1 p=0.26 I² =19.9%

Test for overall effect z=1.05   p=0.3

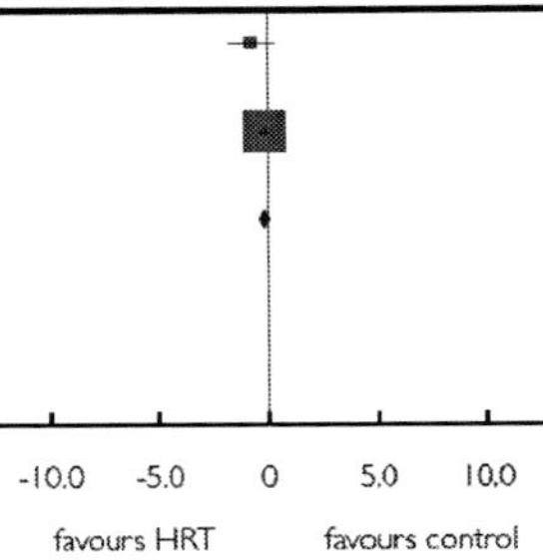

-10.0   -5.0   0   5.0   10.0

favours HRT   favours control

Figure 19.2. Estrogen (any dose) versus placebo or no treatment; outcome = BMI; reproduced with permission from Kongnyuy et al.,[5] © Cochrane Collaboration

Review: Oestrogen and progestogen hormone replacement therapy for peri-menopausal and post-menopausal women: weight and body fat distribution
Comparison: 02 Oestrogen plus progestogen (any dose) versus placebo or no treatment
Outcome: 01 Weight (kg)

Study	HRT N	HRT Mean(SD)	control N	control Mean(SD)	Weighted Mean Difference (Fixed) 95% CI	Weight (%)	Weighted Mean Difference (Fixed) 95% CI
Armstrong 1996	46	64.90 (13.30)	55	68.60 (9.50)		1.0	-3.70 [-8.29, 0.89]
Gallagher 1991	16	66.14 (13.46)	13	67.54 (12.22)		0.2	-1.40 [-10.76, 7.96]
Hartmann 1995	12	72.90 (17.40)	10	73.30 (17.90)		0.1	-0.40 [-15.23, 14.43]
Jensen 1987b	32	64.00 (11.00)	35	69.00 (15.00)		0.5	-5.00 [-11.26, 1.26]
Jensen 1987c	21	66.80 (9.50)	23	70.30 (12.80)		0.5	-3.50 [-10.12, 3.12]
Khoo 1998	46	67.68 (10.84)	47	70.19 (12.10)		1.0	-2.51 [-7.18, 2.16]
Komulainen 1997	175	71.27 (13.49)	213	70.90 (12.23)		3.1	0.37 [-2.22, 2.96]
Limpaphayom 1996	32	54.34 (11.60)	42	61.35 (16.66)		0.5	-7.01 [-13.46, -0.56]
Speroff 1996	553	66.76 (10.22)	136	64.90 (10.97)		5.1	1.86 [-0.17, 3.89]
Writing 1996	124	61.40 (7.70)	64	62.40 (8.30)		3.5	-1.00 [-3.44, 1.44]
Kanaya 2003	1380	70.20 (14.10)	1383	70.80 (14.60)		18.0	-0.60 [-1.68, 0.48]
Perez-Jaraiz 1996	23	64.60 (7.10)	25	62.80 (6.70)		1.4	1.80 [-2.11, 5.71]
WHI 2002	6744	75.20 (17.20)	7115	74.90 (16.80)		65.1	0.30 [-0.27, 0.87]
Total (95% CI)	9204		9161			100.0	0.04 [-0.42, 0.50]

Test for heterogeneity chi-square=18.76 df=12 p=0.09 I²=36.0%
Test for overall effect z=0.17 p=0.9

-10.0 -5.0 0 5.0 10.0
favours HRT   favours control

Figure 19.3. Estrogen plus progestogen (any dose) versus placebo or no treatment; outcome = weight; reproduced with permission from Kongnyuy et al.,[5] © Cochrane Collaboration

Review: Oestrogen and progestogen hormone replacement therapy for peri-menopausal and post-menopausal women: weight and body fat distribution

Comparison: 02 Oestrogen plus progestogen (any dose) versus placebo or no treatment

Outcome: 02 BMI

Study	HRT		control		Weighted Mean Difference (Fixed)	Weight	Weighted Mean Difference (Fixed)
	N	Mean(SD)	N	Mean(SD)	95% CI	(%)	95% CI
Hartmann 1995	12	28.10 (5.10)	10	28.20 (4.90)		0.2	-0.10 [-4.29, 4.09]
Komulainen 1997	175	27.51 (4.77)	213	27.73 (4.77)		3.2	-0.22 [-1.17, 0.73]
Mijatovic 1998	14	26.00 (3.90)	13	26.00 (4.60)		0.3	0.00 [-3.23, 3.23]
Myrup 1992	11	23.70 (2.70)	24	26.50 (6.00)		0.3	-2.80 [-5.68, 0.08]
Tonstad 1995	39	23.60 (2.80)	29	24.30 (2.70)		1.7	-0.70 [-2.02, 0.62]
Walsh 1998	70	25.63 (3.21)	85	26.12 (3.63)		2.5	-0.49 [-1.57, 0.59]
Wimalawansa 1995	12	25.30 (2.94)	9	24.90 (2.97)		0.4	0.40 [-2.16, 2.96]
Wimalawansa 1998	15	25.00 (3.17)	14	26.00 (2.20)		0.7	-1.00 [-2.98, 0.98]
Kanaya 2003	1380	27.70 (5.30)	1383	28.00 (5.40)		18.0	-0.30 [-0.70, 0.10]
WHI 2002	6704	28.80 (6.00)	7080	28.80 (5.90)		72.7	0.00 [-0.20, 0.20]
Total (95% CI)	8432		8860			100.0	-0.10 [-0.27, 0.07]

Test for heterogeneity chi-square=7.62 df=9 p=0.57 I²=0.0%

Test for overall effect z=1.16 p=0.2

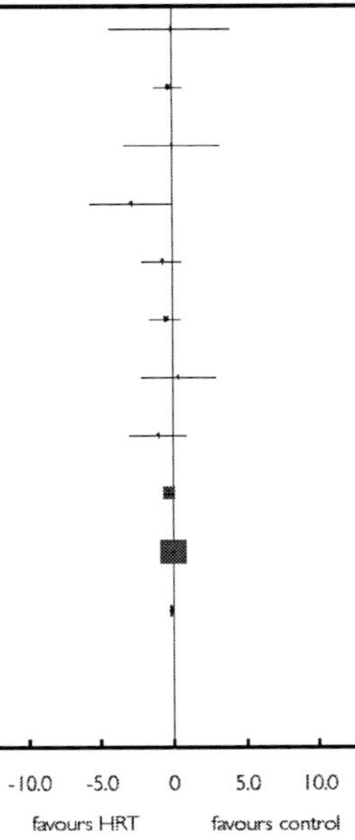

-10.0 -5.0 0 5.0 10.0

favours HRT   favours control

Figure 19.4. Estrogen plus progestogen (any dose) versus placebo or no treatment; outcome = BMI; reproduced with permission from Kongnyuy et al.,[5] © Cochrane Collaboration

References

1. US Census Bureau. Global *Population at a Glance: 2002 and Beyond.* Washington, DC: US Census Bureau; 2004 [www.census.gov].

2. Office for National Statistics and Government Actuaries Department, UK [www.gad.gov.uk].

3. Rees M, Purdie DW. *Management of the Menopause. The Handbook.* London: Royal Society of Medicine Press; 2006.

4. Reynolds RF, Obermeyer CM, Walker AM, Guilbert D. The role of treatment intentions and concerns about side effects in women's decision to discontinue postmenopausal hormone therapy. *Maturitas* 2002;43:183–94.

5. Kongnyuy EJ, Norman RJ, Flight IHK, Rees MCP. Oestrogen and progestogen hormone replacement therapy for peri-menopausal and post-menopausal women: weight and body fat distribution. *Cochrane Database Syst Rev* 2007;(2):CD001018.

6. Williams LT, Young AF, Brown WJ. Weight gained in two years by a population of mid-aged women: how much is too much? *Int J Obes (Lond)* 2006;30:1229–33.

7. Guthrie JR, Dennerstain L, Dudely EC. Weight gain and the menopause: a 5-year prospective study. *Climacteric;*2:205–11.

8. Wing RR, Matthews KA, Kuller LH, Meilahn EN, Plantinga PL. Weight gain at the time of menopause. *Arch Intern Med* 1991;151:97–102.

9. Sternfeld B, Wang H, Quesenberry CP Jr, Abrams B, Everson-Rose SA, Greendale GA, *et al.* Physical activity and changes in weight and waist circumference in midlife women: findings from the Study of Women's Health Across the Nation. *Am J Epidemiol* 2004;160:912–22.

10. Guthrie JR, Dennerstein L, Taffe JR, Ebeling PR, Randolph JF, Burger HG, *et al.* Central abdominal fat and endogenous hormones during the menopausal transition. *Fertil Steril* 2003;79:1335–40.

11. Gill JM, Malkova D. Physical activity, fitness and cardiovascular disease risk in adults: interactions with insulin resistance and obesity. *Clin Sci (Lond)* 2006;110:409–25.

12. Sammel MD, Grisso JA, Freeman EW, Hollander L, Liu L, Liu S, *et al.* Weight gain among women in the late reproductive years. *Fam Pract* 2003;20:401–9.

13. Sternfeld B, Bhat AK, Wang H, Sharp T, Quesenberry CP. Menopause, physical activity, and body composition/fat distribution in midlife women. *Med Sci Sports Exerc* 2005;37:1195–202.

14. Rocca WA, Grossardt BR, de Andrade M, Malkasian GD, Melton LJ. Survival patterns after oophorectomy in premenopausal women: a population-based cohort study. *Lancet Oncol* 2006;7:821–8.

15. Garnero P, Jamin C, Benhamou CL, Pelissier C, Roux C. Effects of tibolone and combined 17beta-estradiol and norethisterone acetate on serum C-reactive protein in healthy post-menopausal women: a randomized trial. *Hum Reprod* 2002;17:2748–53.

16. Writing Group for the Women's Health Initiative Investigators. Risks and benefits of estrogen plus progestin in healthy postmenopausal women: principal results from the Women's Health Initiative randomized controlled trial. *JAMA* 2002;288:321–33.

17. The Women's Health Initiative Steering Committee. Effects of conjugated equine estrogen in postmenopausal women with hysterectomy: the Women's Health Initiative randomized controlled trial. *JAMA* 2004;291:1701–12.

18. Limpaphayom K, Taechakraichana N, Jaisamrarn U. Hormonal replacement and lipid changes in postmenopausal women. *J Med Assoc Thai* 1996;79:10–15.

19. Jensen J, Riis BJ, Strom V, Nilas L, Christiansen C. Long-term effects of percutaneous estrogens and oral progesterone on serum lipoproteins in postmenopausal women. *Maturitas* 1989;156:66–71.

20. Speroff L, Rowan J, Symons J, Genant H, Wilborn W. The comparative effect on bone density, endometrium, and lipids of continuous hormones as replacement therapy (CHART study). A randomized controlled trial. *JAMA* 1996;276:1397–403.

21. Espeland MA, Stefanick ML, Kritz-Silverstein D, Fineberg SE, Waclawiw MA, James MK, *et al.* Effect of postmenopausal hormone therapy on body weight and waist and hip girths. Postmenopausal Estrogen-Progestin Interventions Study Investigators. *J Clin Endocrinol Metab* 1997;82:1549–56.

22. Armstrong AL, Oborne J, Coupland CA, Macpherson MB, Bassey EJ, Wallace WA. Effects of hormone replacement therapy on muscle performance and balance in post-menopausal women. *Clin Sci* 1996;91:685–90.

23. Gallagher JC, Kable WT, Goldgar D. Effect of progestin therapy on cortical and trabecular bone: comparison with estrogen. *Am J Med* 1991;90:171–8.

24. Good WR, John VA, Ramirez M, Higgins JE. Double-masked, multicenter study of an estradiol matrix transdermal delivery system (Alora(tm)) versus placebo in postmenopausal women experiencing menopausal symptoms. Alora Study Group. *Clin Ther* 1996;18:1093–105.

25. Lindheim SR, Notelovitz M, Feldman EB, Larsen S, Khan FY, Lobo RA. The independent effects of exercise and estrogen on lipids and lipoproteins in postmenopausal women. *Obstet Gynecol* 1994;83:167–72.

26. Jensen J, Riis BJ, Christiansen C. Cyproterone acetate, an alternative progestogen in postmenopausal hormone replacement therapy? Effects on serum lipids and lipoproteins. *Br J Obstet Gynaecol* 1987;94:136–41.

27. Jensen J, Riis BJ, Strom V, Christiansen C. Continuous oestrogen-progestogen treatment and serum lipoproteins in postmenopausal women. *Br J Obstet Gynaecol* 1987;94:130–5.

28. Hartmann B, Kirchengast S, Albrecht A, Laml T, Bikas D, Huber J. Effects of hormone replacement therapy on growth hormone secretion patterns in correlation to somatometric parameters in healthy postmenopausal women. *Maturitas* 1995;22:239–46.

29. Khoo S-K, Coglan MJ, Wright GR, DeVoss KN, Battistutta D. Hormone therapy in women in the menopause transition: randomised, double-blind, placebo-controlled trial of effects on body weight, blood pressure, lipoprotein levels, antithrombin III activity, and the endometrium. *Med J Aust* 1998;168:216–20.

30. Komulainen M, Tuppurainen MT, Kröger H, Heikkinen AM, Puntila E, Alhava E, *et al.* Vitamin D and HRT: no benefit additional to that of HRT alone in prevention of bone loss in early postmenopausal women. A 2.5-year randomized placebo-controlled study. *Osteoporos Int* 1997;7:126–32.

31. Kanaya AM, Herrington D, Vittinghoff E, Lin F, Grady D, Bittner V, et al; Heart and Estrogen/ progestin Replacement Study. Glycemic effects of postmenopausal hormone therapy: the Heart and Estrogen/progestin Replacement Study. A randomized, double-blind, placebo-controlled trial. *Ann Intern Med* 2003;138:1–9.

32. Perez Jaraiz MD, Revilla M, Alvarez de los Heros JI, Villa LF, Rico H. Prophylaxis of osteoporosis with calcium, estrogens and/or eelcatonin: comparative longitudinal study of bone mass. *Maturitas* 1996;23:327–32.

33. Myrup B, Jensen GF, McNair P. Cardiovascular risk factors during estrogen-norethindrone and cholecalciferol treatment. *Arch Intern Med* 1992;152:2265–8.

34. Tonstad S, Ose L, Gorbitz C, Djoseland O, Bard JM, Fruchart JC. Efficacy of sequential hormone replacement therapy in the treatment of hypercholesterolaemia among postmenopausal women. *J Intern Med* 1995;238:39–47.

35. Wimalawansa SJ. Combined therapy with estrogen and etidronate has an additive effect on bone mineral density in the hip and vertebrae: four-year randomized study. *Am J Med* 1995;99:36–42.

36. Mijatovic V, Kenemans P, Jakobs C, van Baal WM, Peters-Muller ER, van der Mooren MJ. A randomized controlled study of the effects of 17beta-estradiol-dydrogesterone on plasma homocysteine in postmenopausal women. *Obstet Gynecol* 1998;91:432–6.

37. Walsh BW, Kuller LH, Wild RA, Paul S, Farmer M, Lawrence JB, *et al.* Effects of raloxifene on serum lipids and coagulation factors in healthy postmenopausal women. *JAMA* 1998;279:1445–51.

38. Wimalawansa SJ. A four-year randomized controlled trial of hormone replacement and bisphosphonate, alone or in combination, in women with postmenopausal osteoporosis. *Am J Med* 1998;104:219–26.

39. The Writing Group for the Estradiol Clotting Factors Study. Effects on haemostasis of hormone replacement therapy with transdermal estradiol and oral sequential medroxyprogesterone acetate: A 1-year, double-blind, placebo-controlled study. *Thromb Haemost* 1996;75:476–80.

40. Haarbo J, Marslew U, Gotfredsen A, Christiansen C. Postmenopausal hormone replacement therapy prevents central distribution of body fat after menopause. *Metabolism* 1991;40:1323–6.

41. Avenell A, Broom J, Brown TJ, Poobalan A, Aucott L, Stearns SC, *et al.* Systematic review of the long-term consequences of treatments for obesity and implications for health improvement. *Health Technol Assess* 2004;8(21).

42. Brown TJ. Health benefits of weight reduction in postmenopausal women: a systematic review. *J Br Menopause Soc* 2006;12:164–71.

Chapter 20

Weight management: the role of drugs for obesity

Mike Lean

After centuries of confusion, misinformation and mythology amongst doctors as much as the general public, weight management (Box 20.1) has come of age in the 21st century. There are now evidence-based guidelines[1,2] and in the UK an effective and cost-effective evidence-based weight management programme, Counterweight,[3] has been established for routine use to save a cash-strapped NHS money.

The stimulus to manage obesity properly within routine medical services has arisen from several origins. As in other branches of medical practice, such as evidence-based protocols for pain relief, the development of safe, effective drugs for obesity has been a powerful driver. But before this could happen, there had to be the recognition by doctors, health service planners and pharmaceutical companies that obesity is a serious and debilitating disease.

Like other multifactorial diseases, obesity responds in part to diet and lifestyle interventions. At a public health level, the greatest impact will come from small changes in diets and physical activity patterns, both for obesity prevention and for its clinical management. The same is true for other diseases such as asthma (allergen avoidance) and hypertension (sodium restriction and physical activity). However, it is plain to see that diet and lifestyle interventions are not always adequate, and many people are unable to adhere to restrictions to their preferred diets and inactivity. Pharmacological and surgical interventions are both necessary when lifelong control of obesity is not otherwise possible.

Of course, in the context of this book on obesity and reproductive health, the information in this chapter clearly pertains to the nonpregnant situation. Drugs for obesity or even weight loss have no place in the treatment of pregnant women because of risks to nutrient supply. Weight loss drugs have rarely been studied specifically in the context of reproductive health: there is only evidence for use of orlistat in women with polycystic ovary syndrome (PCOS).[4]

Box 20.1. Components of 21st century evidence-based weight management

1. Primary obesity prevention
2. Weight loss (3–6 months)
3. Maintenance of weight loss (life-long)
4. Identification and effective management of obesity-related risk factors and symptoms (including health optimisation for people unable to lose weight)

Diet and lifestyle management

Drug therapy for obesity is only ever acceptable as 'adjunctive therapy' to add to optimal diet and lifestyle improvement, or, more correctly, optimal *advice* for diet and lifestyle improvement. There is evidence now to define the goals of advice that will be most effective in controlling obesity, improving health outcomes and providing a basis for effective adjunctive drug therapy.

Low-fat diet

The recent obesity epidemic is associated with a huge increase in fat within the human food chain – up to an average of 40% of calories in many Western countries. Dietary fat as a proportion of calories correlates with prevalence of obesity while high-starch carbohydrate diets are associated with thinness. Reducing dietary fat to < 30% of calories, or < 25% for some people, is hard but effective in preventing weight gain, and simultaneously improving cardiovascular disease (CVD) risk factors.

This form of diet has been used in all the large, long-term trials in weight management[5,6] and as the dietary component of all recent pharmaceutical trials for obesity (STORM,[7] XENDOS[8] and RIO-Europe[9]). All cardiovascular risk factors improved. Low carbohydrate diets can certainly produce short-term weight loss, but this is partly water-depletion, and long term results are poor.

Physical activity and avoiding physical inactivity

There are two complementary and additive components to boost energy expenditure. Current recommendations are to maintain 30 minutes additional physical activity (moderate or intense, so enough to become breathless and/or break sweat) on at least 5 days a week. This is primarily to improve cardiovascular function and promote heart health but there are many additional benefits, including sleeping better, avoiding depression and reducing appetite. Many people who are obese find this difficult to achieve without a period of training, and hard to maintain without regular encouragement and professional contact. Some may need more physical activity than this to overcome their high drive to eat excessively, in order to lose weight.

A more fundamental measure, i.e. minimising physical inactivity, may be sufficient to prevent early excess fat accumulation, at least early in the disease. Restricting time spent watching TV or on computers has been shown to prevent weight gain in children.[10]

Combined low-fat diet and physical activity

Addressing only one side of the energy-balance equation commonly results in compensatory adjustment of the other, such that weight loss is avoided. For weight loss, there is usually a need for a substantial conscious effort to reduce energy intake. Physical activity helps to preserve muscle mass but does not contribute much to weight loss.

For weight maintenance – to avoid gain or regain – the evidence indicates that the best results come from a combination of small changes to reduce energy intake (primarily by reducing fat intake) and to increase energy expenditure, simultaneously.[11] The absolute level of changes required almost certainly varies among individuals. As a starting point, to reduce fat intake and energy intake by around 100 calories a day and to increase physical activity by about 100 calories a day (e.g. by walking an extra 2000 steps a day) seems reasonable.[12]

The medical benefits of these quite modest modifications of energy intake and energy expenditure are very substantial. These can be seen most clearly in the Diabetes Prevention Program (DPP)[5] and the Finnish Diabetes Prevention (FDP)[6] studies which gave essentially identical results, both reducing the incidence of new diabetes by 58% over a 4 year period, together with improvements in all the other risk factors. It is this combination of modestly reduced energy intake while maintaining physical activity that forms the basis of the Counterweight programme.[3] In routine care settings when all referred patients are included, and these include many patients with health risk, the overall results are more modest with a weight loss of around 3–4 kg, and about 40% of the participants achieving weight loss greater than 5 kg over 1 year. Once again, however, the benefits in terms of risk factors within Counterweight was substantial. Efforts to increase physical activity of obese patients are usually of low value until they have achieved some weight loss by dietary restriction.

Which drug and when

There are drugs licensed for use in the UK, including phentermine and diethylpropion, which dates from the appetite suppressant era. These drugs have been used very widely and have not been shown to have frequent or serious adverse effects but they were not subjected to the currently required levels of testing for efficacy or safety. These drugs thus do not feature in clinical guidelines.

Three drugs are now well studied in large international research portfolios and have been shown to be both safe and efficacious in weight management when given together with a structured programme of supervised dietary restriction and physical activity. These are orlistat, sibutramine and rimonabant.

Orlistat

Orlistat is an intestinal lipase inhibitor. It is essentially not absorbed by the gastrointestinal tract and operates entirely by reducing the absorption of consumed triglyceride in food. It is therefore the first choice of drug for patients who are able to tolerate it and the limiting factor is that its mode of action, blocking 30% of fat absorption, produces intolerable steatorrhea if fat consumption exceeds about 20–25 g per meal. Around 7–8 g of fat can be malabsorbed without any symptoms by most people. This effect is to reduce energy intake by around 200 calories per day. There is an additional benefit if patients are able to adhere to a diet containing only 60–80 g of fat daily in that this almost inevitably results in reduced energy intake anyway.

The clinical benefit of orlistat has been shown in a large number of well-conducted clinical trials (reviewed in 2006 by Lean and Finer[13]). It produces a weight loss on average around 3 kg more than placebo, with the same diet and exercise programme. Unfortunately, the clinical trials have all been conducted in such a way that treatment was continued even in non-responders, for up to 4 years in the case of the XENDOS trial.[14] This has the effect of contaminating the treatment arm with patients who would normally have the drug stopped at an earlier stage in treatment. Even with this problem, the clinical benefit from the additional weight loss is very substantial in the case of XENDOS: there was a further 37% reduction in incidence of new diabetes over 4 years,[14] compared with a diet and exercise programme very similar to the DPP study. The additional benefit in terms of cardiovascular risk factors is consistently positive. How the drug is likely to perform in routine practice is best seen from an analysis[15] that excludes patients who fail to lose weight (they should have the drugs stopped at a very early stage, as in routine practice) and this analysis shows improvements in blood pressure, lipids and glucose tolerance broadly equivalent to or exceeding that seen by the introduction of separate drugs for these conditions (Figure 20.1).

Because orlistat is not absorbed into the body and it therefore has essentially no adverse effects, it is now available over the counter in a number of countries. The limiting factor for its effectiveness in routine use is always the ability of the patient to comply with very strict fat restriction. This limits the usefulness of orlistat to perhaps 25% of patients for long-term use. Its value is very substantially increased in the context of a managed and well-presented multi-component weight management programme, such as that in the Counterweight programme, which allows patients to continue on treatment more or less indefinitely.

Sibutramine

Sibutramine was initially developed as an antidepressant and shares some of the pharmacological actions of the serotonin re-uptake inhibitor fluoxetine. It was not found to be sufficiently potent as an anti-depressant but, possibly because of its additional noradrenaline uptake inhibition, it was effective in reducing body weight. This mode of action is different from the appetite-suppressant drugs that cause release of transmitter in an uncontrolled way, leading to, among other things, addiction in some cases. The important adverse effects of the releasing agents commonly include hypertension and this is not seen with re-uptake inhibitors. For this reason, sibutramine is a much safer drug for obesity and weight management than other structurally related compounds. As well as enhancing satiety, thereby reducing the need to eat without damaging appetite between meals, sibutramine has a modest action increasing energy expenditure and thereby reducing the compensatory fall in metabolic rate that occurs with weight loss.[16]

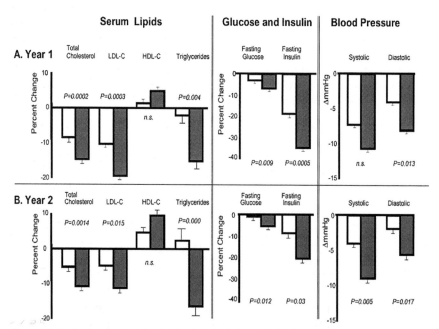

Figure 20.1. Cardiovascular risk reduction in patients treated with diet, exercise and orlistat; reproduced with permission from Rissanen *et al.*[15]

From its mode of action, sibutramine can be expected to reduce energy consumption by around 300 calories a day and to save approximately 100 calories a day from compensatory reduction in metabolism. It would therefore be expected to lead to around 4–6 kg weight loss over a 3–6 month period in comparison with placebo. On the other hand, to reduce metabolic rate by 300 calories a day, and match a reduced food intake at this level, would entail a weight loss of around 13 kg. It can therefore be predicted from mode of action that sibutramine should be able to maintain the body weight 13 kg below baseline if that can be achieved by diet, exercise and drug. The clinical trials show that sibutramine does exactly as predicted. Dose-ranging trials found effective weight loss with 10 and 15 mg a day and low levels of adverse effects. Above this dose, the adverse effects became problematic.

The weight maintenance value of sibutramine is of much greater value to patients and can be seen, firstly, in a study by Apfelbaum and colleagues[17] when the initial weight loss was achieved with a very low calorie diet and the randomisation then to placebo or sibutramine showed weight regain with placebo but stabilisation at around 12–13 kg below baseline on sibutramine. A longer term study, the STORM trial,[7] used a study design which more closely mimicked use in routine practice. Sibutramine together with a diet and exercise programme was given to patients at the outset in an open fashion, and they lost around 13 kg on average. Randomisation after 6 months showed, as expected, that a placebo drug allowed the weight regain whereas maintenance on sibutramine allowed very effective weight maintenance for 2 years when the trial ended. There is no reason to think that the effect of the drug would not continue indefinitely.

Together with the reduction in body weight, there was a parallel for waist circumference and an improvement in all the cardiovascular risk factors with the exception of blood pressure, which did not change. The lack of effect on blood pressure is attributed to the noradrenaline re-uptake action of sibutramine but this may in fact not be an important consideration for two reasons. Firstly, weight loss achieved by other means including surgery has not proven to be effective in controlling the elevated blood pressure in obese patients in the long term. This may indicate that prolonged obesity has reset the neuro-endocrine regulation of blood pressure in a rather permanent way, or alternatively, that there are permanent vascular stiffness changes with prolonged obesity which cannot be reversed by weight loss. Secondly, randomised controlled trials of sibutramine plus diet and exercise in the management of obese hypertensive patients has shown that the blood pressure falls equally with weight loss, whether patients are given sibutramine or placebo.

Sibutramine is absorbed into the body so it has some potential adverse effects. These have been collected from the clinical trials and found to be generally mild and self-terminating and to occur early in treatment. The number of patients withdrawn from clinical trials because of adverse effects is very small and no different from placebo (Table 20.1).

Table 20.1. Patients withdrawn in all controlled long-term trials with sibutramine; data from Sharma[18]

Adverse effect	Patients withdrawn		P value
	Placebo	Sibutramine	
Hypertension	0.6%	1.1%	0.21
Palpitations	0.0%	0.2%	0.22
Tachycardia	0.0%	0.6%	0.048
Vasodilatation	0.0%	0.1%	0.48
Total	8.7%	9.0%	Not significant

Sibutramine is therefore clearly an effective and safe agent for weight management as an adjunct to diet and exercise therapy. It produces a sense of satiety which is noticeable to patients, particularly those who are troubled by having an excessive appetite or urge to eat. It currently has a licence that appears to restrict its use to 1 year of treatment. There is in fact inadequate understanding by regulatory authorities since withdrawal of the drug inevitably leads to a resurgence of an otherwise uncontrollable urge to eat and to an aggravation of a whole range of health problems. There is never any suggestion that sibutramine use should be restricted on safety grounds and long-term clinical trials do not show any loss of its effectiveness over at least 2 years, which is longer than most drugs given for the management of diabetes or hypertension or other medical problems. It is hoped that this licence limitation will be changed but in the meantime it is reasonable on the basis of a large body of evidence to continue treatment that is technically off licence, provided there is adequate supervision of patients.

Rimonabant

A number of patients eat not because they are hungry or have a big appetite but through boredom or for 'comfort'. This observation led to the development of rimonabant, the first available cannabinoid receptor antagonist (CB1). The receptors are found in various parts of the brain, including the hypothalamus where its action is to reduce the drive to eat. It may also have peripheral actions that are believed to modify cardiovascular risk profiles. Clinical trials with rimonabant have been conducted in a number of settings, including patients with hyperlipidaemia, diabetes and 'uncomplicated' obesity, and all used exactly the same study design and produced almost identical results. However, as always, weight loss was lower in patients with existing diabetes, perhaps because they had already been through a phase of weight loss with the help of dieticians. The degree of weight loss produced by rimonabant is very similar to that seen with the other agents, of the order of 4–5 kg more than the placebo arm, both with diet and exercise programme. The benefit in terms of cardiovascular risk is again broadly similar to that seen with other effective drugs in the management of obesity (Table 20.2).

Rimonabant is absorbed into the body. It is a new class of drug and little is known about its hazards in long-term use, but the adverse effect profile in clinical trials has been good. There is some evidence that it may affect mood and this is perhaps understandable from its mode of action: blocking an activity that people use to improve their mood. Rimonabant has not been studied in patients with a history of depression and this remains of some concern, although the clinical trials did not show any worsening in mood and depression scores in the clinical trials. However, because of concerns over potential effects on mood, the US Food and Drug Administration (FDA) has not yet given approval for its use in the USA. The European Agency for

Table 20.2. Cardiovascular benefits with anti-obesity drugs acting on the central nervous system

	Sibutramine (STORM trial[7])	Rimonabant (RIO-Europe trial[9])
Waist circumference	−10%	−4%
High density lipoprotein	+18%	+8%
Triglyceride	−23%	−15%
Systolic blood pressure	—	−1%

the Evaluation of Medicinal Products (EMEA) will review evidence on rimonabant in due course, but at present rimonabant can be prescribed in the UK. Depressed mood is common in obesity, but although few cases have been reported in patients taking rimonabant it is wise to monitor the patient's mood.

It is tempting to suggest that rimonabant may be particularly suited to patients who do not appear to have a large appetite but eat for comfort or reward. Clinical trials have yet to be performed that will show whether this differential is valid. At present it can only be said that rimonabant offers a third line of management for patients unable to tolerate or unable to gain benefit from orlistat or sibutramine. The main advantages and disadvantages of rimonabant are summarised in Table 20.3. There is as yet no evidence that combining drugs for obesity produces improved results although this might be considered likely given that they all use different modes of action.

Future therapies

Looking into the future, there is a large number of neuroendocrine pathways that affect appetite and which could potentially lead to effective agents in weight management. From first principles however, the human appetite and the drive to eat is extremely well defended by evolutionary processes that oppose weight loss (even in people who are obese). It is likely that a drug affecting any one of these pathways will have only a modest effect of the order seen with currently available drugs. It is also likely that compensatory mechanisms will soon establish themselves to limit the weight loss that is achieved by any one drug. With any drug use in the management of obesity it remains the diet and exercise programme that generates and maintains most of the weight loss – the effect of the drug is to tip the balance in favour of the patient who cannot muster the necessary level of self-control or compliance.

Cost–benefit considerations

Detailed health economic analyses have not been conducted with these drugs and somewhat erroneous analyses have been based on the clinical trials, which are, of course, biased because many of the patients on the treatment arm do not in fact lose weight and should in routine practice have the drug stopped. Nonetheless, the multiple clinical benefits seen with quite modest weight loss are often of the level that would take the place of or avoid treatment with one or two drugs for blood pressure, one or two for lipid lowering, one or two for diabetes and would also be expected to reduce the need for analgesics and anti-anginal drugs. The improvement in mood and reduction in 'depression' with weight loss may reduce the need for drugs for these conditions.

It would seem desirable that doctors evaluate the overall health profiles of patients in relation to their body mass index (BMI) or waist circumference and then recognise

Table 20.3. Advantages and disadvantages of rimonabant for treating obesity

Advantages	Disadvantages
• Reduces internal rewards for repeated (addictive) eating • Cardiovascular risks reduced • Once-daily administration	• Absorbed – central nervous system adverse effects could aggravate depression • New drug – limited long-term experience

Table 20.4. Useful definitions of obesity

Application	Definition
For epidemiology WHO (1995)[19]	BMI 18.5–25 kg/m² = normal BMI 25–30 kg/m² = overweight BMI > 30 kg/m² = obese
For clinical decisions and health promotion Lean et al. (1995)[20]	Professional help: waist > 88 cm (women); > 102 cm (men) Personal action: waist > 80 cm (women); > 94 cm (men)
To understand and manage obesity Sattar et al. (2006)[21]	The disease process of excess fat accumulation, caused by gene–environment interactions, with multiple organ-specific pathological consequences

the dynamic nature of the disease of obesity (defined in Table 20.4). The current usual practice within primary care is to introduce drugs one-by-one by complications of obesity and then at a very late stage in the disease to think about treating the underlying weight problem. A very strong case can now be made for much earlier intervention to check weight gain, including some weight loss if possible. If that requires a long-term drug intervention then this may have major health benefits as well as being economically preferable to poly-pharmacy for the complications of obesity. It would seem that some of the regulatory and guideline decisions made about drugs for obesity have not always been informed by sufficient expert opinion from those involved in weight management, and there remains prejudice against the long-term use of the drug to prevent worsening of obesity and its complications. This has arisen despite our acceptance now of expensive drugs such as statins and anti-hypertensives, which have only modest effects on reducing absolute incidence of death or cardiovascular outcomes. It will, of course, be an advantage when the results of long-term trials with cardiovascular endpoints are available for drugs in the management of obesity. However, before that evidence is available, we would be right to look at all other available evidence, including collateral evidence that suggests it is very likely that effective weight management will have a major net health gain.

References

1. Scottish Intercollegiate Guidelines Network. *Obesity in Scotland: Integrating Prevention with Weight Management*. No 8. Edinburgh: SIGN; 1996.
2. National Institutes of Health, National Heart Lung and Blood Institute. *Clinical Guidelines on the Identification, Evaluation and Treatment of Overweight and Obesity in Adults – the Evidence Report*. Bethesda MD: NIG; 1998.
3. The Counterweight Programme [www.counterweight.org].
4. Jayagopal V, Kilpatrick ES, Holding S, Jennings PE, Atkin SL. Orlistat is as beneficial as metformin in the treatment of polycystic ovarian syndrome. *J Clin Endocrinol Metab* 2005;90:729–33.
5. Knowler WC, Barrett-Connor E, Fowler SE, Hamman RF, Lachin JM, Walker EA, et al. Diabetes Prevention Program Research Group. Reduction in the incidence of type 2 diabetes with lifestyle intervention or metformin. *NEJM* 2002;346:393–406.
6. Tuomilehto J, Lindstrom J, Eriksson JG, Valle TT, Hamalainen H, Ilanne-Parikka P, et al. Finnish Diabetes Prevention Study Group. Prevention of type 2 diabetes mellitus by changes in lifestyle among subjects with impaired glucose tolerance. *NEJM* 2001;344:1343–50.
7. James WP, Astrup A, Finer N, Hilsted H, Kopelman P, Rossner S, et al. Effect of sibutramine on weight maintenance after weight loss: a randomised trial. STORM Study Group. *Lancet* 2000;356: 2119–25.

8. Torgerson JS, Hauptman J, Boldrin MN, Sjostrom L. XENical in the prevention of diabetes in obese subjects (XENDOS) study: a randomized study of orlistat as an adjunct to lifestyle changes for the prevention of type 2 diabetes in obese patients. *Diabetes Care* 2004;27:155–61. Erratum in: *Diabetes Care* 2004;27:856.

9. Van Gaal LF, Rissanen AM, Scheen AJ, Ziegler O, Rossner S; RIO-Europe Study Group. Effects of the cannabinoid-1 receptor blocker rimonabant on weight reduction and cardiovascular risk factors in overweight patients: 1-year experience from the RIO-Europe study. *Lancet* 2005;365:1389–97. Erratum in: *Lancet* 2005;366:370.

10. Sharma M. School-based interventions for childhood and adolescent obesity. *Obes Rev* 2006;7:261–9.

11. Wyatt HR, Grunwald GK, Seagle HM, Klem ML, McGuire MT, Wing RR, *et al*. Resting energy expenditure in reduced-obese subjects in the National Weight Control Registry. *Am J Clin Nutr* 1999;69:1189–93.

12. America on the Move [www.americaonthemove.org].

13. Lean M, Finer N. ABC of obesity. Management: part II – drugs. *BMJ* 2006 14;333:794–7.

14. Heymsfield SB, Segal KR, Hauptman J, Lucas CP, Boldrin MN, Rissanen A, *et al*. Effects of weight loss with orlistat on glucose tolerance and progression to type 2 diabetes in obese adults. *Arch Intern Med* 200;160:1321–6.

15. Rissanen A, Lean M, Rossner S, Segal KR, Sjostrom L. Predictive value of early weight loss in obesity management with orlistat: an evidence-based assessment of prescribing guidelines. *Int J Obes Relat Metab Disord* 2003;27:103–9.

16. Walsh KM, Leen E, Lean MEJ. The effect of sibutramine on resting energy expenditure and adrenaline-induced thermogenesis in obese females. *IJO* 1999;23:1009–15.

17. Apfelbaum M, Vague P, Ziegler O, Hanotin C, Thomas F, Leutenegger E. Long-term maintenance of weight loss after a very-low-calorie diet: a randomised blinded trial of the efficacy and tolerability of sibutramine. *Am J Med* 1999;106:179–84.

18. Sharma AM. Sibutramine in overweight/obese hypertensive patients. *Int J Obes Relat Metab Disord* 2001;25 Suppl 4:S20–3.

19. World Health Organisation Expert Committee. *Physical Status: the Use and Interpretation of Anthropometry*. WHO Technical Report Series 854. Geneva: WHO; 1995.

20. Lean ME, Han TS, Morrison CE. Waist circumference as a measure for indicating need for weight management. *BMJ* 1995;311:158–61.

21. Sattar N, Lean M, editors. *ABC of Obesity*. Oxford: Blackwell Publishing; 2007.

Chapter 21

Interaction of lifestyle factors with obesity in the genesis of pre-eclampsia

James M Roberts, Lisa Bodnar and Thelma Patrick

Introduction

Obesity is increasing at epidemic proportions in developed countries. Obesity has long been recognised as a risk factor for pre-eclampsia. Recent studies have resulted in two important findings. Firstly, if pre-eclampsia is examined as a continuous function of body mass index (BMI) the increase is monotonic and nearly linear and increases at all BMIs (Figure 21.1). Secondly, the relationship is present not only in mild pre-eclampsia occurring at term but is also present in severe pre-eclampsia.[1] The relative risk in a low-risk obese population (no evident hypertension or diabetes) in the USA is about three-fold. Combined with the prevalence of obesity (BMI > 30 kg/m^2) in about 35% of women, this leads to an attributable risk of almost 35% for obesity. If

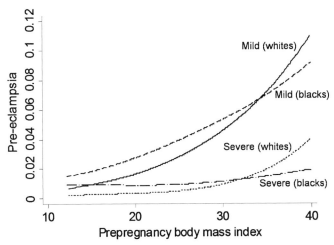

Figure 21.1. Association between prepregnancy body mass index and the unadjusted prevalence of mild and severe pre-eclampsia by race/ethnicity (Collaborative Perinatal Project, 1959–66); the analysis is of pregnancies in 19 135 white and 19 053 black women; curves were estimated by calculating predicted probabilities based on an unadjusted multinomial logistic regression model; reproduced with permission from Bodnar *et al.*[1]

abnormal BMI is extended to include overweight (BMI > 25 kg/m²), the attributable risk approaches 50%. Thus, obesity is a major risk factor for pre-eclampsia and an effort to understand the relationship and pathogenic factors underlying the increased risk is a major focus of our laboratory. These studies are targeted to identify modifiable factors and to identify the subset of women who are obese and at risk for pre-eclampsia. It is important to remember that with a relative risk of 3 and an incidence for pre-eclampsia of 3.6% in our low-risk population, over 90% of women who are obese will not develop pre-eclampsia. What might be different about the subgroup that develops pre-eclampsia?

The possibilities explaining the increased risk of pre-eclampsia in a subset of women who are obese can be listed as follows:

1. Only certain kinds of fat accumulation relate to pre-eclampsia: visceral versus subcutaneous obesity; percentage of body fat; fat accrual.

2. Obesity with different metabolic consequences influences the frequency of pre-eclampsia. Pre-eclampsia is more common with increases in: insulin resistance; abnormalities of lipids (especially free fatty acids); inflammation; and oxidative stress.

3. Obesity and pre-eclampsia are not causally related but have one or more common causes and not all causes of obesity relate to pre-eclampsia.

4. Obesity must interact with other factors to result in obesity – there are potentially an enormous number of these factors, including relationship to lifestyle factors.

The relationship to lifestyle factors has not been extensively studied. It is clear from the epidemiology of cardiovascular disease that there are many factors influenced by obesity that are associated with an increased risk of cardiovascular disease in later life. Many of these have the advantage of being at least theoretically modifiable. If these same factors influence the risk of obesity to increase the frequency of pre-eclampsia, the potential to modify these factors would be very desirable. Weight loss during pregnancy is not encouraged in current practice. It is also, of course, very difficult to modify obesity in any setting. Modifying lifestyle factors that interact with obesity to increase the risk of pre-eclampsia would be an alternative approach that has another relevant advantage. It is possible that the relationship between obesity and pre-eclampsia is not causal. If obesity and pre-eclampsia are not causally related but share a common cause, preventing obesity will not necessarily prevent pre-eclampsia. However, if there were potentially modifiable lifestyle factors that when present with obesity lead to pre-eclampsia, modifying these factors would be useful regardless of whether or not pre-eclampsia and obesity are related causally. With this motivation, this chapter will explore the potential relationships of lifestyle factors to pre-eclampsia in women who are obese. Guided by factors identified as important in cardiovascular disease, we will explore the impact of diet, physical activity, stress, sleep disorders and smoking to increase pre-eclampsia in women who are obese. The strategy will be to examine the relationship to cardiovascular disease and what is known about these lifestyle factors in pregnancy and pre-eclampsia. Since many of these factors also contribute to obesity, this relationship will also be explored where appropriate. The chapter is clearly hypothesis generating.

Diet

Diet and cardiovascular disease

Poor nutrition is a major contributor to cardiovascular disease. Diets high in antioxidants, fruits and vegetables, B vitamins, omega-3 polyunsaturated fatty acids (PUFAs), fish and seafood, whole grains and dietary fibre protect against heart disease, and excessive intakes of saturated fat, trans-fatty acids, refined grains and sweets increase the risk of heart disease.[2] Following decades of research, healthy diet is now a cornerstone of cardiovascular disease prevention.

Diet and pre-eclampsia: the importance of periconceptional nutrition

Despite the similarities between pre-eclampsia and cardiovascular disease, few investigators have studied the role of diet in the pathophysiology of pre-eclampsia.[3] Each nutrient or food described above as relevant to cardiovascular disease has a biologically plausible relationship with components of the pre-eclampsia disease process. The experience with periconceptional folic acid supplementation to reduce neural tube defects has drawn attention to this period as especially important for micronutrient adequacy. In addition to being a time of rapid cell growth and differentiation, a major oxidant challenge occurs at 8–10 weeks of gestation. At this time the maternal blood supply begins to perfuse the intervillus space with a resulting increase in pO_2 and evidence of oxidative stress.[4] Vitamin C, vitamin E and the carotenoids are important physiological antioxidants, and fruits and vegetables are the major food sources for these nutrients. The consumption of less than the recommended vitamin C level and fruit and vegetable servings in the year before delivery increased the likelihood of pre-eclampsia.[5] This was supported by another study in which women with the highest quartile of serum vitamin C concentration at an average of 18 weeks of gestation a had lower rate of pre-eclampsia (0.59; 95% CI 0.38–0.93) than women with lower vitamin C concentrations.[6] Results of supplementation with vitamins C and E have not been as consistent. In a small group of primarily low-risk women with abnormal uterine artery Doppler velocimetry at 22 and 24 weeks of gestation, supplementation with 1000 mg of vitamin C and 400 iu of vitamin E reduced pre-eclampsia by two-thirds.[7] However, in a larger study by the same authors of the same supplementation to women at high risk for pre-eclampsia, the treatment was not successful.[6] In another study of the same antioxidants at the same doses, pre-eclampsia was not reduced in approximately 900 low-risk women.[8] The inconsistency of these results compared with dietary studies may indicate differences in populations but probably also reflects the important difference between food intake and dietary supplementation. The failure of antioxidant therapy in these studies may also underscore the importance of periconceptional antioxidants since the average date of recruitment in all of these studies was 18 weeks of gestation, well past the oxidative challenge associated with the establishment of the intervillus circulation.

Dietary fibre, mainly contributed by whole grains, fruits and vegetables, modulates glucose homeostasis/insulin sensitivity, lowers blood lipids, reduces blood pressure and may have anti-inflammatory properties.[9] No studies have assessed dietary fibre intake and risk of pre-eclampsia.

Foods high in refined sugars, including soft drinks, which are low in important vitamins and minerals, may replace nutrient-dense foods in the diet and also may have an independent role in contributing to the pathophysiology of pre-eclampsia. Indeed, Clausen et al.[10] reported that women who consumed greater than 25% of energy from sucrose in the second trimester were 3.6 (95% CI 1.3–9.8) times as likely as low sucrose consumers to develop pre-eclampsia. The same study demonstrated an increased risk of pre-eclampsia (2.6; 95% CI 1.3–5.4) in women with increased intake of PUFA.

Diet and obesity

Obesity is associated with an imbalance in energy intake and energy expenditure. Traditionally, obesity has been viewed as a state of overnutrition, in which micronutrient adequacy was assumed because of presumably high food intake. Nevertheless, data from healthy adults and children suggest that micronutrient concentrations in blood are negatively associated with BMI and other measures of body fatness.[11,12] For instance, in a cross-sectional study of 19 068 healthy men and women, plasma ascorbic acid concentrations were inversely related to waist:hip ratio (WHR), even after adjusting for BMI, age, supplement use, smoking and socio-economic status.[13] Observations were only partially explained by dietary ascorbate intakes. Anderson *et al.*[14] conducted a prospective cohort study of 3071 individuals in the CARDIA study and determined that BMI at baseline predicted a lowering of serum carotenoids concentrations 7 years later in nonsmokers. As far as is known, these associations have not yet been tested during pregnancy. There are preliminary data that suggest prepregnancy overweight is associated with reduced concentrations of key micronutrients for pre-eclampsia prevention, including plasma ascorbic acid, serum carotenoids (Figure 21.2) and serum vitamin E in early gestation.

Furthermore, obesity is associated with increased intake of soft drinks,[15] which in the USA are sweetened with fructose. Fructose does not stimulate insulin and is associated with lower leptin concentrations.[16] It can induce the metabolic syndrome in animals[17] and increased intake is associated with obesity and the metabolic syndrome in humans.[16] It is interesting that in the Clausen study of Norwegian women cited above, soft drink intake accounted for much of the increased caloric intake associated with an increased risk of pre-eclampsia.[10] In checking with the authors, they concluded that sucrose was the major sweetener in Norway at that time. However, if a similar relationship exists between pre-eclampsia and intake of soft drinks in US women, this would represent a large intake of fructose.

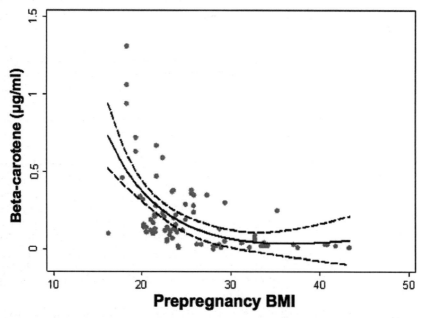

Figure 21.2. Serum beta-carotene concentration as a function of prepregnancy body mass index; samples ($n = 93$) were obtained at 20 weeks of gestation; the solid line represents the point estimate and the dotted lines represent the upper and lower 95% confidence bands

Physical activity

Physical activity and cardiovascular disease

Regular physical activity is important to general wellbeing and is recommended as a preventive for cardiovascular disease.[18] Cardiovascular disease is associated with a sedentary lifestyle.[19,20] The Women's Health Initiative study illustrates the relevance of physical activity to cardiovascular health and disease in women. Findings from this study document that in a group of racially diverse women, either walking or vigorous exercise reduces the incidence of cardiovascular events, and, conversely, inactivity increases the risk of such events.[21]

There are many changes with physical activity that favour cardiovascular health. Physical activity is inversely linked to cholesterol concentration,[22] blood pressure,[23] BMI,[24] glucose intolerance[25] and fibrinolytic activity.[26] There is evidence that even modest activity can increase insulin sensitivity[27,28] and modify other components of the metabolic syndrome.[29] It is increasingly evident that inflammation is a major pathophysiological feature of cardiovascular disease. A sample of 13 748 adult participants was identified from the Third National Health and Nutrition Examination Survey (NHANES III) to assess the association of C-reactive protein and leisure-time physical activity.[30] An inverse, dose-dependent relationship was identified for C-reactive protein and physical activity. In addition, activity was directly associated with serum albumin concentration and inversely with fibrinogen concentration and white blood cell count. Thus, the results from this study support findings from other studies that physical activity favourably affects concentrations of acute phase reactants.[31–33]

Physical activity and pre-eclampsia

The similarities between cardiovascular disease in later life and pre-eclampsia, and the fact that physical conditioning and pre-eclampsia have opposite effects on critical physiological functions, suggest that, as with cardiovascular disease, exercise may reduce the risk of pre-eclampsia. The available data, although historical and observational, support this concept. Even occupational and leisure-time physical activity in early pregnancy have been associated with a reduced incidence of pre-eclampsia, as compared with women who are less active.[34,35] A case–control study of pregnant women, 201 of whom were pre-eclamptic and 383 of whom were normotensive, assessed the type, intensity, frequency and duration of physical activity performed during the first 20 weeks of pregnancy and during the year before pregnancy.[36] Women who engaged in any regular physical activity during early pregnancy, compared with inactive women, experienced a 35% reduced risk of pre-eclampsia. When the level of activity was considered, those who engaged in light or moderate activities and those who participated in vigorous activities experienced a reduced risk of 24% and 54%, respectively, relative to inactive women. Brisk walking (average walking pace ≥ 3 miles per hour), when compared with no walking at all, was associated with a 30–33% reduction in risk of pre-eclampsia. Recreational physical activity performed during the year before pregnancy was associated with similar reductions in risk of pre-eclampsia. These data suggest that regular physical activity, particularly when performed during the year before pregnancy and during early pregnancy, is associated with a reduced risk of pre-eclampsia.[36]

There are no published controlled randomised clinical trials examining the effects of prenatal exercise on biochemical markers for endothelial dysfunction, placental dysfunction or oxidative stress.[37] Our group has such a randomised trial in process, for women with a history of pre-eclampsia, toward a goal of reducing the recurrence of pre-eclampsia. Based on the interaction of obesity and physical activity described below, exercise may be an especially important determinant of pregnancy outcome in women who are obese.

Physical activity and obesity

Reduced physical activity is a well-recognised and major contributor to the epidemic of obesity. Additionally, however, there are other important interactions between these lifestyle factors. The relationship of obesity and physical activity to cardiovascular risk markers in women was explored in the Women's Health Study data. Lower levels of physical activity and higher levels of BMI were independently associated with adverse levels of nearly all lipid and inflammatory biomarkers. High BMI showed stronger associations than physical inactivity. Women who were obese and inactive had nearly ten times the risk of increased inflammatory markers as a referent group of women who were physically active and of normal weight. However, in all BMI categories, physical activity was associated with more favourable cardiovascular biomarker concentrations.[38,39] A more recent analysis explored the relationship of obesity and physical activity to major cardiovascular events in women. In a multivariate model adjusting for cardiovascular risk factors, overweight and obesity were significantly associated with increased risk of coronary heart disease, whereas increasing levels of physical activity were associated with a graded reduction in coronary heart disease risk. When a joint analysis of BMI and physical activity was conducted with women who had a healthy weight and were physically active as the reference group, the relative risks of coronary heart disease were highest for women who were obese and sedentary (3.44), decreased to 2.48 for women who were obese but active, and decreased even more (1.48) for women who had a healthy weight but were sedentary. Similar findings were reported when the analysis was focused on WHR and physical activity.

Exercise appears to have a specific effect on visceral fat, which is considered to have greater risk than subcutaneous fat. In a study of individuals with graded exercise, sedentary individuals increased their visceral fat by 9% while low amounts of exercise prevented significant accumulation of visceral fat. The highest amount of exercise resulted in a 7% decrease in visceral and subcutaneous abdominal fat.[40,41]

Obesity and physical inactivity independently contribute to the development of coronary heart disease in women. These findings emphasise the importance of understanding both the weight and activity status in exploring the risk of pre-eclampsia in women who are obese. If the interactions in pre-eclampsia are similar to those in cardiovascular disease, increased activity should reduce the risk of pre-eclampsia in women who are obese.

Stress

Stress and cardiovascular disease

The detrimental effects of stress on the cardiovascular system have been documented through research in animals and humans.[42] Acute stressful events such as earthquakes are associated with a temporally associated increase in coronary events and stroke.[43] It is proposed that two systems primarily mediate the effect of the stress response on cardiovascular function: the hypothalamic–pituitary–adrenocortical (HPA) axis and the sympatho-adrenomedullary system (SAS).[43] Individuals with confirmed cardiovascular disease or its risk factors respond differently to these two systems. Although humans are physiologically equipped to respond to acute stressors, chronic (long-time) stress disrupts the HPA axis and the SAS, resulting in harmful effects on human health. Studies in people with pre-existing coronary disease or essential hypertension consistently show a positive relationship between stress reactivity and subsequent clinical outcomes, including stroke.[44,45] The heightened output from the HPA and SAS associated with chronic stress serves to produce a variety of other changes that have been strongly linked to coronary artery disease, including signs of increased inflammation,[46] central obesity, hyperinsulinaemia, diabetes, hypertension, platelet activation[47,48] and endothelial dysfunction.[49]

Stress and pre-eclampsia

The literature on stress and pregnancy is limited to statements of hypotheses and retrospective case–control analyses of specific forms of stress, taking advantage of certain life stresses or historic occurrences that increase stress, particularly job stress.

Job stressors provide a means of assessing the risk of stress exposure and pregnancy outcome. The approach to defining a particular job as high stress or low stress has varied. For example, in one study the occupational database developed by Karasek[50] for such categorisation was used, while in others both the pressures of the job and the control over decisions regarding the job were considered in the analysis. In spite of these methodological differences, the findings are quite comparable. When considering all working women, regardless of parity, there is a 1.5 to 2-fold risk of pre-eclampsia in the context of high-stress jobs across studies. When these analyses are limited to primiparous women, the likelihood of pre-eclampsia in high stress or high job pressure/low control work roles ranges from 2 to 2.5 times more, relative to women in roles that are perceived to impose less stress.[51–54]

Stress and obesity

Stress is associated with obesity in several ways. Stress influences eating patterns and may impact both weight and health when altered over time. Increased salivary cortisol is associated with both psychological stress and mechanisms affecting hunger. In a study of women exposed to stress, women who were categorised as high cortisol reactors consumed more calories on the stress-exposure day compared with low reactors but ate similar amounts on the control day. In terms of taste preferences, high reactors ate significantly more sweet food across days. Further, increases in negative mood in response to the stressors were also significantly related to greater food consumption.[55]

In addition to the effect of stress on caloric intake, central fat distribution is related to greater psychological vulnerability to stress and cortisol reactivity. Women classified by high or low WHR, as a surrogate measure for central adiposity, were evaluated using laboratory challenges. Women with high WHR rated the tasks as more threatening, performed more poorly on them, and reported more chronic stress. These women secreted significantly more cortisol during the first stress session than women with a low WHR. Furthermore, women who were lean and had a high WHR lacked habituation to stress in that they continued to secrete significantly more cortisol in response to now-familiar challenges (days 2 and 3) than women who were lean and had a low WHR.[56]

The Brown University Medical Student Study examined self-proclaimed stress eaters versus stressless eaters for weight change over time by following students during a baseline control period as well as during two examination periods. Stress eaters tended to gain more weight and demonstrated increases in nocturnal levels of insulin, cortisol and blood levels of total/high density lipoprotein (HDL) cholesterol ratio, during examination periods, controlling for the baseline control period.

From our current understanding of stress and cardiovascular disease, obesity and pre-eclampsia, we posit that several measures of stress are pertinent to understanding the interaction of stress, obesity and pre-eclampsia. Both acute and chronic stress should be considered. Personality factors related to stress and experiences that sensitise a person to day-to-day situations as unfavourable, hostile, or discriminatory must also be considered, as such factors are the lens through which the stressor is perceived. Finally, according to the stress-buffering hypothesis, social support is believed to mitigate the relation between negative life events and disease states.

Sleep disorders

Sleep disorders and cardiovascular disease

Sleep disorders are associated with an increased risk for cardiovascular disease. Hypertension, coronary artery disease, stroke, arrhythmias and heart failure are all more common with disordered sleep.[57] The frequency of cardiovascular disease in women increases with decreasing duration of sleep. When compared with women sleeping 8 hours a night, women sleeping 5 hours a night have 1.5 (95% CI 1.1–1.9) times the risk of cardiovascular disease.[58] Sleep disorders may contribute to cardiovascular disease in several ways. The most direct and well-established effect is through intermittent hypoxia associated with the obstructive sleep apnoea syndrome (sleep apnoea).[59] In this syndrome individuals suffer intermittent airway obstruction with consequent hypoxaemia during sleep. This is frequently manifested as snoring. Individuals with obstructive sleep apnoea matched for BMI with individuals without this disorder have an excess of adverse cardiovascular findings including increased diastolic blood pressure and increased dyslipidaemia.[60] Sleep dysfunction is also an independent risk factor for insulin resistance and the metabolic syndrome.[61] The relationship to abnormal insulin resistance persists with adjustment for BMI and manifests a dose response with the insulin resistance increasing with increasingly dysfunctional sleep.[62] However, there are probably also other effects of disordered sleep than intermittent hypoxia. For example, insulin resistance is increased in experimentally sleep-deprived individuals who would not be expected to experience intermittent hypoxaemia.[63] Alterations of autonomic input, immune function and neuroendocrine disruptions associated with fragmented sleep are also relevant.[61]

The mechanisms by which sleep disorders lead to cardiovascular disease are best explored for obstructive sleep apnoea. The intermittent hypoxia is associated with oscillation of sympathetic outflow. To a certain extent, the hypoxia re-oxygenation resembles the hypoxia reperfusion syndrome and is consistently associated with free radical production.[64] Of special relevance to the pathogenesis of pre-eclampsia, this excess free radical production is associated with biochemical evidence of endothelial dysfunction.[65]

Sleep disorders in pregnancy

Many events in normal pregnancy affect sleep adversely, with 66–94% of pregnant women describing changes in sleep patterns.[66] The change in sleep during pregnancy is not very well studied but is probably a complex interplay of the effects of reproductive hormones on respiratory drive and 'mechanical factors' related to the increasing size of the fetus and physiological changes of increased extracellular volume and oedema.[66,67] The origin of the sleep abnormality varies with the duration of gestation. In early pregnancy, it is primarily increased urinary frequency while as pregnancy advances other features such as difficulty in the use of usual sleep postures and gastro-oesophageal reflux become important. Finally, in late gestation, the genesis appears to be at least partially due to airway obstruction. Sleep apnoea, as indicated by snoring, increases to more than 50% of women compared with 32% of nonpregnant controls ($P < 0.05$).[68] This is, of course, a form of sleep disorder especially relevant to cardiovascular disease including hypertension and metabolic syndrome, two of the components of the pre-eclampsia syndrome.

Sleep disorders in pre-eclampsia

The relationship of sleep disorders to cardiovascular disease suggests that sleep disruption might also be relevant in pre-eclampsia. There are several lines of evidence supporting such a relationship. Snoring is more common in pregnancy and even more common in pre-eclampsia. Several studies have documented increased snoring in women with pre-eclampsia.[68-71] In a study comparing pre-eclampsia and normal pregnancies, snoring was present in 85% of women with pre-eclampsia and in 55% of women with normal pregnancy outcome ($P > 0.001$).[68] In another study in which pregnancy outcome was compared between women who did or did not snore, pre-eclampsia occurred in 6–7% of women who snored compared with 4% of women who did not ($P < 0.05$). Interestingly, a similar relationship was found for pregnancies with small-for–gestational-age (SGA) infants. SGA was present in 7.1% of women who snored and 2.6% of those who did not ($P < 0.05$).[71] An important relationship in both of these studies was the fact that women who snored were heavier than women who did not. However, not all of the snoring effect is explained by obesity. In the latter study, multivariate analysis indicated an independent effect of snoring on pre-eclampsia and SGA when BMI was accounted for in the model.[71] The studies above were largely by self-report. More objective assessments of sleep abnormalities support these findings. Women with pre-eclampsia, gestationally age-matched normal pregnant women and normal nonpregnant women were observed with overnight monitoring of sleep pattern and arterial oxygenation. With this objective assessment, women with pre-eclampsia had a significant doubling of time with inspiratory flow limitations compared with normal pregnant women.[70]

Another finding implicating airway obstruction in the genesis of pre-eclampsia is the observation that the haemodynamic response to obstructive respiratory events during sleep is augmented in women with pre-eclampsia.[72] Women with pre-eclampsia responded to these episodes with a significant ($P < 0.007$), 50% greater, increase in blood pressure than normal pregnant women.[72] Whether this is causal or a response to pre-eclampsia pathophysiology could not be determined but it does indicate a substantial effect of obstructive episodes on the vasoconstrictor response in pre-eclampsia.

Obstructive sleep apnoea can be treated with continuous positive airway pressure. This has been attempted in a small study of women with pre-eclampsia. Eleven women with pre-eclampsia were monitored overnight and all manifested sleep-induced upper airway flow limitation on the pretreatment night. Auto setting airway continuous positive pressure at a mean of 6 ± 1 cmH$_2$O eliminated flow limitation on the treatment night. This was associated with marked reduction in blood pressure compared with the pretreatment night ($128 \pm 3/73 \pm 3$ versus $146 \pm 6/92 \pm 4$; $P < 0.007$).[73]

In summary, pregnancy increases the risk of sleep apnoea and this is further increased in pre-eclampsia. As would be expected, obesity also contributes to the frequency of sleep disturbances. Preliminary data indicate that the airway obstructive problem can be successfully treated in pregnancy and more specifically in women with pre-eclampsia. The correction of the problem reduced blood pressure substantially, consistent with the increased pressor response to obstruction that is present in women with pre-eclampsia.

Obesity and sleep disorders

Obesity is quite commonly associated with obstructive sleep apnoea. Of those with obstructive sleep apnoea, 60–90% are obese, and approximately 40% of individuals who are obese have sleep apnoea.[74] The relationship is more striking in women. Sleep apnoea is less common in women (1.2% versus 3.9%) and even less common premenopausally (0.6%). Virtually all sleep apnoea in premenopausal women is associated with obesity.[75] Although there have not been a great number of intervention trials, it is encouraging that a 10% reduction of body weight was associated with a 26% reduced frequency of apnoeic or hypoxaemic sleep events.[76]

Smoking, obesity and pre-eclampsia

Smoking is one of the leading risk factors for cardiovascular disease. It is also associated with an increased risk of virtually every abnormal pregnancy outcome with the exception of pre-eclampsia.[77] Numerous epidemiological studies indicate a reduced frequency of pre-eclampsia in smokers with a modest dose–response relationship with pre-eclampsia less common as the amount of smoking increases.[77-84] An interesting exception to this finding is a study in a Japanese population. The investigators found that in women with a prepregnancy BMI ≥ 24 kg/m^2, 47% of women who developed pre-eclampsia smoked prior to pregnancy while only 7% of women who did not develop pre-eclampsia were smokers.[85] This BMI is not elevated by US standards and, in preliminary experiments, we examined smoking history in the US population with high BMI, defined by US standards as > 30 kg/m^2. In 387 women who were obese (26 with pre-eclampsia), we found an association of prepregnancy smoking with an increased risk of pre-eclampsia ($P = 0.07$) that with this small number of women with pre-eclampsia did not achieve our chosen level of statistical significance, although the results demonstrated no evidence of the protective effect of smoking.

Interaction of lifestyle factors

There are interactions between most of the lifestyle factors with each other and with obesity. Stress, obesity,[86,87] smoking,[88] sleep disturbances,[89] high unsaturated fat diets[90,91] and reduced physical activity[30] are all associated with inflammatory activation. Sleep is also induced by inflammatory cytokines.[89] Stress is associated with increased eating of comfort foods, which in animal studies leads to visceral obesity.[92] A similar relationship is also present in humans[93] and has been suggested to contribute to the metabolic syndrome.[94,95] Furthermore, smoking increases the frequency of snoring[96,97] and sleep deprivation leads to a reduction in the anorexigenic hormone leptin, an increase in the orexigenic factor ghrelin, and an increased appetite, especially for calorie-dense foods.[98] In a study of pregnancy and sleeping disorders, smoking was an important behaviour. Inadequate sleep was twice as common in pregnant women who were heavy smokers compared with non-smokers.[99]

Summary

Obesity is associated with an increased risk of pre-eclampsia. Obesity affects and is affected by lifestyle factors that clearly contribute to cardiovascular disease and for which there is emerging evidence of a similar association with pre-eclampsia. Most of these factors are at least in theory modifiable. Investigations are warranted to test whether some or all of these factors interact with obesity to result in pre-eclampsia.

Acknowledgements

This research was partially supported by the National Institute of Child Health and Human Development (PPG 2PO1HD30367, 5MO1 RR00056).

References

1. Bodnar LM, Catov JM, Klebanoff MA, Ness RB, Roberts JM. Prepregnancy body mass index and the occurrence of severe hypertensive disorders of pregnancy. *Epidemiology* 2007;18:234–9.
2. Albert NM. We are what we eat: women and diet for cardiovascular health. *J Cardiovasc Nurs.* 2005;20:451–60.
3. Roberts JM, Balk JL, Bodnar LM, Belizan JM, Bergel E. Nutrient involvement in preeclampsia. *J Nutr* 2003;133:1684S–92S.
4. Jauniaux E, Watson AL, Hempstock J, Bao YP, Skepper JN, Burton GJ. Onset of maternal arterial blood flow and placental oxidative stress. A possible factor in human early pregnancy failure. *Am J Pathol* 2000;157:2111–22.
5. Zhang C, Williams MA, King IB, Dashow EE, Sorensen TK, Frederick IO, et al. Vitamin C and the risk of preeclampsia – results from dietary questionnaire and plasma assay. *Epidemiology* 2002;13:409–16.
6. Poston L, Briley AL, Seed PT, Kelly FJ, Shennan AH. Vitamins in Pre-eclampsia Trial C. Vitamin C and vitamin E in pregnant women at risk for pre-eclampsia (VIP trial): randomised placebo-controlled trial. *Lancet* 2006;367:1145–54.
7. Chappell LC, Seed PT, Briley AL, Kelly FJ, Lee R, Hunt BJ, et al. Effect of antioxidants on the occurrence of pre-eclampsia in women at increased risk: a randomised trial. *Lancet* 1999;354:810–16.
8. Rumbold AR, Crowther CA, Haslam RR, Dekker GA, Robinson JS, Group AS. Vitamins C and E and the risks of preeclampsia and perinatal complications. *N Engl J Med* 2006;354:1796–806.
9. Erkkila AT, Lichtenstein AH. Fiber and cardiovascular disease risk: how strong is the evidence? *J Cardiovasc Nurs* 2006;21:3–8.
10. Clausen T, Slott M, Solvoll K, Drevon CA, Vollset SE, Henriksen T. High intake of energy, sucrose, and polyunsaturated fatty acids is associated with increased risk of preeclampsia. *Am J Obstet Gynecol* 2001;185:451–8.
11. Neuhouser ML, Rock CL, Eldridge AL, Kristal AR, Patterson RE, Cooper DA, et al. Serum concentrations of retinol, alpha-tocopherol and the carotenoids are influenced by diet, race and obesity in a sample of healthy adolescents. *J Nutr* 2001;131:2184–91.
12. Wallstrom P, Wirfalt E, Lahmann PH, Gullberg B, Janzon L, Berglund G. Serum concentrations of beta-carotene and alpha-tocopherol are associated with diet, smoking, and general and central adiposity. *Am J Clin Nutr* 2001;73:777–85.
13. Canoy D, Wareham N, Welch A, Bingham S, Luben R, Day N, et al. Plasma ascorbic acid concentrations and fat distribution in 19, 068 British men and women in the European Prospective Investigation into Cancer and Nutrition Norfolk cohort study. *Am J Clin Nutr* 2005;82:1203–9.
14. Andersen LF, Jacobs DR Jr, Gross MD, Schreiner PJ, Dale Williams O, Lee DH. Longitudinal associations between body mass index and serum carotenoids: the CARDIA study. *Br J Nutr* 2006;95:358–65.

15. Bray GA, Nielsen SJ, Popkin BM. Consumption of high-fructose corn syrup in beverages may play a role in the epidemic of obesity. Am J Clin Nutr 2004;79:537–43. Erratum in: *Am J Clin Nutr* 2004;80:1090.

16. Elliott SS, Keim NL, Stern JS, Teff K, Havel PJ. Fructose, weight gain, and the insulin resistance syndrome. *Am J Clin Nutr* 2002;76:911–22.

17. Nakagawa T, Hu H, Zharikov S, Tuttle KR, Short RA, Glushakova O, et al. A causal role for uric acid in fructose-induced metabolic syndrome. *Am J Physiol Renal Physiol* 2006;290:F625–631.

18. Bassuk SS, Manson JE. Physical activity and cardiovascular disease prevention in women: how much is good enough? *Exerc Sport Sci Rev* 2003;31:176–81.

19. Dubbert PM, Carithers T, Sumner AE, Barbour KA, Clark BL, Hall JE, et al. Obesity, physical inactivity, and risk for cardiovascular disease. *Am J Med Sci* 2002;324:116–26.

20. Kohl HW 3rd. Physical activity and cardiovascular disease: evidence for a dose response. *Med Sci Sports Exerc* 2001;33(6 Suppl):S472–83; discussion S493–4.

21. Manson JE, Greenland P, LaCroix AZ, Stefanick ML, Mouton CP, Oberman A, et al. Walking compared with vigorous exercise for the prevention of cardiovascular events in women. *N Engl J Med* 2002;347:716–25.

22. Nieman DC, Brock DW, Butterworth D, Utter AC, Nieman CC. Reducing diet and/or exercise training decreases the lipid and lipoprotein risk factors of moderately obese women. *J Am Coll Nutr* 2002;21:344–50.

23. Whelton SP, Chin A, Xin X, He J. Effect of aerobic exercise on blood pressure: a meta-analysis of randomized, controlled trials. *Ann Intern Med* 2002;136:493–503.

24. Kayman S, Bruvold W, Stern JS. Maintenance and relapse after weight loss in women: behavioral aspects. *Am J Clin Nutr* 1990;52:800–7.

25. Mourier A, Gautier JF, De Kerviler E, Bigard AX, Villette JM, Garnier JP, et al. Mobilization of visceral adipose tissue related to the improvement in insulin sensitivity in response to physical training in NIDDM. Effects of branched-chain amino acid supplements. *Diabetes Care* 1997;20:385–91.

26. El-Sayed MS, Sale C, Jones PG, Chester M. Blood hemostasis in exercise and training. *Med Sci Sports Exerc* 2000;32:918–25.

27. Henriksen EJ, Saengsirisuwan V. Exercise training and antioxidants: relief from oxidative stress and insulin resistance. *Exerc Sport Sci Rev* 2003;31:79–84.

28. Hawley JA. Exercise as a therapeutic intervention for the prevention and treatment of insulin resistance. *Diabetes Metab Res Rev* 2004;20:383–93.

29. Carroll S, Dudfield M. What is the relationship between exercise and metabolic abnormalities? A review of the metabolic syndrome. *Sports Med* 2004;34:371–418.

30. Ford ES. Does exercise reduce inflammation? Physical activity and C-reactive protein among U.S. adults. *Epidemiology* 2002;13:561–8.

31. Smith JK, Dykes R, Douglas JE, Krishnaswamy G, Berk S. Long-term exercise and atherogenic activity of blood mononuclear cells in persons at risk of developing ischemic heart disease. *JAMA* 1999;281:1722–7.

32. Mattusch F, Dufaux B, Heine O, Mertens I, Rost R. Reduction of the plasma concentration of C-reactive protein following nine months of endurance training. *Int J Sports Med* 2000;21:21–4.

33. Geffken D, Cushman M, Burke G, Polak J, Sakkinen P, Tracy R. Association between physical activity and markers of inflammation in a healthy elderly population. *Am J Epidemiol* 2001;153:242–50.

34. Saftlas AF, Logsden-Sackett N, Wang W, Woolson R, Bracken MB. Work, leisure-time physical activity, and risk of preeclampsia and gestational hypertension. *Am J Epidemiol* 2004;160:758–65.

35. Marcoux S, Brisson J, Fabia J. The effect of leisure time physical activity on the risk of pre-eclampsia and gestational hypertension. *J Epidemiol Community Health* 1989;43:147–52.

36. Sorensen TK, Williams MA, Lee IM, Dashow EE, Thompson ML, Luthy DA. Recreational physical activity during pregnancy and risk of preeclampsia. *Hypertension* 2003;41:1273–80.

37. Weissgerber TL, Wolfe LA, Davies GA. The role of regular physical activity in preeclampsia prevention. *Med Sci Sports Exerc* 2004;36:2024–31.

38. Mora S, Lee IM, Buring JE, Ridker PM. Association of physical activity and body mass index with novel and traditional cardiovascular biomarkers in women. *JAMA* 2006;295:1412–19.

39. Bruunsgaard H. Physical activity and modulation of systemic low-level inflammation. *J Leukoc Biol* 2005;78:819–35.

40. Slentz CA, Duscha BD, Johnson JL, Ketchum K, Aiken LB, Samsa GP, et al. Effects of the amount of exercise on body weight, body composition, and measures of central obesity: STRRIDE – a randomized controlled study. *Arch Intern Med* 2004;164:31–9.

41. Slentz CA, Aiken LB, Houmard JA, Bales CW, Johnson JL, Tanner CJ, et al. Inactivity, exercise, and visceral fat. STRRIDE: a randomized, controlled study of exercise intensity and amount. *J Appl Physiol* 2005;99:1613–18.

42. Vanitallie TB. Stress: a risk factor for serious illness. *Metab Clin Exp* 2002;51(6 Suppl 1):40–5.

43. Kario K, McEwen BS, Pickering TG. Disasters and the heart: a review of the effects of earthquake-induced stress on cardiovascular disease. *Hypertens Res* 2003;26:355–67.

44. Dallman MF, Gold PW, Lightman SL, Mittleman MA, Musselman D, Pollock DM, et al. *Cardiovascular Consequences of Chronic Stress.* Paper presented at NHLBI Working Group, 2004; Bethesda, Maryland, USA.

45. Henry JP. Psychological and physiological responses to stress: the right hemisphere and the hypothalamo-pituitary-adrenal axis, an inquiry into problems of human bonding. *Integr Physiol Behav Sci* 1993;28:369–87; discussion 368.

46. Seematter G, Binnert C, Martin JL, Tappy L. Relationship between stress, inflammation and metabolism. *Curr Opin Clin Nutr Metab Care* 2004;7:169–73.

47. Brydon L, Magid K, Steptoe A. Platelets, coronary heart disease, and stress. *Brain Behav Immun* 2006;20:113–19.

48. Camacho A, Dimsdale JE. Platelets and psychiatry: lessons learned from old and new studies. *Psychosom Med* 2000;62:326–36.

49. Rozanski A, Blumenthal JA, Davidson KW, Saab PG, Kubzansky L. The epidemiology, pathophysiology, and management of psychosocial risk factors in cardiac practice: the emerging field of behavioral cardiology. *J Am Coll Cardiol* 2005;45:637–51.

50. Karasek R, Brisson C, Kawakami N, Houtman I, Bongers P, Amick B. The Job Content Questionnaire (JCQ): an instrument for internationally comparative assessments of psychosocial job characteristics. *J Occup Health Psychol* 1998;3:322–55.

51. Klonoff-Cohen HS, Cross JL, Pieper CF. Job stress and preeclampsia. *Epidemiology* 1996;7:245–9.

52. Landsbergis P, Hatch M. Job stressors and gestational hypertension. *Epidemiology* 2000;11:95.

53. Landsbergis PA, Hatch MC. Psychosocial work stress and pregnancy-induced hypertension. *Epidemiology* 1996;7:346–51.

54. Marcoux S, Berube S, Brisson C, Mondor M. Job strain and pregnancy-induced hypertension. *Epidemiology* 1999;10:376–82.

55. Epel E, Lapidus R, McEwen B, Brownell K. Stress may add bite to appetite in women: a laboratory study of stress-induced cortisol and eating behavior. *Psychoneuroendocrinology* 2001;26:37–49.

56. Epel ES, McEwen B, Seeman T, Matthews K, Castellazzo G, Brownell KD, et al. Stress and body shape: stress-induced cortisol secretion is consistently greater among women with central fat. *Psychosom Med* 2000;62:623–32.

57. Budhiraja R, Quan SF. Sleep-disordered breathing and cardiovascular health. *Curr Opin Pulm Med* 2005;11:501–6.

58. Ayas NT, White DP, Manson JE, Stampfer MJ, Speizer FE, Malhotra A, et al. A prospective study of sleep duration and coronary heart disease in women. *Arch Intern Med* 2003;163:205–9.

59. White DP. Pathogenesis of obstructive and central sleep apnea. *Am J Respir Crit Care Med* 2005;172:1363–70.

60. Ip MSM, Lam KSL, Ho CM, Tsang KWT, Lam WK. Serum leptin and vascular risk factors in obstructive sleep apnea. *Chest* 2000;118:580–6.

61. Punjabi NM, Polotsky VY. Disorders of glucose metabolism in sleep apnea. *J Appl Physiol* 2005;99:1998–2007.

62. Punjabi NM, Shahar E, Redline S, Gottlieb DJ, Givelber R, Resnick HE, et al. Sleep-disordered breathing, glucose intolerance, and insulin resistance: the Sleep Heart Health Study. *Am J Epidemiol* 2004;160:521–30.

63. VanHelder T, Symons JD, Radomski MW. Effects of sleep deprivation and exercise on glucose tolerance. *Aviat Space Environ Med* 1993;64:487–92.

64. Pack AI. Advances in sleep-disordered breathing. *Am J Respir Crit Care Med* 2006;173:7–15.

65. Robinson GV, Pepperell JC, Segal HC, Davies RJ, Stradling JR. Circulating cardiovascular risk factors in obstructive sleep apnoea: data from randomised controlled trials. *Thorax* 2004;59:777–82.

66. Santiago JR, Nolledo MS, Kinzler W, Santiago TV. Sleep and sleep disorders in pregnancy. *Ann Intern Med* 2001;134:396–408.

67. Sahota PK, Jain SS, Dhand R. Sleep disorders in pregnancy. *Curr Opin Pulm Med* 2003;9:477–83.

68. Izci B, Martin SE, Dundas KC, Liston WA, Calder AA, Douglas NJ. Sleep complaints: snoring and daytime sleepiness in pregnant and pre-eclamptic women. *Sleep Med* 2005;6:163–9.

69. Izci B, Riha RL, Martin SE, Vennelle M, Liston WA, Dundas KC, et al. The upper airway in pregnancy and pre-eclampsia. *Am J Respir Crit Care Med* 2003;167:137–40.

70. Connolly G, Razak AR, Hayanga A, Russell A, McKenna P, McNicholas WT. Inspiratory flow limitation during sleep in pre-eclampsia: comparison with normal pregnant and nonpregnant women. *Eur J Respir Dis* 2001;18:672–6.

71. Franklin KA, Holmgren PA, Jonsson F, Poromaa N, Stenlund H, Svanborg E. Snoring, pregnancy-induced hypertension, and growth retardation of the fetus. *Chest* 2000;117:137–41.

72. Edwards N, Blyton DM, Kirjavainen TT, Sullivan CE. Hemodynamic responses to obstructive respiratory events during sleep are augmented in women with preeclampsia. *Am J Hypertens* 2001;14(11 Pt 1):1090–5.

73. Edwards N, Blyton DM, Kirjavainen T, Kesby GJ, Sullivan CE. Nasal continuous positive airway pressure reduces sleep-induced blood pressure increments in preeclampsia. *Am J Respir Crit Care Med* 2000;162:252–7.

74. Namyslowski G, Scierski W, Mrowka-Kata K, Kawecka I, Kawecki D, Czecior E. Sleep study in patients with overweight and obesity. *J Physiol Pharmacol* 2005;56 Suppl 6:59–65.

75. Bixler EO, Vgontzas AN, Lin HM, Ten Have T, Rein J, Vela-Bueno A, et al. Prevalence of sleep-disordered breathing in women: effects of gender. *Am J Respir Crit Care Med* 2001;163(3 Pt 1):608–13.

76. Peppard PE, Young T, Palta M, Dempsey J, Skatrud J. Longitudinal study of moderate weight change and sleep-disordered breathing. *JAMA* 2000;284:3015–21.

77. Castles A, Adams EK, Melvin CL, Kelsch C, Boulton ML. Effects of smoking during pregnancy. Five meta-analyses. *Am J Prev Med* 1999;16:208–15.

78. Zhang J, Klebanoff MA, Levine RJ, Puri M, Moyer P. The puzzling association between smoking and hypertension during pregnancy. *Am J Obstet Gynecol* 1999;181:1407–13.

79. Xiong X, Wang FL, Davidge ST, Demianczuk NN, Mayes DC, Olson DM, et al. Maternal smoking and preeclampsia. *J Reprod Med* 2000;45:727–32.

80. Sibai BM, Gordon T, Thom E, Caritis SN, Klebanoff M, McNellis D, et al. Risk factors for preeclampsia in healthy nulliparous women: a prospective multicenter study. The National Institute of Child Health and Human Development Network of Maternal-Fetal Medicine Units. *Am J Obstet Gynecol* 1995;172(2 Pt 1):642–8.

81. Sibai BM, Ewell M, Levine RJ, Klebanoff MA, Esterlitz J, Catalano PM, et al. Risk factors associated with preeclampsia in healthy nulliparous women. The Calcium for Preeclampsia Prevention (CPEP) Study Group. *Am J Obstet Gynecol* 1997;177:1003–10.

82. Lain KY, Powers RW, Krohn MA, Ness RB, Crombleholme WR, Roberts JM. Urinary cotinine concentration confirms the reduced risk of preeclampsia with tobacco exposure. *Am J Obstet Gynecol* 1999;181:1192–6.

83. Klonoff-Cohen H, Edelstein S, Savitz D. Cigarette smoking and preeclampsia. *Obstet Gynecol* 1993;81:541–4.

84. Conde-Agudelo A, Althabe F, Belizan JM, Kafury-Goeta AC. Cigarette smoking during pregnancy and risk of preeclampsia: a systematic review. *Am J Obstet Gynecol* 1999;181:1026–35.

85. Kobashi G, Ohta K, Hata A, Shido K, Yamada H, Fujimoto S, et al. An association between maternal smoking and preeclampsia in Japanese women. *Semin Thromb Hemost* 2002;28:507–10.

86. Berg AH, Scherer PE. Adipose tissue, inflammation, and cardiovascular disease. *Circ Res* 2005;96:939–49.

87. Greenberg AS, Obin MS. Obesity and the role of adipose tissue in inflammation and metabolism. *Am J Clin Nutr* 2006;83:461S–5S.

88. Peterson MC. Circulating transforming growth factor beta-1: a partial molecular explanation for associations between hypertension, diabetes, obesity, smoking and human disease involving fibrosis. *Med Sci Monit* 2005;11:RA229–232.

89. Majde JA, Krueger JM. Links between the innate immune system and sleep. *J Allerg Clin Immunol* 2005;116:1188–98.

90. Grimble RF. Nutritional modulation of cytokine biology. *Nutrition* 1998;14:634–40.

91. Grimble RF, Tappia PS. Modulation of pro-inflammatory cytokine biology by unsaturated fatty acids. *Zeitschrift fur Ernahrungswissenschaft* 1998;37(Suppl 1):57–65.

92. Dallman MF, Pecoraro NC, la Fleur SE. Chronic stress and comfort foods: self-medication and abdominal obesity. *Brain Behav Immun* 2005;19:275–80.

93. Moyer AE, Rodin J, Grilo CM, Cummings N, Larson LM, Rebuffe-Scrive M. Stress-induced cortisol response and fat distribution in women. *Obes Res* 1994;2:255–62.

94. Bjorntorp P. Do stress reactions cause abdominal obesity and comorbidities? *Obes Rev* 2001;2:73–86.

95. Chrousos GP. The role of stress and the hypothalamic-pituitary-adrenal axis in the pathogenesis of the metabolic syndrome: neuro-endocrine and target tissue-related causes. *Int J Obes Relat Metab Disord* 2000;24;Suppl 2:S50–55.

96. Grunstein R. Snoring and passive smoking – a counterblast? *Am J Respir Crit Care Med* 2004;170:722–3.

97. Franklin KA, Gislason T, Omenaas E, Jogi R, Jensen EJ, Lindberg E, *et al.* The influence of active and passive smoking on habitual snoring. *Am J Respir Crit Care Med* 2004;170:799–803.

98. Spiegel K, Tasali E, Penev P, Van Cauter E. Brief communication: Sleep curtailment in healthy young men is associated with decreased leptin levels, elevated ghrelin levels, and increased hunger and appetite. [summary for patients in *Ann Intern Med* 2004;141:I52]. *Ann Intern Med* 2004;141:846–50.

99. Kaneita Y, Ohida T, Takemura S, Sone T, Suzuki K, Miyake T, *et al.* Relation of smoking and drinking to sleep disturbance among Japanese pregnant women. *Prev Med* 2005;41:877–82.

Section 5

Consensus views

Chapter 22

Consensus views arising from the 53rd Study Group: Obesity and Reproductive Health

Research

The growing rates of obesity raise important issues specific to women and reproductive health with an urgent need for research on prevention and treatment.

1. More research is required on the effect of obesity on clinical effectiveness, cost effectiveness and quality of life in all aspects of reproductive health.

2. More research is required on the effect of weight loss on clinical effectiveness, cost effectiveness and quality of life in all aspects of reproductive health.

3. There is a need to investigate the impact of obesity on diagnosis and management of common gynaecological problems, including contraception.

4. More research is required to determine causes of the documented epidemiological links between obesity and gynaecological neoplasia.

5. More research is required to identify predictors specific to developing weight-gain related reproductive, obstetric and long-term gynaecological disease such as body composition and distribution, ethnicity, activity, lifestyle and psychosocial factors, with the recognition that these may differ for different conditions.

6. More research is required to identify the mechanisms that determine poor pregnancy and neonatal outcomes in relation to maternal obesity; for example, through investigation of biomarkers, dietary and clinical risk factors, and with the use of relevant animal models.

7. There is an immediate need for prospective randomised studies in pregnant women who are obese to assess the effects of diet, physical activity and lifestyle changes on maternal, fetal and neonatal outcomes, including long-term follow-up studies assessing the impact on the health of the child in later life.

8. Optimal weight gain in pregnancy needs to be clarified in subsets of the population, with the recognition that weight gain is partly dependent upon maternal body mass index (BMI) at the start of pregnancy. Measurements of the weight of women who are obese during pregnancy should be performed to guide policies on weight change during pregnancy. Research is also required to define optimal methods of assessment of body fat in women, with the recognition that

BMI, especially in pregnancy, is a poor index of adiposity. Researchers should also be aware that birth weight is a poor index of neonatal adiposity.

9. Research is required into the clinical benefit of low-dose aspirin (75 mg/day) during pregnancy in women who are severely obese.

10. Research is required to determine the optimal gestation for screening women who are obese for impaired glucose tolerance and whether early detection and management improves outcome.

11. Research is required into the impact of weight-loss strategies on long-term health outcomes in women in their post-reproductive years.

Education and training

12. A public health programme is required to inform women of the potential effects of obesity on reproductive health related to risk to both themselves and their offspring and in the short and long term; for example, obesity levels in mothers is a major determinant of heaver (overgrown) babies; weight gain between pregnancies, even within a normal BMI, increases the risk of numerous pregnancy complications in a subsequent pregnancy.

13. The implications of obesity, nutrition and lifestyle on reproductive, obstetric and gynaecological health should be included in continuing medical education programmes for all healthcare professionals, including reference to anaesthetic and surgical risk where appropriate.

14. Prevention of childhood obesity is a priority. In particular, barriers to physical activity in girls and young women should be addressed.

Clinical

The management of obesity requires a multidisciplinary approach. Healthcare practitioners should encourage women who are overweight to adopt healthy lifestyles practices, including improving diet quality and physical activity patterns. Stepwise programmes with realistic time-related goals are required, starting with modification of lifestyle, progressing to pharmacotherapy and ultimately obesity surgery.

15. Referral letters and health records across reproductive health should include information on measured and documented body weight and BMI. Waist circumference should be recorded as a supplementary measure of adiposity in those with a BMI < 35 kg/m². **Clinical Practice Point (CPP)**

16. Women who are obese attending for reproductive health care should have access to a referral pathway to appropriate healthcare professionals for supporting the adoption of a healthy lifestyle. Women should be referred to a nutritionist in cases where clinicians lack the knowledge and/or time to provide adequate counselling. Disordered eating and eating disorder psychopathology should be assessed and specific psychological input offered. **CPP**

17. Pharmacotherapy, including metformin, is not a substitute for weight loss or lifestyle improvement in women with polycystic ovary syndrome (PCOS) or adolescents. Metformin has little benefit in the most overweight and its role in the management of infertility requires further evidence. **Grade B**

18. In accordance with the guidelines of the British Fertility Society (BFS),[1] it is inadvisable that women with a BMI greater than 35kg/m² should receive fertility investigations or treatment until they reduce weight to BMI < 35kg/m² because of the reduction in successful outcomes and the increased risk to pregnancy and offspring. **Grade B**

19. All women seeking pregnancy should be encouraged to maintain BMI in the range 20–25 kg/m² as this may increase chances of pregnancy and reduce pregnancy complications. Ethnic differences need to be considered when assessing the effect of BMI – in particular, south Asians are considered overweight when BMI greater than 23 kg/m². Women with a BMI greater than 30kg/m² should be advised to reduce weight to a BMI less than 30 kg/m² before receiving assisted reproductive technology (ART) therapy/ovulation induction. **Grade B**

Gynaecology, contraception and the menopause

20. An appropriate care pathway is required by a multidisciplinary team for women who are severely obese. In particular, such women should be sent for pre-operative/antenatal anaesthetic assessment. **CPP**

21. Non-surgical treatments for benign gynaecological problems should be considered for women who are obese, such as the levonorgestrel-releasing intrauterine system (LNG-IUS). Women who are obese requiring surgery should have access to appropriately equipped facilities and specialist services. **CPP**

22. Obesity surgery should be considered in young women of reproductive age when all other therapy has failed (BMI greater than 40 kg/m² or 35–40 kg/m² plus other disease, such as type 2 diabetes mellitus – see the NICE clinical guideline on obesity;[2] if BMI is greater than 50 kg/m², bariatric surgery should be considered as first-line therapy). **Grade B**

Pregnancy

23. Maternal weight and height should be measured at the booking visit to the antenatal clinic in all women and throughout pregnancy in women who are obese. Inter-pregnancy weight change should also be recorded. **CPP**

24. Women with severe obesity (BMI greater than 35 kg/m²) plus one additional risk factor for hypertensive disease should be prescribed aspirin 75 mg/day from 12 weeks. **CPP**

25. Prepregnancy counselling for women who are severely obese (BMI greater than 35 kg/m²) in subfertility, recurrent miscarriage and diabetic clinics:
    a) consider high-dose folic acid (5 mg/day)
    b) discuss the importance of healthy diet and exercise in pregnancy and the need to avoid excessive weight gain; consider referral to a dietician and screening for diabetes. **CPP**

26. Early booking visit to plan pregnancy management for all women who are obese:
    a) consider low-dose aspirin (75 mg/day) in the presence of additional clinical risk factors (other than obesity) for pre-eclampsia
    b) consider antenatal thromboprophylaxis in the presence of additional clinical risk factors for venous thromboembolic (VTE) disease. **CPP**

27. A detailed anomaly scan and serum screening for congenital abnormality should be recommended in all women who are obese. **CPP**

28. Glucose tolerance testing at 28 weeks of gestation, with the potential for repeating in later pregnancy, should be considered in all women who are obese. **CPP**

References

1. R Kennedy, C Kingsland, A Rutherford, M Hamilton, W Ledger. *Implementation of the NICE Guideline – Recommendations from the British Fertility Society for National Criteria for NHS Funding of Assisted Conception.* Leeds: British Fertility Society; 2006 [www.fertility.org.uk/news/documents/HumanFertilitypaper.pdf].

2. National Institute for Health and Clinical Excellence, National Collaborating Centre for Primary Care. *Obesity: the Prevention, Identification, Assessment and Management of Overweight and Obesity in Adults and Children.* London: NICE; 2006 [www.nice.org.uk/CG043fullguideline].

Index